D1613538

DIVINE
FEMININE

THE JOHNS HOPKINS UNIVERSITY
STUDIES IN HISTORICAL
AND POLITICAL SCIENCE
119TH SERIES (2001)

1. Joy Dixon
Divine Feminine:
Theosophy and Feminism
in England

THEOSOPHICAL SOCIETY LEEDS LODGE

YOU ARE

Cordially Invited

to attend the Lectures announced in this Syllabus.

All who are interested in the study of Religion, Philosophy, and Occultism, or the investigation of the Powers latent in man and the invisible worlds around him, will find these Lectures full of interest and information.

Admission Free.

QUESTIONS INVITED.

COLLECTION.

JOY DIXON

DIVINE FEMININE

Theosophy and Feminism
in England

BBfAL

The Johns Hopkins
University Press

BALTIMORE AND

LONDON

© 2001 The Johns Hopkins University Press
All rights reserved. Published 2001
Printed in the United States of America on acid-free paper
2 4 6 8 9 7 5 3 1

The Johns Hopkins University Press
2715 North Charles Street
Baltimore, Maryland 21218-4363

www.press.jhu.edu

Library of Congress Cataloging-in-Publication Data

Dixon, Joy, 1962–
Divine feminine : theosophy and feminism in England / Joy Dixon.
p. cm. — (The Johns Hopkins University studies in
historical and political science 119th ser.)
Includes bibliographical references and index.
ISBN 0-8018-6499-2 (alk. paper)
1. Theosophical Society (Great Britain)—History. 2. Feminism—Religious
aspects—Theosophical Society (Great Britain)—History of doctrines. 3. Feminism—
England—History. I. Title. II. Series.
BP573.F46 D59 2001
299'.934'0820941—dc21

00-009881

A catalog record for this
book is available from the British Library.

Contents

Illustrations

Preface

This project had its beginnings in a paper I wrote many years ago as a postgraduate at the University of Sussex. I was working on a study of representations of the women's suffrage movement in the popular press, tracking down caricatures of the "shrieking sisterhood" in magazines like *Punch* and in comic novels. Much of what I found was predictable: the suffragette (according to the comic novelists at least) was a woman of a certain age, sexually frustrated, resolutely unfashionable, and possibly hysterical. But there were other, more surprising elements in the picture: the typical suffragette was also (again according to the comic novelists) a vegetarian, an animal rights activist, and a devotee of the Higher Thought, Cosmic Consciousness, or the Masters of the Wisdom. Turning to the classified advertisements in suffrage newspapers, I discovered a feminist culture that had been largely ignored by historians. Central to that culture was a self-conscious attempt to create a feminist spirituality. There were advertisements for women's spiritualist seances, lectures on the Divine Feminine, and prayer circles that met to offer intercessory prayer on behalf of women imprisoned for suffrage militancy. In the midst of all of this activity, one organization occupied a prominent place: the Theosophical Society, which had its headquarters in India and had been founded by one woman (Helena Petrovna Blavatsky) and led by another (Annie Besant).

Since that discovery, I have been preoccupied with the effort to understand the place of spirituality in general, and theosophy in particular, in the English feminist movement. This book is the result of that preoccupation.

Part I, "Domesticating the Occult," traces the process by which both eastern mysticism and women's spirituality were created and consolidated, focusing on the ways in which gendered understandings of eastern spirituality were shaped by the contingencies of the historical moments in which they emerged. On the most obvious level, to domesticate is to tame, and there were many efforts to tame the power of the occult, to assimilate it into existing religious and scientific systems, or to force it to accommodate itself to class and social hierarchies. At the same time, "eastern" occultism was an exotic import—a product of colonial trade which arrived in England along with cashmere shawls and Benares ware. But to domesticate occultism was also to locate it in the home, to make it the peculiar province of women and a "feminine" spirituality.

The process of domestication was erratic. Chapter 1, "The Undomesticated Occult," lays out the challenge that H. P. Blavatsky and her mysterious trans-Himalayan Mahatmas posed to those who wished to assimilate this new eastern wisdom into European culture, and especially into the rational and masculine language of late Victorian science. It also explores the contradictions inherent in the founding of the Theosophical Society, which were never fully resolved. These contradictions were reflected in the differences between the two founders: Henry Steel Olcott, the organizer and practical man of business who envisioned the society as a kind of religious and philosophical debating club, versus Blavatsky, the mystic, occultist, and seer who emphasized the society's function as a school of occult development and who bolstered her claims with impressive displays of "phenomena." The differences between Blavatsky and Olcott were reflected in the society's peculiar sense of its own mission: to proclaim publicly occult or esoteric truths, truths that by definition are secret, hidden, and known only to the initiated.

After this early phase (which ended in 1885, when the Society for Psychical Research published a damning report on Blavatsky and her followers), members of the Theosophical Society turned to new strategies. Chapter 2, "The Mahatmas in Clubland: Manliness and Scientific Spirituality," explores another effort to domesticate the occult, this time by distancing the society from scandal and sensation. During this period the Theosophical Society in England was dominated by upper- or upper-middle-class men; it was an eminently "clubable" creed. The Theosophical Society in the 1880s and 1890s was a quasi-public/quasi-private organization in the tradition of more mainstream late Victorian voluntary associations. As such, it was dominated and controlled by respectable gentlemen who stamped their impress on the society and its teaching. These men emphasized theosophy's scientific claims and its celebration of the "manly" virtues of rationality and independent judgment.

There were various efforts to maintain this version of theosophy, as part of a public culture of rational discussion implicitly and explicitly defined as masculine, in the face of challenges from those who saw theosophy as a feminine form of spirituality. This is the central theme of

Chapter 3, "'A Deficiency of the Male Element': Gendering Spiritual Experience." With Annie Besant's conversion to theosophy in 1889 the Theosophical Society gained a new public prominence. Over time, and particularly after Besant's election as president in 1907, the character of the organization changed dramatically. Besant reanimated its Esoteric Section and demanded greater commitment and energy from members. Besant's "neo-theosophy" was criticized both as feminine and as a submission to "Oriental despotism," and many of the respectable gentlemen who had formed the core constituency a generation earlier abandoned the society during this period.

In the end, the conflicting factions reached a modus vivendi on the basis of a sexual division of spiritual labor that distinguished between feminine modes of mystical experience and a more virile, magico-clerical occult tradition. But because the vision of gender relations on which these divisions were based was itself internally divided, the version of feminine spirituality that emerged was a contradictory one. The supposedly virile tradition of occultism also contained contradictions, and was in fact often stigmatized as effeminate. In the scandal that came to be known as the Leadbeater Case, the Theosophical Society's leading occultist was accused of the sexual abuse of young boys in his charge. The occult tradition thus became entangled in explosive debates about sexuality—and especially male homosexuality. This is the subject of Chapter 4, "'Buggery and Humbuggery': Sex, Magic, and Occult Authority."

Part II, "Political Alchemies," explores the role of these new visions of spirituality in feminist political culture in England. Like the utopian socialists a century earlier, many theosophists emphasized that political change needed to be accompanied by moral and ethical transformation. Just as the alchemists had attempted to turn lead into gold, theosophists attempted to spiritualize politics. Chapter 5, "Occult Body Politics," focuses on esoteric understandings of the body and their political implications. Theosophists—and particularly women within the Theosophical Society—drew on the immanentist teaching of the One Life to oppose liberal definitions of the distinctions between individual and community, secular and sacred, and public and private. For many women, this immanentist vision sustained a feminist culture in which personal and political transformation were inextricably linked. Although this immanentist theology could authorize a range of progressive political projects, it also drew on some of the most conservative readings of so-called eastern mysticism to develop a new spiritual and political vision that hovered ambiguously between socialism and fascism.

Chapter 6, "The Divine Hermaphrodite and the Female Messiah: Feminism and Spirituality in the 1890s," places discussions of feminism and spirituality in the Theosophical Society and in the wider feminist press in the context of debates in which Hinduism and Buddhism were praised as manly creeds, while Christianity was defended as an especially feminine form of spirituality. These alliances and conflicts shaped the ways in which many English feminists defined their relationship to empire and to non-Christian religious traditions.

Chapter 7, "A New Age for Women: Suffrage and the Sacred," traces the intersections between esoteric spirituality and the women's suffrage movement. Through a series of case studies, this chapter argues that for women as diverse as Charlotte Despard, Eva Gore-Booth, Dora Marsden, and Gertrude Colmore, the suffrage movement was only a means to an end. Their ultimate goal was less the enfranchisement of women than the enfranchisement of the spiritual.

In the 1920s and 1930s women in the Theosophical Society in England embraced increasingly conservative versions of feminism. At the same time, the locus of theosophical feminism shifted from England to India. Chapter 8, "Ancient Wisdom, Modern Motherhood," makes visible the exchanges between this strand of English feminism and its Indian counterpart. In England the turn to a concern with women as wives and mothers helped to consolidate the conflation of women and spirituality with the private realm of home and family. Simultaneously, it was assimilated to eugenic concerns with "racial motherhood." In India a similar rhetoric functioned very differently, exploiting nationalist constructions of "Indian womanhood" to authorize an expansive cultural and political role for high-caste women. The comparison between theosophical feminism in England and in India reemphasizes the contingency of "womanhood," the "East," and the "spiritual," categories that have all too often been reified and essentialized.

There were many different and competing understandings of all of these terms in circulation between 1880 and 1930. This book traces the debates over each of them and asks how and under what circumstances particular constructions of "womanhood," the "East," and "the spiritual" came to be accepted as natural and true. My real interest is in the material, historical, and cultural factors that shape both faith and doubt. In today's New Age movement, one of theosophy's most important legacies, these debates continue in a new context. In some cases, the impact of feminism and postcolonialism has changed the terms of the discussion beyond recognition. In others, the assumptions that underpinned nineteenth-century works are still present and unexamined. In more mainstream conflicts between secularists, religious fundamentalists, and religious liberals, we find the same diversity. The questions that drive this project are as relevant at the turn of this century as they were at the turn of the last. I hope, therefore, that an exploration of some of the historical roots of these debates will also illuminate our own historical situation.

Note on Transliteration
In the text, I have eliminated diacritical marks on proper names and on words such as *Vedanta* that are commonly used in English, either in scholarly or theosophical writing. In passages quoted from primary sources, I have retained the use of diacritical marks in order to preserve the flavor of the original. I have, however, standardized the typographical conventions for such marks both in order to achieve consistency and to conform to current practice. So, for example, *Vâhan* becomes *Vāhan*.

Acknowledgments

This book marks the end of a long process; to get to this point I have incurred many debts, personal and professional. For guidance, encouragement, and the occasional impossible challenge, my thanks are due to those who were my teachers and have become my friends: at the University of Sussex, to Eileen Yeo, who supervised the master's thesis that sparked my interest in this area; at Rutgers: The State University of New Jersey, where I completed my Ph.D., to Michael Adas, John Gillis, Don Kelley, and Bonnie Smith. I am grateful to the Rutgers Center for Historical Analysis, and especially to Phyllis Mack and the participants in the center's "Varieties of Religious Experience" seminar in 1996–97, which provided an ideal setting in which to spend a year's study leave and rethink the project. Above all, I am grateful to Judith R. Walkowitz, who supervised the Ph.D. dissertation that was the real beginning of this book and who did so much to shape my writing and my thinking, and to Leonore Davidoff who, since her term as a visiting professor at Rutgers, has been a continuing source of support and inspiration. At the University of British Columbia, I would like to thank my colleagues in the history department, especially Bill French and Jim Winter, and my colleagues in nineteenth-century studies, especially Pamela Dalziel and Maureen Ryan.

For financial and institutional support, my thanks are due to the British Council, for a Commonwealth Scholarship that allowed me to begin my postgraduate work at the University of Sussex; to the organizers of the European Summer University (Berlin) in 1988, who allowed me to participate in their workshop on "Gender and History"; to Rutgers University; to the Social Sciences and Humanities Research Council of Canada; and to the University of British Columbia. I am also grateful to the staff, both in the history department and in the library, at Sussex, Rutgers, and UBC for their assistance over the years.

For their kindness and generosity to an outsider, I would like to thank the staff and officers of the Theosophical Society in England, of the society's Blavatsky Lodge, and of the library and archives at the society's international headquarters in Adyar, Chennai, India. Special thanks go to the Theosophical Society in England and to the Adyar Library and Research Centre, The Theosophical Society, Adyar, Chennai, 600 020, India, not only for allowing me access to their collections but also for permission to reprint unpublished material. Unfortunately, I was unable to get permission to reprint materials from the Blavatsky Lodge, but I am grateful to that organization for the opportunity to consult its collection. Thanks also to the Theosophical Publishing House for permission to reproduce an illustration. Unless otherwise noted, all information on membership in the Theosophical Society is taken from the membership registers, Office of the General Secretary, Theosophical Society in England. Thanks are also due to the Society for Psychical Research, whose archives were then located in London, both for granting permission to reprint materials and for making my research there a pleasure; and to the Hacker Papers, University College London Library. I am also grateful to the staff at the Johns Hopkins University Press, especially to Michael Lonegro and my editor, Henry Tom, for their support and assistance in the last stages of this project. Thanks also to Lys Ann Shore, whose highly professional work at the copy-editing stage made that part of the process as painless as possible.

Portions of chapters 4 and 6 appeared in an earlier version in "Sexology and the Occult: Sexuality and Subjectivity in Theosophy's New Age," *Journal of the History of Sexuality* 7, no. 3 (1997): 409–33 (© 1997 by The University of Chicago; now published by the University of Texas Press). A portion of chapter 8 appeared in "Ancient Wisdom, Modern Motherhood: Theosophy and the Colonial Syncretic," in *Gender, Sexuality and Colonial Modernities,* ed. Antoinette Burton (London: Routledge, 1999).

The effort to pursue historical work in this area has been made immeasurably easier thanks to the efforts of the journal *Theosophical History,* which, under the able direction of Leslie Price and James Santucci, has helped create a supportive environment for research and has also made available an enormous amount of invaluable primary and secondary material. I owe a special debt to Leslie Price, for his assistance over the years in locating key material and for his willingness to read and comment on the entire manuscript. I would also like to thank Ted Daly of the TS in Canada, for guiding me to valuable materials.

For friendship and support during my visits to London, I thank Tony Claydon, Jeremy Gregory, Stephen Church, Maria Sophia Quine, and Sarah King. For help of various kinds, and for advice, commentary, criticism, and kindness over many years, my thanks go to Nancy Anderson, Meg Arnot, Mike Ashcraft, Kelly Boyd, Catherine Candy, Clare

Collins, Francisca de Haan, Linda Dowling, Gretchen Galbraith, Kali Israel, Jan Lambertz, Lara Perry, Erika Rappaport, Tori Smith, and John Tosh. For generously agreeing to read parts of this manuscript at its various stages, and for showing me kindness and support, I thank Lucy Bland, Antoinette Burton, Barbara Ramusack, Peter van der Veer, Gauri Viswanathan, and Pamela Walker, among many others. To those who read all of the manuscript, sometimes more than once, it is impossible to convey the extent of my gratitude: Mark Bevir, Nadja Durbach, Kim Gunning, Lisa Merrill, Alex Owen, and Denise Quirk. To Hilary Mason—who has read this manuscript almost as many times as I have, and whose support has made all the difference—I can only say thank you yet again. And finally, I thank my parents, Mary Anne and Arthur Dixon, who taught me many things, not the least of which is that religious belief can matter tremendously in people's lives. This book is dedicated to them.

DIVINE

FEMININE

Introduction

On September 3, 1911, at precisely 10:59 A.M., Annie Besant, president of the Theosophical Society and Vice President Grand Master of the Supreme Council of Universal Co-Freemasonry, laid the foundation stone for the new Theosophical Headquarters in London, just off Tavistock Square in Bloomsbury. The day and time were carefully chosen so that "the influence of the ruling planets should bless the work with power and success," and the ceremony was conducted with full Masonic rites. The foundation stone had been ceremonially incensed as the Theosophical Society's general secretary played music from Wagner's *Parsifal* on the organ; it had been laid and tested by the perpendicular, the plumb line, and the level; now corn, wine, oil, and salt were scattered on the stone with the requisite invocations.

Co-Masonry, a form of Freemasonry that admitted women, was (unofficially) a "subsidiary activity" of the Theosophical Society in England. The Co-Masonic procession at the groundbreaking ceremony added more than just the charm of pageantry to the occasion; these invocations and rituals were designed to produce specific spiritual effects. The temporary hall on the site had been converted into a Masonic Temple for the occasion, and the ceremony had begun at 9:45 A.M. with an appeal to the Great Architect of the Universe. The Brethren were then marshaled into a great procession, which marched around the grounds to be used for the new building. The Brethren wore their Masonic regalia, the women dressed in white robes along with the aprons, collars, and jewels of their rank. It was a solemn occasion, as the "blue of the Craft, the bright scarlet of the Rose Croix, the tesselated sashes of the Royal and Holy Arch, the black and silver of the 30°, and the white and gold of the 33° passed by." As church bells pealed in the background, the ceremony concluded with a chorus of "God Save the King" (Masonic version), and the procession re-formed in reverse order and returned to the lodge, which was closed in due and ancient form.[1]

A few months earlier, on June 17, 1911, a very different procession had moved through London: at the last of the great suffrage marches,

The groundbreaking ceremony at the TS London Headquarters in 1911.
(Adyar Library and Research Centre)

the Women's Coronation Procession, forty thousand women from all of Britain's suffrage societies had paraded through London, along with their male supporters in the Men's Leagues. The Women's Coronation Procession was a counterpoint to the largely male royal processions held to celebrate the coronation. The procession dramatized, before the eyes of a watching empire, both women's patriotism and their exclusion from the political nation. It mobilized a range of symbolic and material resources in a spectacular display of women's solidarity in pursuit of their political goal.[2]

Both processions symbolically claimed a measure of urban space as their own. The suffrage marchers traced a public, political space for women on the streets of the capital, from the Embankment to the Albert Hall. The Co-Masons, in contrast, marked out a more circumscribed space on Tavistock Square, a space that was sacred and ceremonial rather than directly political. (The site is occupied today by the British Medical Association.)

There were also important links between the two processions, links that have not been traced by historians. Most histories of the suffrage movement have given short shrift to women's religiosity. Religion is treated primarily as a language that women used to express more "real" (for which read secular and political) concerns. Women's politics and women's spirituality have been dealt with in separate literatures, and only a few attempts have been made to map the relationships between them.³ So, for example, the artist Pamela Colman Smith appears in one tradition as a minor figure in the Suffrage Atelier (formed in 1909 to mobilize women's art as suffrage propaganda). She appears in an entirely separate tradition as the artist who executed A. E. Waite's vision for what has become known as the Rider-Waite tarot deck, the most popular and best known such deck in England or North America.⁴

This historiographical division of labor erases the connections between spirituality and politics in feminist political culture—connections that were clear to contemporary critics. It is no accident that Miss Miniver, the suffragette caricatured in H. G. Wells's 1909 satire *Ann Veronica,* preaches the Higher Thought along with feminism, socialism, vegetarianism, and the Simple Life. A feminist spirituality was a crucial component of much feminist politics, and it was one of the sites at which feminist politics—for better or worse—was constituted and transformed.

Esoteric religion—what we might now call alternative or New Age spirituality—provided a crucial space for the articulation of this unorthodox vision. Although many men and women in the mainstream churches supported the women's suffrage movement, the conservative churchmen who dominated both Anglicanism and Nonconformity proved slow to endorse women's rights. Esoteric and occult organizations seemed more receptive: for example, in the issue of *The Suffragette* the Women's Social and Political Union published to commemorate the death of Emily Wilding Davison, the movement's first martyr, it was the Occult Church of the Seers in Brighton which rushed to announce "a Requiem, with music, for the repose of the soul of Emily Davison."⁵

The Theosophical Society (TS) was the largest and most influential of these esoteric or occult organizations. It was founded in New York in 1875 by the Russian émigrée Helena Petrovna Blavatsky and the American lawyer Henry Steel Olcott. In 1879 the founders moved to India, and in 1882 the new society's world headquarters were established at Adyar, near Madras (now Chennai), in south India. According to theosophical tradition, the true founders of the society, who provided Blavatsky with her inspiration and authority, were the Mahatmas, or Masters of the Great White Lodge, an occult brotherhood located in Tibet that drew its members from the most spiritually advanced "Adepts" throughout the world.

The "First Object" of the Theosophical Society, and the only item to which members were required to subscribe, was a commitment "to form a nucleus of the Universal Brotherhood of Humanity without distinction of race, creed, sex, caste or color." The society's other two objects were equally comprehensive: "to encourage the study of comparative religion, philosophy and science" and "to investigate the unexplained laws of nature and the powers latent in man." Officially, the TS (then as now) had no dogmas, but it did develop a distinctive set of teachings, which most members identified as theosophy. These teachings emphasized an immanentist and evolutionary vision of spirituality: the universe, seen and unseen, was One Life, which evolved to consciousness (in a series of immensely complicated cycles) through a diversity of forms, governed by the mechanisms of karma and reincarnation. These teachings, theosophists claimed, were the divine wisdom, the esoteric truths of all religions, philosophies, and scientific systems. This was an ancient wisdom which, they argued, had been best preserved in the great spiritual traditions of the East. The result was to produce a kind of generic "eastern mysticism," one that has had a significant impact on modern New Age movements, many of which have borrowed their terminology and basic concepts from theosophical teachings.

Theosophists also tended to emphasize the importance of ancient, written texts at the expense of popular ritual and customary practice, and they privileged Hindu and Buddhist texts over Judaic, Christian, or Islamic ones. In the twentieth century many theosophists began to anticipate the coming of a New Age, which was to be ushered in by a new Messiah: Jiddu Krishnamurti, the World Teacher. Not all members of the Theosophical Society agreed with all these claims; the society was always characterized by great diversity among its members. And because the only test for membership was a commitment to the First Object, many men and women joined the society even while they remained skeptical about the truth of many theosophical teachings. It was also possible, and at times even encouraged, for members to become theosophists while continuing to identify themselves as Christian, Buddhist, or Hindu. Since theosophy claimed to unify all religious traditions, members could believe that there was no inherent conflict between the divine wisdom and the particular forms it took within different religious traditions.

The accounts theosophists provided of Asian religions were much criticized, both by scholars and by orthodox Hindus and Buddhists. The orientalist F. Max Müller, for example, criticized Blavatsky for blurring the distinctions between Buddhist and Vedantic teachings. He also dismissed her claims about the existence of esoteric Buddhism as without foundation. Although the theosophists often explained the rhetoric of the New Age and of the World Teacher with reference to

Hinduism's Avatars or the Buddhist teaching of the Bodhisattva, others have argued that this rhetoric emerged out of messianic and millennialist traditions that were primarily of Christian origin.[6] Theosophists were undeterred by such arguments, for they claimed to be uncovering a hidden tradition that had become inaccessible to academics and ordinary believers alike, and had been preserved only among initiates.

The small group of English spiritualists and Freemasons who formed the first branch of the TS in Europe grew to hundreds and, by the 1920s, to thousands of members. By 1911, when theosophists began building their new headquarters, the society was engaged in a wide range of activities that proclaimed theosophy's affiliation to progressive politics broadly defined, as well as its innovative approach to religious practice. A vegetarian guesthouse was opened across the square for the use of members, and over the weeks and months that followed, the temporary hall erected on the headquarters site was home to a bewildering variety of theosophical activities. The Knights and Companions of the Order of the Round Table met there regularly, as did the Poor Children's Clothing Guild. The Temple of the Rosy Cross worked its mystic rites, while the League of Redemption debated changes to the Criminal Law Amendment Bill and organized its campaign for the abolition of the so-called white slave trade.

Theosophy's links to the English feminist movement were particularly marked. In June 1911 a contingent of theosophists had marched, under the banner of Universal Co-Freemasonry and in full Masonic regalia, as part of the Women's Coronation Procession.[7] Led by Annie Besant, they took their place alongside the Women Writers' Suffrage League, the Women's Tax Resistance League, the Fabian Women's Group, and the Church League for Women's Suffrage.[8] In the suffrage procession Charlotte Despard marched as president of the Women's Freedom League (WFL); in September she took her place in the Co-Masonic procession as Assistant Deacon. The suffrage procession itself was organized by the theosophist Kate Harvey, also a member of the WFL and a close associate of Despard.[9]

The affiliations between religion, especially esoteric religion, and feminist political culture were neither accidental nor idiosyncratic. As Philippa Levine has noted, few of the women who entered the feminist movement rejected religion entirely. A significant minority of the women in Levine's sample (around 8 percent) experienced spiritual conversions, which she takes as an indication that religion played an important role in their lives.[10] In *Becoming a Feminist* Olive Banks studied a representative list of prominent feminist women from the nineteenth and early twentieth centuries. Of the women in her sample who were active from the 1890s to the 1930s, almost 10 percent—Annie Besant, Ursula Bright, Charlotte Despard, Flora Drummond, Eva Gore-Booth, Annie Kenney, Dora Montefiore, and Emmeline Pethick-Lawrence—actually joined the Theosophical Society at some point in their careers. Not all these women can be usefully characterized as theosophists, but their membership in the TS signifies, at the very least, an interest in "matters spiritual" and an openness to unorthodox forms of religiosity. Given theosophy's minority status, this percentage is remarkably high: prominent feminists were hundreds of times more likely to join the TS than were members of the general population.[11]

If we add to this number those women in Banks's study whose lives included a substantial engagement with unorthodox forms of spirituality more broadly defined, such as Emily Wilding Davison, Mary Gawthorpe, and Dora Marsden, the percentage climbs even higher. One might also include Eleanor Sidgwick, who devoted many years of her life to the Society for Psychical Research, founded to explore the scientific evidence for spiritual claims. Of the other women Banks lists, many devoted considerable time and energy to creative and original religious work. Frances Power Cobbe, for example, was better known in her own day for her writings on theism than for her feminism; Christabel Pankhurst spent her later years writing and preaching on the Second Coming; and Maude Royden was the minister at London's City Temple in the 1920s.

Some studies note the links between theosophy and the women's movement. They tend to conclude that theosophy was attractive to women because it offered a "feminine" form of spirituality and a celebration of the balance between male and female principles (the yang and the yin) in cosmic and human development.[12] This argument allows us to see the appeal of movements like theosophy to women who were active feminists, but it also begs crucial questions. It risks implying that an appropriately feminine (or feminist) form of spirituality was already waiting to be mobilized for political ends. Other important questions, such as how and under what circumstances spiritual claims are made available for feminist ends, can only be answered when both "women's spirituality" and the concept of the "spiritual" are subjected to a rigorously historical analysis. The spiritual was itself a site of struggle; feminist versions of theosophy or esotericism existed in tension with other, often explicitly antifeminist interpretations of the esoteric tradition. Women's spirituality emerged from these struggles as a precarious, contradictory, and unstable formation; its mobilization within feminist political culture was also inflected by these struggles.

These women were attempting to articulate a feminist spirituality at a time when explicitly religious issues were becoming increasingly marginal to public political debate. According to Hugh McLeod, religion at this time was increasingly understood as a matter of private conscience rather than as the basis for public life. James Obelkevich, in his review of the English case, characterizes this process as the privatization of religion.[13] Even though religious issues no longer dominated parliamentary debate, religious beliefs continued to shape extraparliamentary political culture, especially feminist culture, in crucial ways. Many of those who campaigned for "votes for women" would not have viewed feminist politics as a secular activity. *The Co-Mason*, for example, argued that the women's suffrage procession was a "sacramental" act.[14] That claim was tied to an understanding of feminism that rejected a privatized spirituality and instead attempted to sacralize the public sphere.

The tendency to conflate both women and the spiritual with the private is partly the legacy of early nineteenth-century evangelicalism, which helped to shape the divisions between public and private within middle-class culture and to identify both women and spirituality with the ostensibly private sphere of the home.[15] Even so, religion also provided women with access to the public sphere. Believing themselves to be the morally and spiritually superior sex (a notion that was always partial and contested), some women tried to lay claim to moral and spiritual authority in public as well as in private. Throughout the nineteenth century, women put religion to many and various uses: Primitive Methodists defended women's preaching, utopian socialists called for a "Female Messiah," and women in the spiritualist movement used their role as trance mediums both to subvert and confirm separate-spheres ideology. Excellent studies in each of these areas reveal the difficulty of generalizing about the relationship between women and religion during this period.[16] Sectarian and theological differences are not trivial ones, and close attention must be paid to the ways in which women and women's concerns were interpolated into different religious traditions, each of which provided women with different degrees of room to maneuver. In the same way, the Theosophical Society and the esoteric tradition offered women very specific opportunities while foreclosing others.

I am primarily concerned to trace the dynamic structures of gender and sexuality, especially as they related both to feminist politics and to the feminization of religion during this period. It is crucial, however, not to lose sight of how these structures were imbricated in others, equally dynamic: changing notions of class and race both undergirded and undercut these other debates. If we return to the contours of the space ceremonially marked as sacred in the Co-Masonic procession in

September 1911 we can see, embedded in the building itself, important claims about the prestige, purpose, and meaning of theosophy and the Theosophical Society. These claims, which articulated particular kinds of class and racial privilege, provided a crucial context for the elaboration of both a women's spirituality and a feminist political theology.

The late nineteenth-century occult revival came in many guises. Some, such as certain forms of astrology or fairground fortunetelling, were relatively popular and democratic. Others, like the magical Order of the Golden Dawn or the Theosophical Society itself, were more self-consciously elitist. The TS deliberately constructed itself as a religion for the "thinking classes." It appealed above all to an elite, educated, middle- and upper-middle-class constituency. The new headquarters were therefore intended to reflect the dignity of the society in concrete and visible ways. An early proposal to build on Malet Street, just behind the British Museum (probably the site now occupied by Senate House, University of London) was rejected by the planning committee because of insufficient space.[17] The new buildings, arranged to evoke a Celtic cross, were to contain four small halls and a central amphitheater, the offices of various theosophical enterprises, and some self-contained flats for members of the society. If the Theosophical Society was entitled, on the basis of its dignity and importance, to be considered the "'Royal Society' of Occultism," then it deserved a worthy headquarters.[18]

In the division between the "classes" and the "masses," the TS was clearly on the side of the classes—a political, economic, cultural, and intellectual elite dominated by a relatively small and cohesive set of familial and marital networks. This was a rich recruiting ground for the many heterodox movements that flourished in late Victorian and Edwardian culture. On the "physical plane," social class and its associated cultural capital regulated access to the mysteries. This was as true of the occult as it was of the perhaps equally esoteric discourses of medicine and the law.

The construction of the new building also revealed the links between theosophy and progressive politics. The work was to be organized on Guild Socialist lines, an experiment in the direct employment of labor overseen in part by the Labour M. P. George Lansbury, who was a member of the TS Headquarters Building Committee. Against the backdrop of a lock-out of unskilled workers in the building trade, the Theosophical Society, for Lansbury, stood as an example of new possibilities in the relationship between capital and labor.[19]

In 1911 members of the Theosophical Society believed that they were about to lead the world into a New Age, spiritually and politically.

Artist's sketch of the proposed TS Headquarters.
(Adyar Library and Research Centre)

These grandiose ambitions were never realized. The society never even took possession of its new headquarters, which were commandeered by the Ministry of Munitions during the 1914–18 war and eventually sold. In 1934 the society finally acquired permanent headquarters (less central and less impressive, though still respectable) on Gloucester Road. By that time, the society's prestige and political purchase had declined substantially. But in 1911 members of the TS were actively engaged with some of the most pressing issues of the day.

One of the functions of the Theosophical Society was to bring together men and women with a range of progressive and humanitarian interests. This oppositional, radical culture was largely populated by those men and women dismissed by H. M. Hyndman of the Marxist Social Democratic Federation as "old cranks, humanitarians, vegetarians, anti-vivisectionists and anti-vaccinationists, arty-crafties and all the rest of them." Historians have just begun to map the contours of this oppositional culture, and we have as yet only an imperfect understanding of the networks that linked alternative spirituality to these political movements. Theosophy provided one way of theorizing the connections between causes as apparently diverse as women's suffrage, antivivisection, pacifism, anti-imperialism, and socialism. Theosophists were among those men and women who constituted themselves as the humanitarian conscience of the middle class, a dissident minority who worked in a variety of parallel organizations to critique the dominant bourgeois values and culture.[20] These organizations occupied a privileged place, at once inside and outside of elite culture.

The history of theosophy also needs to be set in the context of the history of imperialism. Recent research in that field has called into question the division between "Home" and "Empire" that still underpins conventional understandings of British domestic and imperial history. Modern British history should be viewed in the context of what Ann Stoler has described as an "imperial landscape" and Mrinalini Sinha has called the "imperial social formation."[21] By the late nineteenth century improvements in transportation and communication had brought Europe and Asia into relatively close proximity. Travel between England and India was still the privilege of a small and mostly affluent group, and was still structured by the constraints of gender and race, caste and class. It had become more frequent, however, as travelers and tourists, pilgrims and professionals crossed and recrossed the globe.[22] The encounter between England and India, which was sometimes reified in the pages of theosophical magazines and pamphlets, was also forged through multiple personal encounters within the TS, both at home and abroad.

By 1911 the Theosophical Society in England was ready to take what members believed was its proper place in this imperial landscape, politically and architecturally. The time had come, Annie Besant claimed in her 1911 presidential address to the society's convention, for the TS in England to have "a worthy Headquarters in the Metropolis of the Empire." "You must," she argued, "from your geographical position, from your place in the world-empire, occupy the leading place in the Movement so far as the English-speaking lands are concerned, and it is not quite consonant with the dignity of the Movement that you should have to meet always in a hired house."[23] As befitted a headquarters in the

"Metropolis of the Empire," the new building was to be designed, and its erection supervised, by Sir Edwin Landseer Lutyens, fresh from commissions in Rome, where he had designed the British Pavilion for the international exhibition, and South Africa (the Johannesburg Art Gallery and the Rand war memorial). Sir Edwin's services were obtained through the good offices of his wife, Lady Emily, who was an active and prominent member of the TS.[24]

The racial politics of empire were crucial in framing the context for the emergence of a feminine/feminist spirituality within the Theosophical Society. Recent studies of religious syncretism emphasize both its crucial role in religious life generally, and the extent to which it is structured by relations of power.[25] The inequalities of power that structured exchanges in the colonial context mark theosophy's syncretizing impulse as a distinctively colonial one. Theosophists claimed to uncover the esoteric truth of traditions from beneath their exoteric accretions, to rescue a form of knowledge that had fallen into degraded forms in modern-day India. Theosophy was therefore a kind of middle-brow orientalism (in Edward Said's sense), which reinscribed divisions between eastern mysticism and western science.[26]

As Richard King points out, recent scholarship in both Buddhist and Hindu studies has tended to reject characterizations of those traditions as inherently or essentially mystical, and has instead emphasized their diversity. But, King argues, current debates within the comparative study of religion, and especially of mysticism, continue to reproduce the image of a mystic East that functions as the mirror image of a secular and rational West.[27] East and West, in this context as in others, are clearly imaginary entities. As Dipesh Chakrabarty emphasizes, however, that they are imaginary does not diminish their appeal and power.[28] My use of terms like *East* and *West*, or *eastern mysticism,* is always intended to signal their ambivalent and ambiguous status—as imaginary entities that nonetheless have had very real effects in both England and India. Even as we draw attention to the historical processes that produced the supposed dichotomy between East and West, we are forced to recognize the power of that dichotomy in the organization not only of knowledge but also of experience.

This is not to deny that such experiences were sincere, deeply felt, and powerfully motivating, or that these were genuine efforts to develop modes of spirituality that embraced diversity and advocated respect for a variety of traditions. The operations of what we might call the colonial syncretic could also permit a critique of imperialism and of English political and cultural life.[29] This spiritual vision, which turned eastward for inspiration, can be characterized in the same terms that

Reina Lewis uses in her study of women, orientalism, and empire, as "a series of identifications that did not have to be either simply supportive or simply oppositional, but that could be partial, fragmented and contradictory."[30] The Theosophical Society was a crucial source of unofficial information about India and Sri Lanka; theosophists were also among the very few in Europe who ventured to suggest that Hinduism and Buddhism might contain spiritual truths that Christianity had forgotten. Syncretic religion was therefore one of the many contact zones where relations between colonizer and colonized were renegotiated, and in which both parties could be transformed.[31]

Since claims about spirituality are so often aligned with claims about the absolute or transcendent, an appeal to the spiritual can become a powerful cultural and political resource. The image of the mystic East, for example, played an important role in the arguments of many Hindu reformers and Indian nationalists. Similarly, in modern England, religion has often been crucial to women in both public and private life, even and perhaps especially in a supposedly secular age.[32] In many histories of feminist political culture, however, the continuing significance of these spiritual claims is ignored. Historians tend to employ a hierarchy of explanation that assumes, rather than demonstrates, the analytic priority of the political or the economic over the spiritual. The point is not to overturn that hierarchy, but to suggest that we need to complicate our understanding of the historical contexts that shape both political and spiritual allegiances, the formation of political subjectivities, and the relationship between secular and sacred in modern political cultures.

The spiritual is not posited here as an ontological category, but as a cultural formation: culturally and historically, the spiritual, like the political or the economic, is precipitated out of the diverse and competing claims that are made about it. Debates over where to draw the lines between secular and sacred themselves constitute the field within which both of those concepts take shape and acquire their power. The spiritual needs to be understood in dynamic rather than static terms, and in its relationship to other discursive constructions, not in isolation.[33]

There are, however, significant limitations to the effort to make the spiritual a category of historical analysis. A recent article by Sandra Holton puts the case bluntly: "Divine intervention is not capable of being established as a historical 'fact.'"[34] Holton draws our attention, not just to the nature of divine intervention, but also to the nature of the historical fact. She goes on to discuss Dipesh Chakrabarty's claim that "investment in a certain kind of rationality and a particular understanding of the 'real' means that history's, the discipline's, exclusions

are ultimately epistemological."[35] The history of spirituality is, therefore, irrevocably bound up with the history of rationality itself. In a
study of Victorian spiritualism, Alex Owen makes a similar point, arguing that to reduce spiritualist experience to the simple dichotomy of
"real/nonreal" ignores the ways in which reality is constituted in relative
and consensual terms.[36]

This is not to suggest that all truth-claims about the nature of the
divine or of the material world are equally fictive (and therefore equally
true). It is, instead, to explore how such truth-claims work, to insist
that the power relationships embedded in these claims be open to scrutiny. Divine intervention is not a historical fact, but the belief (or disbelief) in divine intervention has had powerful historical effects. Science
and religion are not monolithic packages to be accepted or rejected.
They are dense bundles of beliefs and practices that emerge in particular historical contexts. My study of theosophy is an effort to illuminate
those historical contexts. In so doing, I have attempted to evade what
Michel Foucault characterized as Enlightenment blackmail, which demands that "one has to be 'for' or 'against' the Enlightenment. . . . You
either accept the Enlightenment and remain within the tradition of its
rationalism (this is considered a positive term by some and used by
others, on the contrary, as a reproach); or else you criticize the Enlightenment and then try to escape from its principles of rationality (which
may be seen once again as good or bad)."[37]

I am therefore not primarily concerned with what theosophical
teachings "really meant," or with whether or not they were "really
true," but with the range of readings that were historically available,
and with the factors that enabled both belief and disbelief. The conflict
between science and religion has not only (or always) been a conflict
between truth and error; it has also been a conflict between different
kinds of prestige, authority, and privilege. Similarly, the characterization of alternative spirituality as pseudo-spirituality or as a cut-and-
paste religion often invokes unexamined aesthetic and intellectual
standards, which have themselves been produced within the structural
inequalities of our own society, most prominently the inequalities of
class, race, and gender.

Theosophists, no less than their contemporaries working within the
frameworks of orthodox Christianity or natural science, were making
important claims about the relationship between spirituality and power.
Theirs was an attempt to articulate and enact new ways of living and
being, an effort to live, as the theosophist Esther Bright put it, "beyond
the magic circle of custom."[38] The space "beyond the magic circle of
custom" is also, of course, from another perspective, the space occupied

by the lunatic fringe. How and why movements come to occupy such a space is preeminently a historical question: the relationship between the cultural center and its periphery is continually being renegotiated, as both center and periphery are defined and redefined over time. This book offers one history of that relationship.

Part One

DOMESTICATING
THE OCCULT

Chapter One

The Undomesticated
Occult

In December 1885 the committee appointed by the Society for Psychical Research (SPR) to investigate "occult phenomena" in connection with theosophy published the results of a one-and-a-half-year-long study. The SPR report concluded that Mme. Blavatsky was to be regarded "neither as the mouthpiece of hidden seers, nor as a mere vulgar adventuress; we think that she has achieved a title to permanent remembrance as one of the most accomplished, ingenious, and interesting imposters in history."[1] To reach this conclusion, the SPR committee had spent hundreds of hours gathering testimony from theosophists and cross-examining the most prominent members of the Theosophical Society in England. They had even sent an investigator, Mr. Richard Hodgson, B. A. of Cambridge, to the theosophists' world headquarters in India.

Employing methods worthy of his fictional contemporary Sherlock Holmes, Hodgson collected written and oral statements from both "European" and "native" informants, and amassed a wealth of physical evidence. He conducted a minute calligraphic examination of documents—tabulating instances of the "left-gap stroke" and the "clipped loose d" in order to prove forgery—and he pored over telltale stains or marks on clothes and furniture to find evidence of fraud. Hodgson concluded that whatever the status of the theosophists' spiritual teachings, their claims to have verifiable evidence of the existence of supernatural powers and superhuman beings were completely fraudulent. On the basis of Hodgson's findings, the leaders of the SPR—whose published opinions carried considerable intellectual weight and cultural prestige—dismissed Blavatsky as an ingenious imposter.

In the years that followed this "exposure" of Blavatsky and the Theosophical Society, however, Blavatsky's following continued to grow. Her greatest literary success, *The Secret Doctrine,* which sealed her reputation as one of the nineteenth century's greatest occult teachers, came three years later, in 1888. New lodges were founded, drawing hundreds of devotees, as well as the merely curious, to weekly meetings, and a new theosophical magazine, impudently named *Lucifer,* brazenly

17

noted that the SPR condemnation had done the Theosophical Society a great service. In 1891, just days after Blavatsky's death, the *Pall Mall Gazette* noted that even the Society for Psychical Research could not explain away the greatest of Blavatsky's miracles: that "sincere and clever persons, intimate with Mdme. Blavatsky," continued to "believe her incapable of deceit," and that, contrary to all expectations, "the Theosophical Society grows weekly, runs several periodicals, and boasts thousands of disciples in both hemispheres."[2]

Blavatsky's appeal was that she promised to reconcile virtually all the oppositions of late Victorian society. What had attracted the interest of the Society for Psychical Research in the first instance was the promise of an empirically verifiable spiritual science. Blavatsky did not claim to defy science but to supersede it: the Theosophical Society's motto, "There is no religion higher than truth," reflected the effort to reconcile all religions, philosophies, and scientific systems in a higher synthesis. There was enough of the Enlightenment project here to suggest that theosophy offered a more modern religion as well as a more spiritual science. Blavatsky's superior knowledge of natural law apparently allowed her to manipulate the laws of physics to produce what looked to the uninitiated like miracles: she could create the sound of "astral bells" or materialize a shower of roses out of thin air.

But theosophy was also routinely condemned as un-Christian, unscientific and un-English—not a fit creed for persons of culture and breeding. This was because Blavatsky claimed to offer not only the certainty of science, but also the exotic glamour of a mystic East. Her powers were believed by her followers to be directly linked to ancient spiritual teachings transmitted to her by members of an Occult Brotherhood living in the "trans-Himalayan fastnesses of Tibet."[3] Since Tibet was in this period effectively closed to Europeans, knowledge of the country and its terrain was inevitably partial and fragmentary; for many late Victorians, Tibet was "mysterious Tibet," and Blavatsky offered to solve that mystery.[4] Manuscripts purportedly written by the Mahatmas who belonged to this brotherhood not only conveyed the teachings Blavatsky claimed as the basis of her powers, but also were offered as material evidence of the reality of occult phenomena. Prominent theosophists had claimed to receive letters from these Mahatmas, letters that had been transmitted across the Himalayas from Tibet to India at the speed of electricity and delivered by occult means.

The Mahatmas had chosen Blavatsky, a woman who was a Russian and, as she put it, therefore "*half Asiatic*," to convey these teachings to the world.[5] This was, according to the *Pall Mall Gazette*, "inexpressibly bizarre and paradoxical."[6] Many observers could not believe that the

West, modern, industrialized, and scientific, had anything to learn from the East, which was routinely characterized as backward and mired in superstition. Similarly, Blavatsky's being a woman made her an unlikely authority. In the late nineteenth century women in England were effectively excluded from most professions and many of the major intellectual institutions. Authority, spiritual or otherwise, had come to be represented as the property of European men, not of "Asiatics" and women. One way to read the history of the TS, from its earliest years through the 1930s, is to see it as a series of attempts to create a usable version of both eastern and feminine authority.

The theosophists' claims that an "ancient wisdom" existed in the East and that it was being transmitted to the West through the medium of a woman played off long-standing tropes in English culture. Throughout the nineteenth century, both women and the Orient were looked to as sources of spiritual power and inspiration. Women's special relationship to spirituality and morality had been firmly established, at least for the middle classes, in early Evangelical texts. And from at least the Romantic movement onward, versions of eastern mysticism had provided inspiration to Europeans suffering from the malaises of industrial modernity. However well established, these remained troubled forms of authority. Insofar as the spiritual had become feminized or exoticized, it was a subordinated knowledge; conversely, insofar as the spiritual was a source of authority, it tended still to be associated with western forms of male privilege, such as the clergy and the academic establishment.

Religious authority itself was also being undermined during this period. From the mid-nineteenth century, orthodox Christianity had been called into question by natural scientists, philosophers, and even theologians. In the 1870s and 1880s an evolutionary paradigm that plotted societies along the axis of primitive/civilized was rapidly becoming the common sense of a new anthropology. The mid-nineteenth century belief in the link between civilization and Christianity was beginning to be eroded. In 1871 the publication of both Darwin's *Descent of Man* and E. B. Tylor's *Primitive Culture* had begun the process of unhitching spirituality and religion from the "civilized" end of the axis and linking them more closely to the animistic and mythological world of "primitive man."[7] A new version of the civilizing mission emerged, which emphasized not Christianity but science and technology as the hallmarks of cultural superiority.[8] In its baldest and most vulgar form, this shift to an evolutionary paradigm was interpreted to mean that men (and especially men of the European bourgeoisie) represented the modern, rational, secularizing thrust of progress, while women (and non-

Europeans) represented an atavistic primitivism that was traditional, emotional, and superstitious or religious.[9]

The "secularization of the European mind" in the nineteenth century was an uneven process, which produced new faiths as often as it overturned older ones.[10] Frederic Myers of the Society for Psychical Research was one of those who believed, however briefly, that Blavatsky might possess the answers to his spiritual questions. Myers, like many of the founding members of the SPR, was well educated; at Trinity College, Cambridge, he had been closely associated with Henry Sidgwick, the Knightsbridge Professor of Moral Philosophy and founding president of the SPR. Much of Myers's own research was in experimental and theoretical psychology, and he later played an important role in popularizing Freudian theory for an English audience.[11]

In 1886, in his introduction to the SPR study *Phantasms of the Living*, Myers noted that the SPR investigation of theosophy was part of a larger investigation of the claims of religion in general. If the theosophists' claims had proven to be true, then a prima facie case would have been established for miracles and revelations. According to Myers, "the *emotional* creed of educated men is becoming divorced from their *scientific* creed." For Myers, science alone had not addressed the fundamental questions of human existence: "the obvious deductions of materialistic science are strained or overpassed in order to give sanction to feelings and aspirations which it is found impossible to ignore." He argued that scientific progress had made it impossible for educated men to cling to the superstitions of the past, but science in its present form did not meet the basic emotional needs that even the most primitive religions had evolved to satisfy. Evolutionary biology had explained away the belief in God or gods, but it could not provide the assurance of salvation or the knowledge of life after death. As Myers put it, "Our highest and most complex emotions are traced to their rudimentary beginnings in the instincts of self-preservation and reproduction." And yet, "Death . . . has lost none of its invincible terrors."[12] Myers's understanding of the ultimate questions was still an implicitly Christian one; these were not the central concerns of all religious traditions. Myers also reinforced the notion that the crisis of faith involved only those men whose education and upbringing had made the faith of their fathers inadequate in a more modern age. Although the SPR, like the TS, attracted a significant minority of women—Eleanor Sidgwick was the most prominent woman member—the reference to educated *men* in the society's manifesto was not accidental. The late Victorian crisis of faith was implicitly presented as a genteel and masculine dilemma.[13]

Men like Myers were searching for a scientific and empirically verifiable spirituality, but they were also drawn to the glamour and the mystery that Blavatsky represented. Myers and his colleague Edmund Gurney, in particular, were impressed by the theosophists' claims, so much so that the psychical researcher J. H. Stack complained in October 1884 that "I tried to convert Myers and Gurney yesterday; I am afraid my arguments had not much effect: they are still under the spell of Mme. Blavatsky."[14] In Blavatsky's presence, as Frank Podmore of the SPR put it in 1892, "the very air teemed with mystery."[15]

Blavatsky's appeal was a combination of mystery and scientism. The vision of the East and of India mobilized within the TS in the late 1870s and 1880s was simultaneously the glamorous and exotic India of conservative orientalism and the India of the liberal reform tradition, evolving toward a more English, and therefore supposedly more modern and scientific, version of civilization.[16] In these early years, theosophy and Blavatsky attempted to occupy both poles of the primitive/civilized axis simultaneously and to confound easy distinctions between science and religion, West and East, male and female, civilized and primitive. Blavatsky traded on the fact that theosophy could not be fully domesticated, that it was not (quite) civilized. She unabashedly drew on western rationalist norms for authority and at the same time forced her interlocutors to participate in, or at least to acknowledge, her critique of those same norms. She also deployed (as it suited her purposes) all the stereotypes that linked spiritual power to the primitive and uncivilized. In effect, Blavatsky and her Mahatmas represented a vision of the mystic East that could be both respectable and exotic.

Blavatsky's own history displayed many of the same contradictions that later characterized the society she helped to found. Born in the Ukraine in 1831 of an aristocratic Russian family, Blavatsky had traveled widely in Europe, Egypt, and the Americas. Her biographers disagree about her activities, but she claimed to have spent at least some of those years studying occultism in a Tibetan monastery. She arrived in New York in 1873 and two years later, with the American lawyer Col. Henry Steel Olcott, founded the Theosophical Society. In 1879 Blavatsky and Olcott traveled to India, establishing a new world headquarters for the Theosophical Society, first in Bombay, and then at Adyar, a suburb of Madras.[17]

Mme. Blavatsky, or HPB, as she became known within the TS, remains an enigmatic and controversial figure. The more respectable members of her society spent much of their time apologizing for her behavior—her outspokenness, her vulgarity, and her refusal to abide by the niceties of drawing-room etiquette. Some wondered audibly why the new revelation had not been conveyed through someone rather more

H. P. Blavatsky in 1889.
(Adyar Library and Research Centre; photograph by Enrico Resta)

genteel, to which Blavatsky responded, "I DO NOT CARE ABOUT PUBLIC OPINION. I despise thoroughly and with all my heart Mrs. Grundy."[18]

If Mrs. Grundy was the personification of respectable opinion, then Blavatsky was buoyed in her campaign against Grundyism by an aristocratic upbringing. Intimately connected to the Russian elite, she cultivated aristocratic connections even after renouncing her claim to any title on becoming an American citizen. Simultaneously a democrat and an aristocrat, she was at home and yet not at home in the official Anglo-Indian society of Ootacumund and Simla. Can you imagine, she wrote, with heavy irony, "my graceful, stately person, clad in half Tibetan half night-dress fashion, sitting in all the glory of her Calmuck beauty at the Governor's and Carmichael's dinner parties; H. P. B. positively courted by the aide-de-camps! . . . hanging like a gigantic nightmare on the gracefully rounded elbows of members of the Council, in pumps and swallow tail evening dress and silk stockings smelling brandy and soda enough to kill a Tibetan Yak!!" And yet, there she was, "presiding Juno and Minerva-like over the whole of the Ooty high officials."[19] Underscoring her own rejection of both bourgeois respectability and the ideal of the aristocratic lady of fashion, Blavatsky represented herself as standing outside convention.

The references to her "half Tibetan" dress, and her "Calmuck beauty" also exemplify HPB's curious claims to represent, hybrid-fashion, a reconciliation of opposites. The few years spent living with her father when he was the governor of Russia's Kalmuck Buddhists had, it seemed, laid a "Kalmuco-Buddhisto-Tartaric" cast over her features; that claim, repeated often enough, shaped how others perceived her. Prominent in Olcott's memory of his first meeting with her, for example, was this "massive Calmuck face," with "its suggestion of power, culture, and imperiousness."[20] "Half Asiatic" when it suited her, she could also claim to be "European born" and as such, "brought up as much as any one else in the worldly notions of truth and honour."[21] She exploited the Slavophile strain in Russian culture in similar ways, portraying herself as a literal embodiment of East and West.[22]

Blavatsky also moved between man and woman. Far from womanly, she made her womanhood a crucial part of her transgressive public persona: "I am repeatedly reminded of the fact, that, as a public character, a woman, who, instead of pursuing her womanly duties, sleeping with her husband, breeding children, wiping their noses, minding her kitchen and consoling herself with matrimonial assistants on the sly and behind her husband's back, I have chosen a path that has led me to notoriety and fame; and that therefore I had to expect all that befell me."[23] However, her being a woman gave her public character its unsettling charge. There were times when she presented herself in conventionally feminine terms: for example, representing herself as a passive medium for the transmission of her Masters' teaching. At other times she claimed a masculine persona, as when she spoke of an "indweller," an "interior man" who could be identified either with her higher consciousness or with the overshadowing spirit of one of the Masters themselves.[24] When she published her mystical treatise, *The Voice of the Silence,* a few years after the publication of the SPR report, she inscribed the flyleaf of her own copy, "From H. P. B. to H. P. Blavatsky, with *no* kind regards," confirming this sense of a doubling or splitting of her gendered self-representation.[25] Awkwardly situated with regard to both "true manhood" and "true womanhood," Blavatsky exploited that situation to claim spiritual authority as a man (HPB) and spiritual powers as a woman (Helena Blavatsky).

Finally, in contrast to those who by implication were the enervated products of modern civilization, Blavatsky personified, for both her critics and her admirers, the exuberance and the power of the natural world, unspoiled by civilization. In a memorial published after her death in 1891, she was described as a "mountain torrent" that flooded the valleys with the spiritual wisdom of the Himalayas.[26] There was a sense of the inhuman in these descriptions, of something primordial and even grotesque: as W. T. Stead, the editor of the *Pall Mall Gazette* and a convinced spiritualist, put it, she was "a kind of Rabelaisian fantasy of Gargantuan proportions."[27] Years later one admirer recalled her as "the last of the mammoths" and said that "only the cave-temples of India can describe her." In her outward appearance, "she suggested the *monsterism* of those strange forms Blake drew; whose clothes, hair, gestures, seem part of the rocks and trees which surround them; who walk girdled with the Zodiac and hold converse with the gods."[28]

More prosaically, at the time of the SPR inquiry, Blavatsky was in her mid-fifties, overweight, and suffering from Bright's disease, which frequently confined her to a bath chair. Self-educated, she had a reputation as a polymath, and had at least a passing familiarity with a wide range of academic specialties. Aside from her native Russian, she spoke English, French, German, and some Italian, and she claimed to be able to read a fair amount of Sanskrit. Blavatsky's great strength was that she could appear able to "converse with the gods" at the same time as she spoke in the language of science and civilization. Her written work drew on sources ranging from Schopenhauer and Leibniz to the Kabbalah, the Purānas, and Chaldean mythology, from Haeckel and Darwin to Herbert Spencer and Michael Faraday. Blavatsky somehow managed to contain these contradictions within her carefully stage-managed persona. She charmed, overawed, and exasperated the sober, serious, and respectable men of both the Theosophical Society and the Society for Psychical Research, who were both attracted and repelled by Blavatsky and her mysterious Mahatmas.

In the late 1870s and the early 1880s British theosophists, unlike Blavatsky, were precisely the sort to worry what Mrs. Grundy might say. On their way to India in 1879 Blavatsky and Olcott had visited London and had met with those seekers who constituted the British Branch of the Theosophical Society. Led by the barrister Charles Carleton Massey, who had been present at the founding meetings of the movement in New York, a small group had been meeting in London to discuss theosophy since January 1877.[29] The British Theosophical Society was formally organized on June 27, 1878, when members were inducted under the obligation of secrecy and provided with the grips, passwords, and signs by which they were to recognize each other. The group was a loosely knit collection of spiritualists, Freemasons, and Rosicrucians, and (although its by-laws provided that "persons of either sex are eligible for admission"), with the exception of Emily Kislingbury, entirely male.[30] Other women joined soon afterward, notably Francesca Arundale, whose nephew and adopted son George was one day to become president of the TS, but women remained very much in the minority. Borrowing much of its structure and ritual from Masonic sources, the British Branch of the TS preserved the elite, male character of Freemasonry.

Massey and the others were impressed by Blavatsky's ability to produce apparently miraculous "phenomena" at will, but they were less enamored of her capacity for self-promotion. When Massey found his name in the newspapers in connection with occult phenomena, he complained that the incident had cost him his legal practice. The group tended to reject what they saw as Blavatsky's "aggressive policy," and emphasized study and self-discipline rather than propaganda.[31] Real success awaited the arrival of Mr. and Mrs. Sinnett from India in 1883. Alfred Percy Sinnett was largely responsible for disseminating the Theosophical Society's teachings in England, through the publication of *The Occult World* (1881) and *Esoteric Buddhism* (1883). Both works proved immensely popular, and the latter became the talk of fashionable London.[32] Sinnett also published novels that dramatized, though rather ponderously, theosophical teachings in a country-house setting (in *Karma* [1885] the theory of reincarnation is introduced through a kind of parlor game during a house party at the castle Heiligenfels, home of the Baron Friedrich von Mondstern).

Sinnett was the editor of the Anglo-Indian civil service newspaper, the *Pioneer*, published from Allahabad. His prominence within the Theosophical Society, and within London society more generally, was the result of his personal contacts with Blavatsky and, more important, with the Masters whom she claimed were guiding forces behind her work. These Masters had been variously identified in early theosophical writings, but by the mid-1880s they had been firmly located within a specifically Hindu tradition, as "Mahatmas," or great souls, who, as Blavatsky explained it, "by special training and education, [have] evolved those higher faculties and [have] attained that spiritual knowledge which ordinary humanity will acquire after passing through numberless series of reincarnations during the process of cosmic evolution."[33] Two of these Mahatmas, with whom Blavatsky claimed to have studied during her much disputed travels to Tibet, had taken a special interest in the Theosophical Society.[34]

Sinnett and his wife joined the TS while still in India, in 1879. A year later Blavatsky and Olcott visited the Sinnetts in Simla, where Blavatsky provided demonstrations of her training by the Mahatmas. These exhibitions became known as the "Simla phenomena" and were immortalized by Sinnett in *The Occult World*. Some of the phenomena were simple—for example, her ability to make cigarette papers appear and disappear. Others were more elaborate, as when she produced, apparently by magic, a cup and saucer required for an unexpected extra guest at a picnic. Sinnett, eager for more direct contact with the Mahatmas, asked Blavatsky if she could, by some occult means, deliver a letter that he had written to "the Unknown Brother" in Tibet. Blavatsky agreed to pass letters back and forth, and Sinnett's personal correspondence with the Mahatmas Koot Hoomi (KH) and Morya (M) began. Along with Sinnett, another Anglo-Indian member of the Simla Eclectic Theosophical Society, A. O. Hume, also began corresponding with the Mahatmas. Where Sinnett was a Tory and a staunch imperialist, Allan Octavian Hume was a radical and a liberal; in the late 1880s he was to be instrumental in organizing the first meetings of the Indian National Congress.[35]

The correspondence—thirteen hundred pages of which was deposited in the British Library's rare manuscript room in 1939—continued from 1880 to 1885. In 1883 Sinnett compiled the teachings offered in the early letters and published them as *Esoteric Buddhism*. The original letters were often scrawled on mismatched scraps of paper; stationer's shops, KH explained, were not a Tibetan institution.[36] Many of KH and M's notes were actually annotations on Sinnett's own letters, which were returned to him with marginal commentary in blue and red pencil. The Mahatma Letters themselves were transcribed and compiled by the theosophist A. T. Barker, who published them in 1923, two years after Sinnett's death.

The Mahatma Letters are curious documents. Their origin and provenance are, of course, open to dispute. Based on his study of the handwriting in the letters, and of their peculiarities of spelling and idiom, Richard Hodgson of the Society for Psychical Research concluded that the letters were forgeries, produced by Blavatsky and her confederates in response to Sinnett's request for direct contact with the Masters. Hume always remained cautious and skeptical, but Sinnett believed them to be authentic communications from beyond the Himalayas, written and delivered by occult means. As a consequence of his belief, he was forced to negotiate the paradoxes of this peculiar variant of orientalism: he was being asked to acknowledge as spiritual superiors beings whom he, as an Anglo-Indian during the British Raj, also saw as his "racial" inferiors.[37] It was one thing to encounter the "ancient wisdom of the East" through the writings of scholars, but it was another to have to deal with what he believed were actual native pandits. Reading the Mahatma Letters as Sinnett read them, as letters from real Mahatmas, underscores the complex renegotiations of authority that were at stake in this encounter.

If the author of the letters was Blavatsky herself, ventriloquizing Mahatmas who lived in Tibet (as Hodgson argued), the problem of interpretation is no less complicated. In this reading, Blavatsky's fictional personas—Morya, the gruff Punjabi, and the scholarly Kashmiri, Koot Hoomi Lal Singh—allowed her access to both an authoritatively masculine and an exotically eastern voice. Morya and Koot Hoomi could thus be invoked to authenticate Blavatsky's own pronouncements. Blavatsky staked her authority on her ability to speak on behalf of what she characterized as an ancient tradition of eastern wisdom: modern Hindus, she argued, should be "less sycophantic to their Western masters, less in love with their vices, and more like their ancestors in many ways." If they valued their own culture and learning rather than imitating their self-styled superiors, she went on, they wouldn't need "an old Western hippopotamus of a woman to prove the truth of their Shastras!"[38] If Blavatsky did write the letters, they become not (as Sinnett believed) the tangible proof of ancient eastern wisdom, but a complex appropriation of the ambiguous authority of the East in the orientalist imagination.

The authenticity of the Mahatma Letters was not necessarily the most important issue: as A. O. Hume put it, in one of his more skeptical notes to Master KH, "*even when I was fully persuaded you were a myth, . . . even then my heart yearned to you as it often does to an avowedly fictitious character.*" The Mahatma Letters played with notions of their own fictitiousness in sophisticated ways, calling attention to the Mahatmas' status as inventive inventions: having been "'invented' ourselves," the Masters noted, they "repay the inventors by inventing" increasingly complicated "imaginary" doctrines as a way of avoiding accusations of inconsistency or internal contradiction in their teachings.[39]

The Mahatma Letters were part stage spectacle and part scholarly artifact. Their final resting-place, in the manuscript room of the British Library, was an uncanny fulfillment of Morya's prophecy in Letter 29: "Ah Sahibs, Sahibs! if you could only catalogue and label *us* and set us up in the British Museum, then indeed might your *world* have the absolute, the desiccated truth."[40] But that final domestication was still a long way off. In 1885 Blavatsky and her Masters also embodied the glamour of the imperial exotic, the same glamour that was simultaneously drawing crowds to the spectacle of India-on-stage at London's Gaiety Theatre, where the "Indian Dramatic Company," which included acrobats, dancers, jugglers, and snake-charmers, was in the middle of a successful run.[41]

Blavatsky's accounts of the Masters, and of her relationship with them, were contradictory and confusing.[42] She sometimes borrowed the Mahatmas' authority to bolster her own: "Maybe I am now speaking *under inspiration*," she wrote to Sinnett on one occasion, "and you better not pooh-pooh my advice."[43] But the letters themselves continually undermined Blavatsky's authority as well as their own, emphasizing her unreliability, her incomplete understanding, her tendency to become "weak-headed when left to herself."[44] These are complicated narrative maneuvers, and it is no wonder that Sinnett's and Hume's correspondence with the Mahatmas M and KH continually returned to the question of the Mahatmas' authority.

The key question in this context was the extent to which Morya and Koot Hoomi measured up to the standards of British "civilization." Allan Hume posed this question most clearly, rejecting what he saw as oriental despotism in spiritual matters. Hume was a convinced liberal, broadly sympathetic to Indian nationalist demands for self-government. However, his agenda was assimilationist, and his sympathies tended to go to the most westernized elites within the nationalist movement.[45] According to Blavatsky, Hume treated the Masters "as if they were native clerks."[46] When Hume dreamed of mounting a scientific-cum-military expedition into Tibet to find the Masters and prove their existence, the Mahatmas ridiculed his temerity, declining the offer of his services as "General School Master for Tibet, Reformer of ancient superstitions and Saviour of future generations." Hume's letters, KH complained, had been "a monument of pride, the loud echo of that haughty and imperative spirit which lurks at the bottom of every Englishman's heart." Hume, it was suggested, was unable to reconcile his own secular authority over "native clerks" with the deference required of a humble postulant in matters spiritual.[47]

Hume eventually broke off the correspondence with Blavatsky's Mahatmas, but his behavior had raised a crucial question. How, KH asked, were men like Sinnett and Hume to take spiritual "dictation" from a Hindu, whose race "you have not yet learnt even to tolerate, let alone to love or respect." Perhaps the Mahatmas needed to be sanitized for western consumption? How many Anglo-Indians "would ever consent to have 'a nigger' for a guide or leader. . . . The prejudice of race is intense, and even in free England we are regarded as an 'inferior race.'" Fully cognizant of the kind of spiritual teacher Sinnett hoped for, KH added ironically that he would be careful, should he and Sinnett ever meet, to "create an atmosphere of sandal-wood and cashmere roses" which would presumably fulfill Sinnett's most exotic expectations.[48] Sinnett's more conservative (and even unabashedly racist) orientalism thus enabled a different, closer, and in some ways more deferential relationship with the Mahatmas than did Hume's liberalism. Where Sinnett's belief in racial difference allowed him to be convinced that his so-called racial inferiors could possess a knowledge the more civilized Englishman had lost in his ascent in the racial hierarchy, Hume's assimilationist convictions left less room for this interpretation.

Sinnett's orientalism took him only so far, however. He also wanted to be able to hold M and KH to the standards of probity and good manners that he felt were appropriate in Anglo-Indian society. Alas, KH informed him, "we have no *gentlemen*—now at all events, that would come up to the Simla standard—in Tibet, though many honest and truthful men."[49] Unlike Sinnett, the Mahatmas were unimpressed by "'Englishmen of the better sort,'" and "their hearts are rather for the natives."[50]

The tensions between western spiritual seekers and their recalcitrant "masters/servants" were central to the Theosophical Society's development from the beginning. English theosophists continually returned to the question of how and to what extent they would be guided by Asian religious authorities. When Sinnett returned to England, having lost his position at the *Pioneer*, he became prominent in what was by then known as the London Lodge of the Theosophical Society. There the conflict between East and West was restaged yet again. By this time Sinnett had staked his public reputation—with the publication of *The Occult World* and *Esoteric Buddhism*—on the existence of the Mahatmas and the validity of their teaching. Problems arose when Sinnett's commitment to his Masters came into conflict with the teachings of the new president of the London Lodge, Anna Bonus Kingsford. Kingsford was, with her colleague Edward Maitland, the author of *The Perfect Way* (1882). Like theosophy, *The Perfect Way* taught reincarnation and karma, but its emphasis was on Christian esotericism rather than Hinduism or Buddhism. Like Blavatsky, Kingsford claimed to have been "inspired" with the teachings conveyed in *The Perfect Way*. Kingsford's account of her "inspiration," however, was much closer to the model of passive, trance mediumship—in which a (usually female) medium served merely as a channel through whom the spirits could speak[51]—

than was Blavatsky's. The alliance between Kingsford and the TS was always an uneasy one: an anonymous review of *The Perfect Way* that appeared in *The Theosophist* in 1882 made the gendered oppositions between Kingsford's "esoteric Christianity" and theosophy's "esoteric Buddhism" very clear: "Occult philosophy, or esoteric Buddhism, is a stern uncompromising system of reason and logic; Christianity, a scheme of thought which throws reason and logic altogether overboard and rests its claims entirely on sentimentality—it is a religion in fact for women and not for men."[52] Conflict seemed inevitable.

Blavatsky and Kingsford clashed early in Kingsford's career in the Theosophical Society. Blavatsky's letters to Sinnett are bitingly sarcastic on the subject of the "divine Anna" who provided a stark contrast to Blavatsky's decidedly unfeminine style.[53] In 1884 Sinnett and Kingsford became involved in an acrimonious public disagreement about the role of the Masters and their teaching in the Theosophical Society, and Kingsford and Maitland left the TS to found the Hermetic Society.[54] After their departure the London Lodge was free to devote itself more fully to the teachings Sinnett had received from India and the Mahatmas.

Blavatsky argued that it was English "race-superiority" that had caused much of the trouble. Of George Wyld, for example, who left the TS during this period to pursue his own brand of Christian esotericism, she claimed that he wanted "to make believe, I suppose, that his Jesus was an Anglo-Saxon Aryan."[55] Those who remained within the TS in Britain declared themselves "for" the Mahatmas: members of the society formally recognized the superiority of eastern to western knowledge in things spiritual. They also reinstated a masculine rather than a feminine authority. Mr. Finch (head of his class in mathematics at Cambridge) was elected the new president, Sinnett continued to dominate the society both publicly and privately in his businesslike capacity as the "importer" of theosophy to England, and the decidedly unfeminine HPB and her male Masters were confirmed as the inspiring force of the TS.[56]

One result of this shift was to confirm the tendency of many British theosophists to look for a Mahatma in every Indian member they encountered. When Mohini M. Chatterji of the Bengal Theosophical Society arrived in London in the early 1880s, he was forced to negotiate his own claims to spiritual authority in the shadow of the mystic East. Chatterji, a Brahman lawyer and graduate of the University of Calcutta, came to London at a time when caste and religious restrictions against travel for caste Hindus, though weakening, were still in force.[57] Chatterji was therefore one of only a few prominent Indian theosophists to vist England in this period. The *Pall Mall Gazette* made much of his exotic and erotic appeal: "There was a splendour as of some astral oil about his dusky countenance and thick black locks; while his big, dark eyes were as piercing as those of Madame herself. Men gazed upon Mohini with awe, and ladies with enthusiasm."[58] Chatterji himself sometimes participated in the cultivation of this exotic image, as when he and Bertram Keightley, also a lawyer but a graduate of Cambridge, prostrated themselves at the feet of Mme. Blavatsky on the platform of Charing Cross Station, to the bemusement of other travelers.[59] Chatterji constantly confronted the tendency of the metropolitan press and public to construe the Hindu body as an exotic spectacle.[60] But that same tradition of romantic orientalism also invested his body, the specifically male body of a Hindu and a Brahman, with an almost magical power and spiritual authority.

At the same time, the TS provided a forum in which Chatterji could mobilize other constructions of his identity: as a man of letters and of significant professional accomplishments, and as a spiritual teacher entitled to respect. In his published writings Chatterji emphasized the philosophical aspects of theosophy, downplaying its more sensational side.[61] Many British theosophists did turn to Chatterji for spiritual leadership. In 1886, for example, some of the more earnest members began meeting under his guidance as the Oriental Group for the study of esoteric philosophy.[62] The TS thus proved an appropriate site for the enactment of what Mrinalini Sinha has described as the recuperation by Indian men of a "colonial masculinity," and what Inderpal Grewal identifies as a new mode of patriarchal power in relation to colonial modernity.[63]

Chatterji's claims to authority, whether based on his embodiment of the glamour of the mystic East or on his scholarly attainments, were not undisputed. Blavatsky claimed in a letter to Patience Sinnett (A. P. Sinnett's wife) that Chatterji had been made conceited by "those who may be too inclined to see in him a MAHATMA *en herbes*." He would do better, she suggested, to remember his place: he was to be a disciple and not a guru.[64] A descendant of the Hindu reformer Rammohun Roy, Chatterji later married the niece of the poet Rabindranath Tagore; he was thus well placed in liberal and reformist Hindu circles. Under the circumstances, it is perhaps not surprising that he chose in the end to pursue his career as a scholar and a teacher outside the Theosophical Society.[65]

By 1885 the Theosophical Society in England had consolidated a set of claims that reified an ancient eastern wisdom as a source of knowledge that was supposed to transcend both Christianity and science. Nonetheless, the struggle to domesticate the mystic East continued.

The tensions between the respectable and exotic faces of eastern mysticism that had emerged in Sinnett's relationship with the Mahatmas were now to be contained by the reorganization of public and private activities within the TS. The society's activities were effectively separated into two distinct arenas. Occultism was to be pursued secretly among committed theosophists, while the public face of theosophy was to be eminently respectable. On HPB's instructions, Sinnett began to develop an "inner ring" of students who were to receive more privileged communications. As this group advanced in confidence and esoteric knowledge, they also adopted a more public program and began to hold open meetings, abandoning the secret signs and passwords that had characterized their earlier gatherings.[66] Sinnett was critical of these quasi-Masonic rituals, which he believed only served to alienate the educated and cultured audience to which he hoped to appeal. According to Sinnett, "the leaders of the Psychic Research Society were intensely careful to keep all its proceedings on the level of upper class culture." He believed—quite rightly, as it turned out—that Blavatsky and Olcott would shatter the rapport he had established with the leaders of the Society for Psychical Research, because they were not "in tune with the taste of cultivated Europeans."[67]

The Society for Psychical Research had been founded early in 1882 to make "an organised and systematic attempt to investigate that large group of debatable phenomena designated by such terms as mesmeric, psychical, and Spiritualistic."[68] Explicitly modeling themselves on the Royal Society, members of the SPR hoped that by applying the latest techniques of nineteenth-century science they would be able to reach definite conclusions on such crucial issues as the immortality of the soul; questions that had defeated the philosophers and theologians of the past were now to be "solved in the market-place, by the Method of Averages and by tables of statistics." They claimed that their efforts were a reflection of "the democratic tendency of modern science," and that "the public are for the first time being made *participators* in scientific work." But their position with regard to this public was a highly privileged one: "for the first time they [the people] appear as the sources of the evidence, as the actual material (so to speak) of the experiments."[69] The members of the general public were not joint participants in the SPR scientific inquiry, but the subjects who provided the experimental data for that inquiry.

Empirical in their orientation and experimental in their approach, members of the SPR attempted to establish spirituality on a scientific basis. In the effort to establish the boundaries of what was and what was not scientific investigation of the paranormal, the debate over the

TS helped to drive out many of the believers and to establish the claims of the SPR to the disinterested pursuit of truth.[70] The conflict between the TS and the SPR, however, cannot be reduced to a simple triumph of the true and scientific over the false and superstitious. Both organizations operated in a shadowy borderland between science and religion. In this period some of the most advanced scientific techniques were enmeshed in complex relationships to what we have come to know as the irrational. For example, Hodgson's painstaking "calligraphic analysis" was closely allied to the occult arts of palmistry and graphology.[71]

The early contacts between the SPR and the TS were carried on at precisely the level of upper-class culture that Sinnett had hoped for: social calls were made and dinners were hosted at the Athenaeum Club.[72] The two groups drew on roughly the same constituency, and there was a considerable overlap in membership. As with other scientific or literary societies founded to pursue similar goals, the TS and the SPR exchanged journals and speakers on a regular basis.[73] In May 1884 the council of the SPR appointed a committee to take evidence in an investigation of "phenomena connected with Theosophy." This committee issued a provisional *First Report* in December 1884, stating that the evidence presented by the theosophists deserved serious and systematic attention. Hodgson was dispatched to India in November 1884. After a three-month investigation at the TS headquarters at Adyar and in other parts of India, Hodgson returned to England in April 1885. Just before he arrived at Adyar, the *Madras Christian College Magazine* had published certain letters that it claimed had been written by Mme. Blavatsky to M. and Mme. Coulomb, a handyman and housekeeper recently expelled from the TS headquarters. If genuine, the Coulomb letters amounted to an admission by Blavatsky of deliberate and extensive fraud in the production of occult phenomena. Blavatsky herself insisted that the letters were, at least in their incriminating aspects, forgeries. An investigation into the authenticity of these letters, and into other claims made by the Coulombs, occupied much of Hodgson's time in India.

The Coulombs' claim was supported by certain physical evidence found at the Adyar headquarters, including trapdoors and sliding panels in the Shrine Room where letters from the Masters had occasionally been "precipitated." The Coulombs insisted that these had been constructed at Blavatsky's request and explained the ways in which they had been used to deceive those who had witnessed occult phenomena. The theosophists argued that these contrivances had been constructed secretly by M. Coulomb in order to incriminate Blavatsky and to discredit her and her movement.[74] In return for the deception, the theoso-

phists claimed, the Coulombs had been well paid by Christian missionaries who saw the Theosophical Society as a threat to their spiritual
monopoly.

After hearing Hodgson's report, the SPR Committee on Theosophy
weighed the evidence and then announced that Blavatsky's phenomena
were produced through fraud, and that evidence as to the existence and
power of the Mahatmas could be put down to deliberate deception, hallucination, or "unconscious misrepresentation." The committee stressed
that while it had no means of checking Hodgson's findings, it was satis-
fied as to the "thoroughness" and "impartiality" of his investigation.
Hodgson had established a case for the possibility of an alternative explanation of the occult phenomena—that such phenomena could have
been produced by "ordinary physical means." Since "explanations by
trickery . . . or any other such explanations, were possible," and the
accounts provided by the Coulombs were "plausible," the committee
saw no reason to pursue the matter further.[75] Psychical researchers, as
Eleanor Sidgwick argued in *Journal of the SPR* in 1885, had to discard
as evidence all those phenomena that could be proved physically possible, whether by fraud, hallucination, or other means, without invok-
ing occult agency.[76] Theosophical phenomena had failed to measure up
to the stringent and demanding definition of verifiability applied by
the SPR.

The theosophists, no less than the psychical researchers, used science
to authorize their claims. Sinnett had argued in *The Occult World* that
occultism showed that "the harmony and smooth continuity of Nature
observable in physics extend[ed] to those operations of Nature that are
concerned with the phenomena of metaphysical existence."[77] He attempted to render the chaotic materials that had been presented to him
in the Mahatma Letters into a "scientific" form accessible to an English
audience, but he lacked Blavatsky's uncanny ability to play both sides
against the middle. As Frank Podmore of the SPR wrote in 1892, Sinnett "expound[ed] the new Gospel in language which would have been
appropriate in a treatise on kitchen-middens or the functions of the
pineal gland. . . . The mystery evaporated or crystallized into what
seemed mere matter-of-fact." Podmore noted that Sinnett's *Esoteric
Buddhism* had managed to treat the new revelation with all "the precision of an actuary."[78] While theosophists made extensive claims for the
scientific nature of their creed, unfortunately for Sinnett and theosophy,
his common-sense understanding of "scientific" and of "experimental
proof" was very different from that of the Society for Psychical Research. The SPR model was the laboratory: psychical researchers emphasized careful experimentation, elimination of variables, and the

scrupulous recording of data. Sinnett, in contrast, relied on the rhetoric of science but operated with a much less strict understanding of scientific rigor.

Even so, Sinnett fared far better at the hands of the psychical researchers than did most of his Indian colleagues. Indian witnesses were approached with suspicion from the beginning, and the efforts of some of the Indian members of the TS to establish their scientific and professional credentials had little impact. Mr. G. N. Unwale, for example, cited his scientific education, his familiarity with electrical and magnetic devices, and his knowledge of the techniques of prestidigitation as grounds for expertise, to no avail.[79] In tabulating evidence, the galley proofs of the *First Report* graphically illustrated the attitude of the SPR to Indian testimony. The witnesses were arranged by nationality, with the "Occidentals" (further broken down on the preceding page, in descending order, as "English," "American," "Russian," and "French") on one side and "Orientals" on the other.[80] In private correspondence with other members of the SPR, J. H. Stack noted that "slow progress of the cause amongst Anglo-Indians many of whom are highly educated and its rapid progress amongst uneducated superstitious and credulous natives is *prima facie* against it." While Sidgwick dismissed this comment with a scrawled "unimportant," Stack's claim that "there is no country in the world where confederates and witnesses could be purchased so cheaply as in India and where false testimony is so common" created a sense of doubt about the usefulness of Indian testimony.[81]

Indian mystics were not fellow inquirers into spiritual mysteries, but the objects of scientific study. As A. O. Hume, who became a member of the SPR in May 1885, had it in his earlier work, *Hints on Esoteric Theosophy No. 1*, "the comparatively delicate or feeble organization of Easterns—the result partly of climate, partly of vegetarian diet—is more favourable to the development of psychical power than the more robust animal food-fed organizations of the Western." Hume also noted a hereditary factor in psychical ability, and argued that "adeptship having been known for at least 4,000 years in India . . . while it has been absolutely unknown in the West, there are an infinitely greater number here, specially capable for such development than in Europe, or at least Western and Central Europe."[82] Similarly, members of the SPR argued that the psychological and "psycho-neural" constitution of the Indian peoples made them more susceptible to hypnotic suggestion, more likely to experience hallucinations and therefore to lay claim to psychic powers. The obvious lesson was, as the *First Report* put it, "in psychical research, experiment on Orientals."[83]

Sinnett endorsed these claims, arguing that "taking races into account, the people of India as a race, are immensely more susceptible to mesmerism than Europeans; probably because, as a race, they are on *a somewhat lower level of cosmic evolution*." His comments drew a furious response from Blavatsky: "why can't you ever write about India or Indians without allowing your pen to run away with your ineradicable prejudices at the expense of truth and fact?" Sinnett's position was, she argued, a misunderstanding of esoteric facts: "if, as a race, they are lower than Europeans it is only *physically* and in the matter of civilisation or rather what you yourselves have agreed to regard as civilisation—the purely external, skin deep polish, or a *whitened sepulchre* with rottenness inside, of the Gospel." European civilization concealed its narrowness, its materialism, and its bigotry under a veneer of polite behavior; any man unlucky enough to be the product of both Christianity and civilization was, according to Blavatsky, "an object to be hardly, if ever trusted."[84]

Blavatsky herself refused to participate in the SPR investigation, denying the authority of the "psychic asses" and their "*ungentlemanly, disgusting, Scotland yard* secret proceedings."[85] She was perhaps wise to refuse to allow herself to be transformed into the raw data for the scientific investigation of spirituality by the SPR, for women, too, tended to be the investigated rather than the investigators in psychical research. The SPR "Census of Hallucinations," for example, had revealed that women were roughly 50 percent more likely than men to have had, or to claim to have had, psychic experiences in the form of "sensory hallucinations."[86] The SPR did not take kindly to Blavatsky's refusal to participate in its study and exacted its own revenge. As Hodgson concluded in his report, "not to speak of the positive qualities which she habitually manifested, there are certain varieties of personal sacrifice and religious aspiration, the absence of which from Madame Blavatsky's conduct would alone suffice to remove her ineffably far from the St. Theresa type."[87]

Not all of the Theosophical Society's witnesses fared so badly. One of the major difficulties of compiling evidence in the case was that 1ere were European gentlemen pledging their honor to what appeared to be outrageous claims. As the *First Report* had it, the evidence available rendered it "impossible to avoid one or other of two alternative conclusions: —Either that some of the phenomena recorded are genuine, or that other persons of good standing in society, and with characters to lose, have taken part in deliberate imposture."[88] Many of the witnesses were professional, well-educated, well-connected men, very much the sort who formed the constituency of the SPR itself. Sinnett and Stack, for example, had been friends and colleagues since the 1860s, and Sin-

nett suggested in his *Autobiography* that it was Stack who first introduced him to Blavatsky's *Isis Unveiled*.[89]

Unlike spiritualist mediums (who were often working-class women)
or Indian "conjurers," Fellows of the Theosophical Society could and
did invoke their racial, gender, and class privileges in a demand to be
treated with respect; courtesy and professional protocol made it difficult to subject them to rigorous cross-examination or to surround them
with severe test conditions.[90] As the theosophist General Morgan put it,
"if it is considered that natives from their blind admiration of Madame
Blavatsky are out of Court, the same argument cannot apply to European Gentleman." Surely, he demanded, the testimony of "clever men"
like Sinnett (and himself) could not be dismissed or ignored.[91] The production not only of occult phenomena but of the truth of those phenomena was therefore socially and culturally situated. Alex Owen has
noted that the rules that governed the family seance—trust, intimacy,
and sincerity—tended to avert suspicion, creating a setting that imposed its own implicit test conditions.[92] For theosophists, and to a lesser
extent for members of the SPR, the social milieu within which the TS
operated functioned in a similar way. In scientific circles more generally
during this period, as Christopher Hamlin has noted, "rhetoric and reputation, not rigour" often formed an important part of the basis for
judging scientific claims.[93] However committed they were to the empirical tradition, the SPR investigators were reluctant to challenge too directly the complex sets of associations that linked their scientific inquiry to elite models of manliness.

In the event, such gentlemen were cleared from charges of dishonesty
in the SPR report, but only at the expense of their dignity. According
to Hodgson, the theosophical witnesses were "as a whole excessively
credulous, excessively deficient in the powers of common observation;
and too many of them prone to supplement that deficiency by cul-
pable exaggeration."[94] Olcott's dignity suffered more than most. Some
years earlier A. O. Hume had complained that neither he nor Sinnett
could take Olcott as a guide in things spiritual "because we both know
that we are intellectually his superiors."[95] What Sinnett and Hume saw
as Olcott's naive and simple faith proved to be his downfall. Sinnett
claimed that the real break between the TS and the SPR came on June 30,
1884, when Olcott "got up, uninvited, and made a speech in his worst
style," which set everyone's teeth on edge. As a result of Olcott's faux
pas, Sinnett went on, the leaders of the SPR "seem to have grown anx-
ious to shake themselves free from theosophical associates liable to bring
social discredit upon their undertaking."[96] Blavatsky once again sprang
to Olcott's defense: "We want *theosophists* not aristocratic noodles

who expect respect and honours only because their blood is crossed with that of lords and M.P.'s. What have they hitherto done to merit them? Made us the *great honour* of joining the Society? It is an honour to them, not in the least to the MASTERS." Nonetheless, she criticized Olcott for his desire to appeal to a worldly court, the SPR, and for his willingness to take the "Dons" as arbiters. Olcott's mistake, she argued, was his eagerness to cram those same Cambridge dons with what, by their standards, were "*cock and bull* stories."[97]

Sinnett later argued that Hodgson's methods were ill-judged, and that "his unfamiliarity with India and Indian ways" had "led him into many serious mistakes."[98] Hodgson's irreverence and his cavalier treatment of the Masters and their phenomena constituted an insult to the true Hindu's "veneration of things sacred," and Indian theosophists had responded to this insult by deliberately misleading and confusing Hodgson and his investigation.[99] Theosophists ridiculed the arrogance of the attempt to conduct psychical research "in harmony with prevailing modes of thought, by the help of measuring tapes and calligraphic experts," and asked, "Why should such persons [as Mahatmas] desire to convince sceptics of their existence? Did they come like book pedlars, to offer their goods, or have they been *asked* to give the West some of their ancient knowledge?"[100] Theosophists argued that to dismiss the claims of the TS was an insult to the ancient teachings of "Aryan Philosophy," appropriating to themselves whatever cultural authority such philosophy held.[101] Their opponents, on the other hand, saw the apparent unwillingness of the Mahatmas to give up their secrets as an affront to the dignity and honor of the British Raj. As Charles Massey, by then a member of the SPR and thoroughly disillusioned with theosophy, put it, "the knowledge we aspired to was a jealously guarded secret . . . these mysterious Adepts of the East . . . [revealed] a contempt for the European mind, which seemed to deny all hope to persons of our race and education."[102]

The Scottish theosophist W. T. Brown recorded a rebuke from one of the Masters to those who, in the spirit of an imperious western science, demanded irrefutable proofs of their existence: "If an Eastern, especially a Hindu, had even half a glimpse but once of what you had he would have considered himself blessed the whole of his life."[103] In any case, the theosophists, and the Masters themselves, argued that phenomena produced under test conditions that would satisfy the Society for Psychical Research were governed by their own laws, which prevented their taking place in the clinical, materialistic, and skeptical world of the laboratory. Furthermore, the very search for proof was itself undesirable. When Sinnett had requested the definitive proof of the materialization of that day's London *Times* at his home in India, he had been rejected. "Precisely because the test of the London newspaper would close the mouths of the skeptics," wrote KH, it was inadmissable: "See it in what light you will—the world is yet in its first *stage* of disenthralment" and therefore unprepared to have spiritual truth forced upon it.[104]

For those who were drawn to the ancient wisdom that theosophy claimed to convey, the result of the Theosophical Society's encounter with the SPR was, paradoxically, to increase rather than decrease the mystique of the Mahatmas. Beyond the range of western natural science lay the dazzling possibilities of supernatural science. Those elements of spirituality which had been despised as primitive, feminine, or exotic were refigured in ways that simultaneously rejected and confirmed the evolutionist paradigm.

By the beginning of the twentieth century explosive discoveries in the sciences, and especially in physics, had begun to shatter some of the confidence in scientific naturalism that had authorized the SPR investigation. It was no longer clear that the basic laws of nature had been discovered: new research on X-rays, natural radioactivity, and the electron overturned established understandings of mechanics and "confirmed," or so theosophists argued, what Blavatsky and her Mahatmas had been saying all along.[105] In a range of fields, new paradigms emerged that transformed received understandings of the dichotomy between the "primitive" and the "civilized": in anthropology, the more pluralist and relativist approach of Franz Boas; the work of Henri Bergson in philosophy; Freud's innovations in psychoanalysis. All these works addressed, though in more sophisticated and influential ways, the same kinds of issues that had emerged as crucial in the early years of the Theosophical Society. The history of the TS suggests that the possibility of thinking through these new paradigms had begun to emerge by the late 1870s and early 1880s.[106]

Within the TS the supposed conflict between science and spirituality was reframed as a conflict between the "modern civilization of the West" and the "ancient wisdom of the East." This vision was deployed in part in an effort to undermine assumptions about the "superiority" of European, and especially British, civilization over Asian, and especially Indian, backwardness. The hierarchies of class and caste, gender and race, together provided the framework within which the authority of the mystic East was shaped and contested. The early history of the Theosophical Society in England was a series of struggles over *which* gender, class/caste, and "racial" identities would become the markers of (spiritual) authority. In the 1880s relationships of class and of gender were, in Judith R. Walkowitz's words, a "contested terrain" in both "fact and fantasy." Economic change was accompanied by the emergence of new social actors, prompting a range of efforts to redefine the "natural" basis of these relationships.[107] And there were threats on other fronts: if the 1880s witnessed a "New Imperialism," it was in part a response to a shifting political landscape in India. There an emergent urban middle class formed the vanguard of a new nationalism, calling into question British claims to racial and cultural superiority.[108] These conflicts formed the ground on which the late nineteenth-century occult revival, of which Blavatsky was the most notorious and influential exemplar, posed its challenge.

Chapter Two

The Mahatmas in Clubland

Manliness and Scientific Spirituality

Blavatsky died in 1891, six years after the Society for Psychical Research published its "Report on Phenomena Connected with Theosophy," investigating the Theosophical Society. In the mid-1890s the TS underwent the first of a series of major schisms, and from 1895 there were at least two separate theosophical movements, each claiming to be the true heir to the society that Blavatsky's Masters had inspired in 1875. The Theosophical Society (Adyar), with Olcott as president, retained possession of the society's name, its journal *The Theosophist,* and its international headquarters at Adyar. William Quan Judge, who was a leading figure in the TS in America and one of the original members of the TS in New York in 1875, led the bulk of American and Irish theosophists into what eventually became the Universal Brotherhood and Theosophical Society. When Judge died less than a year later, he was succeeded by an American woman, Katherine Tingley, who reconstituted the American TS as a utopian community in Point Loma, California.[1]

The Judge crisis, as it came to be known in the TS (Adyar), once again revealed how claims to spiritual authority were embedded in competing and unstable hierarchies. What emerged within the TS in England was a self-consciously "gentlemanly" variant of theosophy, which emphasized above all theosophy's rational, scholarly, and scientific character. Blavatsky's phenomena were pushed aside to make way for a new concern with her metaphysical writings, and especially with *The Secret Doctrine,* which she published in 1888. Theosophy's esoteric side—letters from the Masters, precipitations and materializations, initiations and Masonic rites—was literally occulted, kept private and hidden from public view.

The Theosophical Society came to resemble most other late Victorian literary and scientific societies, so that it became necessary to remind members that the TS was different from, say, the Royal Geographical Society, and that the cost of joining was far more than the payment of an annual fee.[2] Theosophy was, after all, a spiritual movement. But for all that, the TS itself had been transformed into a kind of gentle-man's club. When the socialist and suffragette Clara Codd joined the Theosophical Society in 1903 it was, as she recalled in her autobiog-raphy, "very like a man's club itself then," with "a comfortable smoking room, full of deep leather armchairs."[3] Members of the Theosophical Society in England had surrounded themselves with the appurtenances of gentlemanly decorum. Safely ensconced in Albemarle Street, in the heart of London's clubland, these mostly male theosophists conducted learned discussions of the *Bhagavad Gita,* the Egyptian roots of Ma-sonic ritual, the occult significance of four-dimensional hyper-solids, and the exact dimensions of the (very recondite) "auric egg," with the Mahatmas at a safe distance.

We know relatively little about the relationship between gender and religion in late nineteenth-century England; we know even less about the specific relationships between masculinity and religion. Most stud-ies of men's relationship to religion in this period have focused on men who underwent a crisis of faith—agnostics, atheists, freethinkers, and secularists—and few of these studies have made gender a central theme. But the extent to which religiosity was feminized in nineteenth-century England, either ideologically or in terms of actual church mem-bership, remains unclear. Jeffrey Cox's study of the borough of Lam-beth provides clear evidence that women outnumbered men in the pews by a small but significant percentage, but he also notes the difficulty of assessing the significance of this fact. The proportion of men attending church services was higher in middle-class districts than in working-class areas, but that was true of a range of social institutions, not just religious ones. Some Nonconformist chapels seem to have attracted higher numbers of men than did the Anglican churches, but no clear pattern emerges to link either theology or church organization to these differences.[4] Despite what has been described in the American context as "the ideological difficulties presented by the identity between piety and femininity," many English men continued to go to church.[5] Why men go to church, what they do there, and how that spiritual praxis is implicated in the renegotiation of masculinity remains, for the most part, unexplored territory.

In the 1890s a new variant of eastern mysticism, the East as the locus of a manly and rational spirituality, became a key element in the scien-tific spirituality of the Theosophical Society in England. This scientific spirituality was used to authorize a particular kind of spiritual author-ity and spiritual experience. Scientific spirituality was modeled on the academic study of religions: techniques developed within the emerging sciences of anthropology and the comparative study of religions (especially through philology) were redeployed in the service of a more "modern" spirituality. Members of the Theosophical Society were participating in a kind of amateur orientalism, which made an important contribution to alternative discourses on South Asia in the late nineteenth century.[6] Like the early anthropologists, theosophists made evolution a central organizing principle of their study of religion. Just as Sir James Frazer's *Golden Bough* (first published in 1890) attempted to impose order on an enormous mass of unruly data by reconstructing the story of human development as the story of progress from magic, through religion, to science, so theosophists attempted to impose a different kind of order on similar material, reinterpreting all religions, philosophies, and scientific systems in the light of an ancient wisdom. From comparative philologists like F. Max Müller, who has been called "the founder of the scientific study of religion," theosophists drew an emphasis on texts, and particularly on the most ancient texts, which were privileged as authentic, while contemporary forms of worship were redefined as corrupted or debased.[7]

While the TS lacked academic respectability, it had a certain popular appeal, and theosophical writings reached an audience that more scholarly works failed to attract. Enough eminent scholars took the trouble to rebut theosophy's claims that the society gained, however tenuously, the appearance of participating in scholarly debate. As one alarmed critic of the TS noted, A. P. Sinnett's *Esoteric Buddhism* had sold more copies than Max Müller's erudite *Essays;* Max Müller responded by taking Sinnett's work seriously enough to publish a rebuttal of it. Max Müller's own theory of phonetic types had been criticized for relying on "occult" explanations, and he may have welcomed the opportunity to rehabilitate himself as an academic authority in the wake of Andrew Lang's devastating critique of the mythological, even mystical, elements of his own theories of language.[8]

Max Müller's rebuttal shored up academic boundaries by placing the TS firmly outside of them. A similar impulse can be traced in the work of J. N. Farquhar, who became professor of comparative religions at Manchester University in 1923. In his survey *Modern Religious Movements in India,* Farquhar devoted over eighty pages to demolishing theosophy's academic credentials. Like Max Müller, Farquhar was writing at a time when the scientific and theological still jockeyed for position within the comparative study of religions; his own book was based on a 1913 series of lectures to students training for the mission field, designed to give them "a good knowledge of the religious history, beliefs and customs of the peoples among whom they expect to work." The bulk of the work theosophists had done on the "exposition of religions" was, Farquhar argued, "unscientific and seriously misleading," it "filled men's heads with froth instead of knowledge." He called instead for an explicitly Christian exposition of the world's religions, arguing that the study of comparative religions should lead to the conclusion that all religions found their fulfillment in Christianity.[9]

Unlike Max Müller and Farquhar, who wrote about Asian religions as Christians and therefore as "outsiders," theosophists went to Asian religions looking for spiritual truth. At the same time, theosophists used the approaches developed within these academic disciplines to establish a more scientific spiritual praxis. A technical vocabulary drawn from variants of Hinduism and Buddhism, combined with the vocabulary of modern science, not only provided theosophists with a claim to professional status in the spiritual world, but also helped to establish the belief that theosophy was neither emotional nor sentimental. "Emotion," after all, as one scientizing theosophist put it, was only "the cognitional aspect of the rate of change of the intensity of vortical activity in the dimorphites."[10] At the same time, this approach inevitably foreclosed certain possibilities, even as it enabled others: the textualization of "authentic" spirituality required the abstraction of texts from their social contexts, and the privileging of an intellectual apprehension of spiritual truth tended to exclude the emotional and experiential aspects. This scientific spirituality also became embedded in particular forms of sociability: since it privileged an intellectual engagement with texts as the means to spiritual enlightenment, it also fostered the lecture and the discussion group as central modes of spiritual practice. The lecture hall, the reading room, and the library became central features of theosophical lodges, both in London and the provinces. Various efforts were also made to rationalize and bureaucratize the TS along the lines of a scientific or literary society.

The first step in reconstituting the TS in a scientific mode was to separate theosophical principles from theosophical phenomena. Principles, which could be printed, published, annotated, and debated, became the public emphasis of the society. The formation of the Blavatsky Lodge in 1887 was partly the result of this emphasis on propaganda and theosophical principles. According to Bertram Keightley, one of its founding members, the Blavatsky Lodge was intended to rescue the TS from the "dilettante class or high society men" who dominated Sinnett's London Lodge. Theosophy, Keightley argued, was not for the "kid gloves and swallow-tail coats," but for earnest and dedicated (and presumably professional and middle-class) students of spiritual mysteries.[11] The lodge was also H. P. Blavatsky's bid for organizational as well as charismatic authority, and it provided her with a dedicated group of helpers.[12] While ordinary members of the lodge promised only to study and defend theosophy, the most committed members pledged themselves to work actively on behalf of Blavatsky and her society. Thanks to the work of the Blavatsky Lodge, the magazine *Lucifer* was launched in 1887; Blavatsky's *The Secret Doctrine* appeared a year later.

Phenomena, the fruits of practical occultism, were to be carefully hidden from public view. When the Esoteric Section of the Theosophical Society was formed in 1888, many of the most active members of the Blavatsky Lodge were among the first to join. The ES provided a formal structure for Blavatsky's practice of forming small groups of chelas, or pupils, to whom she gave special instruction. The formation of the ES consolidated Blavatsky's charismatic authority and also provided a school of practical occultism. Before the formation of the ES, members who wanted to pursue practical occultism had been tempted by magical orders like the Golden Dawn, which emphasized a western mystery tradition. The ES was an ostensibly eastern rival to the Golden Dawn and served to reassert the Theosophical Society's special connection to a specifically eastern wisdom.[13]

The Esoteric Section was officially entirely separate from the Theosophical Society proper, although a probationary period in the TS was necessary before one could apply to the ES. At the same time, this official separation was always complicated by the terminology used by the TS itself: the ES was persistently referred to as the "Inner" and the TS as the "Outer" society. Since the ES was believed to be a direct link to the Masters who were the society's true founders, charismatic authority within the ES could always threaten to destabilize the organizational structure of the TS itself.

The formation of the ES marked a new departure in the scope and scale of theosophical activities in England. Walter R. Old, vice president of the Blavatsky Lodge, announced that "since the formation of the Esoteric Section, the work of the society in England, as elsewhere, has gone rapidly forward; the practical work of the British Section having been done almost exclusively by Esotericists."[14] If the ES was the inner core of the TS, then the inmost part was the Inner Group within the ES: twelve disciples (six men and six women) to whom HPB gave oral instruction beginning in 1890.[15] Most prominent among these was the woman whom Blavatsky appointed as the chief secretary and recorder of her Inner Group teachings, Annie Besant.

"Red" Annie Besant was one of the most prominent and notorious women of her day. In 1873, at the age of twenty-five, she had simultaneously lost her faith and separated from her husband, an Anglican vicar. By 1874 she had joined the National Secular Society, and she soon became one of the free thought movement's most popular speakers and writers. In 1877, in a sensational trial, she and the secularist Charles Bradlaugh were convicted of obscenity for disseminating birth control literature (the conviction was later overturned on a technicality). From secularism, Besant moved to socialism, working closely with W. T. Stead in campaigns against the exploitation of child and female labor and the regulation of prostitution, and on behalf of the trade union movement.[16] In 1889 Stead, the crusading editor of the *Pall Mall Gazette,* gave Besant Blavatsky's *The Secret Doctrine* to review, and on reading it she knew that she had found "the very Truth" for which she had been seeking.[17] Besant's conversion brought the society tremendous publicity, and forced many people to reconsider the SPR verdict against it. Some years later, when the TS was facing yet another public scandal, W. T. Stead's *Borderland* (a new review of things occult and spiritual) announced that as long as Besant "remains faithful" to the society, "so long will Theosophy command the attention and excite the interest of multitudes far beyond the circle of its members."[18]

Annie Besant was not the only one drawn to the Theosophical Society by Blavatsky's *The Secret Doctrine.* If the ES and the Inner Group were the most private face of the TS during this period, the publication of *The Secret Doctrine* in 1888 was its most public one. In two massive volumes, which together total almost fifteen hundred pages, *The Secret Doctrine* claimed on its title page to be "the synthesis of science, religion, and philosophy." Extending and revising the material presented in her earlier *Isis Unveiled* (1877), Blavatsky laid out in dizzying detail a history of the birth and death of universes, and of the evolution of humanity over countless millennia. By October 1888 the first edition of *The Secret Doctrine* had sold out, and a second edition was being printed.[19]

The Secret Doctrine was the most thorough and ambitious of Blavatsky's efforts to render spiritual enlightenment in textual form.[20] It is also a highly complex text, and its authorship has long been disputed. Blavatsky described herself not as the "author" but rather as "the writer"; in many passages of the work she claimed to serve only as the amanuensis of her Masters. The text was a series of commentaries on the "Stanzas of Dyzan," purportedly the oldest manuscript in the world, though not (unfortunately for those who would have liked to verify her sources) available in any European library. Like the "Stanzas of Dyzan" themselves, *The Secret Doctrine* was intended to appeal not to the "ordinary comprehension of the physical brain" but to the "inner faculties," and it resisted a logical and analytical critique.[21] Expressed through a symbolic language that, as E. L. Gardner later put it, at once "revealed and re-veiled," the "truths" in the work were endlessly deferred: *The Secret Doctrine* offered one turn of the key, but in most cases it was "useless to attempt to explain the mystery in full." Even the most devoted theosophists noted that Blavatsky's work was often cryptic and contradictory; less sympathetic observers, like Edward Carpenter, claimed that "no words can describe the general rot and confusion of Blavatsky's *Secret Doctrine*."[22]

Blavatsky outlined an emanationist view of the physical universe, as a manifestation or externalization of the Absolute. As she explained in *The Key to Theosophy* (1889), "We believe in a Universal Divine Principle, the root of ALL, from which all proceeds, and within which all shall be absorbed at the end of the great cycle of Being."[23] The story of the physical universe was therefore the story of the progressive unfolding of spirit in matter. This unfolding took place through two primary mechanisms, both keystones of late Victorian social and cultural theory. The first was a gendered dichotomy embedded in the "absolute universality of that law of periodicity, of flux and reflux, ebb and flow, which physical science has observed and recorded in all departments of nature." The second was the "obligatory pilgrimage for every Soul" through a racialized cycle of incarnations: as individual sparks of the spirit descended into matter, they moved through a complex evolutionary series of "Root Races" and "subraces." The Lemurian, "the first physical man," appeared in the middle of the Third Root Race, 18 million years ago; the "degraded" descendants of the Lemurians survived among the indigenous peoples of Australia. Moving into the even more complicated subdivisions of branch or family races (and their countless "little tribes, shoots and offshoots"), *The Secret Doctrine* located present-day northern Europeans in the fifth (Teutonic) subrace of the Fifth or Aryan Root Race.[24]

Blavatsky attacked both materialist science and Christian orthodoxy. "Occult sciences," she wrote, "claim less and give more, at all events, than either Darwinian Anthropology or Biblical Theology."[25] As recent studies have shown, the highly materialist, scientific naturalism of T. H. Huxley and his followers was only one of many competing scientific paradigms, and scientists as well as their lay audience continued, with varying degrees of success, to incorporate conceptions of spirit into scientific discourse.[26] The power of Blavatsky's *The Secret Doctrine* lay in its ability to assimilate and rework new scientific developments through an elaborate constellation of spiritual beliefs: Blavatsky promised to harmonize the demands of faith with the dictates of reason, by claiming to transcend both. Theosophists offered a creative rereading of nineteenth-century science, seeking the esoteric truths that lay behind a range of scientific texts, just as they sought the esoteric truth of Buddhism or Christianity.

The Secret Doctrine was written for the most serious students of Blavatsky's teaching; readers willing to wade through its copious notes proceeded, in breathless leaps, from the Zodiac of the Maya to the *Rig-Veda* to the Kabbalah, and from Louis Büchner's *Force and Matter* to Herbert Spencer's *Principles of Biology*. The proliferation of commentaries and manuals that attempted to explain *The Secret Doctrine* testified to the heavy demands the work placed on its readers. In 1889 Blavatsky published a more accessible catechism, *The Key to Theosophy*, which provided comparatively straightforward answers to common questions. The *Key* also provided an extended discussion of "practical theosophy," which was to bear fruit some years later in the form of theosophical Leagues of Service, dedicated to a variety of philanthropic and political activities.

If *The Secret Doctrine* appealed, at least superficially, to the intellect, Blavatsky's *Voice of the Silence,* published in 1889, appealed to an understanding that was represented as beyond reason. Just as *The Secret Doctrine* claimed to be based on the "Stanzas of Dyzan," *The Voice of the Silence* claimed to be a translation from a text in an ancient and now forgotten sacerdotal language, Senzar, that had been preserved within Mahāyāna Buddhism. The text was the "Book of the Golden Precepts," and a selection of its treatises was offered (with annotations) to "the few real mystics in the Theosophical Society."[27] Like its title, the book itself was characterized by what Blavatsky's contemporary, the Harvard philosopher William James, described as "self-contradictory phrases." This, he argued, "prove[s] that not conceptual speech, but music rather, is the element through which we are best spoken to by mystical truth." James chose a series of passages from Blavatsky's *Voice of the Silence* to illustrate his point: " . . . the soul will hear, and will remember. And then to the inner ear will speak THE VOICE OF THE SILENCE. . . . the VOICE unbroken, that resounds throughout eternities, exempt from change, from sin exempt, the seven sounds in one, the VOICE OF THE SILENCE. *Om tat Sat.*" "If they do not awaken laughter as you receive them," James wrote, "[these words] probably stir chords within you which music and language touch in common"; such mystical states haunted "a verge of the mind," and called into question the authority of the rational consciousness.[28]

In the last years of her life, then, Blavatsky produced a range of texts that authorized a range of spiritual modes. Blavatsky also provided further teachings to her closest and most trusted followers in the Esoteric Section and the Inner Group. *The Secret Doctrine* was the only book

Blavatsky wrote during the late 1880s that was primarily scholarly in tone, and even that required some rehabilitation before it could straightforwardly be described as "rational." The "manly and intellectual" character of the TS in the 1890s was, therefore, only one of many possible responses to Blavatsky's legacy. The emphasis on the quasi-public/quasi-private, "clublike" atmosphere of the TS was also a selective response to the emergence of competing public and private activities in the Theosophical Society in Blavatsky's last years.

Shortly after Annie Besant joined the Theosophical Society, Blavatsky and the TS headquarters were moved to Besant's house at 19, Avenue Road, St. John's Wood.[29] Many of the most dedicated theosophists made their homes at this address, providing Blavatsky and the TS with an efficient staff and a devoted band of disciples. By 1890 the new Blavatsky Lodge building was under construction in the garden—a corrugated iron shell, its wooden interior walls painted in blue with the symbols of the Zodiac and six of the great world religions by the artist R. A. Machell. At the same time the house was renovated to suit its new purposes. Offices and workrooms were added, along with a short secret passage from HPB's bedroom to the chamber used by the ES. There was yet another, even better hidden room, the Occult Room, reserved for the activities of the Inner Group.[30] The Avenue Road headquarters was a quasi-public venue as well. When the Blavatsky Lodge moved to the new headquarters in 1890, 250 people were present at the inaugural meeting.[31]

The rules that governed life at headquarters were posted under the signature of HPB herself. According to these rules, the pursuit of practical theosophy demanded the cultivation of right thought, right feeling, right speech, right action, and right living. On a more mundane level, it required that residents rise no later than 8 A.M., and that lights be extinguished by midnight.[32] Blavatsky's rules for resident members highlighted the multiple functions of the Avenue Road address: a domestic establishment, a business and administrative headquarters, and an occult training school. As one member of the household recalled, "there were dangers and difficulties in conducting a species of conventicle wherein occult training and domestic affairs elbowed one another in a quite uncomfortable manner." According to Arthur A. Wells, "the supposed interference of the Masters in the domestic affairs of Avenue Road became simply comic, even to her most devoted disciples."[33]

On 8 May 1891 the household at Avenue Road lost its most important member when Blavatsky died or, as the theosophical newsletter *The Vāhan* put it, "abandoned a physical instrument that could no longer be used." Her body was unostentatiously conveyed to the crematorium at Woking where, after a short address and a brief silence, "the Theosophists disposed of the worn-out garment that their friend and teacher had worn for one incarnation."[34] A year later they celebrated the anniversary as White Lotus Day, and two hundred people gathered in the lecture hall at Avenue Road to hear readings from *Light of Asia* and the *Bhagavad Gita*. Afterward members were invited to visit Blavatsky's room, where they could view the chair where she was sitting when she died, the pen she had used to write *The Secret Doctrine*, her last dinner service, and her last cigarette.[35]

The newspapers had a field day with Blavatsky's obituary. For three days after her death, the story of the "Prophetess of the Buried Tea-Cup" and her "strange, erudite medley of abracadabras" dominated the *Pall Mall Gazette* (which, as one critic noted in disgust, had taken theosophy "under the shadow of its wing").[36] Although many people predicted that the Theosophical Society would not survive the death of its revered teacher, the TS continued to flourish and even to expand. But in the absence of the charismatic and flamboyant Blavatsky, it did so, at least initially, in a much more routinized way.

In 1890 and 1891 the British and European Sections of the TS were reorganized. In 1890 a section register was compiled, and diplomas were issued to members. The first annual convention of the European Section was held in 1891.[37] The bureaucratization of the society met with some resistance. The London Lodge declined to enroll in the new section, remaining directly affiliated to the Adyar headquarters, on the grounds that "we desired at our meetings to study and cultivate the exalted spiritual teaching of Theosophy, and to have as little as possible to do with external business and formal routine."[38] In 1893 William Quan Judge argued that the society "came to its high point of energy without votes, without rules, supported and sustained by unselfish effort," and warned the English theosophists not to "mummify it with red tape. . . . There is a tendency in this country to choke effort with forms and regulations."[39]

In 1894 a letter to the "Enquirer" column of *The Vāhan*, the English society's recently established newsletter, argued that it was "a great pity that a movement which has such exalted and unworldly aims as the Theosophical Society, should be associated with such petty and formal details as subscriptions, committees, bye-laws, registers, and other kinds of red-tape, just like any other cut-and-dried society."[40] In response, some members wrote to defend the need for just such details. James Pryse, an American printer who ran the Theosophical Society's press in London, was one of the most forthright: "The Society is not based on moonshine, and its ranks are not recruited from the moon-stricken."[41] The TS had grown too large to be governed informally and now required not only an administrative and bureaucratic structure but also a stable and predictable source of revenue in the form of subscriptions if it was to continue in active work. The move into this commercialized public space was perceived by some older theosophists as a betrayal of theosophy's earlier purity, and at least one member of the society recalled nostalgically the days when Mr. and Mrs. Sinnett had generously and unobtrusively paid all expenses in connection with the meetings of the London Lodge, and "the commercial element seemed to evaporate in thin air."[42]

The society had acquired its own printing facility, the H.P.B. Press, which, under Pryse's management, employed "the pick of the women compositors in London" to do all the London printing for the TS. After a year's work, the press had produced 117,000 pamphlets and leaflets. Copies of theosophical texts were offered to hotels and ocean-going steamers; the "Press Gang" worked to introduce theosophy into the columns of journals and newspapers, and in just over two years contributed more than two thousand articles and letters to the public press. Subscribers to *The Vāhan* were encouraged to contribute articles and instructed in the niceties of writing "copy" for the printers.[43] No wonder, as one alarmed critic of the TS pointed out, that theosophy was "now so common a subject of conversation, and . . . is ever presenting itself in the periodic and other literature of the day."[44]

G. R. S. Mead was general secretary of the TS in England from 1891 to 1898. Under his leadership, the English society was rapidly becoming a respectable organization. Mead, who joined the TS in 1887, began his theosophical work as Blavatsky's private secretary. W. B. Yeats described him as having the intellect of "a good sized whelk," but other members of the TS had a higher opinion of this abilities, regarding him as one of their preeminent scholars.[45] Born in 1863 into a military family, George Robert Stowe Mead was a graduate of St. John's College, Cambridge, and used the TS as a forum in which to pursue his studies in philosophy and early Christianity, such as his English translation of the gnostic gospel *Pistis Sophia*, which he published in the theosophical magazine *Lucifer*.[46]

By the 1890s the TS, and especially its Avenue Road headquarters, resembled a well-run gentleman's club, with a discreetly efficient staff and a growing library. When the society was founded in 1875, Olcott had drawn up a circular laying out its aims, the first of which was "a serious attempt on the part of each member to study and develop his 'inner psychic self.'" Opposition to "materialism and dogmatic theology" and encouragement of "the institution of a Brotherhood of Humanity" followed.[47] By 1890, as Jill Roe has noted, "the objects had assumed something like their present rather bland form": (1) to form the nucleus of a Universal Brotherhood of Humanity, without distinction of race, creed, sex, caste, or color; (2) to promote the study of Aryan and other eastern literatures, religions, philosophies and sciences, and to demonstrate their importance to humanity; and (3) to investigate unexplored laws of nature and the psychic powers latent in man.[48] Words like *study* and *investigation* were key markers of the society's reorientation to scholarly efforts, and the demotion of things psychic from first to third place, along with the deletion of the commitment to "develop" that psychic self, was part of the same project.

Mead's efforts to remake the English society in his own image, however, received a severe setback in 1894, when the *Westminster Gazette* published a series of articles by Edmund Garrett exposing what Garrett described as "theosophistry" in the TS. Quickly issued in book form as *Isis Very Much Unveiled, the Story of the Great Mahatma Hoax*, Garrett's articles turned what had been a private scandal within the TS into a highly public one.

The scandal had been brewing for some time. When Blavatsky died, Besant had been expected to succeed her as Outer Head of the Esoteric Section (the Masters were assumed to be the Inner Heads). At the center of the controversy lay a new series of letters from the Mahatmas, which had been received since Blavatsky's death, and which many members believed had been forged by William Quan Judge. Shortly after HPB died, while both Judge and Besant were in London, Annie Besant received "precipitated" letters from the Masters stating that "Judge's plan is right" and urging her to cede control of the ES to Judge. As a result, Besant agreed to share the Outer Headship with him. Accusations surfaced at Adyar that Judge had forged the new Mahatma Letters, and he was offered a choice between resignation or full investigation. The charges against Judge, however, became entangled with the question of the existence of the Mahatmas from whom he claimed to have received his instructions. To preserve the society's neutrality on the question of the existence of the Masters, the charges were dropped.[49]

In August 1891 Annie Besant, in her heavily publicized farewell address to the National Secular Society at the Hall of Science, had staked her reputation on the existence of the Mahatmas and the authenticity of their letters:

> You have known me in this hall for sixteen and a half years. (Cheers.) You have never known me to tell a lie to you ("No, never," and loud cheers.) My worst public enemy has never cast a

slur upon my integrity. ("Never," and cheers.) I tell you that since Mdme. Blavatsky left I have had letters in the same handwriting as the letters which she received. (Sensation.) Unless you think dead persons can write, surely that is a remarkable feat. You are surprised; I do not ask you to believe me; but I tell you it is so.[50]

Garrett insisted that Besant, by virtue of her public claims on behalf of the society and its teachings, most notably this announcement at the Hall of Science, had constituted herself as a "professional Honest Person" whose credentials should be subject to public examination.[51]

In Besant's closing statement in her lecture at the Hall of Science, "Why I Became a Theosophist," she claimed that

> an imperious necessity forces me to speak the truth, as I see it, whether the speech please or displease, whether it bring praise or blame. That one loyalty to Truth I must keep stainless, whatever friendships fail me or human ties be broken. She may lead me into the wilderness, yet I must follow her; she may strip me of all love, yet I must pursue her; though she slay me, yet will I trust in her; and I ask no other epitaph on my tomb but
> "SHE TRIED TO FOLLOW TRUTH."[52]

Her changes of allegiance, which her critics might otherwise construe as feminine inconstancy, Besant represented as "loyalty to Truth," here allegorized as feminine. As a woman with a public reputation to defend, Besant used the conventional personification of Truth as female as her license to speak. Her status as a "professional Honest Person," as Garrett put it, was thus crucial to her negotiation of her persona as a woman in public.

Garrett's case rested on the rhetoric of financial fraud and stock-jobbery, presenting the TS as a Barnum & Bailey sideshow that duped the credulous into paying for spurious miracles. *Isis Very Much Unveiled* (with its allusion to a different kind of "public woman," the woman "very much unveiled" for public delectation) focused on the commercial underpinnings of the society's success: Blavatsky's "particular line of business" was "Missive-manufacturing," and her miracles had "created the successive 'booms' (as they would be called in a more purely commercial connexion) which have produced the biggest crop of entrance subscriptions from the wonder-loving public."[53] When the *Westminster Gazette* revived the issue on October 29, 1894, and continued to milk it for all it was worth over the next nine days, members of the Theosophical Society began to take sides, issuing statements and circulars, giving interviews to the press, and raising the controversy at lodge meetings and theosophical conferences. Some of Judge's most prominent supporters in England, including many members of HPB's original Inner Group, formed a new lodge, the HPB Lodge of the Theosophical Society.[54] In a much quoted (though supposedly private) circular that Judge issued to the members of the ES on November 3, he claimed that the Masters had ordered him to depose Besant, and he made it clear that opposition to him was opposition to the Masters. The circular itself was headed "By Master's Direction."[55]

Given her high public profile, Besant herself was remarkably absent from this public debate. This was partly because since 1893 she had spent much of her time away from London and in India. But she was also trying to police the boundaries between public and private within both the ES and the "outer" Theosophical Society. The Masters and Master's Orders, she claimed, were privileged, private, and sacred. Judge's carelessness with documents circulated under a pledge of secrecy had brought the TS into public disrepute.[56] Besant, still the "professional Honest Person," confined her public statements to the claims she had made at the Hall of Science, since those were already in the public realm. In her absence, the debate within the English society quickly acquired an almost entirely masculine character.

Some English theosophists were only too willing to agree that to reject Judge was to reject the Masters, and to do just that. The members of Stoke-on-Trent Centre, for example, were "of the opinion that the unpleasant circumstances through which the Theosophical Society is now passing may be largely attributed to the idolatrous adoration of Mahātmās." Such behavior was clearly to be discouraged: "The cringing, slavish prostitution of man's rational faculties to 'Masters' cannot but demoralize the whole Society, and tend to make its members the laughing stock of the civilised world." They feared that the TS was becoming a "Mahātmic Church," and they opposed "the deification of 'Masters,' with the elevation of certain persons (no matter who they may be) to the position of mouthpiece or prophet."[57] Independence and rationality could not coexist with the Masters and their prophets.

Judge's claims to occult authority and spiritual leadership were also characterized by his opponents as an attack on the "manly" qualities of theosophy. "Surely," as the theosophist Robert Holt put it, "before thus renouncing all the prerogatives of manhood, and consigning our very thoughts to an eternal subjection, common prudence demands that we should seriously consider what manner of man it is who pretends to be the Arch-Pope of our society."[58] The true theosophist, Judge's opponents agreed, bowed to no authority but that of the inner or higher self. According to Mead, "the spirit which questioned was a right spirit, and neither in H. P. B. nor in anyone else ought we to place blind and unreasoning reliance."[59]

The question of eastern versus western authority became a crucial part of these debates. A decade earlier George Wyld had resigned from the British Theosophical Society on the grounds that this "Oriental practice of secrecy" appeared to him to be "childish and effeminate."[60] In 1895, however, the images associated with both East and West were quite different. Judge did criticize Besant's increasing reliance on Hindu advisers, such as the Brahman Gyanendra N. Chakravarti, a professor of mathematics in Allahabad and an ardent Hindu nationalist, whom Besant considered a "Master in the flesh."[61] Judge denounced Chakravarti, who was teaching Besant "Bengali Tantrik" philosophy, as an agent of "Black Magicians" and argued that Besant's policies were turning the Theosophical Society's attention away from the glories of ancient India and toward what he saw as the degraded India of the present. Modern India he described as the India of "Yogis and Fakirs, its hide-bound castes, its subtle and magnificently intellectual theology, its Hatha Yoga and all the dangers attending that."[62]

Judge denigrated modern India and rehabilitated the West as a source of the divine wisdom. He said the Master told him that "the T. S. movement was begun by Them in the West by western people, and that it is not Their desire to turn it into a solely eastern movement nor to have us run after the present East." The key to continuing Blavatsky's work was *the establishment in the West of a great seat of learning where . . . western occultism, as the essence combined out of all others, shall be taught.*[63] As Arthur Lillie put it in his own exposé of the TS, "Mr. Judge proposes to dethrone the fine 'old wisdom religion of India' as well as Mrs. Besant, its chief expounder." The Mahatmas, Lillie pointed out, "no longer 'live in India.'"[64] Bertram Keightley, now general secretary of the new Indian Section, denounced Judge's circular as a violation of the First Object, the commitment to Universal Brotherhood. Judge's goal, he argued, was to elevate the West over the East spiritually as well as materially. Not only that, but also Judge had stirred up trouble in India itself, by exploiting anti-Brahman feeling and exacerbating caste hostilities.[65]

Judge's November 3 circular had cast the "subtle and magnificently intellectual theology" of modern Hinduism in a negative light. For his opponents, it was precisely the emphasis on intellectual, rather than emotional, apprehension of spiritual truth that was the appeal of theosophical teaching. In October 1891 B. A. had written to the "Enquirer" column of *The Vāhan* to ask what use theosophy might be "to those who are lacking in intellectual capacity," since it was "such a difficult subject that none but the intellectual can gain any comprehension of it." The initial replies had stressed the importance of purity of life and the pursuit of spiritual truth, but Mead added an editorial caveat, lest the importance of study be neglected: "it should be distinctly remembered that no real student of life should seek excuses for 'intellectual laziness.'"[66]

Judge and his followers, in contrast, emphasized the importance of making theosophy a vital force in their lives. According to W. A. Bulmer, honorary secretary of Yarm-on-Tees Centre and the editor of *The Northern Theosophist,* Mead and his set were creating a new breed of "Theosophical tadpoles" who were "all head": "They would settle every question by appeal to the brain. Logic chopping is their favourite occupation."[67] Working side by side with the "tadpoles" were the "red tapers," who were strangling the life out of the society. A "few wire-pullers" had foisted a "whole super-structure of spurious laws and regulations" on the membership; this was not theosophy but a "Holy Mother Church."[68]

These mutual recriminations often carried clear racial overtones; they were also implicitly debates over the content and character of manliness itself. James M. Pryse made his case against Mead and the metaphysicians in an impassioned letter to the "Enquirer" column of *The Vāhan:* "Who are you. . . . that you should talk loftily of 'metaphysics' and decry the 'miracles' of some saint the tense strings of whose pure being vibrate silvery and sonorous from plane to plane . . . until even the things of darkness and of matter obey his godlike will?" Pryse valued miracles over metaphysics and portrayed his opponents as anemic intellectuals who were too cowardly to face the realities of Judge's spiritual power. Pryse himself, in increasingly purple prose, looked to the heroes of the western mystery tradition for inspiration, back to the "steel-clad seekers for the Holy Grail" and "the mailed Templars who with sword and lance fought mightily under the red cross of the Four Powers of the Hidden Majesty." He saluted those "western warriors who fought for the Cause," hailing that "nobler past out of this cultured present when beings, having something of the outward semblance of men, keep well to the rear when danger comes and talk of philosophy and of the indestructibility of noumena."[69]

Pryse had drawn the battle lines very clearly: miracles rather than metaphysics, European crusaders rather than eastern pandits, emotion rather than reason. In drawing these lines, he also invoked an alternative model of masculinity: not the independent, self-controlled, and rational manliness of the gentleman and scholar, but the virile masculinity of the mail-clad warrior. This was a model that, as Gail Bederman has demonstrated, was rapidly gaining ground within an American elite struggling to maintain its class and racial hegemony.[70] Following Judge, his fellow American, Pryse elevated western spirituality over what he characterized as the intellectual sterility of the East and thereby recovered, as a new, more virile form of masculinity, precisely the emotional and "irrational" elements his opponents rejected. Where Mead and the Avenue Road leadership argued that esoteric philosophy and *The Secret Doctrine* could stand on their own intellectual merits, the "Judge-ites" argued that to make theosophy an intellectual creed was to drain it of its spiritual power.[71]

The members of the Dublin Lodge issued a statement supporting Judge, which became an important symbol of the pro-Judge campaign in the British Isles.[72] When the secession of Judge and his supporters was reported in *The Vāhan* in August 1895, the Dublin Lodge was prominent among them.[73] The Dublin theosophists were a small but close-knit group, many of whom lived together in monastic style at the residential headquarters of the Dublin TS, at 3, Upper Ely Place, a house taken by a young engineer for the Dublin Board of Works, Frederick J. Dick.[74] Closely linked to the Anglo-Irish literary renaissance through George Russell (better known as Æ) and W. B. Yeats, an occasional visitor to the lodge, the Irish theosophists were busy developing a mystery tradition of their own. F. J. Dick reported on their activities in May 1895:

> The subject of "Theosophy in Ancient Ireland" has been occupying a good deal of our attention lately, and it is interesting to note that some recent examples of folk-lore unearthed in the West of Ireland after thousands of years of preservation solely by oral tradition, correspond not only in minute details with those of Ancient America and elsewhere, but with occult teachings. Tales of one-eyed giants whose eyes were put out by red-hot iron, of Druidical wands which consisted of a three-fold fire, etc., have meanings which are only too obvious.[75]

The location of this Irish mystery tradition in a distant and pagan past was characteristic of contemporary efforts by Anglo-Irish Protestants to disconnect Irish patriotism from contemporary Catholicism.[76] It also provided an apparently indigenous source of spiritual authority that stood as an alternative to the distant eastern mysticism represented by Indian Mahatmas.

Irishness was linked here to a personal and emotional investment in the spiritual. A similar invocation of a racial spiritual heritage operated in Annie Besant's writings. In her autobiography, she lamented the fact

Annie Besant.
(Adyar Library and Research Centre)

that she had been born in London when "three-quarters of my blood and all my heart are Irish." Ireland, for Besant, was that "ancient land once inhabited by mighty men of wisdom, that in later times became the Island of Saints, and shall once again be the Island of Sages, when the Wheel turns round."[77] She also claimed an Indian identity that functioned in a similar way: as Nancy Anderson notes, "when she arrived in India, Besant felt as though she had come home, for indeed she believed that, though Western in birth and white of skin, in earlier lives she had been Indian."[78] In these accounts, spiritual authority was linked to particular ethnic or racial identities, which by implication provided access to greater spiritual insights.

There were many competing discourses on race current in England in the late nineteenth century. By the 1880s the myth of the Anglo-Saxon/Teutonic origins of Englishness was becoming dominant. As Paul Rich argues, the Anglo-Saxon ideal accomplished many things simultaneously: it gave British parliamentary democracy a racial heritage, by tying it to ancient Anglo-Saxon tribal institutions; it emphasized the common racial interests of Britain and the settler colonies, including the United States; and it served to oppose more pluralist visions of a Britain that included the Celtic peoples of Scotland, Ireland, and Wales. By the 1890s the Anglo-Saxon ideal also served to legitimate "the belief in an inherently racial divide between British and Indian culture [which] was shared even by relatively progressive observers."[79]

The supposed virtues of the Anglo-Saxon ideal were many—a racial instinct for liberty and justice, a practical bent, and a love of order—but a tendency to mysticism was not apparently among them. The opposition between the "spiritual Celt and the philistine Anglo-Saxon" had been elaborated at considerable length in Matthew Arnold's *On the Study of Celtic Literature* (1867), a racial dialectic that, according to Robert Young, also coded the Celtic as feminine and the Anglo-Saxon as masculine.[80] Similar images, which catalogued and categorized racial types in terms of temperament, can be traced in Sinnett's work and in the Mahatma Letters, and were elaborated and developed in *The Secret Doctrine*.[81]

Within the TS, these kinds of claims helped produce a racialized map of secularization, and of resistance to it. The opposition between a secular West and a spiritual East was replicated within Britain, in the form of a secular England (especially in the south) and a spiritual Celtic fringe. In the south of England, these racial oppositions were transformed into sexual ones, in which women represented the spiritual, while men bore the burdens of secularization. The theosophist Isabel Cooper-Oakley (well known outside the TS for her fashionable millinery business and her Dorothy Restaurants in the West End)[82] suggested that the Anglo-Saxon man was the least spiritual of all Britain's inhabitants: "It is a curious fact that in those parts of Great Britain where the Anglo-Saxon race is practically unmixed Theosophy seems to take no root, the chief strength of the T. S. lying in districts where Danish, Celtic, &c., elements had modified the Anglo-Saxon stock. In the South of England the women predominated, whilst in the North it was the men who were the principal strength of the T.S."[83] The impression that emerges from the writings of English theosophists is that India and the "Celtic fringe," along with women, were the repository of a spirituality that English men had forfeited in exchange for material progress.

One way of recovering those qualities associated with both the Celtic and the Indian within Anglo-Saxon Englishness was to emphasize the common heritage of all these races within an Indo-European or Aryan framework. From the 1850s to the 1870s British orientalists, and especially comparative philologists, elaborated a complicated theory of racial origins that identified the English with the Aryans of North India. That myth of racial origins could and did have racist and reactionary consequences, but it could also reinforce the sense of a common racial heritage and link the English with Aryan elites at least.[84] Those theosophists who remained loyal to Adyar and Avenue Road continued to exploit these older notions of Aryanism to defend the (imperial) connection between England and India, which Judge wanted to abandon.

The obverse of the rational Anglo-Saxon was the mystical Celt or the Hindu pandit. The racialized map of spirituality and secularism dominant within the TS thus helped to consolidate a generic oriental-mystical authority. When Ernest T. Hargrove wished to intervene on behalf of Judge in 1895, he did so in the persona of "The Chinaman," Che-Yew-Tsäng.[85] Hargrove later claimed that he wrote under a nom de plume as he wanted his work to be judged on its merits, not on the basis of his personality. His critics argued, however, that Hargrove's choice of pseudonym, though initially a trivial matter, "became really important when 'The Chinaman' masqueraded as an Oriental mystic, and intervened as such, with an implied claim to authority, in the dispute about Mr. Judge."[86] That the "masquerade" as an "Oriental mystic" carried with it "an implied claim to authority" testified to the power of this orientalist vision of a generic eastern mysticism within the English TS.

The debate over the Judge crisis was articulated as a conflict between two different modes of manly spirituality, both inflected by racial or ethnic stereotypes. One was a scholarly practice, in which the most important relationship was the one between the reader and the written word, a route to spiritual enlightenment that had been fully textualized and abstracted from its social context. The other was structured around the personal and social relationship between teacher and pupil, stigmatized on the one hand as the oriental despotism of guru and chela, and valorized on the other as the way of the western warrior.

After the Judge crisis was resolved by the secession of Judge and his largely American (and Irish) followers, the TS in England began to rethink its public role and strategy. Besant, now firmly in control of the Esoteric Section, spent most of her time in India. Mead had the field to himself, and he dismissed earlier efforts as "unintelligent propaganda," arguing that members now realized that "our main duty is to try to fit ourselves by study and training before we proclaim ourselves instructors of others." The emphasis was to be on sound scholarship rather than on occultism and phenomena, and Mead claimed that "there is no longer any considerable demand for pseudo-magical treatises or works that pretend to mysticism."[87] A year later, in 1898, he praised the society for its avoidance of "*too* popular propaganda" and argued that "the making of members was not the main object of the Theosophical Society, which should consist of real students who will work steadily and without being *bizarre*."[88]

This was also a reaction against the activities of Judge's supporters in England and of Katherine Tingley, Judge's successor, who toured Europe on a "Theosophical Crusade" in the late 1890s. An account of Tingley's crusade in *Borderland* noted that educated opinion in London "has but scant sympathy with an attempt to introduce what may be regarded a kind of Salvation Army proceeding into the Theosophical Society. Mrs. Tingley with her purple, embroidered banner, and sensation boom, creates at headquarters in Avenue Road, the same kind of shudder that General Booth, with his drums and his cymbals, his banners and his bands, produces in Lambeth Palace."[89] All this was anathema to the Adyar theosophists, who rejected Tingley's "sensationalism" in favor of an emphasis on the austerities of theosophy's "spiritual philosophy."[90]

In the 1890s it was Tingley's Universal Brotherhood association, and not the Adyar TS, which was most closely associated with active work among the masses. The English theosophists who seceded with Judge, unlike their counterparts in the Adyar society, modified their statement of the society's First Object to read "brotherhood without distinction of . . . social class," reflecting their desire to appeal to a broader audience. The secessionists also included theosophical strongholds in the East End, such as Bow Lodge, whose members were active in outreach at the university settlement house at Toynbee Hall.[91] Tingley herself emphasized that her Universal Brotherhood and Theosophical Society was more committed to active philanthropic work than was her rival's organization, and claimed that her message, unlike Besant's, was for the poor as well as the rich.[92]

The rejection of "Tingleyite" forms of propaganda was part of the larger process by which the Adyar TS defined more precisely its intended audience. But the attempt to bring occultism before the public without an overly popular propaganda and to attract attention without being sensational was inevitably an awkward business. In the late 1890s the Theosophical Society in England decisively turned away from the emerging mass public and began to cultivate a more select clientele.

This effort was reflected in the decision to move the London headquarters of the TS from Avenue Road to Langham Place and then to Albemarle Street. These moves were undertaken with an eye to the society's credibility and public dignity, and it was hoped that a more central location, preferably near Oxford Street and Piccadilly, would improve the organization's profile.[93] The new general secretary of the TS, the Hon. Otway Cuffe, third baronet and sometime superintending engineer, Public Works Department, Burma, was clear on this point.[94] "It should be borne in mind," he told the 1899 convention, "that the fitting housing of the Section in this city is a matter which in a manner affects the standing of the society in the eyes of the public, and consequently directly reacts on the whole movement."[95] A similar philosophy governed the activities of local lodges as well, for members were reminded of the importance, when arranging public lectures, of "the hiring of rooms of good class and situation," for "if second or third rate rooms are secured the audience is usually unsatisfactory."[96]

However "manly" the rhetoric, it is also clear that theosophical lodges, in London and in the provinces, were eminently hetero-social spaces. The effort to re-create them as gentlemanly spaces had a clear impact on the kinds of experiences that both men and women had there. The TS in England began to compile membership registers in 1889, and of the 305 members recorded in 1889 and 1890 (which included many of the older members from the 1880s whose membership had never been officially entered on a master list), only 103 were women. Throughout the 1890s men continued to dominate the TS numerically, but women were a significant minority, forming roughly one-third of the membership.[97]

Women who did join the society seem to have had a relatively high level of education for the time. Jill Roe's study of theosophy in Australia notes that the census of 1911 suggested that women in the TS there were the best educated women of all religious groups in Australia at the time, and better educated on the whole than male theosophists.[98] Some of the most prominent women in the English TS, such as Isabel Cooper-Oakley and Henrietta Müller, were graduates of Girton, but it is not clear how typical they were. Women did not, however, play a public or prominent part in the life of the society. Internationally, the offices of president and vice president were held by men until Besant became president in 1907; at the national level, the highest office in each section was held by a man, with the lone exception of New Zealand, where Miss Lilian Edger, the first woman in New Zealand to take an M.A. degree, was general secretary. In England the office of general secretary was occupied by a succession of men until 1905.[99] Nationally and internationally Besant was by far the most prominent woman in the Theosophical Society, but the power she exercised as head of the ES left few public traces.

At the provincial level, in local lodges and centers, the pattern is less clear, but where records survive, it appears that lodge life was dominated and directed by men. These local lodges attracted a diverse audience drawn from local spiritualists, anarchists, antivivisectionists, and food reformers. The local groups tended to be small and were sometimes rather haphazardly administered. The Brighton Lodge, founded in 1890, began its work with a grand total of seven members, three of them men. At the first meeting, all the men were elected to official posts: Edward Ellis became president, and Mr. W. Liebenhaar, Esq., secretary-treasurer; Dr. King and two of the women members of the tiny lodge were appointed to the lodge council. The rules and regulations that governed local lodges, however, were often honored more in the breach than in the observance, as when the secretary noted that "owing to a misunderstanding the officers were omitted to be elected."[100]

The Sheffield Centre of the TS was founded in 1895 and chartered as a lodge the following year. Although the Sheffield Centre attempted to preserve a more democratic system, when the lodge was chartered and officials had to be elected, those positions also went to men. By November 1895 the center was deep in earnest study of the nature of the Ego, though their efforts were occasionally derailed, as when Mrs. Entwhistle, a first-time visitor, broke into the discussion with a display of trance mediumship. By January members were complaining that meetings were insufficiently studious, and a program of directed study was adopted, with a rotating chair to keep the meeting in order. A week later, with Mrs. Pexton in the chair, the group began working their way through Miss Elizabeth Moulson's explanatory notes on points arising out of the previous week's discussion. Miss Moulson's notes—giving, for example, the dates of the Dark Ages, a definition of Neo-Platonism, and figures for the numbers of Christians and Buddhists in the world— indicate the intellectual level at which discussions were conducted. How comfortable women and less educated men were in such a milieu is unclear. The rough and tumble of intellectual debate could leave at least some women at a disadvantage. The minutes for a meeting in Sheffield in 1896, for example, produced the following laconic entry from C. J. Barker, the lodge secretary (and later Moulson's husband): "Vegetarianism discussed. L. M. [Elizabeth Moulson] obstreperous, & sat on by the company generally, retired feeling squashed."[101]

During these years the TS provided women with significant social and intellectual opportunities. But the clublike atmosphere of the society also imposed certain limitations. Club culture was notoriously anti-feminist: as Brian Harrison has argued, "the existence of pubs, clubs and club-like institutions prevented Victorian and Edwardian wives of all classes from occupying more than a segment of their husband's time." For middle- and upper-class men, London's clubland reinforced the spatial and social segregation of the sexes that was also characteristic of the institutions from which clubland drew its clientele—the public schools, Oxford and Cambridge, and professional institutions. Clubland therefore functioned as an exclusionary space within metropolitan culture. In the colonies gentleman's clubs also functioned to exclude the "natives" from British society.[102] In the last decades of the nineteenth century some women's clubs were founded, catering largely to the needs of single, professional women. Some of these, like the Pioneer Club, founded in 1892, served an explicitly feminist constituency; others were more socially oriented.[103] Mixed clubs of various kinds also existed; one of the most famous was the Men and Women's Club, founded by Karl Pearson in 1885. As Judith R. Walkowitz has demonstrated, however, women could be at a considerable disadvantage, even in these self-consciously mixed spaces.[104]

Many men in the Theosophical Society explicitly defined theosophy as manly, in contrast to what they represented as a weak and womanly Christianity. Charles Webster Leadbeater, for example, who became one of the most prominent and notorious members of the TS worldwide, claimed that theosophists had no truck with "the cheap, namby-pamby, backboneless sentimentalism which is always overflowing into vague platitudes and gushing generalities."[105] Arthur A. Wells, one of the English Section's general secretaries in the 1890s, made the point (with its gendered implications) even more clearly, arguing that anyone foolish or weak enough to imagine that their problems could be solved "by some mystic 'washing in the blood of Jesus'" would be better off outside the Theosophical Society, for theosophy was "a *man's* religion, and does not deal in soothing powders and lollypops."[106]

Some efforts were made to give women the resources to flourish in this atmosphere. Members flocked to Practice Discussion Classes and Debating Societies organized by local lodges and by the London headquarters. These exercises were designed to "afford help in enabling students to express themselves suitably on Theosophical subjects."[107] The Social Committee at headquarters established an Afternoon Debating Society in 1906, which made a special effort to appeal to women who might be unused to public speaking. Resolutions included "That greater likeness between men and women is desirable" and "That it is desirable in the interest of the State that women should now share men's work on all governing bodies, and fit themselves to enter Parliament at some future date."[108]

Mead and his allies had won a significant battle. But if, over the course of the Judge crisis and throughout the 1890s, a manly version of intellectual spirituality triumphed, that triumph hardly outlasted the century; the forces represented by Mead had won the battle but they were to lose the war. As women gained more confidence, and grew in numbers within the society, they began to challenge the hegemonic image of the theosophist as a gentleman and a scholar. In 1898 Mead already detected signs of trouble:

> Our questioners are not playing fair with our pandits, and the editor finds it difficult to keep things in proportion. For one question on any other subject we have at least ten on matters astral. Now these psychic things can only be answered by one or two people. . . . The editorial sanctum possesses two or three drawers full of questions such as: Can the psychic eye see through a brick wall; if so why so, if not why not? Or: I frequently see specks before my eyes; do you think this is the astral light? Now all these things are important in their own sphere. . . . [but] the thing is out of all proportion.[109]

Lectures on ghosts (or other "matters astral") were, the secretary of the Blavatsky Lodge noted, very well attended, but historical studies of eighteenth-century mysticism did not draw the same crowds. Such "psychical curiosity" was to be lamented, "when not balanced with definite study."[110] There were other signs of things to come: at the North of England Federation (TS) meeting in November 1897, the Esoteric Section, which had not been discussed publicly for some years, was "*the* subject of the Conference."[111]

Since the late eighteenth century, the effort to apprehend the spiritual through scholarship had been a dominant element in European esotericism. By the late nineteenth century, in movements like the Golden Dawn, scholarship was increasingly displaced by new concerns with spiritual "experience."[112] That shift was consolidated in the twentieth century. The emphasis on experience was paralleled in the academic world as well. By 1902 William James had begun to insist that religion was a matter of feeling rather than of belief. In his published work he was "bent on rehabilitating the element of feeling in religion and subordinating its intellectual part."[113]

The emphasis on feeling, so marked in James's account, also came to characterize the TS in the early twentieth century. The shift coincided with the increasing dominance of the Theosophical Society by women, both in the leadership and in the membership more generally. Already in America women appeared to be outnumbering men among theosophists. In 1894 an American observer, Dr. J. D. Buck, noted a curious difference between the English and American lodges: whereas in England the sexes appeared to be represented roughly equally in the society, in America there were ten women to every man. The cause, he claimed, was "the intense absorption of the average American in the race for the 'almighty dollar,' leaving only the women and a few professional men to take part in the thought movements of the age."[114] The Theosophical Society was about to be reshaped once again, in yet another effort to domesticate the occult.

Chapter Three

"A Deficiency
of the Male Element"

Gendering Spiritual Experience

In the late nineteenth century the Theosophical Society, and English occultism as a whole, was a man's world. In the twentieth century esoteric religion was redefined as a paradigmatically feminine experience. Women became emblematic of a personal, emotional, and subjective religiosity, and spirituality was increasingly represented as an essentially feminine enterprise. These associations were popularized and given academic respectability in Jungian psychology. The Jungian psychologist Esther Harding, following Jung himself, elaborated this point in *Woman's Mysteries,* first published in 1935. "Contact with the inner or spiritual world," Harding argued, "is governed not by masculine but by feminine laws." Her definition of the spiritual as personal, subjective, a-rational, and relational is repeatedly tied back to her understanding of the feminine.[1]

One corollary to the claim that religion was the special province of women was that it had therefore become insignificant. As Jeffrey Cox puts it, "Church was for women, and there was a general assumption, which historians have not entirely avoided, that women were unimportant, religion was for women, and religion was therefore unimportant."[2] The supposed feminization of religion also fitted neatly with a renewed emphasis on the private, personal, and subjective character of religious experience. William James's famous definition of religion as *"the feelings, acts, and experiences of individual men in their solitude, so far as they apprehend themselves to stand in relation to whatever they consider the divine"* reflected this emphasis.[3] Since women were popularly believed to be associated with feeling rather than reason, and with the private rather than the public sphere, religion was also understood as primarily experiential and personal. The perceived feminization of religion is therefore a crucial component of the secularization thesis. Historians have now come to recognize that the most simplistic versions of this thesis can only be sustained by a blatant disregard for the evidence.[4] The current reevaluation of the process of secularization allows

67

us to reconsider the links between the private, the spiritual, and the feminine.

These links were actually historical rather than natural phenomena. The history of the Theosophical Society in England provides an excellent opportunity to trace the emergence of these links. After Annie Besant became president of the TS in 1907, the English Section of the society began to be dominated by women, and the kinds of spiritual activity that were celebrated within the TS were characterized, by both critics and supporters, as distinctively feminine. Both of these shifts were a significant departure from earlier patterns within the Theosophical Society. When a register of members was first compiled in 1890 the society's membership was largely male; as early as 1895, however, almost half of new members were female. Between 1900 and 1910 nearly two-thirds of new members were women. After 1910 the fraction climbed even higher, and from 1915 to 1925 between two-thirds and three-quarters of new recruits were women.[5] Simultaneously there was a new emphasis on emotion and devotion rather than study, on personal relationships rather than abstract principles, and on hierarchy and loyalty rather than individual autonomy. Subjective and interior experiences were valued in new ways, and many of these experiences took place in the rigorously private (in the sense of secret or hidden) context of the Esoteric Section. These changes were dramatic enough that some critics began to refer to Besant's "neo-theosophy."[6]

Less clear is the relationship between the literal feminization of the Theosophical Society and the emergence of a more feminine (or even feminist) spiritual practice. In her groundbreaking study of alternative religion in America, Mary Farrell Bednarowski emphasizes the doctrinal and structural elements that drew women to movements like theosophy, including the rejection of an anthropomorphic God and of a traditional, male-dominated, ordained priesthood.[7] More recent studies attempt to locate these features in their specific historical contexts.[8] An exploration of the specific historical context in which women came to dominate the TS in England reveals a surprising result: while the features that Bednarowski identified were characteristic of theosophy in its first fifty years, many of them were least evident at precisely those moments when women dominated the society.

The relationship between women, the feminine, and feminism within the TS in England was not at all straightforward. The transformation of theosophy was not an inevitable result of the increasing numbers of women in the society. Rather, it was the outcome of hard-fought struggles over the content and form of spirituality. These diverse innovations formed an ensemble, which then came to be understood as a more feminine (or, for critics, less virile) religiosity. Critics of Besant's neo-theosophy often argued that it was characterized by a lack of virility, which led to its excessive credulity and heightened sentimentalism. But if this was, as these critics argued, a feminine spirituality, it was by no means a direct consequence of women's presence in the society. The demands made by new women members were various. The changes they called for, though sometimes justified as a way of making women feel more at home in the TS, were drawn from a range of contradictory understandings of women and women's spirituality. The ongoing debates about the meaning of women's presence in the TS, however, did help to consolidate the connections between women and women's spirituality that the concept of feminization serves to naturalize. These two quite different meanings of feminization must remain conceptually distinct.

The first discussions of the need for change in the TS were conducted without much direct reference to feminization. In 1904 *The Vāhan* opened its correspondence columns to a discussion of the "atmosphere" of the society. Ida Ellis wrote to complain of the cool reception she had received when she visited other lodges, criticizing the "ice-cold attitude of 'I understand these things and nothing moves me.'"[9] In the next issue, Minnie Theobald, who had been raised in a spiritualist family and had joined the TS with her parents at the age of twenty, wrote to second Ellis's criticisms. Theosophists, she argued, were too prone to neglect the "careful cultivation of the emotions." "Put aside your books," she urged, "stop the ceaseless working of your brains and learn to feel! To feel the rhythm of the universe, to feel life and love flow from every object that surrounds you, and by experience know Universal Brotherhood."[10] Over the next few years the points raised by Ellis and Theobald were echoed by a chorus of other voices, male as well as female.

In 1906 D. N. Dunlop saw an opportunity to revive, in this more sympathetic context, the debates that had surrounded the Judge crisis ten years earlier. Dunlop, a publicity manager for Westinghouse Electric (and later a prime mover behind the British Electrical and Allied Manufacturers' Association and the World Power Conference) had left the Adyar TS along with his associates in the Dublin Lodge in the 1890s and had spent time in America with Katherine Tingley, Judge's successor. After a falling out with the "Purple Mother" and her Point Loma theosophists, Dunlop had returned to London and to the Adyar TS, but he was not content to leave the English theosophists as he found them. "We have surrendered to books much other activity associated with the life of men," he wrote. "Spiritual culture in the old time came 'as an exaltation of life itself'—not at the expense of life."[11] The crucial point here is not Dunlop's reference to men, which can easily be read as generic in this case, but his participation in a more general call for a renewal of spiritual life within the TS.

There were, however, some hints that the call for a renewed emphasis on the spiritual life of the TS was being tied to the growing presence of women within the society's ranks. In 1907 a letter from G. K. to *The Vāhan* made the new context clear. G. K. argued that the truly spiritual life could not be lived on the intellectual plane alone:

> That is why brilliant lectures, while satisfying the mind, still often leave the inner life in gloom; that is why too often a small Branch meeting of motherly old ladies, whose combined intellect is less than that of a pupil-teacher of a London Board School, has more of the true theosophic spirit. I have often been present where a Branch was composed mostly of women, and most of them unintellectual, and yet I have learned much of Theosophy from their quaint generalisations about nature, human and divine, arrived at not through process of mind, but surely by some process that transcended it.[12]

G. K.'s letter identified what, over the next ten years, would emerge as new oppositions within the Theosophical Society. The life of the mind versus the inner life, intellect versus intuition, a masculine versus a feminine spiritual practice. Women, G. K. suggested, possessed a unique and even superior way to the divine.

The links that G. K. pointed to were reinforced in debates over Annie Besant's election. On January 7, 1907, Olcott, believing himself to be near death, issued a statement from Adyar. He announced that the Mahatmas M and KH had instructed him to appoint Besant as his successor.[13] Olcott's statement raised the constitutional question of whether he had the right to appoint or only to nominate the next president of the TS. But far more important was his linking of his recommendation of Besant to the will of the Masters. Besant would inevitably run as the Masters' candidate. Besant was at this time Outer Head of the ES, standing as Blavatsky's heir in representing the inner, spiritual, phenomenal side of theosophy. If she were also elected president of the Theosophical Society she would, her critics argued, wield unprecedented power. As the leader of the ES, she could use her personal power over members of the Esoteric Section to subvert the democratic process by which the TS was ostensibly governed.

The net result of Besant's election would be to found the TS once again on the authority of the Masters and their representatives. Such a

move, she argued, would open a "new cycle of life, of strength, of progress" in the TS, allowing her to carry on the great work of both Blavatsky and Olcott.[14] In the end Besant was elected by a large majority in
all of the national sections; in Britain the final count was 1,181 votes
for, and 258 against.[15] Her election was one indication of the increasing
power of women in the TS and the extent to which the society was open
to their leadership. But the debates over Besant's election, and not her
election itself, were what constituted women's presence as significant
and Besant's spiritual belief and practice as feminine.

The initial responses to Olcott's circular set the tone for what followed. Besant's supporter Clara Codd remembered that "when the copy
of the Colonel's letter reached our little Lodge in Bath our president
read it to us. 'I suggest,' she said, 'that we do nothing about this. It
sounds to me like just another spiritualistic message.'" At the London
convention that followed, Codd recorded, the same charge was repeated: "The Vice-President, Mr. A. P. Sinnett, told us very pontifically
that he proposed to take no notice, as to him it seemed mediumistic.
Mr. Kingsland got up and called on the Masters to come forward and
let themselves be examined 'like any other phenomena.'"[16] Kingsland's
comments recalled the events of twenty years earlier, when Blavatsky
and the Masters had been investigated by the Society for Psychical Research (see chapter 1). Kingsland positioned himself with the psychical
researchers, on the side of science, objectivity, and rationality. The
charge that Olcott's visit from the Masters was "mediumistic" aligned
Olcott and Besant with spiritualist mediums, who were routinely represented in spiritualist writings as feminine: passive, receptive, often physically frail, young, and female.[17]

Besant's opponents quickly identified her candidacy with a constellation of threats, arguing that she was antidemocratic, irresponsible, and
irrational. She represented the vices of arbitrary, private power, in opposition to the virtues that should govern public life. G. A. Gaskell's
Exeunt Mahatmas! written in the midst of the crisis in 1907, argued
that "the more critical members of the Society are fast recognizing the
danger and inconvenience of being ruled, either personally or socially,
in mundane affairs by superior beings or 'supermen.'" He continued,
"It is not without reason that they cry out that such ruling would mean
the establishment of a Popedom and the dethronement of reason and
common sense. In this broad light of human freedom it does not matter
whether supermen exist or not. The interference of the genuine autocrat, privately or publicly, would be as objectionable as that of his spurious rival." The problem with "Master's Orders," Gaskell concluded,
was that they demanded an uncritical trust in the judgment and sanity

of those recognized as the Master's representatives. He dismissed the account of Mahatmic visitation as a form of collective hypnotism and called upon rationalists to defend their liberty of thought. Gaskell denied not only the truth of the Mahatmas' visit but also the authority Besant derived from it. He and his wife resigned from the TS during this period, although Ellen Gaskell, who had been one of those writing to *The Vāhan* to encourage the development of the "personal element" in the TS, later rejoined.[18]

G. R. S. Mead also objected to being governed by the Masters and their candidate. He "repudiated the pronouncements of these apparitions" in terms similar to those used by Kingsland and Sinnett. Besant's election, he went on to argue, would mean "the death of our constitution and the handing over of the society to the mercy of an irresponsible psychic tyranny." As Outer Head of the ES (in Mead's words, that "most important and intimate office"), Besant as president of the TS would be able to "force other similar pronouncements upon us and hold them *in terrorem* over the heads of the unknowing and timorous."[19] Mead's implications were clear. The "intimate office" of Outer Head of the Esoteric Section rested on private and personal power; this power was not exercised responsibly in public, but rather was wielded irresponsibly in private. And it exploited the weakness, timidity, and lack of knowledge of those who were willing to bend to such "psychic tyranny." As he recalled in 1926, he had opposed Besant's election on the grounds that the ES had become "the inner rot to the whole movement, seeing that it was based on blind obedience to (so-called) 'esoteric orders.'" Mead argued that Besant's election had been engineered "by the teamwork of the E. S. under her orders" and claimed that this "'Esoteric' cabal" was a "camouflaged political caucus, 'pulling' every crisis in the society from within to suit A. B.'s own views and purposes."[20]

Besant turned Mead's own arguments against him in ways that reinforced the dichotomy between a masculine public and a feminine private. Mead's pamphlet she described as a "clever electioneering squib" that "recalls so vividly the political struggles of my youth, with the familiar tricks of half-truths, ignoring of patent facts, and lurid pictures of what will happen if the government candidate be elected."[21] Besant was not above invoking the prestige of the public sphere, as her reference to "the political struggles of my youth" makes clear. But her exclusion from public life, as a woman under an unreformed franchise, also allowed her to represent herself as untainted by the corruption and special pleading endemic in politics.

Her strongest claim to the presidency was her personal link to the Masters, and so, according to Codd, in the face of skepticism expressed at the 1907 convention, Besant could restrain herself no longer: she "gave us a most impassioned address upon the reality of our Masters, many of whom she knew personally."[22] Besant was quite aware of her personal power, having admitted in *The Theosophist* in 1907 that "I know that I exercise a quite unwarrantable power," that she could have defeated Colonel Olcott on any issue in the last decade and a half, and that "it is impossible to neutralise the authority of one to whom thousands look up as to a spiritual teacher."[23] Recognizing all that, she claimed that she remained committed to the constitutional principles that governed the TS, and argued that the society itself would be strengthened by the union of its inner and outer forms. In any case, "I would rather be rejected as my Master's nominee," she announced to members of the British society, "than succeed by disavowing that which, to my mind, carries a far higher honour than any possible election by applauding crowds."[24]

Besant herself stressed that members of the TS should not accept her teachings, or the teachings of the Masters, uncritically. Her presidential address in 1911, however, made clear that her position as the Masters' representative allowed her to affirm even as she renounced personal spiritual authority: "Some of you may say: 'Yes, but you are right.' That may be. It is very likely that I am; for I know, on these matters, far more than any one of you can know. But that is not a reason why you should believe."[25] The dispute over Besant's election, and over the place of the Masters within the TS, was a dispute about what kind of spiritual authority and practice would be institutionalized within the Theosophical Society.

For many ordinary theosophists, access to the Masters and to spiritual experience itself came through the Esoteric Section of the TS. Through carefully structured ritual activities, the ES shaped personal spiritual experiences in new ways. Within the ES, classes were formed for the study of documents specified by Besant as the head of the school. The documents themselves were carefully chosen. The methods of study were clearly laid out as well, for esoteric documents were to be studied by esoteric means. Classes were run through dialogue rather than lecture, and students were not permitted to read from prepared notes. When a point had been satisfactorily elucidated, all were to hold their thoughts upon it, "uniting in a brief meditation." These techniques were intended to develop the powers of thinking and remembering, and to discipline the mind.[26]

These were clearly not ordinary study meetings of the kind that had been typical of the TS in the 1890s. Besant made it clear that when the ritual passwords were exchanged, the members passed through "the psychic gateway," out of the "atmosphere of the world into the atmosphere of the Great Lodge" of the Masters. Behavior was to be "reverent, quiet and controlled. All noise, all unnecessary movement, should be avoided; the voice should be gentle, the mind stilled." The sacred portraits of the Masters themselves should, whenever possible, be displayed in the meeting room and reverently saluted with the silent thought, "Homage to the Divine Teacher." Dissent was not to be openly expressed, as what one student might dislike could be helpful to another. Argument and laughter were discouraged, as "these cause disturbing ripples in the stream of thought." At the end of the meeting, after the chanting of the "sacred word," they saluted the sacred portraits once again, and left the room in silence.[27] It was emphasized that the sounds and words uttered in ES meetings were powerful tools, which could harm an untrained person of impure life who might overhear them.[28]

Even in the wider community that was the TS itself—still governed by democratic structures, run by a bureaucracy, and apparently quite separate from the ES—theosophical life changed to reflect the fact that the TS was not merely a voluntary association but a spiritual community. Besant restored the ceremony of initiation for new members that had fallen into disuse in England, though it had been preserved at Adyar. In 1912 she was "At Home" to seventy new Fellows of the TS in London, who were duly initiated into fellowship and given the signs and passwords.[29] The ceremony, at which only Fellows of the TS were entitled to be present, reinforced the seriousness of becoming a Fellow of the Theosophical Society. The rooms were prepared with incense and fresh flowers, and "soft and tranquilising music" preceded the ceremony, which opened with a short meditation, followed by readings from the world scriptures and various theosophical writings. While the ceremony was not to be confused with the "Great Initiations of the Path of Holiness," it acted as a symbol and reminder of those greater initiations.[30]

Several lodges now introduced devotional services, which supplemented the public lectures that had been the mainstay of theosophical propaganda. The West London Lodge (the first in the TS to be founded almost entirely by women) had been holding meetings "of a more devotional character" for some years.[31] In 1909 the North London Lodge discontinued its weekday lectures and instead held theosophical services on Sunday evenings, which consisted of music, invocations, ethical hymns, and addresses.[32] In December 1914 came the announcement that Sunday devotional meetings were to be held at the TS headquarters in Tavistock Square, which made organized devotion and worship an official part of the society's activities in England.[33] Although some criticized the move as an abandonment of theosophical principles, most members welcomed the new departure.

The outbreak of war in 1914 was a crucial factor in the move to a more devotional emphasis within the TS. Even before the war began, however, this devotional tendency had begun to characterize a range of theosophical activities. There was a new emphasis on what was described in the title of one popular pamphlet as *The Hidden Side of Lodge Meetings*. At least 2,500 copies of this book were sent out to members and local lodges in 1909 in an attempt to popularize a new attitude to lodge meetings among the members.[34] While "to the dim physical eyes all that is visible [at a lodge meeting] is a small band of humble students," to the clairvoyant vision such a meeting was actually a swirling vortex of thought power, spiritual magnetism, and divine energy.[35] Marie Russak's description of the "astral forces" at work during Besant's public lectures in London in 1912 provided a further confirmation of the powerful forces many theosophists believed were active in the Theosophical Society. As Russak described it, the audience in The Queen's Hall was joined by a great mass of nature spirits and by the Great Ones themselves, charging the auditorium with "brilliant force" and producing the effect of "a mass of searchlights flashing brilliantly in and through the transparent rainbow clouds."[36]

The society was changing in other ways as well. While some members had long criticized the Albemarle Street headquarters, claiming that it "savoured too much of snobbery," when the move came, it was not to a less central or less dignified site.[37] Besant took a ninety-nine-year lease on a property in Tavistock Square, and plans were drawn up for construction of a headquarters building, which was expected to cost almost £50,000. Offices for the ES, the Theosophical Publishing House, and various "subsidiary activities" were to be provided, along with self-contained residential suites for members of the society. Special rooms were to be reserved on the third floor for ES meetings and meditation by ES members, and another for any Fellow of the Theosophical Society wishing to use it for meditation or devotion.[38]

The plans for the new building reflected the distance the society had come from the days when it resembled the other gentleman's clubs in Albemarle Street. The ambitious scale on which the Tavistock Square headquarters was planned represented the society's renewed belief in its public mission. The provision of explicitly private spaces, literally walled off from the intrusive gaze of outsiders, simultaneously embedded the society's emphasis on the private and personal aspects of spiritual experience in the building itself. The residential suites and special rooms for the ES and for devotion and meditation displaced the smoking rooms at Albemarle Street and (like the Celtic cross at the core of the original design) helped to designate this as an explicitly spiritual space.

The new headquarters gave concrete form to the initiatives that had been launched under Besant's leadership. These initiatives were also linked to a new element in theosophical teaching: a commitment to belief in the imminent Coming of the World Teacher in the person of a young Telugu Brahman, Jiddu Krishnamurti, who was to be the vehicle of the "Christ that is to be." In 1911 Besant had reorganized the Esoteric Section to acknowledge that the Masters had once again drawn closer to the society they had founded. Those who wished to remain in the ES were required to subscribe to a pledge: "I pledge myself to support before the world the Theosophical Society, and in particular to obey, without cavil or delay, the orders of the Head of the Esoteric Section in all that concerns my relation with the Theosophical movement; to work with her, on the lines she shall lay down, in preparation for the coming of the World-Teacher, and to give what support I can to the Society in time, money and work."[39] The new pledge bound members who took it more closely to Besant, to the Masters, and to the young Krishnamurti.

The "discovery" of Krishnamurti was the work of C. W. Leadbeater. Charles Webster Leadbeater was an Anglican curate who had joined the TS in 1883. Even before he joined, his spiritual interests had been eclectic and radical: he had explored spiritualism, and he also joined the Confraternity of the Blessed Sacrament, an Anglo-Catholic organization that represented the most extreme wing of the Anglican High Church movement. Soon after joining the Theosophical Society, Leadbeater broke with the Anglican Church and traveled to Colombo with Olcott and Blavatsky, where he made a public profession of faith in Buddhism. From Colombo, Leadbeater traveled to Adyar and, according to theosophical tradition, "unfolded and perfected his psychic faculties under the inner guidance of his Guru."[40] He returned to England in 1889 and began to build a considerable following; his accounts of his clairvoyant investigations proved increasingly popular. In 1906 Leadbeater temporarily resigned from the TS after he was implicated in a sexual scandal (discussed at length in chapter 4), but shortly after Besant's election as president of the Theosophical Society he was readmitted and acknowledged as the society's most prominent occultist.

In April 1909, on the beach at Adyar, Leadbeater had encountered a young boy, the son of one Jiddu Narayaniah, a Brahman widower who had retired from the Civil Service a year earlier to work for the TS. The "size and beauty" of the young Krishnamurti's aura impressed Leadbeater, and he announced to his assistant Ernest Wood that this boy would become a great spiritual teacher, greater even than Besant.[41] To support his claim, Leadbeater began the clairvoyant investigations that gave Krishnamurti his long spiritual pedigree: "Rents in the Veil of Time," published in *The Theosophist* beginning in April 1910, provided detailed accounts of Krishnamurti's past incarnations, in which, under the name Alcyone, he could be found serving the Masters, surrounded by a faithful "Band of Servers" made up of loyal theosophists.[42] Mme. Blavatsky had taught that the end of the nineteenth century would roughly coincide with the end of a cycle in the Hindu Kali Yūga, or "Dark Age," and many theosophists expected that the twentieth century would be a "New Age." Besant and Leadbeater added a new and more precise gloss to these claims and dramatically accelerated Blavatsky's timetable.

Besant publicly declared the Coming for the first time in December 1908, at the end of a lecture in Madras. In December 1910 the Theosophical Publishing House at Adyar released *At the Feet of the Master,* Alcyone's account of teaching given to him by the Master KH. The work was immensely popular, and within a few years it had been translated into twenty-seven languages, gone through over forty editions, and sold over a hundred thousand copies.[43] In January 1911 the journal *Herald of the Star* appeared, edited at least nominally by Krishnamurti, and in July 1911 Besant launched the Order of the Star in the East (OSE) to prepare the world for the new Advent. At the Christmas meeting at Adyar on December 28, 1911, the promised World Teacher apparently manifested himself through Krishnamurti for the first time, throwing the atmosphere "into powerful pulsing vibrations of a most extraordinary force."[44]

The formation of the OSE reflected the new mood in the TS. Members of the order vowed to make devotion (along with gentleness and steadfastness) "prominent characteristics of our daily life," and began and ended each day "with a short period devoted to the asking of His blessing upon all that we try to do for Him and in His name."[45] The new general secretary, James I. Wedgwood, argued that there was now a new spirit of warmth and cordiality in the TS, which he linked to "the near coming of the Lord of Love Himself, Who already is shedding His divine benediction over the Society." In his general report for that year, Wedgwood argued further that the OSE had served to counterbalance "the tendency to over-intellectualism, inherent in a scientific and metaphysical Society such as ours."[46] Where late nineteenth-century theosophists had postulated either the inner self or an impersonal Logos (the absolute divine principle) as the highest good, theosophists now pos-

Jiddu Krishnamurti in 1910.
(Adyar Library and Research Centre)

sessed their own, very real object of worship—Krishnamurti. Lady Emily Lutyens, the chief representative of the OSE in England, argued that this was a more human and personal spirituality than theosophy had previously offered: while there are some, she wrote in 1917, who are able to derive inspiration and consolation from abstract ideals, there are also those "who need to see those ideals embodied in a more or less concrete form . . . [these] are hero-worshippers, who see God best when He shows himself through man."[47] Elizabeth Severs spoke of the "curiously drawing power" of Krishnamurti's features and the "strange, indescribable aroma of attraction and of reverence" that clung to his person.[48]

Critics of the movement pointed out that women were especially drawn to Krishnamurti.[49] Even more scandalous was the possibility of a homoerotic element in the adoration evinced by his male followers. Devotion was good, as Wedgwood had argued, but excessive devotion was feminizing. In a scathing review of Edgar Williams's book of poetry, *The Sign of the Star*, Wedgwood claimed that "the poetry is drivel. . . . People of the ultra-devotional order, mentally flabby and revelling in gush and sentiment, are likely to be strongly attracted to this movement: we hope that the work of those who want the movement to be virile will not be eclipsed."[50]

As Wedgwood's remarks indicate, the perceived feminization of theosophy, in terms of both its membership and its character, did not go unnoticed. In November 1913 Capt. A. E. Powell began what became a long and heated controversy in the correspondence columns of *The Vāhan* with an article entitled "Virility in the T.S." According to Powell, "a deficiency of the male element in the Theosophical Society, at any rate in England, has been a noticeable element for some years." Not only were male workers becoming scarce, but "there is a scarcity of those elements which are usually classed as belonging primarily to the male end of the scale." Intellectual rigor, courage, vigor, and alertness: these were the qualities in which, Powell argued, the TS was now sadly lacking.[51]

Although one or two correspondents attempted to refute Powell's claims, the majority of his critics accepted his charges while revaluing the changes that had taken place. Jean Delaire (Mrs. Muirson Blake), author of *A Pixie's Adventures in Humanland* and other occult novels, pointed out that the "transient predominance of the passive, the devotional, the feminine elements" was simply a necessary reaction to the former preponderance of male elements.[52] Delaire and others valorized these feminine qualities, arguing that they were a sign not of weakness but of strength: love, devotion, compassion, and self-sacrifice were to be prized, and it was to the credit of the TS that it increasingly celebrated these qualities. Susan Gay, for example, argued that "Love is believed to be the principle which women chiefly represent, and Love is the note of the new Era." Major C. G. M. Adam linked women's prominence in the society both to the rise of the feminist movement and to Besant's leadership: "It is of course very noticeable that the large majority of members are at present in female bodies. This may be because our President is wearing a female body, and consequently the majority of her followers and devotees of the past were also incarnated as women for that reason; also because the period of Mrs. Besant's presidency has synchronised with the great advance of the Women's Movement generally." E. A. Palmer, on the other hand, agreed with Powell, arguing that theosophists paid too much attention to what "Mrs. Besant says," and not enough to developing their own ideas. This was particularly unfortunate, Palmer suggested, "in this age, when there is so much force abroad, and so much 'virility' amongst women."[53]

As Palmer's comment suggested, the relationship between women's numerical dominance in the society and the society's apparent lack of virility was not a straightforward one. What was an appropriately feminine or masculine spirituality was defined differently in different contexts. Thus, the Order of the Star in the East was not the only activity associated with the Theosophical Society to emerge in preparation for the Coming of the Christ. A range of other ritual and ceremonial orders had also become popular within the society, and each of them positioned women and the feminine in different ways. Through these new orders the working of occult ritual in the TS was Christianized and westernized, drawing increasingly from Europe's medieval past, in addition to India and Sri Lanka, for inspiration. At the same time, the occult tradition itself was virilized, although this was always a partial and uneven process. This virilization was associated with a sexual division of labor in which mysticism, apparently a quintessentially feminine spiritual experience, was to be subordinated to the authority of an occult male priesthood.

One ceremonial organization associated with the TS that admitted women on the same terms as men was the Universal Order of Co-Freemasonry, the first Masonic order to do so. The move toward a *Maçonnique mixte* was begun in France in the 1880s and 1890s, and the theosophist Francesca Arundale was the first English woman to join. After her initiation into La Grande Loge Symbolique Écossaise de France, Le Droit Humain, Arundale brought Besant into the order, and in September 1902 the first Co-Masonic lodge (Human Duty Lodge, No. 6) was consecrated in London. By the mid-1920s there were over forty Co-Masonic lodges in England, more than ten of them in the London area.[54]

Universal Co-Masonry claimed to be returning to the ancient practice from which true Masonic orders derived, and argued that "a movement which professes to be a Brotherhood of Humanity cannot accomplish its object if it refuses entry to one half of the human family."[55] In the first issue of the new order's magazine, *The Co-Mason*, the feminist and theosophist Edith Ward linked Co-Masonry directly to the aims of the women's suffrage movement: Co-Masonry was "part of that great stirring of the whole world which is known as the woman movement. . . . It is neither the rites and ceremonies, nor the titles and banquets, that attract women to Masonry, but a recognition that here is an

English Co-Masons, c. 1902. Besant is at center. Ursula and Esther Bright are
third and fourth from left, respectively; Edith Ward is on the far right.
(Adyar Library and Research Centre)

established channel through which the water of spiritual life may yet
flow freely."[56]

While Co-Masonry was clearly and proudly feminist in its inspiration—witness, for example, the contingent of Co-Masons who marched
in the Women's Suffrage Procession in June 1911—it was no simple
matter to incorporate women into the rhetoric and symbolism derived
from male operative Masonry. Masonic ritual, drawn from the trade of
the stonemason, was saturated with references to chisels, planes, and
plumb-lines, stones, bricks, and mortar—an unfamiliar language for
women (though to be fair, an unfamiliar language to most of their
mainly middle-class male colleagues as well). Early efforts to modify
the Masonic designation of "Bro∴" to read "Ssr∴" were abandoned as
infelicitous, even though they had been preserved in France.

While not technically a theosophical activity, Co-Masonry in En-
gland was dominated by theosophists: Annie Besant was created Vice-
President Grand Master of the Supreme Council and Deputy for Great
Britain and Its Dependencies, and theosophists populated the higher
degrees. The formation of the Star in the East Chapter of Royal Arch
Masonry in July 1911 also served to symbolize Co-Masonry's connec-

tions with the TS and the OSE.[57] The order's journal, *The Co-Mason*,
reflected the overlap in membership and interests until 1925, when the
proprietor of the journal, Miss Bothwell-Gosse, broke with both the
TS and Co-Masonry, and relaunched the magazine as *The Speculative
Mason*.

Where Co-Masonry emphasized women's spiritual equality to support a feminist agenda, other theosophical initiatives had different results. Much of the inspiration for ceremonial activity within the TS
came from the influence of James Ingall Wedgwood, who joined the
society in 1904 and rose quickly to become general secretary in England
in 1911, a position he held until 1913. Wedgwood had trained as an
organist in Nottingham and at York Minster and was studying for Anglican orders when, in 1904, he heard Besant lecture in York. He abandoned his theological studies and joined the York Lodge of the TS, de-
voting himself to theosophy.[58] In 1912, together with Marie Russak, he
founded the Temple of the Rosy Cross (TRC). The TRC was intended
as a ceremonial form of preparation for the Coming of the World
Teacher. The article in *The Vāhan* announcing the formation of the
TRC recalled the splendid ceremonials of medieval England, displaced
first by the "dull hard *régime* of the Puritan" and then by "industrial
greyness and Victorian ugliness." Those ceremonies were now to be revived through the TRC, which was to be "devoted to the study of the
Mysteries, Rosicrucianism, Kabalism, Astrology, Freemasonry, Symbolism, Christian Ceremonial, and the mystic and occult traditions found
in the West." Formed as an adjunct to the Order of the Star in the East,
the TRC was not intended to displace the authority of the wisdom of
the East, but to express it in a western idiom.[59]

These new ceremonial initiatives brought to prominence a new Master with a European pedigree: "the Count," Master Rakoczi, the "Hun-
garian Adept." Rakoczi was known to history as the Comte de St. Ger-
main in the eighteenth century, as Francis Bacon in the seventeenth, as
Christian Rosencreuz in the fourteenth, as Proclus the Neo-Platonist,
and before that as St. Alban.[60] The ritual for the TRC was composed
by Besant under the guidance of the Count, but Besant herself remained
a figurehead and was seldom present at the ceremonies. TRC ceremonials combined European forms with the effort to synthesize the basic truths of all religions and emphasized the new revelation still to
come through Krishnamurti. In a ritual loosely based on the Christian
custom of the lighting of the Advent wreath, for example, candles were
lit to represent the lives of earlier World Teachers, such as Christ or
Buddha, and the ceremony culminated with the dedication of an unlit
candle to represent the next World Teacher. Emily Lutyens's account of

these ceremonies (written years later, after Krishnamurti's refusal of the role of World Teacher and his condemnation of all efforts to institutionalize spiritual truth) reflects her loss of faith in such rituals. While it is still possible to see the appeal of TRC meetings—their emphasis on aesthetic elements, and the reshaping or reinvention of "traditional" forms and ceremonies in a modern context—it is difficult to avoid her implication that this is a manufactured, and slightly ludicrous, spiritual practice: "All the members were clad in long white satin gowns, with crimson and gold trimmings, and wore a headdress which was supposed to resemble that of a Knight Templar. They also carried swords. The idea of the dress was to conceal the sex of the wearer and make all look alike. The effect achieved was very curious. The motto of the Order was 'Lux veritatis,' which George Arundale translated 'looks very silly.'" Lutyens's concluding comments reveal the fusion of authenticity and artifice in these rituals: "I was told that I was a 'great channel' for the influence of the Lord Maitreya (the World Teacher who was to use Krishna's body). I worked myself into a state of spiritual ecstasy at every meeting, always picturing to myself the day when Krishna's 'divine hand' would light that unlit candle."[61]

After a year's work, the TRC's Supreme Temple in London had initiated almost three hundred members, a Grand Temple had been founded in Edinburgh, and Provincial Temples were at work in Manchester and London. This, as Wedgwood pointed out, "is an astonishing record; for it must be remembered that a ceremonial Order must inevitably be costly in its equipment and working, otherwise the ceremonial is ludicrous."[62] Wedgwood's comment draws attention to the class privilege that underlay TRC activities. Like the ritualist movement in the Church of England a generation earlier, the use of ritual and ceremonial in both the TRC and Co-Masonry reflected the affluence of the middle classes: as the American sociologist Thorstein Veblen pointed out at the turn of the century, ritualism was closely connected to the desire of the "leisure class" for "the consumption of goods, material and immaterial."[63]

These ceremonials were also a way to establish a sense of order in a world that seemed to be in profound disorder, for these were the years George Dangerfield once described as the "strange death of liberal England." Labor unrest, the Irish question, constitutional crisis, and the threat of war all preoccupied the nation.[64] The women's suffrage movement, and government intransigence on the issue, was another source of disorder. Gertrude Baillie-Weaver, who was a suffragette as well as a prominent theosophist and a Co-Mason, found in Co-Masonry the reassurance of order in a disordered world. She described the essence of Masonry as "an ordered ritual that images, / Albeit but darkly and as in a glass, / And brokenly, in modes of passing Time, / THAT which can never pass."[65]

Class privilege, and the male privilege that also became associated with these initiatives, was even more clear in the organization that superseded the TRC within the TS: the Liberal Catholic Church. C. W. Leadbeater had rather belatedly discovered that the formation of the TRC, which had taken place outside of his control, had been a misunderstanding of the Master's orders, and in 1914 he ordered that the Temple of the Rosy Cross be closed. The new Liberal Catholic Church (LCC) was intended to blend "theosophical mysticism and Catholic sacramentalism." According to its own official history, the LCC was founded in 1916 when its first presiding bishop, J. I. Wedgwood, was consecrated in London. Almost immediately Wedgwood consecrated Leadbeater, who had relocated to Sydney in 1914, as "regionary bishop for Australasia." Wedgwood and Leadbeater began to compile a new liturgy for their new church, and LCC congregations were soon active throughout Scotland and England.[66]

Leadbeater had already been incorporating an Anglican style of service into OSE practice in Sydney, and with his consecration as bishop he adopted episcopal style as well, rarely appearing without his purple cassock, pectoral cross, and episcopal ring. As with the TRC, full participation in the LCC required a certain level of class privilege and resources. Priests were required "to revert to the apostolic practice of combining spiritual and secular avocations," which was to say that the new church could not afford a paid clergy.[67]

Women were not admitted to the new priesthood. As Leadbeater explained in his *Science of the Sacraments,* published in 1920, one of the conditions of this "mighty gift of grace" was "that it is arranged to flow through the masculine organism." This type of magic was not adapted to work through the female body, and although lay men and boys might make spiritual progress by serving at the altar, even these opportunities were not available to women.[68] In *The Science of the Sacraments* Leadbeater deployed the authority of both occult science and Anglo-Catholic sacramentalism to bar women from the priesthood. Wedgwood used a similar occult-physiological argument to bar women from the LCC priesthood. He reassured his female readers that they had their own special form of priesthood, which was motherhood. (Wedgwood claimed that the relative advantage men possessed in occult development and ceremonial magic was some small compensation for the loss of the "evolutionary influence" of bearing children. He seemed quite unconscious of any contradiction between this position and his claim that the effort to bar women from Freemasonry was "specious nonsense.")[69]

Women in the Liberal Catholic Church were the audience before whom the spectacle of the priestly office was performed, but they remained outside the locus of real power. Wedgwood assured theosophists that it was not necessary that they be advanced occultists or great thinkers to make a positive contribution within the society: only a few could achieve the highest places in the Occult Hierarchy, "whereas many who are full of devotion and goodwill and of average intelligence can be grouped together, and used as collective vehicles for the transmission of high spiritual power."[70] This too, could be read as a feminine spirituality—a spirituality founded on that understanding of femininity which subordinated women to male power and authority. For priests and deacons in the LCC, the virile aspects of spirituality were recovered on this new terrain.

The association of occultism with virility was widespread within the Theosophical Society. Occultists within the TS stressed techniques that could be used to manipulate psychic and bodily states, as well as the external world. Occultism, which provided a shortcut to spiritual progress, was represented as a preeminently masculine activity. Besant's own authority was in some ways undermined by these shifts. In the years following her election as president of the society, she withdrew from active occult and psychic investigations in order to devote her energies to political and other activities. Leadbeater was the authority on things occult during Besant's tenure.[71] Although both Blavatsky and Olcott had suggested that women could become Adepts, this claim was increasingly ignored. In this later period it was argued that the "higher Initiations" were usually taken in male bodies, and this was explained using esoteric theories of biology and physiology.

Insofar as science and the professions were male-dominated activities during this period, occultism was implicitly presented as a masculine practice. Scientific metaphors pervaded almost all discussions of occultism, as in Besant's claim that the use of astral vision was "the same as a physical observation carried on with a microscope, and you have to do it as carefully and as repeatedly." Standards of proof, as defined by occultists themselves, were rigorously applied; neophytes were warned not to confuse true occultism with experiences that were merely "the result of impaired digestive organs."[72] The rhetoric of professionalization was used not only to determine what was and what was not "trained clairvoyance," but also to establish a model of authority based on the teacher/pupil relationship. This forestalled the criticism that uncritical submission to another's spiritual authority was in some sense demeaning or unmanly. The occult was a realm of power, and power was dangerous in undisciplined and ignorant hands; just as a professor of chemistry could not allow students to experiment recklessly, so no true occultist could allow his or her disciples to unleash "subtle forces" that might be beyond their control. The aspiring occultist was therefore required to complete a long and carefully supervised period of training before being allowed to experiment.[73]

There were also more direct ways in which the occult was coded as masculine. A new emphasis on the opposition between occultism and mysticism was used to reinforce the association of occultism with masculinity and of mysticism with femininity. Mysticism, like occultism, led to union with the divine, but it was understood to be a more passive form. Occultism was based on the cultivation of a magical willpower, while mysticism was the path of worship. Over and over again, the same oppositions were rehearsed: occultism had to do with power and wisdom, mysticism with self-surrender and love. Writing in *The Occult Review*, for example, H. J. Strutton argued that "whilst the Power predominates in the Occultist, Self-surrender characterizes the Mystic." In his review of Evelyn Underhill's best selling *Mysticism*, Strutton noted that Underhill, who was at this time a harsh critic of occultism, had made a similar distinction: "The fundamental difference between the two is this: Magic wants to get, Mysticism wants to give."[74] The theosophist Lily Nightingale made a similar point: though both aimed toward the unfolding of the spiritual consciousness, "the Occultist attains the goal by Wisdom, the Mystic by Love."[75] While mystical experience was valued within the TS, it lacked the power and prestige of occultism; when the Esoteric Section was reorganized in 1911, for example, members of the higher degrees of Occult Schools were automatically promoted into the new organization, while those of the Mystic School were not. The path of the mystic was a contemplative and solitary one, and as its fruits were almost wholly subjective, its practitioners were exempt from the discipline and hierarchy of occultism.[76]

An article by Mrs. M. H. Charles that appeared in *The Vāhan* in 1912 made explicit the gendered associations of these dichotomies. The mystic, she argued, who follows the path of devotion and love, is "ever a passive recipient type," and ultimately feminine, while the occultist, following the path of wisdom, exemplifies the "active type" and is represented as masculine. Mrs. Charles's sympathies were clearly with mysticism, and in the same issue of *The Vāhan* she announced the formation of a new lodge, Two Paths Lodge at Reigate and Redhill, which was to be devoted to the pursuit of the Mystic Path and which appears to have had an exclusively female membership.[77]

Mabel Charles's embrace of the more feminine form of mysticism was not, however, simply a capitulation to a new spiritual division of labor within the Theosophical Society; it was a form of resistance to the recovery of male power through an occult priesthood. In February 1912 Charles had published an attack on the TS's new function as Herald of the Star and the association of the TS with new orders and organizations. "What is the position," she asked, "of those members who are of the old *régime,* and abiding by our triple articles of association [the Three Objects of the TS], know nothing of such herald duty?"[78] Her manifesto, published in *The Vāhan* in March 1912, attempted to develop Besant's claims about the Paths of Wisdom and Devotion in directions quite different from those Besant had intended. Charles agreed that the two Paths were best understood by the analogy of sex, but went on to reverse the values implicit in that analogy. "By the analogy of *sex* the Two Paths may be best understood, and especially when they pass from the terrestrial to the celestial stage: in which Love takes the active and Wisdom the passive side."[79] Love or Devotion (the Path of the Mystic) thus ruled over Wisdom (the Path of the Occultist). A few months later Charles upped the stakes in her battle with the TS leadership and began circulating material critical of Besant and Leadbeater to the members of the TS in England. By April 1913 Charles was demanding sweeping reforms in the society, beginning with Besant's resignation as president.[80]

Those women and men who, by education or temperament, identified more closely with some version of the scientific spirituality characteristic of theosophy in the 1890s also continued to reject Besant's spiritual leadership. In America, the Wilmington Lodge of the TS broke away from what it called the "Annie Besant Section" of the society, on the grounds that Besant and Leadbeater had conspired "to suppress and throw into the background the works of H. P. B. and to replace them by sets of unprovable Astral visions, and a mass of trifling and inconsequential small books and pamphlets, which make no appeal to the intellect, and which are filled with scientific and philosophical fallacies." Theosophists, they argued, had become overemotional and credulous, abdicating their free will in exchange for occult honors and initiations.[81]

The new tendencies within the TS became exaggerated with the outbreak of hostilities in 1914. Theosophists saw the war as a final sweeping away of old forms that would usher in the New Age, and as a struggle between good and evil on a cosmic scale. The straightforward identification of Germany with evil was facilitated by the recent secession, in 1913, of much of the Theosophical Society's German Section under Rudolf Steiner, who rejected Krishnamurti and the Order of the Star in the East and founded his own Anthroposophical Society on a revival of an explicitly Christian mystery tradition.[82] The war also presented a tremendous propaganda opportunity. A special "Soldiers and Sailors Literature" fund was created, and books and pamphlets were sent to groups and individuals in the armed forces all over the world.[83] The war created a new public and private demand for spiritual consolation in the face of death and bereavement, and theosophy benefited from the failure of the more mainstream religious organizations to offer concrete answers to spiritual problems. Thanks to the financial support of its members, the TS was able "to take advantage . . . of the opportunity created by the war, and to respond, in some measure at any rate, to the demand for light and leading on the all-absorbing topic of the conditions prevailing after death, so carrying comfort to many of the bereaved."[84]

Historians have traced the widespread loss of faith among civilians and servicemen alike in the face of the unprecedented and apparently senseless deaths during the war. Established religion, as David Cannadine argues, struggled to address fundamental questions about the meaning of war, the assignment of guilt, and the fate of the dead.[85] At the same time movements like spiritualism and theosophy experienced a period of dramatic growth. Theosophy offered clear and unambiguous answers: God was on the side of the Allies, the war was part of the Great Plan to usher in a New Age, and death on the battlefield had won for soldiers spiritual honor and the chance for virtually immediate reincarnation. The Theosophical Society claimed after the war that its propaganda office had been overwhelmed by requests from soldiers and sailors for books and pamphlets on theosophical subjects. The TS office staff reported receiving grateful letters from the front lines that spoke "of the strength and courage given in the darkest hours [by theosophical teaching] and . . . the earnestness and keenness which were the outcome of those urgent days."[86]

While the TS obviously had a vested interest in emphasizing theosophy's appeal to the men on the front lines, theosophy did provide a way of explaining many of the practices soldiers engaged in while in the trenches: the reliance on talismanic objects or the attempt to ward off danger through the repetition of "lucky" ritual behaviors. In his war memoir, *Now It Can Be Told,* Philip Gibbs recorded his encounter with a colonel in the North Staffordshires who believed that the power of his will protected him in battle: "I have a mystical power. Nothing will ever hit me as long as I keep that power which comes from faith. It is a question of absolute belief in the domination of mind over matter. I go through any barrage unscathed because my will is strong enough to turn aside explosive shells and machine-gun bullets. As matter they must obey my intelligence. They are powerless to resist the mind of a man in touch with the Universal Spirit." According to Gibbs, "he spoke quietly and soberly, in a matter-of-fact way. I decided that he was mad."[87] What seemed madness to Gibbs could be meaningful, even if still disputed, within the framework developed within the TS.

David Graham Pole, who occupied himself in the trenches by reading the theosophical classic *Light on the Path*, noted that some officers, "who in ordinary life would not consider it 'good form' to talk about death," were suddenly forced to confront its reality, as they struggled to derive some meaning from their experiences.[88] Graham Pole was shipped home a few months after the war began with his "nerves shattered," and was eventually discharged on medical grounds. Elaine Showalter discusses the ways in which both the medical profession and the experience of war itself contributed to a feminization of the shell-shocked soldier, and this insight seems to capture Graham Pole's experience.[89] Far from becoming hardened or calloused by combat, Graham Pole claimed that, if anything, his emotions were "nearer the surface than they ought to be."[90] There were many ways of responding to death on the front lines, and while Pole's reaction may have been atypical, it was not unique. Men like Graham Pole found great comfort in the devotional and meditational aspects of theosophy, and the reports of the Order of the Star were full of accounts of men and women who used the order's meditation rooms to rest from the strain of the trenches, war hospitals, and munition factories.[91]

The war reinforced and exaggerated disillusionment with the ability of western science and technology to improve human existence, strengthening many people's need to find alternative sources of meaning. Michael Adas notes that the war experience—in particular, the spectacle of a scientifically and technologically sophisticated European civilization drowning the best of its youth in the mud and blood of Flanders—created a new audience for critics of western materialism. Writers like Rabindranath Tagore or Herman Hesse, whose idealized vision of a mystic East, *Siddhartha,* appeared in 1921, found new popularity.[92] Theosophy offered a similar critique, and one that had already been domesticated for an English market. The TS grew substantially during and after the war. Membership in Great Britain and Ireland rose from 2,905 in 1914 to 4,155 in 1918, and the organization continued to expand through the 1920s. On December 28, 1925, at the Star Congress in Ommen, the World Teacher appeared to speak directly to his followers through Krishnamurti, and this increased TS membership in England to over 5,100 members in 1928.[93] Subsidiary organizations, such as the OSE, the Universal Order of Co-Freemasonry, and the Liberal Catholic Church, shared in this growth. In 1918 the OSE in England boasted over 4,000 members, of whom almost 1,500 were not members of the TS. This expansion was also fueled by the well-orchestrated propaganda campaign that began before the war and continued through the 1920s.

The new regime was clearly not welcomed by all members of the society. In the years following Besant's election in 1907, and especially after the decision to readmit Leadbeater to the society, some English lodges had resigned their charters, and the Executive Committee received almost 300 resignations from the society.[94] Six members of the Executive Committee resigned in protest.[95] The short-lived Independent Theosophical League was formed "to uphold the ideal of pure spiritual growth and development taught in the Sacred Scriptures of all peoples, and to assist in disentangling that ideal from psychism and sensationalism of all kinds."[96] G. R. S. Mead left to form the Quest Society, a "clean society . . . that should be genuinely undogmatic, unpretentious, claiming no pseudo-revelations, and truly honest inside and out. . . . 'Esotericism' and 'occultism' were to be eschewed as corrupting rather than helpful."[97] A. P. Sinnett's Eleusinian Society offered another venue for those who, as Harold Wolfe Murray put it, desired something "delightfully stimulating after the droning boredom of the average T. S. middle-class lodge!"[98]

The 1920s brought another round of protests, schisms, and resignations. In America, where the Committee of 1,400 was petitioning Besant to reform the society, Besant was forced temporarily to suspend ES activities. In Australia the T. S. Loyalty League was formed, and it launched the magazine *Dawn*, which published criticisms of Besant and Leadbeater alongside attacks on the OSE and other subsidiary organizations. In 1922 B. P. Wadia, a prominent Parsi member at Adyar, resigned on the grounds that the TS, under Leadbeater's influence, had wandered too far from HPB's original program.[99] Wadia, who left the TS to join Robert Crosbie's United Lodge of Theosophists, claimed that "theosophy as a system of thought put forward by the Masters through H. P. B. has ceased to be a serious subject of persistent study, and that which has taken its place has little resemblance to the original virile, healthy, and profound teachings." What was "virile" and "healthy" about HPB's teachings—their emphasis on seeking "the God within" and on the intellectual seriousness of the task—had been displaced by "pseudo-theosophy," which, Wadia argued, was "a ready-made programme of spiritual advancement, which has become a creed, with its saviour-initiates and eternal hell of lost opportunities."[100]

The complaint that theosophy had lost its virility was not simply a convenient metaphor. What became known as the Back to Blavatsky movement was a reassertion of the norms that historically had clearly been tied to men's numerical dominance within the society and to the self-conscious cultivation of a manly spirituality: study rather than devotion, for example, and the celebration of individual autonomy. The publication of *The Mahatma Letters to A. P. Sinnett* were part of this effort to reassert an earlier version of theosophy. *The Mahatma Letters* was edited by A. Trevor Barker, who left the Adyar society disillusioned by neo-theosophy and ended up as the president of the English Section of the Point Loma Theosophical Society. *The Mahatma Letters*—so different in tone from the reverential references to the Masters in Besant and Leadbeater's writings—served as a clear reminder of those early days.[101]

Other movements founded by members who broke away from the Adyar TS at this time were based on similar norms. The Arcane School, founded by Alice and Foster Bailey in America, revived many of Blavatsky's techniques of self-presentation. As the amanuensis for Djwhal Khul, another member of the Great Brotherhood to which KH and M belonged, for example, Bailey claimed to cultivate an "intense, positive attention," like HPB's, that resisted assimilation to the feminine paradigm of passive mediumship. In its early years the Arcane School catered almost exclusively to men, and the group deliberately appealed to those "who would really work hard and who showed signs of true mental culture." The "emotional, devotional type" who did not qualify for the rigors of the Arcane School was, Bailey claimed, more suited to the Theosophical Society's Esoteric Section, where they would find their level. Bailey, who described herself as "no feminist," self-consciously cultivated a more intellectually oriented esoteric culture and rejected the more emotional and devotional elements the TS had embraced.[102]

In England the concerns that animated the Back to Blavatsky movement culminated in a special convention held in 1924, where the TS leadership was accused of leading the society astray and of governing by occult tyranny. Besant's opponents claimed that the Esoteric Section, which comprised only 15 percent of the Theosophical Society's total membership, had monopolized power within the society.[103] William Loftus Hare, an outspoken and indefatigable opponent of Besant, circulated leaflets and pamphlets condemning the "occult committee" that governed the society, which was dominated by members of the Esoteric Section and included priests of the LCC, a representative of the OSE, and a prominent Co-Mason, not to mention a treasurer (a Mrs. Sharpe) "who openly declares she knows nothing about finance and accountancy." He accused the Executive Committee of manipulating the "ritual of business" to subvert the democratic character of the TS.[104] The TS, Besant's critics argued, had become paralyzed by "its reliance on autocratic and secret control, rather than on the cleansing democratic principles expressed in its Constitution."[105]

It was only rarely that this "autocratic and secret control" was explicitly condemned as feminine. Some women may have benefited from belonging to the ES, which provided an avenue to power within the TS that did not depend on those bureaucratic and organizational skills that women may have lacked. But while women like S. Maud Sharpe, the treasurer who knew no accounting, may have come to power in the TS through a personal relationship with Besant, that avenue was not open to all women. And the male members of the Executive Committee—like Maj. A. E. Powell, the author of *The Ritual of Business*, whose manipulation of that ritual had proved so frustrating to Besant's opponents—benefited equally with their female counterparts from their status as ES officials.

Any discussion of the Esoteric Section is inevitably limited by its secret nature. Loyal members abided by their pledges and refused to discuss what went on in ES meetings after the ritual passwords were exchanged. Documents that were made public were usually released by those who were most critical of Besant and of the ES, members who, as Besant and her supporters constantly reiterated, had broken their pledges and betrayed their trust. In his reply to B. P. Wadia, for example, Subramania Iyer argued that even to raise the question of the role of the ES with regard to the wider society was inappropriate and unfair: the ES, he pointed out, had no official or legal connection with the TS, and no one was required to join it. It was Besant's "private and personal" concern, and as a spiritual teacher she had every right to choose her pupils and the conditions of their training.[106]

Besant argued that the existence of the Masters, and of their disciples in the ES, did not "affect the 'democratic character' of the T. S. with its constitution, its regulations, its organisation as an incorporated Society, with its officers and its General Council." Besant claimed that in order to preserve the democratic character of the TS, she could not accept proposals that would ban members of the ES from holding office in the Theosophical Society or prohibit members of the TS from becoming priests in the Liberal Catholic Church or force them to choose between the OSE and the TS. Any such move would be a limitation on members' freedom. In that spirit, Josephine Ransom's official *Short History of the Theosophical Society* later described this period under the general rubric of "Problems of Neutrality," with Besant as the defender of liberty in the society. That seemed, however, a perverse logic to those who felt silenced or marginalized by Besant's statement that while the Masters claimed no authority over the TS, the society's "true life flows down from the Elder Brothers, who are the unseen and unrecognised First Section."[107]

For others, the society's new activities seemed to open up rich new worlds of spiritual experience. The formation of the Surya Lodge in May 1920 illustrates the powerful pull of those experiences. According to the *Prospectus and Syllabus* the lodge issued in 1922, while "the work of every Lodge has its public side, all good and necessary," the real work of the lodge took place on a higher level, where members pictured the lodge as "pouring itself forth in 'love to all beings' . . . as bathed in radiant rosy sunlight, pouring out in every direction . . . [becoming] an inexhaustible centre springing from the Love of God and bathing ourselves as we strive to become channels for its transmission."[108] The Surya Lodge was dedicated to a "belief in the existence of the Masters in the world and in the Theosophical Society," and its mission was only possible in the context of Besant's claims that under her leadership the exoteric Theosophical Society was coming into a closer, more spiritual relationship to the First Section of the society—the Masters and the Great Lodge. It was also only possible once the experiential had displaced the intellectual mode of apprehending the divine, and once new, more explicitly gendered forms of spiritual authority had been developed and institutionalized.

The new forms of spirituality developed within Besant's TS intersected awkwardly with understandings of manliness and womanliness that were themselves internally divided. In 1913 Charlotte Despard, leader of the suffrage organization the Women's Freedom League, had argued in *Theosophy and the Woman's Movement* that "the spiritual voices which are going out into the world to-day have found their most ardent response in the heart of woman."[109] The spiritual was more heavily contested, the response more complicated, and the woman to whom theosophy appealed more diverse than a straightforward reading of the feminization model would allow.

Chapter Four

"Buggery and Humbuggery"

Sex, Magic, and Occult Authority

Many controversies occupied the Theosophical Society from Annie Besant's election as president in 1907 until her death in 1933: debates over
the Esoteric Section, over Krishnamurti and the Coming Christ, and
over subsidiary organizations like the Liberal Catholic Church and Co-
Masonry. These produced innumerable pamphlet wars, schisms, and
secessions. During all these controversies, disgruntled members of the
TS returned to the role of Besant's most prominent associate, Charles
Webster Leadbeater, in their troubles. The difficulties began early in
1906, when Besant and Leadbeater received copies of a letter signed by
the highest ranking officials in the American Section of the TS (Adyar)
and its Esoteric Section. The letter detailed serious charges. Leadbeater
was accused of "teaching boys given into his care, habits of self abuse
and demoralizing personal practices."[1] At the time when Leadbeater
gave his teaching, the boys in question were fourteen or fifteen years
old. The leaders of the American Section began to agitate for Leadbeater's expulsion from the society. On May 16, 1906, an Advisory Board met
at the Grosvenor Hotel in London to consider the Theosophical Society's response to the charges. Presided over by the president-founder,
Henry Olcott, the committee examined the documents in the case, cross-
examined Leadbeater, and then voted to accept his resignation. The
Advisory Board hoped that it had laid the scandal to rest.

Two years later, however, the society, under Besant's leadership,
voted to readmit Leadbeater on the grounds that his forced resignation
had violated the theosophical commitment to freedom of thought. At
the 1908 convention of the British Section of the TS, the question of
Leadbeater's readmission raised a storm of opposition. A special committee was formed in Britain to prepare a report on the question, a
committee dominated by some of Leadbeater's most outspoken opponents. The special committee's report, which did not support Leadbeater, was suppressed by Maud Sharpe and the Executive Committee
of the British Section, and the Executive Committee voted 9 to 5 in
favor of Leadbeater's reinstatement.[2]

94

The scandal resurfaced a few years later, in 1912, when Jiddu Naray-aniah, the father of Krishnamurti and his brother Nityananda, filed a suit in the court of the district judge of Chingleput claiming that Besant was unfit to hold guardianship of his sons. The charges revolved in part around Krishnamurti's role as the Coming Christ. The most inflamma-tory charges accused Leadbeater of a sexual relationship with the seventeen-year-old Krishnamurti.[3] The scandal was revived yet again, and even more virulently, in the early 1920s when the accusations against Leadbeater were brought up again and amplified. This time, Wedgwood and three of his associates in the Liberal Catholic Church were also accused of "sodomy with boys."[4]

Each of the Leadbeater crises forced members of the TS to confront a range of explosive issues: masturbation, child sexual abuse, and male homosexuality. Each had been the focus of a moral panic in Britain in the preceding years, in which the clergy, medical and legal profession-als, feminist activists, and the popular press had competed to define how they would be discussed. The accusations against Leadbeater were especially troubling for theosophists because they also raised the ques-tion of the relationship of spiritual authority to sexual deviance. Sexo-logical writings had begun to establish close links between spirituality and sexual desire, and the suggestion that Leadbeater was sexually de-viant was used to argue that his spiritual teachings were equally per-verse. Discussions of what was originally known to members as the "X. Case" have tended to focus almost exclusively on the question of Leadbeater's innocence or guilt, on whether he should be praised as a great spiritual teacher or condemned as a so-called sexual pervert. My focus, in contrast, is on the ways in which the discussion of the Lead-beater case engaged with larger debates about the multiple meanings of sexuality, and particularly of male homosexuality, in relationship to spirituality during the first decades of the twentieth century.

Opponents of the Adyar TS saw Leadbeater's prominence as the most glaring evidence of the society's departure from Blavatsky's origi-nal teachings. Alice Leighton Cleather, who had been a member of HPB's Inner Group in London in the 1880s, conflated Leadbeater's spir-itual and sexual "perversions": Besant, Cleather argued, had led the TS astray through her "blind and fanatical support of the sex pervert and pseudo-occultist C. W. Leadbeater, and the promulgation of his delu-sive, immoral, and poisonous teachings."[5] The supposed feminization of the TS (Adyar) was paralleled by a concern over what might be char-acterized as its effeminization; the concern with the declining virility of the society was linked not only to the increased visibility and power of women, but also to the threatening specter of deviant male sexuality.

The relationship between the sexual and the religious temperament was central to all these debates. An important strand in sexological thinking had begun to imply that spiritual experience itself was actually a form of sexual mania. In *Psychopathia Sexualis,* which was first translated into English in the 1890s, Richard von Krafft-Ebing had suggested, for example, that the spiritual and the erotic were in a sense interchangeable: "Religious and sexual hyperaesthesia at the zenith of development show the same volume of intensity and the same quality of excitement, and may therefore, under given circumstances, interchange."[6] The heightened emotional states of sexual arousal and religious ecstasy were, for Krafft-Ebing, virtually indistinguishable. In 1899 the British sexologist Havelock Ellis published the first edition of his study of auto-erotism, which included a section called "The Auto-Erotic Factor in Religion." Ellis endorsed Krafft-Ebing's findings, and cited countless other studies that reached the same conclusions. Ellis's own conclusion provided scant comfort for those who wished to see spirituality as the highest and purest of human emotions:

> There is certainly . . . good reason to think that the action and interaction between the spheres of sexual and religious emotion are very intimate. The obscure promptings of the organism at puberty frequently assume on the psychic side a wholly religious character; the activity of the religious emotions sometimes tends to pass over into the sexual region; the suppression of the sexual emotions often furnishes a powerful reservoir of energy to the religious emotions; occasionally the suppressed sexual emotions break through all obstacles.[7]

How, then, to rehabilitate spiritual authority in this context? If Leadbeater's "sexual emotions" could be characterized as in some way deviant, were his "religious emotions" similarly perverse?

The original charges against Leadbeater were presented in a letter of January 25, 1906, from Mrs. Helen Dennis, the corresponding secretary of the Esoteric Section of the TS in the United States. Dennis's letter included testimony from the mothers of three boys who claimed that Leadbeater had initiated their sons into the practice of masturbation, under the guise of spiritual instruction, swearing them to secrecy.[8] The most telling piece of evidence was a fragment of a letter, purportedly written by Leadbeater to one of the boys in code, that, when deciphered, read in part, "Glad sensation is so pleasant. Thousand kisses darling."[9] Mrs. Dennis (whose son Robert was one of the boys concerned, though her letter did not make that clear) demanded that Besant order a thorough investigation of the charges, and this demand was counter-

C. W. Leadbeater.
(Adyar Library and Research Centre)

signed by Alexander Fullerton and other prominent American theosophists.

In the debate that began in 1906, it was unclear whether Leadbeater was being accused simply of an injudicious (to say the least) attempt at sex education, or of something much worse. That the charges against him involved the possibility of the sexual abuse of boys made the case particularly controversial. Several highly publicized cases in earlier decades had made the "corruption of youth" a key element in representations of homosexuality. The Cleveland Street brothel scandal in 1889–90, involving Post Office messenger boys, and the Oscar Wilde trial in 1895 (stable-lads, newspaper sellers, and bookmaker's clerks) had both helped consolidate this image.[10] The charges against Leadbeater were especially troubling because of his involvement in work with children, not only with those individual young men who became known as Leadbeater's boys, but also through theosophical children's organizations like the Lotus Circles and the Round Table, which Leadbeater had helped found.

Even to hint that masturbation might be a way of dealing with sexual desire was itself shocking and unacceptable; the practice appears to have been almost universally condemned in Victorian England, even by the most radical of medical writers. Havelock Ellis's study of auto-erotism had taken a more sympathetic tone, but his redefinition of spirituality as a form of auto-erotism made him an equivocal ally. Medical warnings about the physical and emotional damage caused by "self-abuse" were seconded by clergymen, and the consequent fears were exploited by quacks who touted patent devices and heroic cures for this affliction. Scores of books and pamphlets encouraged young men to a higher standard of chastity. These pamphlets blended medical rhetoric with religious exhortation, and encouraged boys to store up these sexual energies for a more moral use.[11]

Leadbeater himself argued that the storing up of these sexual energies led only to the build-up of a natural, physical pressure, and that such pressure could lead boys to seek sexual relief either with prostitutes or with each other. By discharging that pressure at regular intervals through masturbation, Leadbeater claimed, the boys could avoid the more serious karmic and moral consequences of illicit sexual encounters.[12] Leadbeater's language was, therefore, not erotic but prophylactic: "If he [one of the boys] finds any accumulation," Leadbeater explained to the Advisory Board, "he should relieve."[13] As William Glenny Keagey argued in his defense of Leadbeater, the term *self-abuse* was misapplied here, since the word "as ordinarily understood connotes a very different meaning from anything that a pure and unprejudiced mind could possibly find in any advice given by Mr. L."[14]

The Leadbeater case took place just as advanced opinion was beginning to call for a more explicit emphasis on sex education and sexual hygiene as the best weapons in the campaign against vice. In 1911, for example, the influential National Council of Public Morals published a manifesto calling for education in physiological knowledge as a cure for national immorality and in the interests of "racial health."[15] It was as yet unclear, however, just how ignorance was to be overcome. In the late nineteenth century, the moral and the scientific/medical stance on sexuality had tended to be in opposition. The campaign against the Contagious Diseases Acts, passed in the late 1860s to regulate prostitution in Britain's port and garrison towns, had pitted a coalition of feminists, working-class radicals, and evangelical reformers against a medical establishment that promoted regulation. Although some doctors cooperated with the antiregulationists, the early nineteenth-century alliance between medicine and morality began to be eroded. Through the 1870s and 1880s libertarians, antivivisectionists, antivaccinationists, and feminist reformers had helped disseminate antimedical propaganda that emphasized medical violence and medical sadism. In the first decades of the twentieth century an uneasy rapprochement between moral reformers and the medical profession took place, as a result of shared concerns about national health and national efficiency.[16]

In 1906, however, it was not at all clear whether the medical/sanitary and the moral could peacefully coexist. Leadbeater also invoked moral arguments, especially in defending masturbation as an alternative to prostitution or homosexuality. Here he could exploit the moral capital built up in campaigns against the Contagious Diseases Acts a generation earlier. Those campaigns had produced a highly politicized social-purity movement that called into question the casual acceptance of prostitution as the outlet for male sexual desire.[17] In this case, Leadbeater's moral authority was pitted against the medical authority of Dr. Dyer, an American physician who had been called in to examine Douglas Pettit, one of the boys involved. Dyer confidently pronounced that self-abuse was the cause of the boy's epileptic fits. He condemned the practice, suggesting that it would have been far better to have taken the boy to a prostitute, and prescribed bromides.[18]

Those theosophists who had been active in campaigning against prostitution and other "social evils" often found it difficult to condemn Leadbeater unequivocally. He had, after all, couched his advice as an alternative to the sexual exploitation of women in prostitution. Thus, Besant was adamant that while she dissented from the Leadbeater advice, "I also dissent from the other popular view which winks at, or even encourages, prostitution. I hold that there is no cure for vice except self-control, and that therefore no advice should ever be given which tends to weaken the rigid rule that to yield to either solitary or associated vice is disgraceful and unmanly." At the same time, Besant rejected the conclusion that "all who make allowance for the strength of this passion and try to minimise its evils are dangerous companions for young boys." She castigated the state for its hypocrisy, noting that "nautch girls" in India and streetwalkers in London were not only tolerated but actively encouraged by those who would presume to judge Leadbeater for immorality.[19] Two women doctors who were prominent in the TS, Dr. Mary Rocke and the antivivisectionist Dr. Louise Appel, also endorsed Leadbeater on this basis.[20]

But Leadbeater's opponents refused to accept that masturbation could be a lesser evil, or that physiological and sanitary questions had any place in the debate. Herbert Burrows, an old socialist ally of Besant's who had joined the TS shortly before she did, was one of those who would admit no role for masturbation in dealing with sex problems. Even if the advice was right, "better that the world should blunder along in its old halting way than that the teaching of the Divine Wisdom should be befouled by the doctrine that the way to escape from the lusts of the flesh is by the path of self-abuse." He emphasized that "once admit that self-abuse is to be the cure for any sexual abnormality . . . and a vista is opened which is nothing less than sexual demoralisation of both sexes."[21] Leadbeater's opponents, then, were forced to concede the high scientific ground and to admit that "the charge was not made on sanitary, but on moral grounds."[22]

Once the question of morality became central, the question of Leadbeater's status as a spiritual leader became a major issue in the debate. Leadbeater's advice, though not explicitly theosophical, was accepted by many Fellows of the Theosophical Society as occult and authoritative. Two of the boys had testified that Leadbeater had led them to believe that the advice was somehow theosophical, and that it was part of their occult training. Leadbeater himself denied, publicly at least, that his advice regarding masturbation was either theosophical or occult. Rather, as Besant put it, "he brought the idea over with him from the celibate priesthood of the Anglican High Church and the Roman Catholics . . . and it has nothing to do with Theosophy or the Theosophical Society."[23]

But Leadbeater's advice could be construed as theosophical in at least two ways. He had defended his actions with the claim that he offered the counsel because his clairvoyant abilities had enabled him to see the problems the boys were facing: as an occultist, he was able to see the "thought-forms" generated by lust and sexual desire, which hovered around boys struggling through puberty. When asked at the Advisory Board whether he had always spoken to the boys *after* they asked him for advice, Leadbeater replied, "I advised it at times as a prophylactic." To Miss Ward's question, "I suppose from what you saw on the other planes?" Leadbeater responded rather ambiguously, "From what I saw would arise."[24]

Leadbeater also emphasized the complex and far-reaching karmic consequences of prostitution and homosexual activities; "associated vice" could produce actions and reactions that could take many lifetimes to work out. The "solitary vice" of masturbation, he argued, was in an entirely different category. It was a physiological preventative, not a sexual act. The occultist needed to maintain absolute sexual purity, but the occasional relief of "accumulated pressure" was not a lapse from purity. "It is of course obvious that the lapse mentioned meant connection with a woman or criminal relations with a man," Leadbeater wrote, "and did not at all include such relief of pressure as suggested in the body of my letter."[25]

Some of Leadbeater's supporters argued that, as an occultist, he was above or beyond ordinary morality. George Arundale, for example, defended him on the grounds that "the extraordinary purity of his own life enables him to handle, as no other teacher, as no other individual, would dare to handle, problems of vital moment to the growing youth."[26] They continually invoked his authority as an eminent occultist in defending his actions. For example, William Glenny Keagey's "General Memorandum" on the subject pronounced Leadbeater's "qualifications for expressing an authoritative opinion on the subject to be exceptional." Keagey referred his readers to Leadbeater and Besant's work *Thought-Forms* and added that laymen had no right to "try" and "sentence" an occultist for "things admittedly claimed to have to do with Occult training."[27] Besant herself argued that occult morality "cares for realities not conventions" and concluded, "I speak on this as an Occultist. 'He that is able to receive it [this teaching], let him receive it.'"[28]

The towering edifice that opponents called neo-theosophy had been founded in large part on Leadbeater's authority as an occultist. His teachings on everything from "occult chemistry" to reincarnation and past-life experiences were enormously popular. The discovery of Krishnamurti, the founding of the Order of the Star in the East, the formation of the Liberal Catholic Church, and the theosophical commitment to Co-Masonry: all were linked in some way to Leadbeater's influence. The *International Theosophical Year Book*, published a few years after his death, remembered him as the "Great Seer whose books have robbed death of its terrors; Master-Scientist of Occultism, who unveiled to the world the hidden side of life; Lover of Humanity and Spiritual Teacher of tens of thousands."[29] Even in 1906, when many of these developments still lay in the future, Leadbeater was already one of the most popular speakers and writers in the TS. His centrality to the TS (Adyar) made it virtually impossible to attack him without attacking the society itself.

Leadbeater's opponents protested his exalted position, arguing that "the reason why such a practice has for a moment met with defenders in our body, is because psychism is with some enthroned above morals," and that those who believed Leadbeater to be a high Adept believed him to be a "'martyr' occultist persecuted for his knowledge!" Besant's stance on the subject "open[ed] the way for any psychic in the Society to justify the teaching of it [masturbation] on his bare assertion that he has seen this or that 'symptom' in a child's aura."[30] The manifesto of the Independent Theosophical League, which broke away from the TS to protest Leadbeater's readmission, emphasized the same point: "any teachings which ignore or violate the moral code accepted in common by all civilised nations on the plea of higher or occult knowledge, is contrary to the laws of true spiritual life."[31]

To many people, this was Leadbeater's greatest fault—that he had abused his spiritual authority to gratify his own prurient desires. But for those who accepted the validity of his claims as an occultist, there could be no question of immorality. Leadbeater himself invoked that authority as a way of protecting himself from investigation: "I consider the inquisition of Mead & others into my private affairs as a gross impertinence," he wrote, and claimed that he had resigned from the TS "precisely in order to leave [his opponents] no excuse for exercising their foul mouths and their prurient minds upon a matter which they could not be expected to understand."[32] His opponents were unable to understand because they lacked occult knowledge; the privacy Leadbeater invoked was not merely personal privacy, but the occult emphasis on secrecy that had been institutionalized in the Esoteric Section of the TS.

Leadbeater's supporters, well organized within the ES, succeeded in burying the documents in the case, and refused to publicize any of the attacks on Leadbeater. Attempts to publish evidence in the case also ran afoul of the obscenity laws, and many accounts rendered words like self-abuse or sodomy as a series of asterisks. A. P. Sinnett, who later admitted that he found the discussions of the Advisory Board "distinctly nauseous," argued at the Advisory Board meeting itself that "I think the promulgation of any indecent phrases is most objectionable. I would no[t] use any term like self-abuse or its equivalent."[33]

Most members of the TS were denied access not only to the evidence in the case but also to knowledge of the issues involved. And the issues themselves were never clearly defined, even for the protagonists. Debates over Leadbeater's spiritual authority and over the extent of his knowledge as an occultist in sexual matters were complicated by these confusions. Debate took place in an atmosphere of moral panic, in which far more serious, unspoken accusations against Leadbeater informed the deliberations. The unwillingness or inability to name precisely the accusations against Leadbeater allowed charges to multiply;

the accusations leveled against him were thus, paradoxically, both amorphous and specific. They encompassed a wide range of attitudes, behaviors, and actions that were united, in the final analysis, only by their relationship to what remained an absent referent: sodomy.

There was, at least in the first instance, no suggestion that Leadbeater's actions fell under the jurisdiction of the criminal law. The original charges referred only to "morally criminal" acts on Leadbeater's part—not legally criminal. In the course of the investigation, however, Leadbeater's critics argued that he had not confined himself to giving advice, but had actually committed sexual assault. This issue was first raised at the Advisory Board itself, where, through a particularly tortured and ambiguous series of questions, the board attempted to determine whether "Mr. Leadbeater simply gave advice or something different." The questions focused on a crucial piece of George Nevers's statement, that he had broken off relations with another young man (referred to as Z). Mead asked Leadbeater to explain a key passage in Nevers's statement. The passage read, "He [Z] did not try to *do* this same thing, but he talked about these matters in a way I did not like and his friendship became distasteful to me." Mead pointed out that Z "did not *do* this same thing." But, he accused Leadbeater, "in your case he states that it was *done*." The conversation that followed, among Mead, Leadbeater, and W. H. Thomas, a member from the north of England who was serving on the national Executive Committee, revealed a profound reluctance to confront the accusations directly:

> *Thomas:* Mr. Mead's question is a most important one. It involves whether Mr. Leadbeater simply gave advice or something different.
> *Leadbeater:* It was not in any way something different in the sense of Mr. Mead.
> *Thomas:* I don't mean that.
> *Leadbeater:* I don't quite know what you mean.
> *Mead:* It is quite clear. When boys practice self-abuse they do it on themselves. This sentence suggests something done by you. . . . I ask for an explanation of this, or if you simply deny.
> *Leadbeater:* I deny anything in the way that is apparently suggested, but certainly not that that suggestion was made. I am not denying that in the least.

Thomas remained unsatisfied and repeated that he "would like to know whether it was simply in the nature of advice or whether there was any action." Here Leadbeater admitted the possibility of "a certain amount of indicative action," but refused to be more explicit until Thomas asked, "I would like to know whether in any case—I am not suggesting sodomy—there was definite action." Leadbeater replied, "You mean touch? That might have taken place."[34] His reply became the subject of much debate. Burrows claimed at the 1908 convention that Leadbeater "admitted something else which both here and in America would bring him within the pale of the criminal law," and argued that "that of course is nothing less than indecent assault."[35]

Leadbeater's counter-claim, that his touch "was as clean as that of a doctor or a mother,"[36] raised the question of motive. At the Advisory Board Colonel Olcott initially denied that Leadbeater's motives were at issue. "There is no feeling on the part of those present," he stated, "that you did not have the feeling in your mind when you gave the advice. I think that everybody here knows you [and] will think your motive was the one you gave."[37] Thomas, however, argued that "the whole of the evidence shows that if it was not a case of direct vice it was a case of gratifying his own prurient ideas."[38] The case therefore shifted from a consideration of "direct vice" to an exploration of the relationship between actions and the subjective states behind those actions. Leadbeater's state of mind—and, by extension, his whole personality—was subjected to searching inquiry. Even when unspoken, the accusation of sodomy was the referent against which Leadbeater's actions were judged.

The pitfalls of a too frank discussion of the issues at stake were starkly revealed in the fate of Curuppumullage (Raja) Jinarajadasa. Jinarajadasa was expelled from the TS in 1906 for circulating a letter among prominent men in the American Section in defense of Leadbeater. Olcott, as president-founder, issued an Executive Notice canceling Jinarajadasa's membership.[39] Jinarajadasa, who was soon readmitted and eventually became president of the TS in 1945, was one of the group known as Leadbeater's boys. In 1888, at the age of thirteen, he had been "discovered" by Leadbeater to be the reincarnation of Leadbeater's younger brother Gerald, and in 1889 he had been brought from Sri Lanka to London. Jinarajadasa entered theosophical circles under somewhat inauspicious circumstances: secretly, and against the wishes of the boy's family, Leadbeater arranged to have him smuggled aboard a schooner anchored in Colombo harbor. His parents were eventually convinced to allow Raja to travel to England with their blessing, and he went on to take a degree in Sanskrit and philology from St. John's College, Cambridge, in 1900.[40]

Because it was circulated in the first instance only among prominent *men* within the TS, Jinarajadasa's letter could afford to be explicit. Jinarajadasa wrote to dispute the assumption, which he believed to be current in theosophical circles, that Leadbeater "had been charged and

proven guilty of the crime that ostracises a man, namely sodomy."
When the letter was reprinted for wider circulation by Veritas during
the 1913 wardship trial, "sodomy" became ". . . . ."—a typographical
convention that, ironically, restored precisely the ambiguity that Jinarajadasa had attempted to dispel. Jinarajadasa's concern was that wild
speculation was filling the gaps left in public discussion of the case.
"When it is hinted that there are charges of a frightful nature against a
man, we jump at one conclusion and think of this charge. I gather that
some think that Mr. Leadbeter [sic] is 'a sexual pervert.' Witness for
instance, his liking every boy. . . . his irritability. . . . [his] antipathy for
womankind."[41]

But to raise the issue of sodomy directly, even if the intent was to
deny that it had taken place, was to reaffirm its explosive centrality in
the debate. Organized around the referent of sodomy, a range of otherwise unremarkable attributes and actions took on new meaning. By the
late nineteenth century, medical and legal opinion had begun to articulate an etiology for the "disease" of homosexuality, and had associated
the condition with a set of symptoms. Krafft-Ebing, for example, had
identified four broad types of men who were involved in same-sex sexual relationships, of which the most relevant in this context is the man
who suffered from "effemination." The "effeminate" man, Krafft-Ebing
argued, "eschews smoking, drinking, and manly sports, and on the contrary, finds pleasure in adornment of persons, art, *belles-lettres*, etc."[42]
Havelock Ellis preserved some of Krafft-Ebing's complicated typolo-
gies, but also offered a newly bifurcated vision of sexual and gender
identity: hetero- versus (true) homo-sexuality, "normal" versus "in-
verted" manifestations of "the sexual instinct."[43] What Krafft-Ebing
had described as "effemination" was presented as characteristic of the
vast majority of homosexual men. Although Ellis was equivocal on this
point, he did suggest that "there is a distinctly general, though not universal, tendency for sexual inverts to approach the feminine type, either
in psychic disposition or physical constitution, or both."[44]

Jinarajadasa's circular clearly acknowledged the recognized markers
of an effeminate subjectivity as Krafft-Ebing and Ellis had defined it:
he admitted Leadbeater's "liking every boy," his "antipathy for womankind," and his highly sensitive nature. Jinarajadasa acknowledged that
these facts, taken together, might lead people to believe that Leadbeater
was indeed a "sexual pervert." But he also insisted that each of them,
taken individually, could be explained in other ways. Elsewhere, Jinarajadasa reaffirmed the centrality of Leadbeater's personality, as opposed
to his beliefs or actions, to the debate: "the whole personality of X
[Leadbeater] is viewed from the hostile standpoint of a prosecution;

sinister motives are attributed to him, his actions are twisted into a wrong perspective, his words are specially underlined and emphasized here and there to bear out the gloomy aspect that the prosecution desires to show."[45]

As another of "Leadbeater's boys" put it, "I can quite understand how numbers of trifling things can be regarded as evidence of conduct of this sort where people are suspicious of it."[46] Among those "trifling things" were many of the practices Leadbeater had explicitly associated with the development of occult power, such as abstention from tobacco, alcohol, and meat-eating. Writing from Benares in 1906, Besant mentioned to Leadbeater that Bertram Keightley's animus against him was motivated in part by Keightley's view that Leadbeater was "narrow and bigoted on vegetarianism and smoking etc." (Keightley also criticized Leadbeater for being "rude to women and so on.")[47] Just as Leadbeater's "antipathy for womankind" could be read as a marker of sexual perversity, so too his spiritual teachings on occultism and the need for purity of life could resonate with Krafft-Ebing's concept of effemination.

The esoteric tradition as it had been developed within the TS also provided more specific links between sexual subjectivity and spiritual powers. Leadbeater himself had publicly and repeatedly linked the control of sexual desire to occult progress. As he put it in 1899, chastity or celibacy was "desirable for occult progress," and the adoption of a celibate lifestyle would be "a matter of course for anyone who was at all in earnest." Using what was perhaps, in light of later developments, an unfortunate choice of words, he added that "every student who really means business takes himself in hand with regard to all these minor and outer matters . . . before he even thinks of presenting himself as an aspirant for anything that can really be dignified by the name of occult progress at all."[48]

Sexual desire was believed to disturb and agitate the astral body, and therefore it needed to be controlled and disciplined before the aspiring occultist began to develop the astral powers.[49] Even more important, theosophists had long taught that the "sexual fluids" themselves had important occult properties and were not to be squandered. Through "divine alchemy," it was argued, "the crude vitality which wells up from our animal natures is converted into spiritual forces of transcendent power and potency."[50] Even more explicit was the teaching of *Hints on Esoteric Theosophy*, published in 1882: "the very nerve substance, destroyed in sexual intercourse, forms part of the matrix in which the powers you seek for [i.e., psychic powers] have to be developed."[51] "The same energy," wrote Bhagavan Das only a few years after the first Leadbeater crisis, was available for either sexual or spiritual use, "hence the indispensable need of celibacy, bramacharya, for occult development, that is, development of super-physical senses and powers."[52]

Sex and spirituality were closely connected because both had to do with the creative forces. G. R. S. Mead made this point at the 1908 convention, with direct reference to Leadbeater: "At all times of great spiritual revival, the foul reflection, the distortion, the perversion of the most Sacred Mysteries accompanies it; at all such times the true Mysteries have been surrounded and be-smirched with the foulest of sex crimes." Sex and spirituality were linked, Mead argued, because "the high Mysteries have to do chiefly with the Mystery of Regeneration."[53] Spiritual progress involved a literal sublimation of sexual energy, the transmutation of the base metal of sexual desire into purer and higher forms of creativity. The same knowledge, in the wrong hands, could also lead—as Mead suggested it had done in this case—to the perversion of spirituality.

In the event, however, the 1908 convention split on the question of Leadbeater's readmission (543 voted for his return, 537 against it, with 650 abstentions), and when the British Section welcomed Leadbeater back to the fold, half the Executive Committee resigned in protest, and almost 600 members left the society.[54] Horatio Bottomley, the editor of *John Bull* magazine, claimed that the Leadbeater crisis had driven "numerous . . . well-known public men"—the society's "best men"—out of the TS. He also reiterated the links between sexual and spiritual perversity: "the Society itself remains and . . . is gathering into its ranks an army of morbid moral degenerates, whose teachings are calculated to undermine the character and sap the manhood of our race." Unless Besant "forthwith disowns the vile Leadbeater we must place her in the same category—that of a spurious religious teacher, preying upon the intellectual slavery of unreasoning and hypnotised disciples."[55]

One significant result of the Leadbeater crisis was to shut down certain kinds of discussion of sexuality, and especially child sexuality, within the Theosophical Society. Before the Leadbeater crisis, the TS had occupied a relatively progressive position on the subject of children and sex education. Evelyn J. Lauder, a theosophist of long standing and a pioneer Co-Mason, had made a strong case for sex education at a TS congress in London only a year before the Leadbeater scandal erupted. She argued that "every parent is morally bound to instruct and guide both boys and girls most clearly and delicately as to the powers of each sex, beginning from a far earlier age than is usually done."[56] The "troubles" the TS passed through as a result of Leadbeater's "advice" did not entirely erode this commitment, but the crisis into which it was plunged made the frank discussion of sex more difficult. As Besant put it, "he will be a bold man who ventures to give such instruction, in the face of the hideous misconstruction with which Mr. Leadbeater has been met. The giving by an elder of a scientific and commonsense explanation would be incredible to a society which can only regard sex through an atmosphere of prudery or vice. In all speech thereon a vicious purpose would be taken for granted."[57] And as Emily Lutyens added later, in the midst of yet another Leadbeater crisis, "Unfortunately the Society has closed the mouth of the one man capable of helping us to unravel this problem [of sex] which may be said to lie at the root of all human relationships—I mean of course Bishop Leadbeater—and for that criminal folly both the T. S. and the world in general will have to pay."[58] In 1923 Christmas Humphreys wrote to *The Theosophist* on behalf of young people to complain that the references in theosophical writings to "transmutation, not suppression" of the sexual desires were vague and unhelpful, and to call for clearer and more practical teaching on the subject. The editorial response was flatly to reiterate that "there is no special teaching in the Society on sex, any more than any other physiological subject."[59]

The image of Leadbeater as a corrupter of youth was reinforced in the 1913 wardship trial in Madras. There, the questions of caste, cultural conflict, and colonial exploitation added new dimensions to the debate. In his suit, which was heard before Mr. Justice Bakewell in the High Court of Madras, Narayaniah claimed that when he had granted guardianship of his sons to Besant, he had transferred that guardianship to her alone. He objected, among other things, to the association with Leadbeater, whom he argued was a morally corrupting influence.[60] Leadbeater's corruption of the boys was simultaneously represented as both spiritual and sexual.

Many of the debates at the trial simply rehearsed the issues raised in 1906. But there were also new and more disturbing accusations. In his original statement, submitted to the district judge of Chingleput, Narayaniah had accused Leadbeater of engaging in a sexual relationship with Krishnamurti. There was, if anything, even more confusion over the exact nature of the charges in this case than there had been in 1906. As Veritas recorded the incident, an Indian servant claimed to have seen Leadbeater commit "***" and it was said that "Lakshman actually said that very word," although Lakshman was later heard to say only that he saw Leadbeater "do something very nasty."[61] Justice Bakewell, however, suggested that what Lakshman had seen was simply a minor infraction of caste rules—Leadbeater had introduced Krishnamurti and his brother Nityananda to the practice of bathing, European-style, without clothes—and not a sexual act. At the same time, however, he concluded that Leadbeater, though innocent of this charge, held opinions that were "immoral" and "such as to unfit him to be the tutor of boys."[62]

Bakewell ruled against Besant, Besant appealed the ruling, and the Appeals Court upheld it. The Chief Justice's decision was also an indictment of Besant's neo-theosophy. "It is scarcely extraordinary," he concluded, "that a man [Krishnamurti's father] whose mind [has] possibly become a little morbid by reason of the atmosphere of mystery and mysticism and alleged extraordinary happenings in which he lived, should have dwelt on something which he saw [as] objectionable and indecent though not criminal, until he became obsessed with the idea that Mr. Leadbeater's conduct in connection with these boys, had been such as to warrant the charge of an unnatural offence."[63] The "atmosphere of mystery and mysticism" that pervaded the Theosophical Society at Adyar was, it seemed, somehow linked to the development of sexual morbidity. The same double indictment of Leadbeater and theosophy was levied by Dr. T. M. Nair in *The Antiseptic*. His article "Psychopathia Sexualis in a Mahatma" concluded that "we have nothing but pity for these sexual degenerates—the Mahatma K. H. and Mr. Leadbeater and the rest."[64] Not only Leadbeater, but also his Masters stood accused.

Krishnamurti too fell under suspicion, although there was no evidence to support the accusation. The notorious occultist Aleister Crowley, who was no friend to theosophists, confessed (with good reason) that he himself was "no prude," but that he drew the line "when a senile sex maniac like Leadbeater proclaims his catamites as Coming Christs."[65] Over fifteen years later the Dutch poet Ernest Michel revived the charge in even more violent terms:

> thou, reincarnators of Christ, polluters of Christ, thou, uranic rats; thou, infertile adulterers; thou, poofy pooches; thou, lesbian curs; . . . Christ . . . thou hast degraded now into a little Indian homosexual, into a nancy boy . . . thou who hast castrated Christ, polluted and soiled him into the filthy catamite . . . these violators of children's innocence . . . these dirty animals, should not they in this "liberal" country be beaten to death with sewer pipes?[66]

What many in the TS viewed as Krishnamurti's gentleness and delicacy was here recast in the most virulent terms. Not only Leadbeater but all his works, including the Coming Christ, were combined in a sexual/spiritual perversity.

The links that were made between sexual and spiritual perversity were revived again in the 1920s with much greater force, but by that time the tone of the discussion had changed. A new vocabulary of sexual pathology had become available, and Leadbeater's critics seized on the opportunity to use it, reviving the old charges and detailing new ones. In the debates of 1906 and 1908 it is possible to trace the contours of the image of the sexual pervert emerging around the axis of sodomy (or its elliptical equivalents), but the language of sexual pathology in this period remained relatively vague and unspecialized. At the 1906 meeting of the Advisory Board, Keightley had suggested a diagnosis of "sexual mania," noting that "there are cases closely analogous," but without going into further detail.[67] At the 1908 convention Burrows claimed that Leadbeater was suffering from "local insanity," the "perversion of the sex-instinct too forcibly restrained."[68] The reference here was to a generalized and unspecified (though clearly sexual) lunacy. In the 1920s, much more would be said, and much more explicitly. The links between a perverse sexuality and a perverse spirituality had also become much clearer.

In 1921 T. H. Martyn, a leading member of the TS in Sydney, Australia (where Leadbeater was living at the time), published an open letter to Besant in which he accused Leadbeater of engaging in mutual masturbation with boys and also implicated some Liberal Catholic priests in the practice of sodomy.[69] Martyn, a Sydney stockbroker whose death in 1924 robbed the anti-Leadbeater forces of an implacable supporter, advocated what Besant's biographer Arthur Nethercot described as a "virile brand of Theosophy," a version that apparently could not include Leadbeater.[70] This time the evidence against Leadbeater seemed unequivocal. Martyn based many of his arguments on a report made by the police in Sydney, which claimed that one of the boys had testified that "Leadbeater encouraged him first to bathe, and then to lie down on his (Leadbeater's) bed [in] the afternoon. . . . Leadbeater lay on the bed with him, and without any words caught hold of the boy's person with his right hand and proceeded to masturbate him."[71] Martyn concluded that he found "staring me in the face the conclusion that Leadbeater is a sex pervert, his mania taking a particular form which I have—though only lately—discovered, is a form well known and quite common in the annals of sex-criminology." In this case, Leadbeater himself was not directly accused of sodomy, but he was closely associated with others who were. James Ingall Wedgwood, who had consecrated Leadbeater as an LCC bishop, was the most prominent. Martyn's open letter made the accusations seem common currency: "Of course while in London I heard about charges of sodomy with boys being made against Wedgwood." He claimed that he had been told that the police were taking action against Wedgwood and three other Liberal Catholic priests.[72] Everything seemed to be confirmed when the

LCC priest Reginald Farrer, a former pupil of Leadbeater's, published a "Confession" that read in part: "The imputation against myself, as well as against Wedgwood, King and Clark, in Mr. Martyn's letter is but too true. . . . I was not strong enough to control my own lower nature, and gave way to a practice that I am now heartily ashamed of." Besant later dismissed this evidence on the grounds that Farrer had recanted, and that his confession was a symptom of hysteria, but it was clear that many had received the impression that the TS was rife with "unnatural vice."[73]

Critics of Wedgwood and Leadbeater began a campaign to provide local police authorities with information on the two men, in America, New Zealand, England, and Holland, as well as in Australia. H. N. Stokes, the editor of the O. E. *Library Critic* (founded in Washington, D.C., as the organ of the theosophical Towards Democracy League), began publishing all the "Private and Confidential" documents in the case, making it virtually impossible for the society's leadership to proceed with business as usual.[74] In England the organizers of the 1924 special convention added Leadbeater to the list of things they wanted to purge from the TS.

The majority of theosophists either attempted to ignore the ruckus or rushed to deny the charges. Ernest Griffiths wrote a long critique of the Martyn letter; like Martyn, he did not mince words. He condemned Martyn's wife as "suffering from a fairly common type of feminine hysteria" and argued that Martyn's own judgment was warped. Griffiths's letter is remarkable for its expression of confident expertise on the subject of sexual deviance. He pointed out that pederasts are "naturally not prone" to making confessions and argued that if the accusations against Leadbeater were true, "then the close intimacy of 'Raja's' early days with Mr Leadbeater would necessarily have involved him in the crimes alleged." "Now," he went on, "'Raja' is a happily-married man, and it is inconceivable that a passive pederast who has subsequently married and lived a normal sex life should still view his early seducer with affection and respect." The most convincing argument, for Griffiths, was a statistical one. Given that the TS held no special brief for "sex-perverts," it was beyond the bounds of probability that the society should be overrun with them: "Here we have four, with Mr Leadbeater, five; besides the hosts of their victims. Really Mr Martyn, it will not pass.—there are too many of them. Since there is nothing in the teachings of either the T. S. or the L. C. C. which is subversive of morals or attractive to the sex-pervert, it is inconceivable that here we should find such a school of immoral practice."[75]

The relationship between theosophy and sexuality, particularly homosexuality, was quite contradictory. The links between sexual and spiritual perversity had been made on numerous occasions, but Leadbeater's supporters had always rejected these interpretations. Yet there were elements in theosophy that could be understood as an affirmation of homosexual desire and identity. Members of the TS, led, perhaps unsurprisingly, by the occult investigations of Leadbeater, had for some time been developing an elaborate understanding of sexuality and sexual identity, especially in discussions of reincarnation and past lives.

Writing in the "Enquirer" column of *The Vāhan* in 1898, Leadbeater explained, "We were told long ago that as a general rule an ego took not less than three, and not more than seven successive incarnations in one sex before changing to the other." He noted that recent occult investigation had confirmed this rule, although a more advanced Ego was likely to prove an exception to it and to be "born into the sex and race which were best suited to give him an opportunity of strengthening the weak points in his character."[76] In the same year Leadbeater and Besant collaborated on an experiment in the clairvoyant reconstruction of past lives. Their subject was Miss Annie J. Willson, the librarian at the London headquarters, who traveled with Besant as her secretary and housekeeper for many years. The result of their investigations was *The Lives of Arcor,* and Arcor's story was eventually incorporated into a later work, *The Lives of Alcyone.* As a result, this British spinster, who rates only brief mention in most histories of the TS, was literally immortalized: her doings could be traced from her first appearance as the son of Herakles (Besant) in the Gobi Sea, c. 70,000 B.C.E., to the elevated status of Besant's wife in China 60,000 years later. *The Lives of Alcyone,* serialized in *The Theosophist* in 1910–11, made similar claims about Krishnamurti/Alcyone and identified over two hundred fifty other members of the TS who had been born and reborn as Krishnamurti's associates.[77] These were the kinds of claims that led critics of Leadbeater and the TS (Adyar) to condemn neo-theosophy as a perversion of Blavatsky's teachings. Joseph Fussell, a prominent follower of Katherine Tingley's brand of theosophy, criticized *The Lives of Alcyone* for its "frequent disgusting allusion to changing sexes" and was outraged by the suggestion that Jesus Christ had been the wife of Julius Caesar in a previous incarnation.[78]

In 1910 Charles Lazenby made an explicit effort to link these discussions with the most recent sexological theories. Lazenby, who was graduated from the University of Toronto with a degree in psychology and philosophy in 1907, went on to study Jungian psychoanalysis in Zurich. He was clearly familiar with Leadbeater's writings on reincarnation and the most recent sexological studies; he was also a personal friend of Havelock Ellis and of the sexual reformer Edward Carpenter.[79] Writing in the independent theosophical magazine *The Path,* published by the recently established Blavatsky Institute, Lazenby began by reviewing theosophical knowledge on the subject of sex and reincarnation: "It seems reasonable that at every seventh incarnation we change from one sex over into the other. We have six lives [which are] masculine and on the seventh our consciousness as individuals in the great world-drama takes on the colouring of the feminine, and in the following six lives we come forth feminine, to again in the seventh take over the colouring of the masculine." Lazenby noted, however, that the purely masculine or feminine is found only at the midpoint of each cycle. At this point in the series of male incarnations, "in his imagination he pictures himself wholly as a man, he cannot imagine being a woman." Thoroughly masculine, "all his desires and sexual emotions centre round the female, and he has a male physical body." Yet at precisely this apotheosis of manhood he "begins to take into his mental body as he grows older some slight colouring of the feminine nature." In Lazenby's view, neither sexual nor gender identity was necessarily derived from physical sex in any straightforward way. "Thirty-five years ago," he wrote, "when the Theosophical Society was founded, there was in the popular mind no other conception than of two sexes, the male and the female, quite distinct and clearly defined. In a materialistic age, when the emphasis is put entirely upon the physical form, this must necessarily be so, but for the occultist the problem is much deeper and more difficult." Scientific studies of sexuality had now confirmed the occultists' position, revealing "the existence in civilization of an intermediate sex which has to be considered and may not be ignored." Reincarnation explained this phenomenon: when the Ego made the transition from one sex to the other, the fit between physical sex and sexual identity became uneven. So on the cusp of the change of sex one finds the male and female "Uranian," people whose physical body belongs to one sex but whose thoughts and desires belong to the other, and whose life "may become slightly discordant."[80]

Theosophists spoke of the Uranian in a way that blurred and combined two quite different uses of the term, which was drawn in the first instance from Plato's *Symposium,* and often carried the connotation of a purely spiritual, or heavenly, love. The German writer Karl Heinrich Ulrichs had popularized the term in the 1860s to refer to those whose lives were characterized by a "congenital reversal of sexual feeling." While Ulrichs had used the term (which was often Germanized as *Urning*) to refer to a more explicitly sexual love, in the 1880s and 1890s it was most commonly associated with the Uranian poets who, according to Linda Dowling, "sang the praises of a mode of spiritual and emotional attachment that was, at some ultimate level, innocent or asexual."[81] In 1908 Edward Carpenter's *Intermediate Sex* had helped revive and popularize Ulrichs's usage.[82]

A second, related use of the term was drawn, at least in esoteric circles, from astrological texts. Writing in the radical feminist paper *The Freewoman* in 1912, for example, Dr. Charles J. Whitby deprecated the "purely sexual application of the word." Whitby referred readers of *The Freewoman* to "a recent article in [Alfred Orage's socialist paper] the *New Age* [which] dealt with persons under the influence of Uranus, the planet which awakens the spirit from lethargy and brings it into strange conditions and hazardous enterprises."[83] In theosophical writings, the two senses of the word seem to have been blurred, so that the Uranian simultaneously represented a spiritualized and celibate (homo)sexuality and a harbinger of the New Age.

So, for example, Mabel Charles, an outspoken opponent of Besant and neo-theosophy, noted that the best theosophists combined the strengths of both manliness and womanliness. She speculated that their natal charts might reveal "Uranus strongly marked," for Uranians, whom she associated with the unwedded, the unattached, the ascetics, "had a tendency to a sort of mental double-sexedness."[84] In 1920 B. A. Ross provided an astrological reading of the Theosophical Society and its founders, which linked the Uranian (in this double sense) to the New Age. The close of the nineteenth century, Ross argued, was the dawn of a new cycle, the Aquarian Age. And the New Age was ruled over by the sign of Uranus. In Ross's account, Blavatsky and Olcott became the true Uranians: "Both of them had Uranus at birth in its own Sign, Aquarius—a very strange coincidence—and so it might be taken that they were the first Uranians, a man and a woman living together unconventionally, ignoring the chatter of the foolish, and selflessly acting up to a standard a century or more ahead of their time."[85] The Uranian, as the term was used among theosophists, was a new human type, a perfect blend of masculine and feminine qualities.

The Uranian was both double-sexed and spiritually advanced. At the same time as the theosophists were elaborating these theories, prominent figures outside the TS were making almost the same arguments about homosexuality. Both Havelock Ellis and Edward Carpenter, for example, had argued that there existed a positive, organic relationship between spiritual development and the "homosexual temperament." According to Ellis's sexological study of homosexuality, *Sexual Inversion,* the most recent anthropological studies confirmed the "aptitude of the invert for primitive religion, for sorcery and divination."[86] Carpenter was even more explicit, arguing that the "blending of the masculine and feminine temperaments" that produced the invert would also "in some of these cases produce persons whose perceptions would be so subtle and complex and rapid as to come under the head of genius, persons of intuitive mind who would perceive things without knowing how, and follow far concatenations of causes and events without concerning themselves about the *why*—diviners and prophets in a very real sense."[87]

In theosophical writing the explicitly sexual elements in these theories were occluded. Even so, many theosophists argued that the emergence of the "intermediate sex" was a sign of the times, a distorted reflection on the physical plane of the enormous spiritual changes that were taking place. As G. E. Sutcliffe put it in his "Scientific Notes" on *The Secret Doctrine,* "Anyone who has carefully studied *The Secret Doctrine,* where the coming changes in the character of the race are clearly outlined, can scarcely be surprised that questions relating to the sex instinct, both normal and abnormal, should periodically be forced to the front, since many are at present in a state of transition with regard to this fundamental aspect of our nature."[88] Fritz Kunz, a former pupil of Leadbeater's, was even more forthright, linking the emergence of an "intermediate sex" with the emergence of the sixth subrace, according to Blavatsky the next step forward in human evolution:

> All sorts of adjustments will come in the New Age. We are going to have this queer, intermediate sex that is now appearing very rapidly. . . . Tramping down out of the invisible worlds is marching a host of new souls that will be born in the bodies of the new race, brave and noble men and women, better than ourselves. They will make us look antique, antiquated, obsolete, these young people with the sun of the dawn in their eyes and the breath of spring in their hair; boys and girls that don't know they are boys and girls, that only know they are souls.[89]

Spiritually as well as physically, the children of the New Age would conform less and less to established notions of the appropriately masculine and feminine. D. N. Dunlop predicted that "the sympathetic cords are evolving in complexity to form a second spinal cord and at the end of 'the next round,' humanity will once more become hermaphrodite, and then there will be two spinal cords in the human body to merge later into one." In the distant future, human beings would no longer have sexual organs.[90] Or, as Lazenby put it, "the reproduction of the species will be by the spiritual will of the divine Hermaphrodite impregnating his own womb, and the children will be born as instruments for loving human service."[91]

Taken together, these claims constituted an alternative or oppositional discourse in which homosexuality was neither pathologized nor necessarily represented as deviant. But theosophists as a group offered, on the whole, a relatively conservative analysis of sex and sexuality. Dunlop may have looked forward to the appearance of the Divine Hermaphrodite in the very long term, but he nonetheless resigned from the society in 1922.[92] Lazenby also rejected Leadbeater's authority, arguing that "hardly a ray of truth pierces the abyssmal slime of psychic illusion in which he dwells."[93] Both Dunlop and Lazenby linked what they saw as Leadbeater's perverse influence to the degradation of Blavatsky's spiritual vision.

Many of Leadbeater's critics assumed that his occult knowledge was based on immoral methods of occult development. The theosophist Alfred Wilkinson, who called for a public inquiry into the activities of Leadbeater and the LCC in the 1920s, argued that it was impossible to combine the life of an occult initiate with the practice of sodomy, which he associated with the "Dark Path" of sexual magic.[94] The Quaker theosophist William Loftus Hare, a driving force behind the 1924 special convention, had heard rumors that there were those who "lauded the bestial indulgences of C. W. L., J. I. W. and others as justifiable on the grounds that 'initiates' had the right to use the 'left-hand path' if they wished"; Hare rejected the possibility.[95] That there was widely believed to be a Dark Path of sexual magic and that some occultists pursued it is indisputable. Alex Owen's recent study of Aleister Crowley provides a clear case of the relationship between magical work and "an exoticized and outlawed sexuality." In the 1920s scandalous tales of Crowley's exploits had begun to appear in the popular press, and Crowley was well on his way to being dubbed "the wickedest man in the world."[96] Gregory Tillett also notes the role that ritual (homo)sexual encounters play in certain occult and magical traditions.[97]

Dion Fortune was one of those who warned of the dangers of such sexual magic, and she accused Leadbeater and his associates of practicing it. Before the war Fortune, whose given name was Violet Firth, had practiced as a lay psychologist and apparently lectured on Freudian psychoanalysis at a London clinic. At one time a member of both the Theosophical Society and the Order of the Golden Dawn, she founded a rival magical order, the Fraternity of the Inner Light, in 1922.[98] Fortune explained the ways in which the sex force—what in Tantric philosophy, she explained, was known as the *kundalini,* or "serpent-fire"— could be deployed to magical ends. Leadbeater, she suggested, was one of those who knew the methods of "stimulating this force, and then directing it into abnormal channels where it will not be absorbed, but remain available for magical purposes."[99] This view of sexual magic was based on a complex occult tradition that viewed the male body as positive and the female body as negative. This was not simply a metaphorical restatement of the oppositions between masculine activity and feminine passivity, but an understanding of the different ways in which male and female bodies served as channels for psychic forces. According to Fortune, in heterosexual intercourse energy flowed through a complete circuit, from the positively charged male body through the negatively charged female body, and thus returned to the divine.[100] Sex between men, or between men and boys, brought the sex power into manifestation without providing a negative (that is, female) channel for its return to the divine, and that power then remained available for magical purposes.

This view of the male and female bodies was widely shared by members of the Theosophical Society. It had been invoked to defend women's exclusion from the Liberal Catholic priesthood. But most theosophists would have viewed this interpretation of their teaching with horror. In what is probably the most controversial and disputed claim in his biography of Leadbeater, Gregory Tillett argues that Leadbeater did teach sexual magic, though only to his closest associates.[101] Clearly many of Leadbeater's critics would have believed this interpretation. The original charges against Leadbeater claimed, after all, that "he does this [teaches masturbation] with deliberate intent and under the guise of occult training."[102] The fear that initiates within the TS were following the Dark or Left-hand Path speaks to the same concerns.

The Liberal Catholic Church also had what could be interpreted as homoerotic aspects. David Hilliard, in his study of the homosexual subculture of Anglo-Catholicism in the second half of the nineteenth century, claims that "Anglo-Catholicism provided a set of institutions and religious practices through which they [homosexual men] could express their sense of difference in an oblique and symbolical way."[103] The LCC, drawing as it did on Anglo-Catholicism for both its membership and its ritual, may have served the same ends. In this context, it was possible to detect a sexual subtext in Leadbeater's description of, for example, the "astral effects" of ordination. According to *The Science of the Sacraments,* after the laying on of hands by the presiding bishop and the assembled priests, "the whole aura of the ordinand expands prodigiously with this direct influx of power from the Christ; every atom within him is shaken as its various orders of spirillae are aroused. . . . When the neophyte's aura is thus dilated and extremely sensitive, the priests pour in their influence."[104] A satirical review published in *The O. E. Library Critic* referred to this work as *The Science of the Excrements,* and other titles were suggested, from *Practical Uses for Choirboys* to *Buggery and Humbuggery in the Church.*[105]

The vicissitudes of the Leadbeater case clearly marked the limits of theosophical thinking on gender and sexuality. Although theosophists were sympathetic to some aspects of the sexual reform movement, the TS was not, as has been said, "a refuge for lesbians and gay men."[106] Peter Washington's characterization of this period, which contrasts the *"fin-de-siècle* frivolity and decadence" of the theosophical leadership with the "high-minded, plain-living heterosexuality" of Rudolf Steiner and his anthroposophy, is similarly misleading.[107] Washington's analysis not only fails to capture the tone in which these debates were carried on, it also replicates the assumptions about "effeminization" and sexual/spiritual deviance that shaped the debates in the first place.

The Leadbeater case and its aftermath revealed the extraordinary power of sexuality in the alternative spiritual world of the late nineteenth and early twentieth centuries. The sexologists' reconfiguration of the relationship between sexual and spiritual subjectivity had produced explosive possibilities. Critics of the Adyar Theosophical Society saw Leadbeater as a symbol of the effeminization of theosophy, and the fear that the public would see a link between initiateship and sodomy—or more generally between sexual perversion and theosophical teaching— added fuel to the fire of the Back to Blavatsky movements within the TS. Leadbeater's supporters, in contrast, identified him as a central figure in the new dispensation that had done so much to raise the profile of the Theosophical Society and to add to its membership rolls. Leadbeater thus occupied an awkward position with regard to the "deficiency of the male element" in the TS. If men within the society recovered their power as men on the basis of their superior claim to occult authority, then the effeminization of the magico-clerical tradition, as it was constituted through the Leadbeater case, made that claim an equivocal and unstable one. The result was not only to further stigmatize homosexuality, but also to consolidate the links between sexual and spiritual identity, which meant that heterosexual norms were to be imposed on the spiritual as well as on the physical plane.

Part Two

POLITICAL ALCHEMIES

Chapter Five

Occult Body Politics

In 1912 James Ingall Wedgwood, then general secretary of the TS in England and editor of *The Vāhan*, reminded his readers that HPB had predicted that theosophy would pass through three periods of growth: the physical, the intellectual, and the spiritual. "Many of us think," he went on, "that the epoch of spiritual predominance commenced when Mrs. Besant was elected to the Presidency, and that this period has been marked by a fuller flow of spiritual life throughout the Society." "Fresh channels of kindred work" had appeared, which were the material evidence of this new spiritual life.[1] What I have described as a domestication of the occult is here inserted in another narrative: the evolution of the TS from its beginnings in the physical phenomena that had intrigued the psychical researchers; through the intellectual phase, which had its heyday under Olcott; to the full flowering of the spiritual under Annie Besant. Theosophy's spiritual phase was not, however, a quietist withdrawal from the world; it included far-reaching political initiatives intended to bring the material realities of the "physical plane" into harmony with the Cosmic Plan.

In the late nineteenth and early twentieth centuries an important utopian element within the British left argued that the moral transformation of the individual was central to social transformation.[2] As Terry Eagleton reminds us, these were the days of decadence as well as the Dock Strike, and of spiritualism as well as syndicalism, in which "the same figures can be found demonstrating for the unemployed and dabbling in occultism."[3] These men and women saw no conflict between the transformation of subjectivity and the transformation of the material world through revolutionary change. The relative invisibility of the spiritual elements of this radical political culture in historical accounts of this period is a legacy of struggles that have their origins in just these years. In the 1880s the socialist movement was actually many movements combined: "Marxism, radical Christianity, anti-industrialism, secularism, ethical Socialism, Fabian and reformist Socialism" all jostled for position.[4] Eventually three main currents emerged, each with its own organization, style, and strategy: Social Democracy, Fabianism, and ethical socialism (the chief vehicle of which was to be the Independent Labour Party). By about 1910 the more scientific versions of socialism—the Marxism adopted by Hyndman and the Social Democratic Federation, and the technocratic-reformism of the Fabians—had triumphed, and ethical socialism retired from the field in disarray.[5]

The historical success of these more scientific socialisms has shaped the historiography of socialism itself. As Mark Bevir points out, the orthodox account implies that "a religious society characterized by primitive rebellions naturally evolves into a secular one characterized by class conflict." Bevir, in contrast, reads "the socialism of the 1890s against orthodox assumptions about modernization and secularization." He traces the contours of a new theology of "immanentism," which underpinned the rejection of classical liberalism and made possible a distinctively new form of collectivism in both the New Liberalism and the socialist revival.[6]

These theological and intellectual shifts cannot perhaps bear all the weight Bevir assigns to them; changing political contexts produced radically different understandings of these ideas, which could be found not only among collectivists but also among their most vociferous opponents. But immanentism did provide some socialists with important political resources. In immanentist theology the divine was represented not as a transcendent Being, separate from creation, but as immanent in an evolving material world. William Jupp, one of the founding members of the socialist Fellowship of the New Life in the 1880s, put it this way: for many of his generation, religion could be summed up as "an impassioned sense of the Unity and Order of the world and of our own personal relation thereto; an emotional apprehension of the Universal Life in which all individual lives are included and by which they are sustained; the communion of the human spirit with the Unseen and Eternal; faith in God as the Principle of Unity."[7]

We know relatively little about the relationship between feminist politics and this immanentist impulse, and even less about the ways in which a feminist investment in this worldview might have affected women's relationship to the socialist movement. There are, however, reasons to believe that something like Jupp's vision of the "Universal Life" and "God as the Principle of Unity" also played an important role in feminist culture. Margaret Shurmer Sibthorpe's *Shafts*, for example, published in London from 1892 to 1900, exemplified the immanentist impulse. David Doughan and Denise Sanchez describe *Shafts* as a "lively but slightly odd feminist 'progressive,' radical paper, becoming increasingly involved with 'higher thought' and a degree of mysticism."[8]

The articles in *Shafts* suggest that what historians have viewed as separate campaigns—animal rights, socialism, feminism, and theosophy—were often viewed by their adherents as different aspects of the same struggle. The same range of progressive causes, often including socialist activities, can also be traced in women's political writings a decade later. The classified pages of virtually all of the suffrage and feminist newspapers of the day, from *The Vote* to *The Suffragette* to *The Free-woman*, reflect these connections; advertisements for reform dressmakers, for vegetarian boardinghouses, and for hats and accessories made without feathers or furs provide clues to a rich set of friendship networks, institutional affiliations, and political alliances that could be justified in terms of an immanentist theology.[9]

The Theosophical Society was an important source for immanentist thinking, and the TS provided a political and spiritual home for a wide variety of feminist initiatives. Immanentism had long been a central component of theosophical teaching. As H. P. Blavatsky put it in *The Key to Theosophy*, "we believe in a Universal Divine Principle, the root of ALL, from which all proceeds, and within which all shall be absorbed at the end of the great cycle of Being." Although she was no socialist, Blavatsky did claim that the TS was a philanthropic organization, dedicated to the practical realization of the idea of brotherhood.[10] Theosophists argued that the boundaries between secular and sacred (material and spiritual, public and private) could not be sustained in the face of the recognition that separateness was an illusion, that in reality there was only One Life. The liberal vision of the state as an association of autonomous individuals was challenged by an organic vision that eroded the boundaries between the individual and the community. This erosion of boundaries also involved a different understanding of the human body. The liberal vision of the body as marking the outer limits of an autonomous and independent self was displaced by an image of a body that was literally as well as metaphysically connected to all other bodies. In its fluidity and permeability this vision of the body has more in common with ideas about the body in the early modern period than it does with the modern model of "possessive individualism."[11]

On the physical plane individual bodies might appear to be separate and unconnected, but on the higher planes—the astral, mental, or spiritual planes—bodies were connected in very real ways. This belief, which we might now call holistic, had a dramatic effect on women's and men's experience of the world. Analogies drawn from the study of electricity or magnetism gave precise "scientific" content to these invisible connections between bodies; the universe was not a collection of discrete parts but one organism. At the heart of the occult body politics that was theosophy's contribution to utopian socialism was the claim to speak on behalf of forms of knowledge that were otherwise devalued: the bodily, the spiritual, the feminine, and the eastern. The political ends to which these claims were put, however, varied enormously. The new immanentist theology did not inevitably produce a more collectivist and reformist politics. A great deal of cultural and political work had to be done to turn the vision of the One Life to those ends.

Theosophy's occult body politics involved a critique of liberal individualism. Modern liberalism, as numerous scholars point out, has claimed since the seventeenth century to be universal and inclusive. Over the same period, liberal democracies have systematically excluded particular groups from full participation in public life. As Uday S. Mehta argues, the central contradiction of liberal universalism is that while it posits that all human beings are free, rational, and equal, these supposedly universal qualities are in practice construed as social rather than natural achievements. Liberal universalism is undermined by "the density of the social norms that are required to support its apparent naturalism."[12] Women, the propertyless, and colonized peoples have all, in different ways and at different times, been consigned to the realm of the unfree, the irrational, and the unequal.

Modern liberalism has taken many forms. For Britain, Mary Poovey has traced how, by the 1850s, the older model of the social body was being displaced by an atomistic vision of society as an aggregation of autonomous individuals.[13] The dominant social and economic theories treated these free and independent individuals as the basic elements of civil society. But, as the political theorist Carole Pateman suggests in *The Sexual Contract,* the existence of civil society is dependent on the existence of a realm of apparently natural relationships within the private sphere.[14]

In the public sphere, the concept of the social body did not disappear, but it was marginalized by a form of liberal individualism that emphasized law rather than love, separateness rather than community, and rights rather than duties. In contrast, in the late nineteenth and early twentieth centuries feminists often posed their critique of the public sphere on the basis of precisely those so-called natural values which liberalism devalued. Indian nationalists in the same period often made arguments that were structurally similar: India's spiritual heritage could become an important ground for a critique of colonial liberalism.[15] For many English feminists and Indian nationalists, the goal was not inclusion in the liberal polity but the re-formation of the polity on a new basis.

The occult body politics developed within the TS was part of this broader critique. Theosophists argued that modern European societies had fetishized the individual and individual freedom. They claimed that the separateness of individuals was an illusion: in reality, "We are All One." In place of the liberal model, theosophists offered a vision of spiritual community. One of their goals was to extend the supposedly natural relationships of the private sphere to the public sphere and to do away with conventional distinctions between public and private. This required a rethinking, not only of the concept of the individual, but also of the concepts of equality and independence embedded in it.

The belief in the One Life was not simply an intellectual apprehension or a political commitment: it was tied to claims about a different kind of bodily experience. These narratives privileged the body and bodily experience as the source of a new personal and political knowledge. The contours of this occult body, which remained relatively consistent from the 1890s onward, can be found in the unpublished autobiographical writings of A. Louise Huidekoper, an English schoolteacher who moved to India in 1914, married a Dutch theosophist, and went to live with him at the theosophists' international headquarters at Adyar. Once in India, Huidekoper became deeply involved with the reform of women's education: she became the principal of Bethune College in Calcutta and worked closely with other theosophists to found the All India Women's Conference (AIWC). She served as the AIWC's educational secretary for several years, and as its president in 1929.[16]

Huidekoper's account of her arrival in India is dominated by a sense of dislocation, which is reinforced by the abrupt abandonment of pagination in her manuscript. This dislocation brought with it a new awareness of herself and her body: "In ordinary civilised life," she wrote, "one never sees bodies, but only clothes." In India, however, she (or her fictional alter-ego, Annie Lambert) became acutely aware of the body: she contrasts the ugliness and ungainliness of her own body with the beauty and rhythmic symmetry of the "moving bronze statues" that she encountered in India. The passage sets up a clear opposition between the European body (clumsy, artificial, awkward) and a fetishized Indian body (natural, harmonious, in tune with its environment).[17]

But with this new awareness of the body came a recognition that in India the encounters between bodies were strictly patrolled: walking the streets in India for the first time, Huidekoper was "partly amused, but mostly distressed" by the way the crowds made way for her and her companion, for no other reason than because they were "mem sahibs." While visiting a noble family in Maratha, she learned the caste rules that regulated these interactions; her host's mother "sat in the doorway of her room, and had chairs put for us, just beyond her threshold, so that we could talk easily together, without our contaminating her apartment!" When she went to live at the headquarters of the TS, Huidekoper came to experience her own body in new ways, coming "into new contact with the unseen world" around her. She learned to be sensitive to the atmosphere around her, to tune in to emotional vibrations as if they were radio waves, to see with her astral vision, and to travel in her astral body. These were profoundly physical experiences: she saw and heard and felt the world in new ways. Huidekoper emphasizes two of the elements that were crucial to theosophy's occult body politics: the sense of the invisible connections between bodies and the perceived need to police those connections.

Huidekoper's experiences were not unique. Adyar was often presented as a forcing-ground for a new relationship to the physical body. Clara Codd, for example, went to Adyar for training before embarking on her career as a lecturer and organizer. She described Adyar as a "spiritual powerhouse," a place where spiritual energies were so strong that many European visitors fell ill of what she called "Adyaritis," a fusing of the spiritual circuits that produced depression or hysteria. Of her own spiritual visions, one of the most powerful is one she recorded seeing at nearby Mylapore where, she claimed, the "thought-forms" manifested in local rituals involving animal sacrifice appeared to her astral vision as towering, twenty-foot-high maggots, teeth dripping with the blood of their innocent victims. Though not material, these apparitions were clearly perceived as real and threatening; only when Codd "chanted the Sacred Word, AUM," did they crumple up and disappear.[18]

These encounters with India had been scripted in advance. Huidekoper, for example, had encountered theosophical writings while in England, and these writings helped shape "India" in her imagination. The occult body she came to inhabit had already been codified and theorized, most prominently by the clairvoyant and occultist C. W. Leadbeater. Leadbeater's account of the workings of the astral body, the chakra system, the aura, and the power of "thought-forms" had been mainstays of theosophical magazines since the 1880s. In 1927 his book *The Chakras* brought many of these teachings together. The most recent edition touts Leadbeater as "the original authority"; this work, like Leadbeater's other writings, has been a major influence on New Age understandings of healing, the body, and sexuality.[19]

Leadbeater claimed that "man *is* a soul and owns a body—several bodies in fact; for besides the visible vehicle by means of which he transacts his business with the lower world, he has others which are not visible to ordinary sight, by means of which he deals with the emotional and mental worlds."[20] The physical body was only one, and among the least significant, of many bodies. The teaching of reincarnation was central to this vision; theosophists distinguished between the True or Higher Self (the reincarnating individuality) and its temporary and imperfect expression in this earth-life (the personality). Moving "upward" through a hierarchy of castes and classes, races and sexes, the indwelling spirit or Ego developed an increasing awareness of and control over its "higher bodies."[21] In this schema, the individual so dear to the heart of liberalism was secured at the level of the reincarnating individuality or Higher Self. It is in this sense that "man *is* a soul and owns a body." For the most part, however, the "body" that "man owns" was not entirely his own and not necessarily under his control; this occult body stood at the center of swirling cosmic energies that penetrated and moved through it. This teaching posed a special challenge to dominant constructions of middle-class masculinity, because men of that class were so heavily invested in ideas of individual independence and autonomy. The persistent emphasis on individual separateness obscured this more significant level at which all beings are connected, at which there is only One Life.

Through the chakras, spiritual, mental, and emotional experiences were refracted through the physical body, and bodily experience reverberated on the higher planes. The term *chakras,* Leadbeater explained, was drawn from the Sanskrit, and signified the "wheel-like vortices" a clairvoyant could detect in the luminous energy field that surrounded the physical body. When awakened, the chakras appeared as "blazing, coruscating whirlpools" that were conduits for energy from the higher planes.[22] The astral world was represented as a place of both danger (for the untrained) and possibility (for the occult expert). As Besant explained in her discussion of the astral plane, most people had little control over the vibrations from the astral world that surrounded them. For them, encounters with the astral world could be overwhelming.[23]

Unfriendly astral "elementals," such as the thought-forms produced by malice, jealousy, or lust (which Besant and Leadbeater had rendered in full-color plates in *Thought-Forms,* published in 1901), could impinge on the astral and mental bodies of the unwary, setting up sympathetic vibrations. Violence, lust, or anger could all be transmitted through the astral realm. Thought-forms were believed to have a very real, if immaterial, existence: a jagged bolt of red lightning, stained with the "dirty brown of selfishness," was, for example, the astral accompaniment to domestic violence. Floating "detached in the atmosphere, all the time radiating vibrations," such forms could eventually be absorbed by the mental body of another.[24] When that happened,

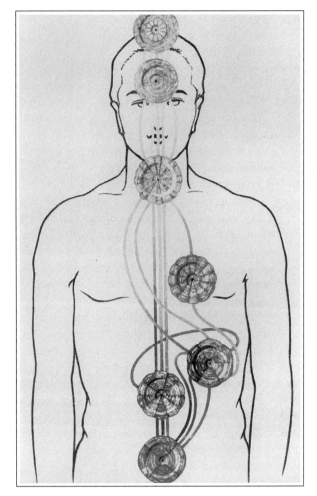

"The Streams of Vitality," from *The Chakras*, by C. W. Leadbeater.
(Theosophical Publishing House, Wheaton, Illinois)

thought-forms could reproduce the thoughts and feelings that had generated them.

Sexual thoughts and desires could also take on a life of their own. These claims resonated with the concern over social purity that had been an important part of feminist activity since the late nineteenth century. Social-purity campaigns grew out of the efforts, under the leadership of Josephine Butler, to repeal the Contagious Diseases Acts. The legislation was an attempt to control the spread of venereal disease through state regulation of prostitution in ports and garrison towns. The Contagious Diseases Acts were condemned by repealers on the grounds that they institutionalized, and gave state sanction to, a sexual double standard and had a severe impact on the poorest and most vulnerable of working women. With the repeal of the acts (in England at least, though not throughout the empire) in 1886, many feminists turned their energies to the reform or purification of public life more generally. The new social-purity campaigns were multifaceted, working to reform the laws on rape and sexual assault, to raise the age of consent for women, to close brothels, and to "rescue" prostitutes from the streets. While some feminists, like Butler herself, deplored the extent to which feminists had aligned themselves with the repressive force of the state, others cited the social-purity campaigns as an example of women's potential to bring about moral and social reform.[25]

The belief in "astral elementals" formed by lust and sensuality gave graphic content to the call for social purity. Codd recalled that Leadbeater himself was once forced to check out of the best room in the best hotel in Auckland when his clairvoyant vision allowed him to "see" that "the walls of that room were covered with darkish red slug-like creatures," the product of "sustained sensuality in the atmosphere." Clara Codd recounted a similar experience; on one occasion, when she could not bear the "feel" of her room in a boardinghouse, she discovered clairvoyantly that it was occupied by a "huge salmon-pink spider-like creature," the astral remnant of lust.[26]

Those who experienced their own bodies not as clearly bounded but as permeable and fluid could take steps to protect themselves. Daily life in the modern metropolis posed special threats: what, for example, might be the consequences (as P. T. asked in *The Vāhan's* "Enquirer" column) if astral bodies were to interpenetrate? Leadbeater's answer was not altogether reassuring: "They [astral bodies] do, however, affect one another considerably in such a case, and if their vibrations are not harmonious a very unpleasant sensation is produced, and serious inconvenience and even great harm may result from such undesirable propinquity when one of the astral bodies is gross and impure." He therefore advised his readers to avoid public transportation whenever possible.[27] Public libraries were another threat. As Leadbeater explained, "a book used in a public library is not infrequently as unpleasant psychically as it usually is physically, for it becomes loaded with all kinds of mixed magnetisms, many of them of a most unsavoury character." The "sensitive person," Leadbeater went on, "will do well to avoid such books, or if necessity compels him to use them he will be wise to touch them as little as may be, and rather to let them lie upon a table than to hold them in his hand."[28] A similar view was expressed in an article that appeared in *The Theosophist* in 1885 and was reprinted in the same magazine in 1900: "From the fingers of every man, from his eyes and from other parts of his body there is a continual flow of an invisible fluid which has been called magnetism, the qualities of which may be extremely injurious to sensitive organizations, when it proceeds from a low, vulgar and selfishly disposed person."[29] These claims were backed by the authority of eastern mysticism, for the writer was identified only as A Buddhist. (This may have been Leadbeater himself, who had recited the Three Refuges and the Five Precepts of Buddhism during a visit to Sri Lanka in 1884.)[30]

In *The Chakras* and elsewhere, Leadbeater held out the promise of techniques and training that could give the individual the power to stand, unmoved, in the center of the cosmic vortex. Those who wished further instruction were advised to seek the advice of occult experts, but Leadbeater offered more general advice, recommending complete abstinence from alcohol and all narcotics (including tobacco, which deadened the vibrations of the astral body) and from meat.[31]

The debates that took place within the TS suggest that the liberal vision of the autonomous and bounded individual body had served as a defense against the promiscuities of modern urban life; in the absence of clear boundaries between bodies, social relationships between individuals had to be handled in new ways. How, then, were contacts between putatively pure and impure bodies to be patrolled? How was virtue to be protected from vice? One answer was derived from the ancient wisdom of the East, the panoply of techniques to be found in caste rules, dietary restrictions, and yogic practices. In these accounts the West (modern, scientific, atomized, artificial, individualistic) was arrayed against the East (traditional, spiritual, holistic, natural, hierarchical). To produce these dichotomies theosophists selected certain possibilities out of the diversity that was South Asia and suppressed others. In *The Nation and Its Fragments,* the political scientist Partha Chatterjee has described such dichotomies as "a false, essentialist, positing of an unresolvable antinomy." Chatterjee emphasizes the need to attend to the diversities within Hinduism at both the elite and popular levels. Other traditions exist that reject the holistic worldview, that oppose the caste system and elite constructions of purity and impurity, and that position the individual, the family, and the community in ways that challenge hegemonic versions of Hinduism. These traditions have appealed to very large constituencies, especially among peasant, non-Brahman, or outcaste groups.[32]

Theosophists drew their understanding of the esoteric meanings of

Hinduism from elite sources. One of the most important of these sources was Indian anticolonial nationalism, which drew in turn on accounts by European orientalists of India's spiritual heritage. Especially in Bengal, where the British presence had been established longest and the expansion of a western-educated male elite had proceeded furthest, nationalist intellectuals argued that while the British might have achieved supremacy in the "outer," material realm, the essence of India had been preserved in an "inner," spiritual realm. There, India's superiority to the West had been maintained.[33] The image of Hinduism on which these claims were based reinforced the cultural and political supremacy of those elite, middle-class and upper-caste groups that articulated it. Since these were also the groups with which theosophists had the most contact, theosophical understandings of caste, of purity/impurity, and of the body were all inflected by this elite bias. While members of the TS had made important contributions to criticisms of the caste system—Henry Olcott, for example, was instrumental in founding pariah schools in India—even there, as Stephen Prothero has noted, "racial condescension" and a "socially reactionary reading of karma" colored these efforts.[34] In TS lodges the neo-traditionalism of Bengali anticolonial nationalism found its echo. "India is in advance in things spiritual, England in things material," Besant declared in a lecture to the Blavatsky Lodge in 1900. "They are two complementary halves which if put together might make the greatest empire ever known."[35]

In the 1890s the lessons to be learned from India's "advanced spirituality" were primarily individual and physical ones. According to Arthur A. Wells, "the physical, mental and spiritual organisation of the Hindoo, unspoilt by beef and brandy-pāni, is a far finer one for spiritual purposes than most of us Westerns possess. . . . Hence, in England, Mrs. Besant lays special stress on the refining of the instrument; the minute care of food and drink, the ceaseless watchfulness over thoughts and desires, which must go to raise us Europeans up to the level where the Soul can feel and act through the renewed brain and bodily senses." Hindus, on the other hand, needed to learn the lessons of western energy and action in order to overcome what Wells implied was a racial tendency to sloth.[36]

But, as G. R. S. Mead hastened to add, to describe "Oriental nations" as spiritually in advance of Europe was misleading: it was "India, and Brāhminical India at that, as distinguished from the India of 299 nationalities," which mattered. "We are told," he said, "that many families of Āryan India enjoy a heredity (physical and psychic) saturated for thousands of years with the atmosphere of religious discipline and soul-culture, and that it is a great advantage to have so easily tamed a vehicle." Those incarnated in "Western bodies" faced a more difficult task.[37] These claims were inserted into an evolutionary schema that consolidated gendered and racialized associations between refinement and purity, on the one hand, and coarseness and (sexual) impurity, on the other. Just as the "families of Āryan India" were believed to possess finer physical bodies than Europeans, other races possessed physical and astral bodies made of coarser material. So, for example, the crude and repetitive rhythms of a "negro camp-meeting" might be ennobling to the participants, because the "psychic currents" set in motion by such music represented the highest that such "lower natures" could attain; in Europe, the "hypnotic effect of the organ and chanting choirs in continental cathedrals" represented the highest that the ordinary Catholic European could attain.[38]

The working classes were also believed to inhabit "coarser" physical bodies. "Social status," Bertram Keightley noted, *"broadly speaking, corresponds to the general level of evolution which the ego in question has reached."* Those reincarnating Egos that had only recently emerged from the animal kingdom inhabited the bodies of the "lowest savages and most backward races"; above them came the slightly older Egos that populated the European working classes.[39] Writing in 1912, Montague R. St. John suggested that "the denizens of our slums are recruited very largely from egos who last incarnated in savage bodies," bodies killed in colonial wars and now returned to England as part of its national karma. Those Egos, it seemed, were motivated only by the lowest forms of desire; they could be stirred by the cruder forms of Christianity that General Booth and the Salvation Army had used so successfully among them, but they were not sufficiently "evolved" to appreciate the higher truths of theosophy.[40]

Future physical development, as Besant put it in 1909, was to be in the direction of "the increased delicacy of the nervous system."[41] Some theosophists linked that future delicacy to a more feminine body: Emily Maud Green, for example, noted in *The Vāhan* that women have "astral and physical bodies capable of responding to higher vibrations than would those of the '*stronger*' sex." For those Egos who had largely exhausted *kāmic* (astral and implicitly sexual) desire, "the less dense and material, and more subtle and pliable *female* physical body, will be the most suitable vehicle." On the next page, A. W. expressed a similar sentiment, drawing attention to "the subtle and refining lessons that a woman's body makes it easier for the ego using it to master."[42]

Discussions of vegetarianism also contained powerful negative images of the body, especially the meat-eating European body. Animal blood was described as a vehicle for "elemental forces," forces "whose nature is helpful only to that which is gross and earthly in the human being."[43] Lilian Lloyd, manager of the Match Girl's Club the TS had founded in East London, pointed out in 1896 that eating meat brought "coarse materials into the physical, etheric, and astral bodies"; a flesh diet "retards the vibrations of these vehicles as to make them not only insensitive, but even opposed, to the demands of the Higher Ego." Similarly, Mead pointed out that a flesh diet "densifies the subtle vehicle, and strengthens the animal passions which are the main impurities which darken and cloud it."[44]

These discussions fostered associations that reinforced oppositions between the coarse, impure, animal bodies of the lower races and lower classes, and the more pure, delicate, and refined bodies of the higher races and upper classes. To the extent that refinement and delicacy were associated with the feminine in the late Victorian and Edwardian image of true womanhood—an image that was itself constructed in relationship to class and racial hierarchies—these associations also aligned masculinity with the impure, coarse, and animalized, and femininity with the pure, delicate, and refined.

For the most part, discussions of vegetarianism in the 1890s focused on the implications of diet for the individual and for his or her spiritual and psychic development. Although ethical questions about the wellbeing of the animal kingdom were occasionally raised, the TS as a whole was not committed to a humanitarian or political program. Philanthropic concerns were not wholly absent: in 1890, for example, the theosophists opened an East End Club for Working Women on Bow Road, which provided inexpensive accommodation, entertainment, and a dining hall for women working in nearby factories.[45] Local lodges in both London and Manchester established children's homes and crèches to assist working women and to improve the condition of working-class children.[46]

These efforts, though justified by an appeal to the society's First Object, the commitment to Universal Brotherhood, were not especially theosophical. Like the philanthropic activities of more mainstream religious organizations, they provided piecemeal solutions to the problems caused by the shortcomings of existing poor relief. Women's activities within the TS during this period were largely confined to those appropriate to the ladies' auxiliary of any voluntary association: cleaning lodge rooms, assisting at headquarters, raising funds, and doing charitable work. While Besant's influence may have drawn theosophists more clearly into the socialist orbit, the TS was not yet in a position to take up large-scale social reforms.

Most of these early initiatives eventually failed for lack of support and lack of funds; when the conflict between Judge and Besant split the TS in 1895, the Adyar theosophists in England abandoned these efforts entirely. As editor of *The Vāhan*, Mead made the society's policy clear: "Theosophy is not *a* religion, and we are not a sect . . . our object is not to establish Theosophical schools, churches, bakeries, printing-presses or soup kitchens."[47] Others, more committed than Mead to social reform, resigned themselves to the inevitable. In 1895 Edith Ward of the Bradford Lodge argued that "we are too small and too weak at present, at any rate, to undertake separate altruistic work. We will do better to help forward the movements at present existing than to set up bran-new [*sic*] agencies of our own."[48]

Members of the TS did help forward other movements. Even in these early years, the TS was a part of a much broader radical community. Edith Ward is a good example of this integration of oppositional politics and alternative spirituality. In the early 1890s she was best known for her uncompromising stand on social purity, a stand she had articulated in *The Vital Question,* a pamphlet published in 1891, a year before she joined the TS. She relied heavily on the language of physiology (along with an overwhelming confusion of mixed metaphors) to condemn male license as a "cancer" eating at the "very heart of the race"; from the middle class "down to the very dregs of the social cauldron," the poisonous roots of a life-destroying tree were eroding "the strength, the manliness, the glory of our Anglo-Saxon race."[49] Ward's racial and physical metaphors hinted at her organic vision, which she was to find elaborated within the TS under the rubric of the One Life.

Ward joined the TS in December 1891, sponsored for membership by Besant and by her friend Mary Pope. In 1891 Ward and Pope were living together in Bradford and working as outfitters in E. Ward & Co., "Manufacturers of Hygienic Underclothing and Makers of Specialities for the Dress Reform." The company, apparently founded by Ward's father and probably owned by her brother Ernest, catered to a specifically feminist market: its Hygiea Corset, for example, was designed to allow women freedom of movement, and its advertising linked reform dress directly to women's emancipation. Reformed clothing, as the company pointed out in a book published in 1886, would allow women to live up to their full mental and physical potential.[50] Together, Ward and Pope represent the entrepreneurial side of alternative spirituality: Ward eventually took up a position at the Theosophical Publishing Society, and Pope taught vegetarian cookery and published vegetarian cookbooks.[51]

Ward also became a lead writer for *Shafts.* In the debut issue she published the first of a regular series of commentaries, "Shafts of Thought."

The article explained the paper's cover illustration—a woman firing the "shafts" of Wisdom, Justice, and Truth from her bow—in the context of recent scientific discoveries in telepathy, clairvoyance, and thought power, and predicted matter-of-factly that these feminist "shafts of light" would carry "germs of purity" into "the dark places of sin, injustice, and ignorance."[52] Ward continued to write lead articles for *Shafts* throughout its run, dealing with everything from animal rights and land reform to temperance and antitobacco campaigns. A member of the Women's Liberal Federation, she campaigned not only for the suffrage, but also for the repeal of the Contagious Diseases Acts in India.[53]

In 1897 Ward and Pope founded the West London Lodge of the Theosophical Society, which met in their home regularly over the next decade. In their theosophical writings, both women emphasized the central theme of Unity. Ward elaborated the importance of Unity as the point where theosophy and modern science meet, and Pope explored Unity as the goal of mysticism.[54] Although both women resigned from the TS in 1909, in the wake of the Leadbeater crisis, in which Ward was a prime mover (see chapter 4), Ward remained active as manager of the Theosophical Publishing Society until she retired in 1917 to devote herself to her work for animal welfare. She also retained her connections to the TS through the Universal Order of Co-Masonry, serving at one time as both secretary and treasurer of the Co-Masonic Order in Britain. As a Co-Mason, she used the order to promote her continuing commitment to equality between men and women.[55]

Other women with feminist commitments also joined the TS during these years, and they often expressed their interest in theosophy in ways that emphasized the immanentist teaching of the One Life. The educational reformer Margaret McMillan, for example, who was then active as a journalist and in the Independent Labour Party, joined the TS in 1891. Although she allowed her membership to lapse a few years later, it is clear that part of the attraction of theosophy for her was its teaching of the One Life.[56] As Carolyn Steedman argues, McMillan found a validation for her own unconventional sense of self in these immanentist teachings. As she wrote in a rather confusing letter to the socialist John Bruce Glasier,

> If you . . . realised that every phase of life and development is a manifestation of One Inner Principle it would be a great deal easier to communicate with you. . . . there are a million types of women none of whom you can truly know till you find out the relation between them all. I pray that . . . you may learn something of the mystery of transition—the transition where all is accom-

plished and all is concealed, and which contemplating you lose
the consciousness of relation and are compelled henceforth to
throw names at people and exhort them to keep certain names (to
wit Labour Church, Theosophite, The Federation etc etc etc).

A friend described McMillan as "not quite a Theosophist, though she
has some of their ideas."[57] The central idea, for McMillan, appears to
have been this emphasis on the "One Inner Principle" that connected
not only the "million types of women" but also the range of activities
in which she was involved.

The immanentist impulse could also become the basis for new kinds
of solidarity between women. Dora B. Montefiore's mystical poetry, for
example, which was also published in *Shafts,* used theosophical imagery
to convey her understanding of spiritual unity. Montefiore was at this
time a well-known member of the Independent Labour Party. In later
life she would identify herself as a freethinker; she came to the painful
conclusion that "the higher life of the spirit" could only be achieved
after a world revolution.[58] Montefiore was admitted to the TS as an
unattached member in 1893 and continued to pay dues until 1900. In
her poetry she emphasized the need to "search through ancient lore for
hidden Light," locating the key to liberation as much in the spiritual as
in the political realm. It was God's thought "that bade / All life thrill
through the Universe" and therefore, by implication, tied all beings together in an indissoluble spiritual bond.[59]

The feminist implications of the effort to formulate an immanentist
and therefore potentially more inclusive vision of spirituality were
made explicit in Montefiore's "My Garden," in which she described a
corner "sacred to the Great God Pan, / Where each lovely bud and
flower lives and loves mid sun and dew." Montefiore drew the political
lesson that all women, "Ladies, Courtesans and Virgins," were equally
precious, equally worthy of a "sister's tending," and equally sacred to
God/Nature.[60] Other articles in *Shafts* exploited a more Christian version of immanentism to argue that women had a spiritual as well as a
political responsibility to become engaged in social reform; if there was
no distinction between the spiritual and the material, then no woman,
however limited her sphere, could really retreat from the world. The
rhetoric of immanentism was one way of transcending the division between secular and sacred, public and private.[61]

A decade later, the connection between immanentism and social reform had become central to theosophical teaching. In 1912 Ethel M.
Whyte reflected on the changes in the TS:

When I joined the Society eighteen years ago, the 'whole duty of' a Fellow that was put before me was that of getting as thorough a grasp as possible of Theosophical teachings, and of introducing them as occasion occurred to friends.

Nowadays something much more strenuous is required. . . . [We must be ready] to see the signs which tell of the dawning of an age of true Brotherhood upon earth, and a response to the mighty Forces behind our movement, which are trying to work through it for the regeneration of mankind. . . . The Kingdom of Heaven is taken by violence at certain epochs, and the time for quiet advocacy of theosophical teachings amongst a small circle of friends has, in my opinion, gone by.[62]

The shift that Whyte identified was linked to a reinterpretation of theosophical teachings on the body: a new emphasis was placed on the social body, on the extent to which individual bodies could not be considered in isolation from one another.

The historical coincidence of women's dominance in the TS and the turn to an explicitly social reading of the One Life makes it possible to draw some connections between these two changes. One factor was the long-standing association between true womanhood and the tasks of caring and nurturing that had made women's contribution vital to Victorian philanthropy. Another was the process, so powerful in the last years of the nineteenth century, that embedded women in the social, making women and women's bodies central to the rethinking of the state and of welfare.[63] Most important, under Besant's leadership the TS catered to a constituency with extensive and multiple connections to socialist and feminist culture. It was in that context that the teaching of the One Life was redeployed as a justification for social reform.

As president of the TS and head of its rejuvenated Esoteric Section, Besant stamped her political impress on the TS as a whole. Her understanding of the immanentist teaching of the One Life had always emphasized its social implications. In a lecture entitled "The Pilgrimage of the Soul," delivered at Harrogate in 1895, Besant had made it clear that "no soul can grow without raising with it the whole human race; no soul can stumble without sending a shock throughout the whole human brotherhood." The end of the soul's pilgrimage, she said, was to become "one of the channels of the Divine Life, by which that life spreads over the human race."[64] She developed the same theme in lecture after lecture. Speaking at The Queen's Hall in 1900 she emphasized that brotherhood exists whether it is recognized or not. Even on the most basic physical level, the transmission of disease through microbes makes nonsense of the belief that human beings can live in isolation from each other. How could any one body be considered truly healthy when surrounded by disease? Occult science, Besant argued, taught that emotions, like microbes, can pass from one body to another. The misery of one was therefore the misery of all.[65]

Throughout her career, Besant continually emphasized that the statement that "all men are brothers" was not simply an empty phrase, but a literal and scientific truth. In an address to new members circulated, with minor variations, since 1911, she emphasized that the call to brotherhood was intimately linked to the theosophical teaching that the universe was a physical manifestation of the Divine Life. The TS did not claim to create the Universal Brotherhood: "Universal Brotherhood is there already; it *exists;* people are brothers whether they know it or not; you can neither make nor destroy it; because all are brothers, because all draw their life from the One Life, the Father-Life of all that is."[66] Conflict and antagonism might exist on the physical plane, where individuals and institutions could express only one aspect of the divine life that animated them, but from the higher spiritual perspective these differences were resolved in a transcendent unity.

There was thus a new emphasis on connectedness, on the bonds that linked members of the TS and linked the TS itself to the larger world. Now, India had a new lesson to teach. In the East, Besant argued in 1900, the idea of individual liberty was not as strong as it was in the West: "There man grows up in the idea of unity with all." Political independence, in the sense of the pursuit of individual rights, was not much cared for; in these "Eastern nations" ruling was to be left to the rulers.[67] Implicit in Besant's analysis was a hierarchical understanding of the political culture of "Eastern nations" that was to become increasingly important to theosophical understandings of the state and society. Her account of the One Life also displaced the individual in favor of the social body. "To be spiritual," Besant emphasized in another lecture that same year, was to be *"conscious in the Self as the Self,* to be conscious in the self is to be a spiritual man, to see It in all and all things in It, to see It in each man."[68]

The task of the Fifth (or "Aryan") Root Race, and especially of its fifth subrace, the "Teutonic" race, had been to develop individualism. The task of the Sixth Race, still centuries away, was the development of the spiritual faculty, and the spiritual faculty was the recognition that all life was One Life. According to theosophy's complicated system of correspondences, the materials for the Sixth Root Race were to be assembled from "the *sixth* sub-race of our present Āryan Race," and the sixth subrace was already beginning to emerge (Besant and Leadbeater had announced) in parts of California.[69] Preparation for the emergence of the new subrace included preparation of a fit environment for the new humanity. The new humanity was also to have a new Messiah. The Coming of the Lord Maitreya through the vehicle of Krishnamurti would mark the formal inauguration of the New Age. Social reform therefore became a spiritual duty. In *The Dayspring,* the journal of the Order of the Star in the East in England, George Arundale announced to members that the head of the order "wishes to draw your attention to the fact that the Order of the Star in the East has the duty of examining all the great world problems in the light of its knowledge of the future and of the general lines of the teaching which the World-Teacher may be expected to deliver to the world when He comes." Relationships between races and religions, between the human and animal kingdoms, between the classes and the sexes were now officially OSE issues.[70]

The expectation of a new race and a new Messiah produced a millennialist anticipation of a New Age. The Theosophical Order of Service (TOS) was founded in 1908 to allow theosophists to organize around social and political issues without violating the TS commitment to neutrality. It was soon harnessed to this millennialist vision. English theosophists formed leagues for social brotherhood; for the abolition of vivisection, vaccination, and inoculation; and for sociology and the social problem. In a few months the TOS in Britain boasted 1,900 members, many of them nontheosophists.[71]

Through the TOS it was possible to translate the teaching of the One Life into political action. All this activity was self-consciously interpreted in the light of the Theosophical Society's role in preparing for the emergence of a New Messiah, a New Race, and a New Age. In 1910 the TOS organizer Elizabeth Severs noted that one of the primary functions of the TOS was to do the "'immediate, insistent work' of preparing for the new Sub-race, the new Root Race, and the coming of the Christ." This work of preparation was a way of recognizing the demands of the body: "Until the Order of Service was founded, the T. S., as an *organised* body, entirely omitted the needs of the body, which, after all, is the medium of communication on the physical plane between man and man, between the soul and the spirit."[72] As Leslie Haden Guest put it, it was "the 'great heresy' of separateness" that had prevented the "realisation of brotherhood . . . as a fact on the physical plane." Universal Brotherhood, Haden Guest argued, was brotherhood "without distinction of vice or virtue, drunkenness or sobriety, dirt or cleanliness."[73] The welfare of the one could not, theoretically or practically, be separated from the welfare of all. Joseph Bibby, a Liverpool

manufacturer and socialist and the editor of *Bibby's Annual,* made a
similar point in 1908. Brotherhood, he argued, was not just an inspiring
ideal but a natural principle: "every thought and every act not only
influences the community for good or ill, but reacts upon ourselves in
the blessing or cursing—a truth we recognise in the law of Karma."
Individual progress and welfare was, therefore, "intimately associated
with the promotion of social good."[74]

This understanding of brotherhood and the One Life authorized a
range of activities. In 1908 the TOS sent delegates to the International
Moral Education Congress in London. Among them were the feminist
and prison reformer Lucy Bartlett and Caroline Spurgeon, a Chaucer
specialist with a degree from the University of Paris. Spurgeon wrote
that "to those who believe in the Unity underlying all things . . . and
who consequently believe that all human progress must take the form
of ever fuller and deeper realisation of this Unity," the congress was a
sign of hope.[75] At the International Anti-Vivisection and Animal Protection Congresses in July 1909 the TOS was represented not only by Besant but also by her fellow theosophists Dr. Louise Appel and Louise
Lind-af-Hageby, both of whom were prominent in the animal welfare
movement outside the TS as well.[76] In 1911 a contingent of theosophists
attended the Universal Races Congress in London, where representatives of colonized peoples came together to articulate their opposition
to imperialism and European claims of racial superiority, and at which
Besant was a featured speaker.[77]

To separate out specifically feminist activities here is to impose a
distinction many theosophists would not have made; one effect of the
teaching of the One Life was to unify this range of activities. But social-
purity campaigns within the TS show one way in which practical political work was combined with this spiritual impulse. In 1909 the TOS
was represented on the Council of the International Federation of the
Abolition of State Regulation of Vice, and in 1912 the TOS League of
Redemption was founded to protect "young women and girls from the
perils which surround them in a great city . . . [and] to help those who
have stumbled to get once more upon their feet and walk along a hap-
pier road."[78] This league, which took as its motto "I have said, Ye are
gods; and all of you are children of the most High," was founded when
Besant urged theosophists to attack "the White Slave Traffic." Members
of the league began drafting and circulating proposed amendments to
the Criminal Law Amendment Act. Arthur St. John, a founding member of the League of Redemption and a leader in the Penal Reform
League (PRL), urged members to study the PRL pamphlet, *Prostitution:*

Its Nature and Cure, and used the combined resources of the TS and the PRL to campaign for change.[79]

Although the London branch of the League of Redemption faltered, the Bath branch took up the cause and raised funds to establish an inexpensive hostel for women and girls in memory of W. T. Stead, whose death on the *Titanic* had prompted a range of memorializations within the social-purity movement. The league also sponsored a series of public lectures to educate people on the subject. Along with these practical and educational activities, the Bath branch urged members to meditate on "Light and Purity" for a few minutes between 10 P.M. and midnight each evening. From this new center of activity, branches were formed in Cheltenham, Bristol, and Manchester, and plans were afoot for national and international campaigns.[80]

An immanentist impulse clearly underpinned these initiatives. One of the prime movers in this campaign was Emily Maud Green of Southampton. Green, who founded the Girls' Crusade in Southampton during the war to protect women from the sexual dangers posed by military personnel in the area, also lectured on sex hygiene for the Church of England and the Free Church Purity Leagues. In a series of mystical stories published in *The Theosophist* during and after the war, Green elaborated her understanding of the essential unity and divinity of all human beings in accounts of life in the venereal wards of a local hospital or among prostitutes.[81]

The conviction that social reform was a spiritual duty, a necessary preparation for a New Age, was reinforced during the war. Across the country, lodge activities included meditation meetings to promote the Allied cause, as well as ambulance classes; the Blavatsky Lodge began providing free vegetarian dinners to women facing unemployment in the St. Pancras area; and theosophical sewing parties in Portsmouth combined their war work with the study of Bhagavan Das's *Science of Social Organization.*[82] In Southampton Green established an Employment Bureau for Women Affected by the War, which was expanded into the Mayoress of Southampton's Committee under the Queen's Work for Women Fund, which was chaired by the president of the local lodge of the TS.[83] The Bow Road Club in the East End was reestablished, and early in 1917 it sponsored an exhibition that included meatless dishes, demonstrations on the feeding and clothing of babies, an introduction to Montessori educational methods, and simple theosophical talks.[84] There was also the League for the Right Settlement of the War, whose object was to attempt to create, through group meditation, an atmosphere conducive to peace, by sending out "thoughts of love and goodwill toward all men, calculated to transmute the vibrations of hate by whomsoever or against whomsoever directed, which are now disturbing and distracting the world."[85]

The rhetoric of the New Age came into its own during the war years. E. A. Wodehouse, a leading figure in the Order of the Star in the East (and the brother of the comic novelist P. G. Wodehouse) claimed, for example, that "the world . . . is at the dawn of a New Era." The stress and conflict of the war had generalized the expectation that a "fairer civilisation" was about to be born; the special contribution of the OSE was to link the Coming of the New Era to the Coming of a New Teacher.[86] The educationalist Beatrice de Normann argued that the TS had been founded to prepare for the New Age, and "as the new wine cannot be put into old bottles there is a great need for destruction and re-construction." The Great War was "the birth throe of the New Age," and out of the destruction of war new forms would emerge, fit for the new spirit, in religion, politics, sociology, and education.[87] The war was only a dim reflection on the physical plane of the tremendous and powerful spiritual forces that were being poured into the world in preparation for the New Age.

Among theosophists, the political and spiritual understandings of brotherhood became increasingly difficult to disentangle. As Emily Lutyens expressed it in *The Sacramental Life*, "The consecrated life is not a life set apart, but a life which is shared by all. To make holy is to make *whole,* to unite the scattered fragments of God's life." The Christian churches, she argued, had distorted the notion of salvation, narrowing it to a personal and individual achievement. In reality, to be saved was "to be healed, to be made whole, ceasing to be separate, becoming one, therefore there can be no such thing as personal salvation." This was true, not simply on a metaphorical level, but literally in occult terms: for the true initiate the self was literally one with all selves, one with the universal consciousness.[88] In this analysis, the boundaries between public and private, political and spiritual, individual and community are blurred almost beyond recognition.

In 1911 Montague R. St. John wrote to *The Vāhan* to send a word of warning to "those ardent and enthusiastic Fellows who would like to prove to the world that it is possible to live according to sixth Root-race principles and ideas, at the present time." Progressive ideals were one thing, but theosophists needed to recognize when enough was enough: he criticized the "simple life fad" (noting that a fruitarian or vegetarian diet was "harmful and onerous" to European bodies) and argued that there was "no reason why members of the Theosophical

Society should attract attention and excite ridicule by dressing in a markedly unconventional and occasionally totally inartistic manner." According to St. John, those men and women who spent too much time among their fellow theosophists were liable to lose touch with the rest of the world.[89] Jessie Davis wrote to second his claims—except on the subject of vegetarianism, which she pointed out was a duty, not a "fad." She noted, "I have heard it said of a Theosophist lacking in any peculiarity: 'He is not like a Theosophist, he is so "well-groomed" and has such common sense.'" Theosophists, she argued, were in danger of relegating themselves to the ranks of "faddists and cranks."[90]

The political meaning of the category of "faddists and cranks," however, remained unstable. In a memorable passage in *The Road to Wigan Pier*, published by Victor Gollancz's Left Book Club in 1937, George Orwell argued that the "worst advertisement for Socialism is its adherents." He objected in particular to "the horrible—the really disquieting—prevalence of cranks wherever Socialists are gathered together." "One sometimes gets the impression," he continued, "that the mere words 'Socialism' and 'Communism' draw towards them with magnetic force every fruit-juice drinker, nudist, sandal-wearer, sex maniac, Quaker, 'Nature Cure' quack, pacifist, and feminist in England." Only the "cocksure Marx-quoting type" of socialist had done more to give the movement a bad name. Orwell's solution was to dispel "the smell of crankishness" clinging to the socialist movement: "If only the sandals and the pistachio-coloured shirts could be put in a pile and burnt, and every vegetarian, teetotaller, and creeping Jesus sent home to Welwyn Garden City to do his yoga exercises quietly!"[91]

Orwell's diatribe could easily have been aimed at those men and women within the TS who had attempted to live out their commitment to the One Life in a political context. Clearly, important links had been forged among humanitarian, left-wing, and feminist causes and a generically eastern spirituality. These links, however, were made historically, and in some cases they were unmade historically as well. By the time Orwell was writing, many members of the TS had already turned away from socialism and socialist or liberal feminism, and had embraced new right-wing movements like Social Credit and even Oswald Mosley's British Union of Fascists. Some historians claim that there was a natural affinity between the occult and fascist or totalitarian ideologies, and argue that insofar as theosophists possessed a political agenda, it was a conservative one.[92] But neither the theosophical theory of the state nor the uses to which it was put was inherent in Blavatsky's work or in a commitment to Universal Brotherhood and the One Life.

This vision of the state, and the politics associated with it, emerged out of a long process of negotiation and was influenced in important ways by the social and historical context.

At the same time the recognition that "All are One" was not necessarily a recognition that all were equal. Many theosophists agreed with Margherita Ruspoli that "order and subordination are necessary." The Occult Hierarchy to which the theosophists' Masters belonged was itself a graded order, based on a clear recognition of the importance of spiritual superiority for leadership. As Ruspoli put it, "Out of a true conception of brotherhood, springs naturally an impassioned loyalty to the Elders who are able and ready to help us."[93]

In the political realm, this understanding of leadership could acquire distinctly authoritarian overtones. The ideal states of Atlantis and Lemuria, according to Besant's detailed description, were well governed by "King-Initiates," highly evolved souls that were absolute autocrats.[94] In an interview with the suffrage newspaper *The Vote*, Besant argued that if the powers of the British monarchy were fully restored, then "great souls" would be sent to fill the office, as had taken place in the case of the Mikado of Japan, "a most advanced soul occupying a position of the highest responsibility."[95] The democratic polity was a necessary stage in humanity's development, but many theosophists argued that its time had passed and it would soon be replaced. Democracy was a temporary phase that did not alter the hierarchical nature of the cosmos, and while it had a part to play in the Great Plan it was not itself an ideal state.[96]

The truly ideal state was a spiritual aristocracy that recognized that all men were not born equal, that there were older as well as younger brothers in the human family. Many theosophists felt no embarrassment about identifying themselves and the middle class more generally with the "elder brethren." As Leslie Haden Guest noted in his pamphlet *Theosophy and Social Reconstruction*, "Those who are older in evolution must recognise where we stand."[97] As president of the TS, Besant targeted the professional middle class as the most effective carriers of her vision. Only those who belonged to the "great Middle Class" were in a position to make the impartial decisions required in the reorganization of the state: "For those of you who belong to the great Middle Class in England, who have a fair sufficiency of the material side of life, who have education, so that your brains have developed, who have acquired the culture which enables people to think impartially and to realise the greatest needs of human-kind, I often think that you are the people best fitted to grapple with these problems."[98] This was consonant with a more general view among the members of the professional class in Britain, the conviction that they were somehow neutral and objective observers of their society, and thus its obvious leaders.[99] If the professional middle class was to emerge as a new spiritual aristocracy, then, theosophists urged, its members needed to cultivate a sense of noblesse oblige, the realization that "it is the weak that have rights, the strong have duties; the weak have claims upon us, the strong have responsibilities."[100] The salvation of society, as Besant put it "was coming, not by the cry of the miserable, but by the self-sacrifice of those in the higher ranks."[101]

Dora St. John, for example, criticized any attempt to proselytize the masses: "Let us spread Theosophy," she wrote, "but not amongst the unevolved—those whom we wish most to help—but among those who are most capable of helping them; let us spread it amongst the social workers, writers, teachers, doctors, politicians. . . . if we can make those who are in authority Theosophists, it will not be many years before the bulk of those under them will not only benefit by the result of such propaganda but be more ready for the teaching itself."[102] Some readers objected to this blunt statement of the case, and particularly to her pejorative use of "unevolved," but Mrs. St. John's letter neatly captured the society's general emphasis. Her husband Montague seconded her concerns, incorporating them into his own brand of socialism: "the true Socialism can and will only come from above . . . any attempt to enforce it from below must prove abortive, and lead to that greatest tyranny of all, the tyranny of the unevolved over the evolved."[103]

Many theosophists argued that the modern state ignored the natural distinctions implicit in the notion of a spiritual aristocracy and imposed in their place the artificial distinctions of class and property. The solution, in Haden Guest's words, was the "reconstruction of a really organically built society."[104] If human society was a living organism, then, as Joseph Bibby put it, "its health and welfare are dependent upon the right co-ordination of all its parts." Further, "whenever the lower elements in its constitution have control of the organism, a condition of disorder arises, which finally issues in the decay of material well-being."[105] In Bibby's conflation of the body politic and the human body, the political and social disorder inherent in democratic notions of equality produced the breakdown of the social organism.

Searching for an organizing metaphor that would include the concepts of organic growth and of a planned and ordered hierarchy, theosophists turned to the idea of the family. The complex relationships between the state and the body, the family and the community, and the "organic" and the "organized" were revealed in one of Besant's public lectures to the English Section of the TS: "A Nation . . . is a natural growth. The Nation becomes a State when it becomes an organised body; when its various functions have their rightful organs; and where the government . . . turns the Nation as an enlarged family into an organised community, working for a common end, trying to realise the general happiness and prosperity for all its citizens."[106] Besant's claim that the liberal idea of the state was an artificial and mechanical one, and that the state should be understood not as a "cold abstraction, but [as] a pulsing, throbbing Life, to be loved and served with enthusiasm, with passion, with uttermost self-sacrifice" was to be taken absolutely literally.[107] The immanentist impulse drew direct and concrete connections between the individual body, the social body, and the body politic: all were part of the same "pulsing, throbbing Life." The idea that society was an evolving organism and that its evolution could be planned and directed by human activity owed much to Herbert Spencer's organicism and even more to the work of T. H. Huxley.[108] The centrality of the family, too, can be linked to Spencer's work: as one of his modern critics has noted, Spencer "accepted as self-evident that a rather idealized family pattern of Victorian England was the resting point of human history."[109]

As a model for the state, the family provided an appropriate setting for the discussions of inequality and of "older and younger brothers" that were central to the theosophists' political program. The ideal middle-class home during this period was governed by a complicated series of rules that established a clear hierarchy between men and women, employers and servants, the old and the young.[110] Although this was clearly an unequal distribution of power, the family itself was believed to be governed not by law but by love. In Besant's words, "moral duties have their basis in the family life, with the parents who are the elders, the brothers and sisters, and the little ones, and the dependents on the family, those are kept right by right emotion, by love, the supreme law."[111] The family was not a group of isolated individuals but a single unit. The different members of the family pursued common aims and profited or suffered together. According to Bibby, this was the rule in any "ordinary well-conducted family," where each member was supported by the "mutual confidence and affection of the others."[112] Such an understanding not only erased the ways in which the patriarchal middle-class family could itself be a site of oppression for women, children, and domestic servants, but also vastly overestimated the extent to which the "ordinary family" lived up to this ideal.

For many theosophists the rhetoric of family was also the rhetoric of caste. As Besant argued in *The Bearing of Religious Ideals on Social Reconstruction* (1916), the ancient Indian ideal of the family was the source of the "social ideal of Hindūism—Dharma." Whereas, in the West, the emphasis on the individual as the basic social unit had produced a society "of mutual contracts, of Rights," the Indian ideal, based on the family, was a "system of mutual obligations, of Duties."[113] Besant called for a return, in both England and India, to a purified caste system, in which "the recognition of real castes" would produce order where there was now only anarchy: in England the anarchy of the individual struggle for existence, in India the anarchy of a caste system modernized into neglect of ancient duties. Teachers would teach, rulers would rule, traders would trade, and those who, by karmic and evolutionary inheritance, were fitted only to serve would serve.[114] In this scheme, everyone would do their evolutionary duty.

This narrow vision of family and caste was translated into a western idiom through organizations like the Order of the Knights of the Round Table, in which Europe's Middle Ages was presented as an exemplar of the organic society. The Round Table (RT) was a children's organization founded within the TS to teach European children the lessons supposedly taught in India by the caste system. RT rituals and ceremonies acknowledged the East as the source of spiritual truth but attempted to cultivate the ideals of service and duty in a form compatible with the European spirit. Girls as well as boys were encouraged to join the Round Table, and women as well as men served as Knights in the order. The RT was designed to revive the spirit of noblesse oblige among the children of the privileged. Its central ethic was a commitment to service and to "the old motto of chivalry: 'Do thy Duty let come what may.'"[115] Just as the revitalization of the caste system was to restore India to its true place in world affairs, so through the revival of chivalry Europe was to be restored to itself. RT activities attempted to resanctify modern life, to provide it with order, structure, and meaning.

Hierarchical and elitist claims had always had a place in theosophy's occult body politics, but this elitism was not necessarily incompatible with a broadly socialist and feminist approach. Writing in *Socialist Review* in 1913, the theosophist H. Brockhouse, who later became a national organizer for the Independent Labour Party, made the case for "socialism and theosophy." Brockhouse anticipated the objection that the "mystic philosophy" could unfit men for "virile action," but he emphasized that the great strength of theosophy was its ability to transform the notion of brotherhood from a "cant phrase, or . . . a vague inspiration" into a "scientific fact." His vision was also tied to his support for the feminist movement: "The strength of the women is in the fact that they urge the claims of human development from the standpoint of sex equality against all the modern artificial barriers which a hidebound, self-satisfied, and prosperous bourgeois Society has erected." He concluded with an invocation of the teaching of the One Life: "Bitter class-strife exists to-day—bitter strife between master and master, also between man and man. But that strife is due to misunderstanding, and an infusion of the higher wisdom may, like oil, calm the troubled waters of the surface, and enable us to see the deeper stream where all men merge in one common life." [116] For a brief period this vision seemed compatible with socialism, especially the ethical socialism of movements like the Independent Labour Party.

But by 1910 the utopian tradition of ethical socialism had been seriously eroded. In the Social Democratic Federation, Henry Hyndman's hostility to feminists, vegetarians, antivivisectionists, and "arty-crafties" of all sorts had succeeded in marginalizing religious and humanitarian concerns. As early as 1896 George Bernard Shaw's "Tract 70" had specifically excluded philosophical and metaphysical questions from the purview of Fabian socialism. In the early 1900s Robert Blatchford and the socialist *Clarion* began a campaign against religion in favor of what Blatchford called determinism. For a brief period surrounding the 1906 general election, ethical socialism enjoyed something of a resurgence, evidenced by the popularity of R. J. Campbell's New Theology, which advocated an immanentist Christian socialism similar to theosophy's vision, but by 1909 even this brief revival was over. [117]

The last bastion of ethical socialism, apart from the TS itself, was A. R. Orage's *New Age*. The "old" *New Age,* before Orage acquired the paper in 1907, had proclaimed that the women's movement, the labor movement, and R. J. Campbell's New Theology were all signs of the same spiritual development. [118] Orage rejected and reworked all those claims. Orage had been a member of the TS in Leeds, and theosophists remained an important element in the *New Age* circle: Leslie Haden Guest, for example, was the paper's drama critic, and the paper was bankrolled by an anonymous theosophical supporter. Orage's advocacy of Guild Socialism also generated considerable support among theosophists. But Orage's Nietzschean mysticism (an all-out attack on what he characterized as sentimentalism) was incompatible with much of theosophy's social vision. Holbrook Jackson, Orage's partner in founding *New Age,* described theosophists in Leeds as "yoga-stricken mugwumps." [119]

Orage and *New Age* were relatively hostile to feminism as well. One woman who wrote for *New Age* on feminist topics was the actress and novelist Florence Farr, who had joined the Theosophical Society in 1902. Farr's feminism, however, was closer to Orage's Nietzschean vision than to theosophy's celebration of the "law of Love." In *Modern Woman:*

Her Intentions (1910), a revision of her articles for *New Age,* Farr called for a "revaluation of all values" in which women would burn through society like the alchemist's fire, turning base metal into gold. Judaism and Christianity, "the patriarchal faith of the goat-worshippers," came under special attack. Tying her claims to eugenic calls for the reinvigoration of the race, Farr called for greater tolerance of women's sexual needs and desires, and an end to the stigma attached to those who were incapable of sexual fidelity. She concluded her discussion of women's sexuality with a discussion of the "old matriarchal village community," which she praised for its sensible combination of sexual temperance with the occasional orgy.[120]

Insofar as immanentism and the One Life found a political home during the 1920s and 1930s, it was on the right rather than on the left of the political spectrum. During these years, members of the TS embraced movements like Guild Socialism and Social Credit, which provided an immanentist critique of liberalism. But these movements did not offer much space for women's concerns. One right-wing organization that did articulate a conservative feminism during the interwar years was the British Union of Fascists, and there were overlaps between theosophical and fascist ideologies. In the late 1920s the Scottish theosophist and anthropologist Alfred Garrett Pape, with some other prominent Fellows of the TS, organized the Centre Group, which claimed to have a small following in both Houses of Parliament. The Centre Group claimed that "Evolution and not 'Class' is the agent of Progress" and called for a recognition of the spiritual basis of politics and citizenship.[121]

Pape stressed the organic nature of society and the need for the right coordination of its various parts, the importance of recognizing an inequality of abilities and powers, and above all the need for an "autocracy of wisdom . . . a Spiritual Aristocracy." Having dismissed democracy as a viable system, Pape intended to make "function rather than numbers" the criterion of "a useful and wise system of valuing votes and voters."[122] Citizens were to be organized on the basis of their contributions to the state, not on the basis of their class position. The role of women in the Centre Group's policy remained vague. The sex problem was to be dealt with "on the lines of constructive and co-operative citizenship," a statement that could be interpreted in a variety of ways.[123] But in a society organized by function, and in which women's function was understood to be different from men's in important ways, women's position was likely to be a subordinate one.

That theosophical claims lent themselves to appropriation by the radical right is undeniable. Pape's functionalism bears at least some resemblance to the suggestion advanced by some members of the British

Union of Fascists—that women would be integrated into the corporate state through the formation of a corporation for women as wives and mothers. At least in Pape's case, it is possible to trace an active cooperation between members of the TS and fascist and anti-Semitic movements. That is not to suggest that the Theosophical Society, by the 1930s, was no longer feminist. But it is necessary to recognize the multiple meanings of feminism in its various historical contexts. As Martin Durham notes, gender ideology within the British Union of Fascists and other British fascist organizations was heavily contested. Although Mosley himself tended to "domesticate" women's contribution to the future corporate state in his writings, a recognizably feminist form of fascism did exist in Britain. Durham argues that the British Union of Fascists made a special effort to recruit women and to develop structures and policies that would appeal to them. In the event, many women within the organization not only took up feminist concerns over motherhood and the birthrate, but also emphasized women's equality to men both as workers and as citizens.[124]

The teaching of the One Life, like the occult body politics that was its corollary within the TS, had no stable political valence. What held this vision together was a critique of the liberal ideal of the individual, and of the state as an association of autonomous individuals. That critique could find a home on both the right and the left; it could sustain both a corporatist and a collectivist vision. It could even sustain, as it did through the 1890s, a recovery of liberal individualism through an emphasis on individual purity and individual self-control. The political purchase of the immanentist vision was thus continually renegotiated in relationship to a changing political context. Theosophy's occult body politics existed in an unstable relationship to the conventional distinctions of left and right in British politics; what persisted throughout these vicissitudes was an immanentist vision of the One Life. The effort to live out this vision called forth a politics of the body that united activities that might otherwise appear separate and unrelated. This version of body politics attempted, with varying degrees of success, to transcend the divisions between public and private, and to develop a politics of transformation. In that transcendence, the transformation of subjectivity was not merely linked to the transformation of the world through material change: the two came to appear as different aspects of the same process.

Under Besant's leadership, in England at least, the TS was an important part of a loosely socialist and feminist political culture. To characterize these men and women as "faddists and cranks" does them a significant injustice. The application of that label is itself a maneuver that defines certain practices and beliefs as trivial, and a certain political praxis as peripheral rather than central. Theosophists claimed, though sometimes on dubious authority, to speak on behalf of forms of knowledge that were otherwise often demeaned or devalued: the body, the spiritual, the feminine, and the East. That these domains were themselves culturally constituted, and that theosophical constructions of them often carried conservative implications, should not prevent us from recognizing that they could also authorize a progressive politics. This history therefore intersects with that of "subjugated knowledges" in the sense in which Michel Foucault, in his later work, defined the term. An excavation of the occult body politics at work within radical political culture is also a contribution to the history of the "insurrection of subjugated knowledges," even as it reveals the instabilities and the dangers of that politics.[125]

Chapter Six

The Divine Hermaphrodite and the Female Messiah

Feminism and Spirituality in the 1890s

Until recently, the 1890s were dismissed as a decade of relative inactivity in British feminism, a quiet period between the campaign to repeal the Contagious Diseases Acts and the emergence of a militant suffrage movement in the early twentieth century. More recent studies suggest that the 1890s were actually a very lively period, in which feminist debate flourished and new kinds of feminist organizations emerged.[1] These new studies have broadened our understanding of late nineteenth-century feminism, shifting the focus away from women's suffrage narrowly defined and toward a range of other issues—women's employment, higher education, marriage and the family, and sexuality and social purity. Among other things, this new scholarship has shown that religious concerns played a significant part in feminist culture.[2]

But many historians remain reluctant to take seriously the spiritual content of nineteenth-century feminism. It is a historical truism that the Victorians and their successors believed motherhood to be a sacred vocation, and women's special excellence to lie in their moral and spiritual superiority. But in most cases, these concepts are invoked only to underscore the gulf between prescriptive ideology and the realities of women's lives. To this end, for example, Susan Kingsley Kent quotes Mona Caird's Hadria, the heroine of *Daughters of Danaus* (1894): "It is such insolence to talk to us—good heavens, to *us!*—about holiness and sacredness."[3] For feminist critics like Caird, who was a member of the TS from 1904 to 1909 and a contributor to G. R. S. Mead's *Quest* magazine, "holiness and sacredness" were not hackneyed platitudes. Caird took men to task for presuming to instruct women on a subject on which women were the true experts; "holiness and sacredness" were, she suggested, far more than mere words to women. Women like Caird were not simply paying lip service to the evangelical legacy of women's moral superiority and spiritual mission, nor were they using a religious vocabulary to express other kinds of political concerns.[4]

Where spiritual rhetoric is recognized on its own terms (that is, as making an explicitly spiritual claim), it is too often read unproblemati-

152

cally as a conservative appeal to Christian orthodoxy. There was no shortage of texts invoking Christianity's claims to absolute truth. But this was not the only influence, or even a dominant influence, within feminist culture in the late nineteenth century. Orthodox Christianity is itself a problematic concept, given the theological uproar of the time. And a too easy conflation of women's religiosity with that orthodoxy erases the considerable work that contemporary feminists did to reshape Christian and other faiths to their own ends. The effort to articulate a specifically feminist spirituality was a crucial part of much feminist activity in England during this period, and a fuller exploration of the spiritual concerns within the feminism of the 1890s yields a richer and more varied picture than is otherwise available.

At the same time, we must recognize that much of the rhetoric about women's spirituality was founded on the assumption of Anglo-Saxon racial superiority and imperial destiny, of class hierarchy, and of the immutability of sexual difference. As women (and some men) struggled to create a feminist culture, they also negotiated its limits. There was a great deal of debate about whether and on what terms less privileged women—colonized women, working-class women, or women engaged in prostitution, for example—were to be incorporated into a feminism informed by notions of women's spirituality. These debates helped shape the visions of women's spirituality that emerged within English feminist culture.

From the mid-nineteenth century, a range of individuals and organizations in England had begun to address different aspects of women's inequality. Some, like the women of the Langham Place group, sought to increase women's employment and educational opportunities, especially in new professions like teaching and office work. Through the *English Woman's Journal* they helped open public debate on a range of issues relating to women.[5] Feminist efforts to reform marriage and divorce law were accompanied by a wider critique of men's behavior within marriage, a critique that spilled onto the pages of the popular press in 1888, when the *Daily Telegraph* received twenty-seven thousand letters to the editor in response to an article that Mona Caird published in the *Westminster Review*.[6]

By the late 1880s and 1890s feminist concerns had forced their way into the public consciousness. So, in 1890, H. P. Blavatsky, who was then resident in London, could write in the theosophical magazine *Lucifer* that "most Theosophists have read Mrs. F. Fenwick Miller's admirable address on the programme of the Women's Franchise League; and many of our Theosophists belong to this League."[7] The Theosophical Society was one of only a handful of religious organizations (the Quakers, the

Unitarians, and the Salvation Army are others) that actively welcomed women's leadership. Blavatsky, theosophy's spiritual founder, was after all a woman, and in England another woman, Annie Besant, was rapidly becoming her most prominent disciple. Yet the TS itself was only welcoming to women in relative terms: in England, only about one-third of the society's members were women, and the English Section was still firmly under the direction of Mead with his brand of "manly" and scientific spirituality (see chapter 2).

Women did, however, join the society in significant numbers. Many of them saw theosophy as sympathetic to feminism and to women's political aspirations. Such women believed that H. P. Blavatsky's teaching, especially in *The Secret Doctrine*, offered new possibilities for rethinking relationships between the sexes. Blavatsky herself had offered no final solutions to the Woman Question. She argued first that the division between the male and female principles was the central organizing principle of cosmic development. The lesson was that "humanity is dual," that both maleness and femaleness had a role to play in the cosmos. The Universal Divine Principle was both sexless and formless; it was "neither Father nor Mother." Manifesting in the universe, this Absolute Spirit created itself as a series of oppositions: positive versus negative, spirit versus matter, masculinity versus femininity. This cosmic sexual order was at once symbolic and actual. At the same time, there was the claim that "esotericism ignores both sexes."[8] The Higher Self, or unconditioned soul, was neither male nor female (or, put another way, it was both male and female), and it occupied the bodies of men and women in turn over the course of millennia. As the Ego or Higher Self developed, passing through numberless lives in both male and female bodies, it began to manifest the highest qualities of both, culminating in the emergence of the spiritual androgyne or "Divine Hermaphrodite."[9]

Blavatsky's vision focused attention on the late nineteenth and early twentieth centuries as a moment of great import in the spiritual and physical evolution of humanity. The end of the nineteenth century roughly coincided with the end of a cycle within the Dark Age (the Hindu Kali-Yūga) and the dawn of a new cycle: humanity, having become fully material, was now to ascend the arc of spirituality. Cosmic polarities were being reversed, and the organization of sex, as the most obvious and fundamental of human polarities, was to change dramatically.[10] The implications of this shift, which were implicit rather than explicit in most of Blavatsky's writings, were seized on by later theosophists as a way of explaining the changes in their society. The apparently profound changes taking place in relationships between men and women, or between Europeans and other peoples, came to be understood as the culmination of "a cyclic law whose period is about twenty-five thousand years in extent."[11]

With Blavatsky's cryptic formulations as their guide, members of the TS continued to debate the Woman Question from the esoteric point of view. The debate involved a series of negotiations over the extent to which Christianity, Hinduism, and Buddhism, and the different traditions within each of those beliefs, were to be considered authoritative. The effort to identify the relationship between Hinduism, Buddhism, and the Woman Question had a troubled history within English feminism, which had long seen Asian women, immured within the harem and the zenana, as the metaphorical epitome of women's oppression. As Antoinette Burton argues, imperial concerns framed the emergence of the British feminist movement in crucial ways. According to Burton, British feminism was founded on the contrasting image of "degraded Indian womanhood," and "by emphasizing Asian women as victims, [this narrative] privileged British feminists as agents of their own liberation."[12] Burton rightly calls attention to the racist underpinnings of these attitudes. But to characterize all of British feminism in this way runs the risk of flattening or homogenizing the historical evidence. We need to explore not just the fact of racism or imperialism but also how these frameworks were produced and reproduced within feminist culture. Imperial feminism was not a monolithic construct, and the historian must be attentive to the cracks in this edifice, to the moments when new possibilities opened up and other possibilities were foreclosed.

Tracking these debates through the Theosophical Society reveals both the instabilities within imperial feminism and the constraints that were placed on the debate. Theosophists were uniquely positioned to contest some of the assumptions of an imperial British feminism. Unlike many of their contemporaries, they were not at all convinced of the superiority either of Christianity or of the Anglo-Saxon race; indeed, as we have seen, they were firmly committed to a recognition of India's superiority to England, at least in spiritual matters. For theosophists and their sympathizers, the easy narratives of progress that underpinned the contrast between English women and their Indian counterparts— from eastern barbarism to western civilization, from primitive superstition to Christianity or secularism, from tyranny to emancipation— were disrupted at many points. In the end, theosophical feminists, at least in the 1880s and 1890s, reinstituted the dichotomies between the "modern," emancipated, English woman and her "degraded" Indian counterpart, and this testifies not only to the resilience of imperialist and racist frameworks, but also to the complex constraints that shaped the emergence of feminist discourses on race and religion.

For many feminists, one of the primary attractions of theosophy was its uncompromising denunciation of Christianity as a key site of women's oppression. The second volume of Blavatsky's *Isis Unveiled* matter-of-factly announced that Christianity was of all religions "the chief opponent of free thought" and went on to trace the ways in which most of Christianity was directly derived from phallic worship and pagan ritual.[13] Alexander Fullerton, a former Episcopal priest and a leading member of the American Section of the TS, argued that phallicism was characteristic not only of Judaism, which he described as sensual and materialistic, but also of Christianity, "whose cross and whose church towers" were thinly disguised monuments to the male procreative function.[14] Blavatsky and Fullerton thus turned on Christianity the criticism that so many European commentators had made of Hinduism—that its sacred symbols venerated male sexuality.[15]

Buddhist women in Ceylon were held up (by a writer using the nom de plume European Buddhist) as free and equal to men; in contrast, Christian women were characterized as oppressed by an "intolerant and despotic Church."[16] In a reinterpretation of the standard view of Asian cultures as stagnant, this writer praised the Sinhalese for their adherence to the noble truths of the Buddha, while criticizing Christianity for burying the ancient wisdom under a degenerate ecclesiasticism. Although these esoteric readings of Hinduism and Buddhism might not have been recognizable to adherents of the exoteric versions of those faiths, theosophists did help to popularize an anthropological critique of Christianity that was otherwise often muted.

But the message offered to women who were only beginning to question Christian orthodoxy was mixed, to say the least. In an editorial "Progress and Culture" published in 1890, *Lucifer* thundered against modern Protestantism and Roman Catholicism, both of which "owe[d] their illegitimate existence . . . to priest-ridden and church-going women." For women to demand franchise reform, however legitimate and just that demand might be, while continuing to attend churches that opposed women's emancipation, was like "boring holes through sea-water." Women had allowed themselves to become willing martyrs to an ungrateful Church.[17] If religion was to be reformed, then women must be reformed. As one writer proclaimed, "*Woman must recover her lost soul*, or the consciousness of it, before she can be less a victim of man's selfish bestiality than now. . . . Through his ritualistic mummery, man has deprived woman of the consciousness that she is an immortal soul inhabiting a physical and mortal body." Deprived of her soul, unconscious of her immortality, woman was simultaneously the helpless victim, the willing accomplice, and the potential savior of man.[18]

Christian womanhood was thus constituted as a problem within the TS. Theosophy, in contrast to a weak, irrational, and sentimental Christianity, was a "man's religion." Women who wished to participate in the society's activities were required to live up to a "manly" standard of rational enquiry, scientific deliberation, and independence of judgment. Women's experience within the TS in the 1880s and 1890s was therefore similar to those of women in other heterodox organizations in the same period: the minority of women within the Fabian Society, for example, also emphasized an egalitarian position—their similarity to men—to establish their right to participate in a group dominated by men and men's interests.[19] So long as theosophists presented the ancient wisdom of the East as a manly creed, and Christianity as weak and womanly, women within the TS were forced to negotiate on inhospitable terrain.

Some women did find opportunities to develop a critique of the society's gentlemanly ethos and assumptions. One such woman, a prominent contributor to both *Lucifer* and *The Theosophical Review* through the 1890s, was Susan E. Gay. A former spiritualist with Swedenborgian sympathies, Gay had a long history of feminist commitment.[20] In 1879 she published *Womanhood in Its Eternal Aspect*, in which she attempted to recognize both sexual equality and sexual difference. A true understanding of women's nature, she argued, must "not only embrace the special, though temporary, physical functions which belong to woman on the physical plane, but must regard her in the far wider sense of a human being, who may be a mother once, but who will be an intelligent living being subject, like man, to higher and purely spiritual laws, forever."[21]

Gay joined the Theosophical Society in May 1890 and immediately began to exploit the possibilities that Blavatsky's teachings, especially those on karma and reincarnation, offered to her feminist project. In October 1890 she published her theosophical-feminist manifesto, "The Future of Women," in *Lucifer*. She argued that reincarnation provided the key to the real meaning of sex: what the uneducated eye took to be a woman was, in reality, only "a SOUL temporarily clothed in the garb of womanhood." To gain a range of experiences, the soul journeyed through both male and female bodies, developing the best and noblest qualities of both sexes. For Gay, conventionally manly men and womanly women were the least developed souls; the true ideal for both sexes was the "spiritual equilibrium" that Christianity's founder had exemplified. From these claims, Gay spun out a far-reaching series of feminist demands. As a crucial first step, men had to free themselves from the mistaken belief that "physical manhood is a sort of freehold possession to be held here and hereafter, which marks off certain souls from certain others known as women, and confers on them all sorts of superior rights and privileges, including the possession and submission of 'wives.'" If men really believed that they might find themselves in female bodies in the next life, they would hesitate before perpetuating women's subordination. Gay therefore criticized those who would confine women to a limited role as wives and mothers, to condemn marital rape, and to call for an end to the sexual double standard.[22]

Gay also wrote, in theosophical magazines and elsewhere, as Libra.[23] Symbolized in modern astrology by the scales or balance, Gay's nom de plume captured the two kinds of balance that were important in her writings: balance in political and social life between men and women, and balance of the "masculine" and "feminine" qualities within the individual human being.

In the end, Gay argued, the final test of any religion was its recognition of women's equality. Theosophy should therefore transcend not only Christianity but Hinduism and Buddhism as well. An anonymous correspondent in *Lucifer* made the same point in 1894: "true religion ... will never create sexual distinctions, and whether these are discerned in the laws of Manu or the epistles of the *New Testament*, all that tends to relegate womanhood to subservience and inferiority must give way to the higher teachings of a Theosophy which fixes its eyes ever upon the Eternal Soul."[24] Gay, who died early in 1918, devoted the last years of her life to revising and publishing at her own expense a life of Christ, *The Prophet of Nazareth*. The book, which received a lukewarm review from Gertrude Colmore in *The Vāhan* in 1917, was part of Gay's continuing effort to rehabilitate Christianity and the position of women within it.

The concepts of reincarnation and karma were central to Gay's analysis, but they were reinterpreted in the context of an esoteric Christianity rather than presented as specifically Hindu or Buddhist teachings. Gay's effort to rehabilitate Christianity was also a rejection of the claims of Hinduism and Buddhism, and reproduced the dichotomy between "degraded" Hindu or Buddhist womanhood and more modern, emancipated, Christian English women. But Gay's complicity cannot simply be reduced to the power of an imperial-racist framework. Her claims were also a response to the form that the newly minted "ancient wisdom of the East" had taken within the TS itself. The version of this ancient wisdom current within the society was the product of a

formidable alliance between English and Indian men who shared a "colonial masculinity." As Mrinalini Sinha has argued, this colonial masculinity reinstated patriarchal power even in the face of racial difference
and the inequalities of colonizer and colonized.[25] This was a fragile alliance, especially since the spiritual authority wielded by Indian men in
the TS was often made contingent on their willingness to enact the
exotic spectacle of the "mysterious Mahatma," which undermined their
performance of English manliness. Even so, this alliance could be used
to turn the ancient wisdom of the East against feminist campaigns.

Gay's claims for a theosophical feminism did not go uncontested.
Blavatsky's teaching could also be deployed as a cosmic justification for
sexual difference and sexual inequality. As the Scottish occultist and
astronomer-royal James W. Brodie-Innes wrote in 1892, "The first emergence of Being from Be-ness was a duality. The one became two—active
and passive, positive and negative, energizing and receptive." While
Brodie-Innes himself resisted the temptation to use the terms *male* and
female in his analysis, others were willing to make that connection.[26] In
1895, for example, Besant argued that two great principles were at work
through all of nature: "one gives impulse, the other nourishes impulse
and builds it into the individual. Call these principles 'active' and 'passive,' or call them life-giving and nourishing; and, if you speak of them
where sex is developed, call them male and female."[27] On the physical
plane male and female were the functional equivalent of active and passive, the life-giving and the nourishing aspects of the universe. Life in
male or female bodies was a special kind of discipline for the soul, an
opportunity to learn the distinctive lessons of manhood and womanhood.[28] Some feminists, like Gay, rejected what they saw as the perni-
cious essentialism of this model. The esotericism in which woman was
symbolic of the soul and man of the "outer Reason" was, Gay argued,
only slightly less mischievous than the more orthodox teaching of wom-
en's inferiority to men.[29]

In Besant's hands, even this more conservative reading of Blavatsky's
teaching could be turned to feminist ends. Not all theosophists, however, were as sympathetic to feminist aspirations as Besant. In 1888 the
Brahman mathematician Gyanendra N. Chakravarti, a Hindu nationalist who enjoyed a brief period as Besant's guru, initiated an acrimonious
debate in *The Theosophist* with his interpretation of the discipline imposed by a female body. Chakravarti wrote to *The Theosophist* in praise
of what he suggested was the "traditional" Hindu woman. "Performance of selfless duty would have been her life-object," he argued. He
claimed that it was a woman's duty to endure even the most abusive
husband because, according to the Shastras, a woman could attain the

highest goal of Moksha "by serving her lord alone— whether good, bad, or indifferent."[30] His article raised a storm of opposition from those who were all too willing to see this as typically eastern barbarism. As one reader wrote, "I thought of joining the Theosophical Society, but if that wretched mixture of senseless superstition and heartless cruelty is Theosophy you may count me in future as one of your enemies."[31]

The changes of sex through reincarnation also had karmic implications, and these could likewise be interpreted to oppose feminist interests. The argument here was double-edged: men were warned not to create karma for themselves that they would have to work off in future feminine lives, while women's oppression was rationalized as a karmic debt they themselves had generated. The American theosophist Dr. Jerome A. Anderson was explicit on this point: "The law of Karma, ever restoring our disturbed equilibrium, is omnipotent and inviolable; and by our very attitude towards the opposite sex, be it that of man or woman, we are creating character traits which may have to be sharply corrected by unpleasant experiences in that opposite sex during our next life."[32] It was perfectly logical to argue as follows: "Suppose A. ill-treats B. his lawful wife, who suffers long and uncomplainingly. The Karma of compensation requires that A. should suffer similarly in his next birth, and this can best be fulfilled if A. be born a female."[33] This argument, advanced by Kali Prasana Mukherji of Barakur, Bengal, provoked strenuous opposition. On one level, his opponents simply asserted, with confidence in their claims to cultural superiority, that such a formulation did not apply to the more modern organization of relations between the sexes in the West. But they also argued that this understanding of karma was not calculated to restore harmony between men and women.[34]

Mukherji's article, "Scraps from a Hindu Notebook," was published in *Lucifer* in 1894. In his discussion of "sex in reincarnation," Mukherji made other claims that were just as fiercely contested. He argued, for example, that the "mental characteristics" of males and females could be clearly and easily distinguished, maleness being characterized by authority, intellect, and a universalizing tendency, while femaleness was characterized by submissiveness, devotion, and an affinity for the particular.[35] An anonymous group of English women responded to Mukherji's article with "Fragments from an English Notebook," in which they argued that the type of woman Mukherji described "is now happily becoming one of a small minority" in England, and that the persistence of the type in India was the result of the "disabilities" under which women suffered there.[36]

It is possible to detect, both in Mukherji's "Scraps from a Hindu

Notebook" and in the "Fragments from an English Notebook," the echoes of a broader intellectual context. Both titles referenced the collected works of the philologist F. Max Müller, published in the late 1860s and 1870s as *Chips from a German Workshop*. Max Müller's orientalist reconstruction of a Hindu golden age still reverberated in Mukherji's rhetoric, which privileged an upper-caste, Hindu-Aryan elite as representative of the Indian past.[37] Indian nationalists, especially those, like Mukherji, from Bengal, had begun to link these claims to a new view of the role of women in the nationalist project. According to Partha Chatterjee's recent analysis of the nationalist movement, while the exigencies of modernity had forced upon men "a whole series of changes in their dress, food habits, religious observances, and social relations," these "capitulations now had to be compensated for by an assertion of spiritual purity on the part of women." Nationalist rhetoric required that masculinity be modernized and that femininity be traditionalized, becoming the repository of the spiritual qualities that were claimed to be the true essence of the nation.[38]

Until the 1920s, when Rukmini Devi rose to prominence within the Theosophical Society, Indian women had little or no public voice within the TS, either in India or in England. English theosophists' encounter with what they believed to be the real India was mediated through a male elite. Insofar as the so-called ancient wisdom of the East was mobilized within the English TS to authorize male privilege and a "manly" spirituality, men benefited most from this rhetoric. Claims about the superiority of eastern over western spirituality were recoded as claims for the superiority of men over women.

In 1901 Emily Maud Green also attempted to explain the differences between English and Indian women in karmic terms. Her analysis illustrates the extent to which feminist arguments within the TS had been shaped in response to the neo-traditionalism in both academic orientalism and anticolonial Hindu nationalism. She argued that the lives and destinies of English and Indian women were divided by karmic and evolutionary necessity. Indian women were understood to be the possession of their lord and master, and therefore, "to India were drawn by kārmic necessity such egos as needed for their further development a life of dependency and obedience, and the evolution of the virtues of wifehood and motherhood. To such egos this would be the 'next step,' the Dharma waiting to be done before aught else could rightly be undertaken." Conversely, she went on, it was by karmic necessity that "to England to-day come the egos who incarnate as the 'modern woman' and are often the leaders of moral reform, the fearless crusaders against old-standing abuses."[39]

G. R. S. Mead pointed out that only in India were branches of the TS segregated by sex, for there "the social customs are such that women can take no part in public affairs." In contrast, the TS in England was committed by the society's First Object to the formation of a nucleus of the Universal Brotherhood of humanity "without distinction of sex"—an object that was loyally carried out, "as may be seen by looking over a list of the officers of its branches and of its principal writers and speakers."[40] Mead's assumption was that sex segregation necessarily implied subordination and could not therefore be part of a feminist program. As Geraldine Forbes makes clear, however, it was precisely through these kinds of separate women's organizations that many Indian women developed and articulated their demands for women's rights.[41] Theosophy's evolutionary framework, which represented feminism as a natural development within English democracy, militated against a recognition of these strategic differences.

The creation of a feminist spirituality within the TS was constrained by the limits of contemporary discourses on race, gender, empire, and religion. Closely related debates were also taking place within feminist culture more broadly. Feminist journals during this period devoted a surprising number of column inches to what might now be characterized as theological, rather than political, debate. Alongside and intimately connected to debates over marriage and morality, women's sexual freedom, and the works of New Woman novelists, we find contention about the nature of the divine, the history of the early Christian church, and the power of prayer.

The journal that gave most attention to these issues was Margaret Shurmer Sibthorpe's *Shafts*. Sibthorpe herself joined the Blavatsky Lodge of the TS in October 1891, at a meeting at which Miss Henrietta Müller spoke on women and theosophy.[42] Passionate discussions of women's spirituality were a central feature in *Shafts* throughout the decade. Christianity in particular came in for close critical scrutiny. In an early issue, an unsigned article "Womanhood and Religious Mis-Education" began a study of the Hebrew Scriptures. They were condemned as exclusively and perniciously masculine, with the possible exception of the early chapters of Genesis, which, viewed esoterically, taught the duality of the divine, its feminine as well as its masculine character. Orthodox Christianity, built on this foundation, was a " 'halved' religion": as a society's religion sets the standard for its social and political life, this half-Christianity had produced the bitter fruit of women's oppression in modern England.[43]

In December and January 1892 Susan Gay, writing as Libra, published a two-part discussion "Womanhood from the Theosophical Point of View," which gave readers a formal introduction to feminist theosophy. The first article outlined the insights into individual development that the teachings of reincarnation and karma offered; the second dealt with the implications of theosophical teaching for "race-production." Employing both an evolutionary and an occult vocabulary, Gay looked toward the day when a purified manhood and womanhood would transcend sexual means of reproduction and produce a true "Master-Race." The key to the emergence of the "Master-Race" (which is not, in this context, explicitly linked either to an Anglo-Saxon or to a European race) was the "occult force represented by *Sakti*," the active feminine and reproductive aspect of Śiva in Śākta Hinduism.[44] This article is clearly evidence of a feminist belief in evolutionary progress. But this was not progress away from a primitive, eastern womanhood and toward a more modern, western one. Instead, the East was idealized as a source of enlightenment, and theosophy's Mahatmas were portrayed as the highest spiritual authorities.[45]

In her later writings, Gay's identification of the Master-Race with Anglo-Saxon womanhood became much more explicit. She also began to characterize Hinduism as especially degrading to women, such that her claims—about the practice of *sati,* for example—were subject to editorial reproof in *The Theosophist.*[46] Both of these shifts can be linked to her turn toward Christian esotericism; the links between the valorization of Christianity, the characterization of Hinduism as degrading to women, and the eugenic impulse were all consolidated within feminist debates over spirituality in the 1890s and early 1900s. In the shorter term, however, Gay's articles on cruelty to children, domestic violence, sexual assault, and the inadequacy of man-made laws in all these areas illustrated the range of her concerns—and implicitly of theosophy's concerns—on the Woman Question and the ways in which a syncretic approach to spirituality could open up new avenues for women's emancipation.[47] Other writers took the same approach. Mrs. A. Phillips's articles "Why Women Are Women" also invoked the "ancient 'Sruti' or Scriptures of the East" to argue that Protestantism's anthropomorphic God was a theological error. Protestant Christianity had become a "cold sexless, therefore motherless" creed in which there was no real place for the Divine Feminine. On the basis of etymological derivations from the Sanskrit, Phillips argued that Christ's sacrifice on the cross, read esoterically, was a symbol of the "perfect marriage union of the male and female" and therefore of women's redemption.[48] Sibthorpe added an editorial note to Phillips's article, calling on her readers to assist in the formulation of a new gospel that would liberate rather than oppress women.

Theosophists, of course, believed that they offered just such a gospel. Not all the readers of *Shafts* were convinced, however, and Sibthorpe, in keeping with her policy of openness to a range of opinion, also published articles that dismissed theosophy as superstitious nonsense.[49] One anonymous correspondent wrote that modern theosophy had been corrupted by "the Oriental taint of contempt for women." The same correspondent wrote again to point out that women in England had been working for women's rights long before the theosophists came along: "it is the insufferable pretension that Theosophists (frequently male) can 'teach' women about themselves, which will never be accepted by the mass of thoughtful women, especially when the teaching is mixed up with such slovenly thinking as is implied in the suggestion that a shifting about of sex touches the problem of the righting of womanhood in any way whatever."[50] These letters returned to the issue that had divided theosophists themselves: that men, rather than women, were most eager to tout the ancient wisdom of the East as the solution to women's problems. Men's appropriation of this rhetoric thus reinforced an already existing skepticism about the value of Hinduism and Buddhism to women's spiritual emancipation.

The debate continued in the paper's correspondence columns for several months, until Sibthorpe put a stop to it with the editorial injunction, "Theosophy certainly contains much truth; it is worth earnest study. Examine all things."[51] But the claim that oriental religions were based on a special and severe contempt for womanhood and that eastern mysticism was peculiarly masculine was worked out in a variety of other contexts as well. The identification of both Hinduism and Buddhism as "Wisdom religions" and of Christianity as a religion of "Love" confirmed a gendered opposition between the faiths of East and West.

While some versions of English orientalism tended to present the East as feminine and the West as masculine, in these religious debates the result was exactly the opposite. Theravada Buddhism in particular was elevated as an ideal type of manly, rationalist religion. As Thomas Tweed argues, Theravada Buddhism had been presented by both European scholars and its Asian supporters as "a rational tradition that emphasizes self-reliance, tolerance, psychology, and ethics."[52] This interpretation of Buddhism was by no means the only one available, but it appears to have been a dominant one in the 1890s. A rationalist version of Hinduism was also readily available. Earlier in the nineteenth century the Bengali Brahman Rammohun Roy had attempted to reconstruct Hinduism on theistic principles, arguing for a reformed Hinduism that could be justified on both rational and utilitarian grounds. In the 1890s Roy's program was preserved in the activities of the Sadharan

Brahmo Samaj, which had a high profile in Europe and America.[53] One of the most popular attractions at the World Parliament of Religions in Chicago in 1893 was Swami Vivekananda's Vedanta, a self-consciously manly version of Hinduism that similarly emphasized self-reliance and scientific rationalism.[54] Within the TS itself, the short-lived alliance with Dayananda Saraswati's Arya Samaj in the 1870s provided a more direct link to the rationalist tradition in reform Hinduism. The alliance foundered when the theosophists' syncretism came into conflict with Dayananda's Vedic Hinduism, but Dayananda's methods, which emphasized the "analytic and grammatical tools needed to understand Vedic Sanskrit," appealed to those who looked to Hinduism for a rational religion.[55]

In contrast, Christianity had been gradually acquiring an association with femininity. The feminization of Christianity was by no means a straightforward process; like the masculinization of Hinduism and Buddhism, it required a selective reading of both historical precedent and contemporary possibilities. Christian manliness could and did incorporate many virtues that were otherwise perceived as feminine: gentleness, compassion, and surrender to God. In the late nineteenth century this understanding of Christian manliness was preserved in evangelical movements like the Salvation Army, which, even with all its military metaphors, remained open to these more fluid notions of masculinity.[56] After 1850, however, the image of a gentle Jesus, meek and mild, was increasingly associated with images of femininity and domesticity. Efforts to virilize Christianity and Christian imagery, most prominently in the effort to popularize a muscular Christianity, were responses to the increasingly powerful association of religion and the spiritual with the peculiarly feminine virtues.[57]

The emergence of a feminist version of spirituality was determined in part by these associations. Conflicts and divisions within the TS in the 1880s and 1890s took shape in precisely these terms: the rejection of Christian mysticism in the theosophists' conflict with Anna Bonus Kingsford and Edward Maitland, for example, was linked to the association between Christianity and the feminine virtues of love and sentiment, on the one hand, and between esoteric Buddhism and manliness, rationality, and science, on the other.

Some women, though they were by no means orthodox Christians, rejected what they saw as the masculine model of spirituality that theosophy represented. One alternative to that model was an esoteric Christianity that valued the "feminine" virtues of love, intuition, and feeling. The feminist Elizabeth Blackwell, for example, Britain's first woman doctor, joined the Christo-Theosophical Society, which based its teachings on a western mystery tradition.[58] The Esoteric Christian Union (ECU) was another organization that many women believed expressed a peculiarly feminine and western religious sensibility. The ECU was founded in 1892 as a channel for the dissemination of the teachings of Kingsford and Maitland. In Maitland's obituary, published in *Shafts* in 1897, Alice M. Callow claimed that "no man of these times has more deeply striven to point out the true and spiritual significance of what is known as 'The Woman's Movement.'" Where the TS declared that knowledge was the royal road to spiritual evolution, and that "there is no Religion higher than Truth," Maitland and the ECU proclaimed that "there is no Religion as high as that of Love."[59] Like the theosophists, Kingsford and Maitland emphasized the duality not only of humanity but also of the individual. In their teachings, however, the symbolic and literal links between love, intuition, and "the Woman," and between wisdom, intellect, and "the Man" were much more explicit. "Woman"— the "woman clothed with the sun" of the New Testament Book of Revelation—became the central symbol of humanity's redemption. "Thus the Heavens eternally witness to the promise of the final redemption of the Earth, and of the return of the Golden Age, and the Restoration of Eden. And the keynote of that desired harmony is to be found in the exaltation on all the universal fourfold planes, physical, philosophical, psychic, and celestial, of the WOMAN."[60]

Christian esotericism did not necessarily require the elevation of Christianity over other creeds. By locating true Christianity in ancient texts and a distant past, Christian esotericism could draw attention to the degradation of Christianity in contemporary Protestant and Catholic churches. The esotericists made similar arguments about the degeneration of Hinduism, but the racist implications were blunted when the same claims were being made about Christianity. Christian esotericism could also lead to a belief that all religions were partial and limited, and that there were many paths to spiritual truth. At the same time, Christianity remained normative and set the standard by which other faiths were to be judged. Even in such cases, however, there was some space for an acknowledgment of the value, and even the superiority, of Hinduism, Islam, or Buddhism. An article published in *Shafts* by A Pioneer (a member of the Pioneer Club, which catered to progressive women) illustrates this ecumenical possibility. Christ Himself, the author argued, had stood against bigotry and intolerance, and even though Hindus worshiped God under another guise, they were nonetheless as pious as any Christian. The article went on to claim that Buddhism included virtually all the basic moral truths taught in true Christianity, and that the standard of morality was higher in Islamic countries than in so-called Christian ones. Given that women's legal and civil status was, on the whole, better protected in non-Christian countries than in Christian ones, the writer concluded that the missionary enterprise was fundamentally misguided. At the same time, there were clear limits to this ecumenical vision, for by assimilating what was good in the "great religions of the East," this reformed Christianity was to become a truly universal religion.[61]

The construction of Christianity as a preeminently womanly religion, and of women and womanly virtues as spiritually superior, could also work in concert with imperialist and racist values to locate true spirituality in the West and to portray western women as the pinnacle of both physical and spiritual evolution. This position found its most influential voice in the work of Frances Swiney. Born into a military family in India in 1847, Swiney was married to a major-general in 1871 and had six children. She was actively involved in the suffrage movement in the 1890s, was president of the Cheltenham Branch of the National Union of Women's Suffrage Societies, and became a member of the militant Women's Social and Political Union.[62] In 1899 Swiney published *The Awakening of Women, or Woman's Part in Evolution,* which received enthusiastic reviews in many feminist publications, including *Shafts.* Sibthorpe described it as the finest book on the subject in almost forty years. She thought it a "clever book" and "unhesitatingly recommend[ed] its perusal."[63] *The Theosophical Review* was less impressed. A scathing review by Bertram Keightley condemned the book as "ill-balanced and injudicious," "imperfect and unripe," and the product of reading that was "more extensive than thorough." Keightley feared that a "great and good cause" had been irretrievably damaged, if not ruined, by Swiney's advocacy.[64]

More recent characterizations of Swiney's work have been equally divided. According to Sheila Jeffreys, "there is no doubt as to the strength of Swiney's feminism. She wrote of women's oppression with passionate rage." Antoinette Burton, in contrast, describes *The Awakening of Women* as "perhaps the most unabashed elaboration of racial feminism in the late Victorian period." Burton argues that the core of Swiney's work was a racial evolutionary model that placed "enslaved Eastern womanhood" at one end and Anglo-Saxon women at the other.[65] Both positions oversimplify Swiney's claims: to understand how and why Swiney's feminism and her racism were connected, it is necessary to explore more fully the explicitly spiritual dimensions of her thought.

However disturbing and eccentric Swiney's works appear today, there was a substantial audience for such writings at the turn of the twentieth century. *The Awakening of Women,* for example, went into three editions, was revised and enlarged over the next ten years, and was translated into Dutch by Martina G. Kramers, at one time secretary to the Dutch National Council of Women, soon after it appeared in English.[66] *The Awakening of Women* introduced all the themes that Swiney elaborated over the next twenty years, undeterred by criticism or incredulity. She characterized motherhood as women's supreme achievement and denigrated the "male element" as a "waste product of Nature." She celebrated the Anglo-Saxon "race," and Anglo-Saxon womanhood in particular, as the pinnacle of evolution; a concern with racial purity dominates the work. Swiney also valorized Christianity as the creed that had done the most to rehabilitate women as equal in "dignity and perfection" to men, making explicit links between women and Christianity's "Law of Love." And she castigated Hinduism as the cause of the "degradation" of Indian womanhood.[67]

Much of the criticism of her work came from theosophists, and Swiney became increasingly adamant that it was theosophy's masculine bias that had led the TS astray. Her relationship to the society was, therefore, always a troubled one. She occasionally lectured to TS lodges, relied heavily on theosophical texts, and borrowed much of her vocabulary from theosophical writings. But she broke definitively with the TS over the question of the ultimate goals of spiritual and racial evolution: where most theosophists posited, at least over the very long term, an androgynous ideal, the Divine Hermaphrodite, Swiney uncompromisingly proclaimed the "Divine Feminine." The masculine was only a temporary and transitional phase between the Eternal Feminine Cause and the Eternal Feminine Effect.[68] For Swiney, there was only one sex, the feminine: men were simply imperfect women, physiologically and spiritually. Under optimum conditions, she claimed, women would reproduce themselves parthenogenetically; the birth of imperfect and partly formed male children was a symptom of racial degeneration.[69] Spiritually as well, there was only one sex. All souls, which were essentially feminine, had to progress first through the masculine, or more material, phase, "the kindergarten of humanity," before embarking on their higher, more spiritual, feminine phase of existence.[70]

Drawing on the biological theories of Patrick Geddes and J. Arthur Thompson, whose *Evolution of Sex* (1889) had argued for sexual difference at the cellular level, Swiney argued that men embodied the katabolic, or destructive, principle, while women embodied the anabolic, or creative, principle.[71] Women's reproductive organs were, for Swiney, a finite approximation of the infinite creative power of the divine, the Eternal Feminine Principle.[72] Swiney's writings thus brought the authority of both science and spirituality to bear in order to valorize an essentialized femininity. In later writings, such as her 1918 book *The Ancient Road,* Swiney argued more explicitly that as the soul made her transition to the higher feminine phase, she had to sacrifice all her most cherished masculine achievements: "This is the feminine phase of the soul, in which the intellect, her dearest and most valued possession, is placed a living sacrifice on the altar of her heart, and she finds her great reward." Swiney was adamant about the need to root out any taint of lower, masculine behavior in women. Many of the leading women in the suffrage movement, "pioneers in feminine emancipation" though they were, appeared more masculine than feminine in their ideals and methods. Those women, she claimed, were relatively young souls that had only just emerged from the masculine phase and were the despair of their "more evolved [that is, more feminine] sisters."[73]

In developing these claims, Swiney drew on a wide range of sources, from biology and sociology to kabbalistic Judaism to Vedanta. Crucial to her arguments were Gnostic Christianity and Egyptology. By the mid-nineteenth century Egypt had been claimed by archaeologists and Egyptologists as a "white" civilization, and this may have made it attractive to Swiney.[74] Both Gnosticism and Egyptian mysticism, she suggested, represented a "sublime feminism," which a degenerate West neglected at its peril. Both had influenced early Christianity, which she described as "feminine" in character. It was from Gnosticism, mediated through Mead's translation of the *Pistis Sophia,* that Swiney derived her understanding of both karma and reincarnation.[75] In her reinterpretation of Christianity, Christ became a female figure, a highly evolved woman who voluntarily sacrificed herself in love "for the race," taking on the lower male form in order to point the evolutionary way forward. At the Second Coming Christ would appear in her true form, a female messiah, the divine daughter who would complete the work begun by the "Son" of God.[76]

The eugenic impulse in Swiney's work was intimately connected to her spiritual vision. In 1904 she joined the Women's Branch of the Malthusian League, which by this time was firmly committed to both feminism and eugenics. Swiney claimed that the work of the Women's Branch was "the greatest reform of the time"; in exchange, the league's journal, *The Malthusian,* began (with some reservations) to reprint her articles and review her books.[77] Since, according to Swiney, the female reproductive organs were an occult link to the Divine Feminine Principle, women, and only women, were responsible for evolution; the female was the "reproducer and evolver of species." The fitness of each individual mother determined the extent to which the child would approximate spiritual and physical perfection. Without "sound brain fibre" there could be no "higher psychic growth": "when a child falls below the mark, it is the embodiment of the mother's own deficiency in metabolism and consciousness. . . . The soul is thus in its cosmic progression . . . let and hindered by the barriers, often artificial and abnormal, of maternal limitation."[78] Among the "artificial and abnormal" barriers to the soul's progression, Swiney identified a range of "racial poisons," from nicotine and alcohol to venereal disease and even sperm (which, she believed, possessed some power for good in moderation, but in excess was a "virulent poison").[79]

Even more important was what Swiney called the "Law of the Mother"—women's abstinence from sexual relations during gestation and lactation. Through the denial of this law, a male-dominated modern civilization had produced "nothing but evil and putrifying [sic] sores." The alarming rise in the incidence of "epilepsy, insanity, idiocy, and congenital diseases" throughout the civilized world could only be halted by the "return to the natural law governing reproduction."[80] Maternal abstinence, the elimination of "racial poisons," and an improvement in the economic conditions of mothers would produce a redeemed and sanctified motherhood. The result would be the gradual elimination of male births (the result of maternal weakness) and the eventual elimination of the male form, which was "the weak link in the evolutionary process."[81] In Swiney's utopia women, having done their part in the physical evolution of the race, would devote themselves to the real business of divine maternity, the production of "thought-children."[82]

What appears in retrospect as a profoundly dystopic vision was mobilized in support of a perverse kind of socialist-feminism. All the world's ills could be linked directly to male supremacy and the abuse of male power. The "first signs of male supremacy" had been "the degraded sister and the enslaved brother; the accumulation of property in the hands of one to the detriment of the others; the exploitation of the many for the gain of the few; the interests of the majority made subordinate to the caprice and gratification of an autocrat." The feminine phase, the truly human phase, would be a democratic, socialist, and communistic society.[83] To the extent that this claim functioned as a critique of a masculine, materialist, capitalist civilization, it could gain considerable currency even among radical and democratic suffragists. Swiney's criticism of both modern Christianity and modern civilization as evil and therefore rotten to the point of putrefaction also served, though in limited ways, to undermine the orthodox Christian "civilizing mission."

Swiney believed that every soul had to pass through the masculine before it entered the higher feminine phase, and her spiritual eugenics was also used to argue for a racist version of global feminism. Those women she saw as most degraded were simply working out the karma forged in their male incarnations. The prostitute was the "fearful nemesis" of the impure man, a "victim of men's lust" because, in an earlier male life, she had sought "the death of his own soul's development" in the brothel. Men's arrogance, despotism, and injustice had to be expiated when they reached the higher feminine: "The tyrant comes on to the woman plane the handmaiden of humanity, the slave and the chattel, the despised and the down-trodden, without political status, without civic rights, without even the rights of personality or individual recognition."[84] The world was now passing out of the masculine phase, and "the woman," the "true human," was now evolving in "the various races of mankind," despite the "corruption, the degradation, and the inefficiency that now exist, and have nearly obliterated the type."[85] There were rare English men who might appear advanced, racially and spiritually, but these men were merely nearing their last male incarnation; all women, whatever their race or class position, were, in terms of their soul's evolutionary journey, nearer to the divine than any man. These were, however, disturbing grounds on which to build a feminist internationalism.

One of the elements that made Swiney's work so appealing was her fervent commitment to sexual purity, her attack on the sexual double standard and male sexual license. Most feminist activists agreed that men's sexual behavior required reform. A few isolated voices defended women's right to sexual pleasure. Some, like Annie Besant before she joined the Theosophical Society, publicly defended the use of birth control; others, even more isolated, advocated "free love." But large numbers of women argued that men should be brought up to meet women's standard of chastity or that they should be taught to emulate women's sexual self-control. For much of the nineteenth century, the "serious Christianity" of Evangelicalism had provided a powerful set of arguments in support of those claims. In the second half of the century, however, Evangelicalism's political purchase had declined, and medical science in contrast threw its weight behind the sexual double standard, defending the regulation of prostitution on the grounds that it met an ineradicable male need. Even middle-class women's vaunted "superior" sexual morality began to be called into question during this period, as some authorities began to characterize celibacy, including female celibacy, as an inherently pathological condition, one that posed a risk to women's mental and physical health.[86]

Swiney defended women's sexual purity in language that seemed simultaneously spiritual and scientific. Her emphasis on the "Law of the Mother" met an important need at a time when marital rape was not recognized as a crime and was rarely criticized in public even by feminists. Swiney's admirer Elizabeth Wolstenholme Elmy had long been an activist on this issue, and her Women's Emancipation Union was the only feminist organization explicitly to address the issue of rape in marriage. Wolstenholme Elmy's enthusiastic support for Swiney's work (she wrote a glowing review of *The Awakening of Women* in *Westminster Review*) testifies to the gap in public discussion of the subject.[87]

Swiney's unabashed glorification of motherhood, her embrace of what we might call "femininism" rather than feminism, and her outspoken racial theories limited her appeal. Single women—unless they wished to identify themselves as potential, psychic, or spiritual "mothers"—were relatively marginalized in Swiney's writings. Many women were not yet ready to sacrifice their hard-won "masculine" qualities of intellect, self-assertion, or autonomy on the altar of the Eternal Feminine. For those women who were searching for a creed that was both scientific and spiritual, and that promised a greater openness to non-Christian and nonwestern beliefs, the Theosophical Society remained an attractive option. Many theosophists seemed open to the effort to blur the lines between the masculine and the feminine, and they too were uncompromising in their defense of celibacy for both men and women.

In the 1880s and 1890s men within the TS had spoken out clearly and forcefully against dominant notions of male sexuality, indicating that some men at least shared the ambivalence toward heterosexual sex that seems characteristic of much of the social-purity movement. Mead described man as a "human soul attached to a beast" and argued that while the sex function was not "unnatural," it was "natural to the animal; natural to man, while the animal predominates—but no longer."[88] The animal in man was to be tamed, made subservient to man's higher desires. Celibacy was not a theosophical dogma, but many theosophists did advocate abstinence from sexual relations, within marriage as well as outside it.

Theosophists encouraged celibacy because, as noted earlier, for those who wished to make significant occult progress, total abstinence from sexual relations was crucial. According to G. V. K., for example, writing in *The Theosophist* in 1896, the "sperm-cell" was virtually identical to the "nerve-cell," a resource crucial to the development of higher psychical and spiritual powers. Along with regular bowel movements, a vegetarian diet, abstinence from alcohol and tobacco, and open-air exercise, G. V. K. hinted at techniques that could purify and transmute sexual energies into higher and nobler forms.[89] Most of these teachings assumed a male audience: the focus was on male sexual energy and male "sexual fluids," and by implication masculine self-control and will-power were what permitted the aspirant to transmute sexual desire into spiritual power.[90] While these teachings could provide useful resources for the reform of men's sexual behavior, they did not necessarily apply to women; it was often assumed that the female body acted as a drag on spiritual and psychic development and that significant occult progress was only possible during a male incarnation.

Some women who were drawn to theosophy because of its masculine associations did find ways to turn these teachings into a defense of female chastity as well. Kate Mills, for example, was a social worker who was closely associated with Karl Pearson's Men and Women's Club in the mid-1880s. Pearson's club was founded to provide a forum for the "objective" and "scientific" discussion of the relations between the sexes, and in the club's discussions Mills was a strong advocate of chastity for both men and women, at least outside marriage. Mills married the theosophist Arthur Cobbald and joined the TS in 1891.[91] Henrietta Müller, another outspoken defender of chastity for both men and women in Pearson's club, also joined the TS during this period. The association between theosophy and a feminist defense of celibacy was important, but it should not be overdrawn. Dora Montefiore, no advocate of celibacy for women, was a member of the TS for most of the 1890s. Montefiore's extramarital relationship with the Independent Labour Party organizer George Belt caused a scandal in socialist and feminist circles in the late 1890s; in private letters at least, Montefiore defended women's right to question conventional sexual morality.[92] Edith Lanchester, who in 1895 would take the dramatic step of entering a "free union" with a fellow socialist, joined the TS in 1892. Although Lanchester resigned from the TS during the Judge crisis in 1894, she retained an interest in esoteric religion and the alternative practices of vegetarianism and the simple life.[93] The most outspoken defense of free love in this period was offered by the Legitimation League in its periodical, *The Adult: The Journal of Sex*. Although *The Adult* burlesqued the theosophists' defense of celibacy on at least one occasion, it often dealt with occult themes. And when *The Adult* launched its Free Press Defense Committee in 1898, the theosophists Charlotte Despard and Herbert Burrows joined Edith Lanchester on the committee.[94]

Theosophy clearly catered to a diverse political constituency. Henrietta Müller appears to have been drawn to the TS precisely because she believed theosophy made no distinctions between men and women, and because it taught that women were as capable as men of exercising the masculine virtues. Müller was clearly an exceptional woman by late Victorian standards. Born in the early 1850s into a relatively well-off family, in 1873 she became one of the first group of women to attend Girton College, Cambridge. She served on the London School Board for Lambeth from 1879, and founded the Society for the Return of Women as Poor Law Guardians. In the mid-1880s she was a member of Pearson's club—the only female member with a university education. In 1888 she founded the feminist weekly, *The Women's Penny Paper*, under the pseudonym Helena B. Temple. The publication boasted that it was "the only paper in the world conducted, written, printed and published by women."[95]

Müller joined the Theosophical Society in June 1891. Before joining she wrote to Mme. Blavatsky and put the question bluntly: "Do women in the Theosophical Society enjoy equal rights, the whole way along the line, with men, or do they not?" Blavatsky's answer, she recounted later, was that the TS made no distinction of sex: what counted was the work to be done, not whether it was done by a man or a woman. Blavatsky also assured her that women as well as men could aspire to the position of Adepts or Mahatmas, and that examples of such women could be found in India and Tibet up to the present day.[96]

Müller's tendency to take an independent line quickly brought her into conflict with prominent theosophists: in what appears to have been her debut lecture within the TS, in October 1891, her analysis of women and theosophy was disputed by theosophical luminaries like Besant and Mead.[97] But the TS did provide Müller with an opportunity to make further contacts not only with Indian women, but with women in Japan and Sri Lanka as well. (Müller's *Women's Penny Paper* had been remarkable among contemporary feminist publications for its attention to the concerns of Indian women and the extent to which it provided at least some Indian women with an opportunity to speak for themselves, through interviews and excerpts from their writings.)[98] Soon after joining the TS, Müller began making plans to accompany Besant on her next tour of India and to make contact with Japanese and Sinhalese women who were working "for the elevation of their sex."[99] In 1895 she initiated legal proceedings to adopt a young Bengali man, Akshaya Kumar Ghose, as her son and planned to use her "ample fortune" to have him educated for the Bar. She hoped that he would eventually enter Parliament and devote his life to social and political reform in India. While the Anglo-Indian papers made scandalous capital out of her supposedly inappropriate public displays of affection for her adult Indian "son," her defenders pointed out that "those who have enjoyed the privilege of intimate friendship with her, need no editorial assurances to convince them of the purity and unselfishness of her motives, however eccentric her actions might at any time appear."[100]

Müller left the TS in 1895, disillusioned over the Judge crisis. Karl Pearson, who encountered her shortly after she resigned from the society, pronounced her "much sobered" and was relieved to discover that the "'occult' sciences . . . have absorbed all her crankiness."[101] From theosophy, Müller turned to Vivekananda's Ramakrishna movement, and then—convinced that the Swami's followers were insufficiently ascetic and that Hinduism was after all irredeemably corrupted by "phallic worship"—to an eccentric version of Christianity.[102] When Müller died in Washington in 1906, the London *Times* noted that for some years she had lived "as a native among the natives in the hills [in India], and she was able to secure in some degree better treatment for the women."[103] During her travels in India, Müller had for the most part avoided Anglo-Indian society, and Indian theosophists may have assisted her in making contacts there. The TS thus offered Müller a range of opportunities: an egalitarian spirituality, contacts with women and reform-minded activists in India and throughout Asia, a sympathetic hearing for her social-purity concerns, the promise of occult techniques for spiritual advancement, and an intellectual and scientific approach to religion.

Debates over the content and implications of a feminist spirituality could reinforce divisions among women and between women and men, but they could also generate new solidarities. The different notions of womanhood that underpinned women's spirituality—women as mothers, as sexually pure, as Christian, as "white," as similar to or different from men—each facilitated different kinds of inclusions and exclusions. The Theosophical Society's version of the ancient wisdom of the East could be mobilized, as it was in Müller's case, to reinforce alliances between Hindu reformers and British feminists. At the same time, the peculiarly "manly" character of the TS in Britain and in India militated against the creation of meaningful alliances between English and Indian women. The theosophical ideal of the Divine Hermaphrodite, along with the gentleman's club culture of the TS in England, could exercise a significant appeal to women whose feminism included a commitment to blurring the lines between the masculine and the feminine. But participation in the theosophical movement also meant that women had to be willing to accommodate to an agenda set by men and organized around masculine values.

The effort to rehabilitate Christianity—the emphasis on a feminine Christ, on the feminine qualities of love and self-sacrifice that were believed to be at the heart of a true Christianity—was also limited in important ways. In the 1880s and 1890s a gendered dichotomy between Love and Wisdom, the heart and the head, became central to advanced understandings of the contrasts between Christianity, on the one hand, and Hinduism and Buddhism on the other. It is possible to detect in these debates a reinforcement of the orientalist construction of the dichotomy between West and East, a crucial resource in the construction of Asian religions as peculiarly male-dominated and therefore exceptionally degrading to women. At the same time, esoteric Christianity, with its focus on the phallicism and misogyny of contemporary Christianity, could also serve to undermine Christianity's privileged position as superior to other world religions and open up new possibilities for feminist alliances across religious barriers.

Chapter Seven

A New Age for Women
Suffrage and the Sacred

Clara Codd was the eldest of ten girls, the daughter of an inspector of schools. After her father died, she worked as a teacher and governess to help her mother support the family. While teaching in Bath, where she was a member of the local lodge of the Theosophical Society, she joined the Social Democratic Federation, although she was disillusioned by its hostility to the "spiritual side" of socialism. When Annie Kenney and Christabel Pankhurst of the Women's Social and Political Union (WSPU) came to Bath on a speaking tour, Codd was asked to help steward the meeting. After the meeting she resigned her post as a governess to work as an unofficial WSPU organizer. A dedicated militant, Codd lectured for the WSPU and spent a month in Holloway women's prison for her suffrage activities. After her release from prison, she was offered a full-time post as an organizer for the WSPU. An inner voice, however, warned her that this was not the path she should take, and she resigned from the WSPU to devote herself to the Theosophical Society.[1]

As a result, Codd has disappeared from histories of the suffrage movement. But she herself did not see her decision to resign from the WSPU as an abandonment of feminism; her work as national lecturer to the TS, no less than her work for the WSPU, was work in the "sacred cause" of "service to humanity."[2] The goals she had pursued within the WSPU continued to inform her theosophical writing and lecturing. As she put it in a lecture to the American Theosophical Society, "there is no subject in the world which Theosophy does not illuminate, and we all know very well that the subject of the sexes is one on which the world stands in crying need of illumination." Sexual difference was a reflection of the great truths "right at the root of the universe." Both the feminine and the masculine principles had a role to play—a notion she believed had been preserved in the Hindu belief in the "Shakti," or feminine power of the deity. She continued to rehearse the arguments about women's spirituality that had echoed through her suffrage propaganda: the importance of women's intuition, women's function as the

Septimus E. Scott, "The Dawn," *Bibby's Annual, 1917.*
(*Author's collection*)

"channel of the Divine mercy and understanding," women's "service and silent self-sacrifice."[3] In 1918 she linked women's struggle for freedom with the emergence of the New Age: "The advance of the new era is showing in as equally a marked a fashion in the outer world of men's obligations and relationships to each other as in the inner world of the religious consciousness. The one is indeed the outcome of the other, for to draw nearer to reality within is also to perceive it more clearly without."[4]

Codd's withdrawal from feminist politics narrowly defined was not a withdrawal from the feminist community. The Bath Lodge was one of the most actively feminist of TS lodges; Codd also maintained close links with the WSPU leadership, and especially with Annie Kenney. In

1912 Kenney joined Codd in the Theosophical Society. A year later Flora Drummond of the WSPU also joined the TS. Kenney resigned from the TS in 1914—as she told Codd while the suffrage struggle was at its height, she had "no time for the Masters now"[5]—but she rejoined the society in 1920. A few months later Kenney and Codd jointly sponsored Grace Roe (one of the chief organizers of the WSPU, along with Kenney and Drummond) and Kenney's sister Jessie as members of the TS.[6]

The secular and spiritual modes of Codd's feminism overlapped in significant ways. Even to draw the distinction between secular and spiritual here may be anachronistic. For women like Codd, feminism was not a primarily secular activity. There were, of course, many women for whom feminism was a secularizing project, and for whom the rejection of religion was a part of their own personal and political transformation. And there were others whose religious faith was nominal or was understood as a personal and private matter rather than as a political resource. But for a significant number of women, and particularly for women in the militant wing of the suffrage movement, spirituality was a constitutive element in their feminist politics. Martha Vicinus argues that it is possible to trace in the activities and ideological statements of the WSPU and other suffrage organizations "a conscious effort . . . to forge a new spirituality, based upon women's traditional idealism and self-sacrifice but intended to reach out and transform not only the position of women in society, but that very society itself."[7] Many feminist writings are best read as a kind of political theology, in which women's oppression was construed as a symbol and symptom of a larger problem, one of cosmic dimensions: the subjection of the spiritual to the material in Edwardian culture. "Disenfranchised womanhood" came to stand, metonymically, for the disenfranchisement of spirituality in a secular, capitalist, materialist, and male-dominated culture. In turn, the admission of women (the more "spiritual" half of humanity) into public life was to be a first step toward the literal redemption of the nation.

The TS was a crucial nexus in this broader project. First, it had an active feminist constituency, and many members dedicated significant time and resources to feminist activities within the society. Second, and more important from the perspective of the history of feminism, was theosophy's indirect influence. One way to illustrate this is to explore how themes developed within the TS were taken up, reworked, and disputed outside the society. To that end, this chapter explores the lives and writings of a disparate group of women who, unlike Codd, were more prominent outside of the TS than within it. Charlotte Despard, Eva Gore-Booth, Dora Marsden, and Gertrude Colmore all used esoteric themes to elaborate a feminist theology. These women represented a range of feminist organizations, and each had different political affiliations and priorities. Despard and Colmore were both deeply committed to the TS; Gore-Booth and Marsden are better understood as Christian esotericists. Each of their political theologies acquired its distinctive features through specific conjunctions between the resources of the esoteric tradition and a changing political context. Together, they provide some indication of the multiple points at which occult and esoteric circles intersected with different elements within the feminist community.

All these women shared the belief that the suffrage movement was in reality a spiritual crusade rather than a primarily political struggle. Paying close attention to the categories they employed, we can see that these categories blur the distinctions between secular and sacred in ways that are often unfamiliar and unexpected. At the same time, the disagreements among these four women tended to revolve around some common axes that are still relevant to contemporary political debates: there were disagreements over the question of women's likeness to men (sameness or difference), over political goals (democracy or hierarchy), over the location of spiritual authority (East or West), and over the subject of political action (individual or collective).

Many of these debates were closely connected to discussions that were taking place within the TS in the early years of the twentieth century. In the 1890s feminist versions of spirituality within the TS had been formulated from a position of relative weakness, constrained by associations that linked Asian religions to masculinity and Christianity to femininity. By 1907 the situation had changed dramatically. On the broader political front, the emergence of the WSPU had put women's suffrage at the forefront of public debate; from all points on the political spectrum an increasingly vocal women's suffrage movement was very much in evidence during the first decades of the twentieth century. Within the TS women's numerical dominance had been accompanied by an attempt to feminize theosophical theory and practice: the spiritual phase of the society's existence, in which love, intuition, emotion, and devotion were increasingly valued, was well under way. There was now much more scope for a feminist celebration of women's difference from men; it seemed increasingly possible to articulate difference without necessarily reinscribing inequality. The egalitarian arguments that had been developed in the 1890s did not disappear, inside or outside the TS. But as what historians describe as maternalist feminism found more favor within the women's movement more broadly, the emphasis on sexual difference, the "dual humanity," acquired new prominence within the TS as well.[8]

As the women's suffrage movement gained momentum, feminists within the TS began to undertake their own initiatives. Mrs. K. E. Roy-Rothwell, for example, proposed the formation of an International Woman's Suffrage League under the auspices of the Theosophical Order of Service. Roy-Rothwell suggested collective meditation on a "definite formula" that could, at stated times, be sent as a thought-form in the direction of the Houses of Parliament.[9] The league never materialized, but less than a year later a League to Help the Woman's Movement was formed at TS headquarters, under the chairmanship of Harold Baillie-Weaver. Regular meetings for meditation and discussion were held "to draw together all those interested in the Women's Suffrage Cause who realise the importance of meditation and right thinking as a force behind this movement."[10] The league's organizers were careful to maintain strict neutrality on the question of tactics and avoided any activities that could be interpreted as a criticism of or infringement on the work of more mundane suffrage societies. Their most practical effort was an attempt to organize a public protest over the forcible feeding of hunger-striking suffragette prisoners—drawing attention not only to the moral, physical, and mental effects of the procedure, but also to its karmic effects on both men and women.[11]

The league also participated in the national Call to Prayer organized by several mainstream religious suffrage societies for the first week in November 1913. The organizers of the Call to Prayer urged all the suffrage societies to arrange at least one meeting to emphasize the spiritual aspects of the women's movement. The theosophical League to Help the Woman's Movement was similar to groups like the Anglican Church League for Woman's Suffrage (CLWS), founded in 1909. Members of the CLWS stressed "the deep religious significance of the women's movement" and held special eucharistic celebrations for suffragists and meetings to discuss the spiritual dimensions of the women's cause. According to the bishop of Kensington, a member of the CLWS, the extension of the suffrage would enable women to bring an explicitly spiritual force to bear upon political life, for women represented the "most hopeful and fruitful of all influences in national life."[12] Some of these initiatives may seem, in retrospect, of dubious political value. But those women and men who believed in the power of prayer, meditation, and right thinking could also believe that they were in the vanguard of an intensely political battle. From their viewpoint, the creation of an appropriate spiritual context for political change appeared to be as crucial as the lobbying of politicians. The Spiritual Militancy League, a nonde-nominational wing of the Women's Freedom League, was formed for the same reasons, encouraging its members to attend church services in order to harness spiritual forces for the women's cause.[13]

In theosophical debates, arguments based on the claim that "human-ity is dual," which emphasized sexual difference and women's special excellence, became increasingly common. Blavatsky's analysis of the masculine and feminine principles at the cosmic level was taken up as a key element of feminist arguments. In an apparently paradoxical move, theosophists and their sympathizers began to claim that men and women were so different precisely because, in essence, they were only different aspects of the same thing. While this claim could underwrite conservative understandings of sexual difference, it could also open up opportunities to destabilize that difference.

So, for example, an anonymous writer quoted *Harmsworth's Popu-lar Science* on the "mystery of sex," an article that summarized the Dar-winian claim that the goal of evolutionary progress was an increase in the differences between the male and female of the species. The theo-sophical writer used this to argue that Darwin had substantiated the occultists' claims: "If these conclusions of science are true of the *out-ward,* how much more so are they of the true *soul nature* in its *differen-tiated* divine principles—*dual* in expression—*One in Unity!*"[14] Invok-ing a spiritual-evolutionary vision of racial hierarchy, this analysis portrayed the English suffrage movement as the culmination of the progress of the "race." It also linked men's interests, racially and spiritu-ally, to the cause of women's enfranchisement, even while underscoring the essential differences between men and women. The result was to give both scientific and spiritual weight to the claim that the women's movement was a movement on behalf of all humanity.

Embedded in this way of thinking about relationships between the sexes was a range of political possibilities. Even with their new empha-sis on duality, however, feminist theosophists continued to stress the potential of both the individual and the race to transcend sexual dif-ference altogether. The theosophist Florence Wyman Richardson ex-plained the implications of the idea of unity as follows: "The magnet has two poles, positive and negative. They are opposite ends of the same thing, and by the complementary use of both we get their com-mon force—magnetism. . . . Only in their perfect equality can they demonstrate the power." The "two poles" of sexual difference—an "ac-tive, initiative, positive, masculine principle, expressing itself in strength and intellect" and "the passive, receptive, negative feminine principle, expressing itself in gentleness and affection"—might seem to confirm the most conservative notions of separate spheres. But Richardson went on to argue that just as each fragment of a magnet contains both a positive and a negative pole, so each individual contained both the masculine and the feminine principle, one expressed and one latent. Through the evolutionary process, which was also a spiritual process, individuals would come to embody both masculine and feminine, to take on "the true image and likeness of God, the divine prototype, the Father-Mother." This was the "inner meaning, the esotericism of the Woman's Movement." The suffrage movement was "the surface ripple of a great race undercurrent, the primal force feminine, pushing and forcing its way to the surface, to take its turn in the objective life of the race."[15] Virtually all the themes theosophists were to exploit politically are present here: the simultaneous emphasis on both the sameness and difference of the sexes, the integration of science and spirituality into a religio-eugenic vision, the refiguring of the divine as "Father-Mother," the power of the Divine Feminine, and the gesture toward a more spiritual New Age in which women would play their proper role in the "objective life of the race."

On both the macro- and the microcosmic level, the gendered division of labor was the basis of all development. The "sex nature in us," Clara Codd wrote, was thus a symbol of and "in connection with, the greatest spiritual verities of the universe." Sexual difference symbolized "that primal hour in the dawn of our universe when the one became two."[16] The masculine and feminine principles could be found at work everywhere, even at the atomic level, where the "ultimate physical atoms" were classified as male (positive and centripetal) and female (negative and centrifugal).[17] Everything from the origins of the cosmos to the smallest atoms was saturated with sexual difference and revealed the need for balance between the masculine and the feminine.

The clear distinction between the masculine and feminine principles was complicated by the diversity of human experience, as Henry Selby Green pointed out: "In real life we do not find men and women showing clear-cut distinctions of type. . . . A man will often show in a very marked degree mental qualities generally regarded as characteristic of a woman; and on the other hand, a woman will show those of a man."[18] According to Annie Besant, humanity was only roughly separated into two sexes: in every individual "one sex predominates and the other is rudimentary." All men and women were, at least potentially, both masculine and feminine.[19] Some theosophists interpreted this teaching as a spiritual injunction to develop the latent side of their personality as much as possible, drawing on the accumulated experience of previous incarnations. For example, James Cousins, the husband of the Irish suffragette Margaret Cousins, described his wife as "the individual who was destined to broaden me into real manhood by stimulating in me the reactions of latent womanhood, and [I was to do her] a complementary service." Cousins was "awake to the presence of a considerable admixture of feminine receptiveness and creativeness in my own make-up, and aware of a certain touch of masculine power and initiative in hers that, when I first saw her masculine handwriting, made me brace myself for adventure."[20]

As Isabelle M. Pagan put it in 1908, "It is well to remember that the fully developed human being is not obtrusively man or woman, but has, in perfection, the finest qualities of both; feminine tenderness, sympathy and adaptability, with masculine strength, endurance and concentration."[21] Edith Ward made a similar argument: "the life of the spirit—which is Unity—must tend in its outpouring to draw men and women together, not to separate them: the perfected humanity must needs be the blending of that which is best in both man and woman and—'in the long years liker must they grow. / The man be more of woman, she of man.'"[22] The ultimate goal was a spiritual androgyny which embodied the best of both male and female qualities.

Theosophical teaching, therefore, could be used to authorize a range of feminist positions. In some cases, however, a commitment to theosophy could lead women to a retreat, not just from organized feminism but from public life altogether. Esther Bright is a case in point. Bright came from a wealthy Quaker family with an impressive feminist record. Her father Jacob was Member of Parliament for Manchester and a consistent supporter of women's rights. He was responsible for the introduction of a Married Women's Property Bill in Parliament in 1869, and in 1870 he introduced the first bill aimed at giving women the parliamentary franchise. Bright's mother Ursula was an early supporter of the campaign to repeal the Contagious Diseases Acts, a prominent figure in the fight for a Married Women's Property Act, and a prime mover in the Women's Franchise League in the 1890s.[23] Living in a household where the American suffragists Elizabeth Cady Stanton and Susan B. Anthony were regular visitors, Esther Bright dreamed of growing up to "fight for a great cause, under a trusted leader, with good comrades at my side."[24] That cause might have been feminism, but instead Bright found her cause in theosophy, and her leader in Annie Besant. In 1893 she joined the Theosophical Society's Esoteric Section and in 1907 she became the secretary of the ES.[25] As one of the leading figures in the ES, Bright exercised enormous influence within the Theosophical Society, yet her activities left virtually no trace in the public record. Whatever feminist activities might have taken place within the intensely privatized world of the ES, they are no longer accessible to the historian.

Other women carried theosophical teaching into a more public realm. The most prominent public exponent of a theosophical feminism during the suffrage years was Charlotte Despard, the president of the Women's Freedom League, which broke away from the WSPU in 1907 in reaction to the Pankhursts' increasingly autocratic leadership. Despard was famous by turns as a romantic novelist, a socialist, a feminist, a pacifist, an Irish nationalist, and a communist. She was born into a well-off, landed family. She married Maximilian Despard, an Anglo-Irish shipping agent with Liberal and Radical sympathies, who had made his fortune in Hong Kong. Despard was well connected, by birth and marriage, to the British establishment. Her brother John French was the field marshal in command of the British Expeditionary Forces in France during the Great War, and the last Lord-Lieutenant of Ireland. A comparison between his life and his sister's indicates the political distance Despard traveled over her lifetime.[26]

Max Despard died in 1890, when Charlotte Despard was forty-six. Soon afterward she opened the first of a series of Despard Clubs (a free clinic and community center) in Nine Elms, Battersea, which Charles Booth's survey of London poverty marked as one of the poorest areas in the city.[27] Despard was elected to the Lambeth Board of Guardians, and joined both the Social Democratic Federation and the Independent Labour Party. She also began to recognize from practical experience the limits that political disenfranchisement placed on the abilities of both women and workers to achieve substantive social and economic reforms.[28] By 1906 Despard was a member of both the Adult Suffrage Society and the WSPU.

Alongside these political involvements, Despard had also undergone a series of spiritual conversions. Her most constant spiritual and political inspiration came from the romantic poetry of Percy Bysshe Shelley, to which she later attributed everything from her passion for social justice and her feminism to her vegetarianism and her belief in reincarnation.[29] During her marriage she followed her husband into a rationalist agnosticism, rejecting Anglicanism and Presbyterianism (both significant influences during her childhood) as harsh and narrow. In India with Max in the 1880s she encountered both Buddhist and Hindu thought, and was particularly drawn to the teaching of reincarnation. Soon after her husband's death, she converted to Roman Catholicism, the religion of many of the working-class Irish women in Nine Elms, and less than a decade later, in 1899, she joined the TS.[30] Membership in the TS allowed Despard to integrate her interest in Buddhism and Hinduism with her commitment to Catholicism, especially after the formation of the theosophical Liberal Catholic Church, in which she became a devout and regular communicant.[31]

Despard's fascination with India predated her association with the TS. Her most successful novel, *The Rajah's Heir* (1890), was set against the backdrop of unrest in India in 1857. The novel traces the adventures of a young Englishman who has the soul of "an old Indian Rajah." Despard represented the young Englishman as an embodiment of the best qualities of East and West. The novel's heroine died tragically; as she expired, she repeated the prophecy she had been given by the Hindu priest Vishnugupta: "They are expecting another revealer. He will be different from any who have gone before him, for the sphere will be larger. New lights have been dawning upon the nations, and new truths, forced painfully from the silence by the higher minds, are waiting to be shown to the people. He will know all this. He will be of the West by his training, of the East by his nature. He will have the science and learning of the New World, and the self-forgetting passion of the Old."[32] In *The Rajah's Heir* Despard sketched out many of the themes she was to embrace in theosophy: the romantic vision of a mystic East that could redeem the West, the promise of a New Age, the coming of a new "revealer," and the utopian vision of spiritual revolution.

Members of the TS also provided concrete and practical assistance for many of Despard's reform initiatives. Participants at a theosophical summer school helped her raise funds for striking women workers; theosophists donated furniture and kitchen utensils to the Despard Arms, an experimental teetotal public house established in North London during the war; and the TS lodge in Bath began raising funds to start a local Despard Arms to continue her work.[33] Despard's suffrage novel *Outlawed,* published in 1908, was coauthored with the one-time theosophist Mabel Collins, who also adapted the novel for the stage.[34]

Despard's feminism was as much spiritual as it was political or economic. In the collection of articles published in 1907 by leading figures in the suffrage movement, *The Case for Women's Suffrage,* Despard's article was the one that most consistently and thoroughly grounded women's political claims in a spiritual context. Her article opened with an invocation of the "great woman-principle" in ancient cosmogonies: "the mysterious Isis of Egypt, Athene-Pallas of Greece, Juno of Rome." As an example of women's beneficent influence in political life, she turned first to the Middle Ages when "abbesses . . . sat at State-Councils" and "holy women, like St. Theresa, and St. Catherine of Siena, were consulted on public matters by kings, princes, and nobles."[35]

Despard emphasized the ways in which women's political contribution was linked to their spiritual authority. Even where she set out to make explicitly economic arguments, as in *Woman's Franchise and Industry*, published by the Women's Freedom League, Despard returned in her conclusion to spiritual themes: "the man and the woman statesman; the man and the woman worker and parent of workers must stand together consciously, different in office and function, equal in their common Humanity, the two sides in truth of the one Being—the Divine Life in which they 'live and move and have their being.'"[36] Despard's belief that men and women were "two sides in truth of the one Being—the Divine Life" was the enabling context not only for her feminism, but for her political vision more generally.

She returned to the theme of the common humanity of men and women over and over again. Despard did not see herself as a feminist; she believed she was fighting not just for women but for all of humanity. "I am not a feminist—indeed I hate the very word," she once exclaimed. "It is my earnest hope that the present women's movement will prove to be a passing phase and that the day is not long distant when it will merge with the men's movement."[37] There was, as she put it in *Theosophy and the Woman's Movement* (1913), "no parting of the ways where men and women are concerned . . . the dual humanity to which, by the divine fiat, authority over the visible universe was given, must work as one; if that universe of matter is to be redeemed and sanctified." In this pamphlet Despard drew both on the tradition of Unity in Duality and on the claim that the soul has no sex to develop arguments for women's emancipation based on both their difference from and their similarity to men.[38]

Nineteenth-century Britain, in Despard's view, had allowed the unrestrained development of the masculine at the expense of the feminine side of humanity. The apparent conflict between men and women—the sense that women were separating themselves from men and acting independently of them—was simply the result of men's ignoring the dual humanity and the need for balance: women were "building up visions of a world in which masculinity should be set in its proper place, in which the voice of the woman, mother and worker, should be heard."[39] A new era was coming, and "if the changes are to be in the direction of true spiritual evolution: if we are to progress towards the angels and not retrogress towards the brutes, woman must be free."[40] The eugenic influence is clear in this passage, yet Despard's was a curious inversion of the Darwinian model.

Progress, for Despard, was the reclamation of a more spiritual past, a past preserved in India even while it had been lost in England. In her view, the most compelling proof of the dual nature of humanity lay in ancient spiritual teachings. As she explained in *Woman in the New Era,* published by the Suffrage Shop, in all the "old mythologies" the role of the "woman principle" is recognized in the creation, preservation, and even the destruction of life. The religions of Egypt and Babylon, Greece and Rome all testified to this duality. Even Judaism and Christianity emphasized the feminine principle, at least in the older, uncorrupted versions of the Genesis story. Despard appealed for authority to the most ancient elements of religious traditions, comparing the oldest "Hebraic Scriptures" with the "modern and corrupt Talmud," and the Christian churches (misled by Saints Peter and Paul) with the teachings of Christ. She believed that this mystic truth had been best preserved in India: the Indian reverence for the "Mother-Father God" had maintained "that early conception of creative power and energy which we, to our loss, have let slip." India therefore became, in Despard's vision, both the past and the future of England.[41]

The political subordination of women to men and of India to England was, by extension, the subordination of the spiritual to the material. The materialism of the Victorian age was the direct result of its masculinity. Men were responsible for industry and the machine age, and for an increasingly materialistic understanding of Christianity. And materialism was "peculiarly hurtful to woman. Either she withers and pines when subjected to its influence, or she takes on qualities which are not her own." Politics, as men understood it, could only "tinker" with the worst symptoms of world problems. The solutions to world problems had arisen elsewhere: "Outside the restless world of politics, in the soul of the mystic, in the spiritual awakening, that like the spring's wind of prophecy is sweeping over the world, and in the intuitive heart of woman, the City Beautiful of the Day that is to be is taking form."[42] When war broke out in 1914, Despard took it as confirmation of the subordination of the spiritual—which she believed was represented by "women and honest workers of both sexes"—to the material, the rule of "physical force."[43]

The women's movement, like the pacifist and labor movements, was therefore quite literally a war of the spirit against the flesh. This was the philosophy at the core of Despard's notion of "spiritual militancy." When M. K. Gandhi visited London in 1909, he met with Despard and discussed his theory of *satyagraha,* or spiritual resistance, which he saw as similar to her own, confirming Despard's sense that the fates of woman and India were tied together in spiritual evolution.[44] Despard saw the suffering of militant suffragists as quite literally a sacrament, an outward and visible sign of an inward and spiritual grace. The militant's action was a baptismal moment that "hallowed and purified her." The recognition of the dual nature of humanity was the first step toward the reunion of matter and spirit; the enfranchisement of women would be accompanied by the enfranchisement of the spiritual principles that Despard believed women represented. It was for this reason that the "universe of matter," including the world of politics, could only be "redeemed and sanctified" by women's full participation in public life.[45]

For Despard, all the causes to which she was to dedicate her life— the socialist movement, the women's movement, the Irish and Indian nationalist movements—were signs of the same set of cosmic changes. A new era was dawning, and in the new era the keynote would be spirituality rather than materialism. Even before she joined the TS, Despard had been hoping for a new revelation, which would bring social and political as well as spiritual revolution. Her first lectures under TS auspices, in 1901, bore the title "The Christ That Is To Be," the same title that Philip Snowden used to popularize his own brand of Christian Socialism.[46] Like Snowden, Despard articulated a millennialist vision in which the themes developed in *The Rajah's Heir* became increasingly prominent. The formation of the Order of the Star in the East and the announcement of Krishnamurti's role as the Coming Christ must have seemed to her like the fulfillment of Vishnugupta's prophecy. In 1910 and 1911 Despard became increasingly active within the TS, and by 1912 she was drawing large audiences to her lectures entitled "The Coming Christ, the Hope of the Ages."[47]

The belief in the inevitability of the Coming Christ and of his inauguration of a new era sustained Despard through the war years. She saw the war as a cataclysmic event that would sweep away the present social and political order "with its rivalries, its competitions, its complexity, its fears, its glorification of worldly success and material grandeur" and bring in its stead the return of "the Divine Mother-Spirit of Love" in national and international life.[48] During this same period, however, Despard became increasingly active in pacifist and international socialist circles and found herself increasingly isolated from her former allies both in the TS and the WFL.[49] As the TS moved increasingly to the right in the 1920s and 1930s, it was no longer clear to Despard that theosophy's New Age would be the democratic and utopian society she had imagined. When, in 1925, the World Teacher at long last "spoke" through Krishnamurti at the Star Congress in Ommem, she was acutely disappointed: "If only we could feel that the Master were behind working through and inspiring the great economic struggle. . . . Impossible to believe. If the *Master* were speaking through him, would he not be with the *People*?"[50] Although Despard remained a member of the TS until after Besant's death in 1933, theosophy no longer provided the spiritual inspiration for her political activities.[51]

In Despard's hands, theosophical teaching was used to underwrite a vision of spiritual solidarity that was closely linked not only to her version of feminism, but also to her socialist and communist convictions. Running through and linking both her political and spiritual writings was her emphasis on a fundamental unity, which existed spiritually even when it was not evident on the material plane. A similar pattern emerges in the writings of Eva Gore-Booth. In other ways, however, Gore-Booth's views were opposed to Despard's. Although the TS provided a sympathetic audience for her work, she rejected much of theosophical teaching and adopted instead an unorthodox Christian esotericism. Further, she was resolutely critical of the concept of the dual humanity, which was crucial to Despard.

Eva Gore-Booth was born into a prominent, Anglo-Irish landowning family. Her older sister Constance, later Countess Markievicz, played a key role in the Irish nationalist Easter uprising in 1916 and was the first woman to be elected to Parliament, in the 1918 election. Her brother was active in the Irish cooperative movement. In 1896, while in Italy, Eva Gore-Booth met Esther Roper, who had been working as an organizer for the women's suffrage movement among women textile workers in Manchester. The two women formed a partnership that lasted until Gore-Booth's death in 1926. In Manchester Gore-Booth joined the executive committee of the North of England Society for Women's Suffrage, and along with Roper became active in the National Union of Women's Suffrage Societies. In 1900 Gore-Booth was appointed co-secretary of the Manchester and Salford Women's Trade Union Council, and she went on to serve on Manchester's Technical Instruction Committee. In the summer of 1903 Roper and Gore-Booth, along with other radical suffragists, formed the Lancashire and Cheshire Women Textile and Other Workers' Representation Committee, for the enfranchisement of working-class women.[52] Both Roper and Gore-Booth continued to work, not only for women's suffrage, but also for the interests of working-class women more generally. During the war both women supported the peace movement and served on the British organizing committee of the Women's International Congress, which was to be held at The Hague in 1915. They also worked for the No-Conscription Fellowship, providing material and moral support to Britain's conscientious objectors.[53]

Despite an extraordinary record of active political work, it is only in the last twenty years that Roper and Gore-Booth have been remembered for their suffrage activism. Before that, Gore-Booth was known only as a mystical poet and playwright, and as a minor player in the Irish literary revival. In contrast, her own account of her life, and the account offered by Roper in the introduction to Gore-Booth's *Collected Poems,* highlighted not her literary or political achievements but her inner, spiritual life, represented as the ground beneath her political and literary activity.[54]

When she first arrived in Manchester, Gore-Booth was attracted to Unitarianism, and she became associated with John Trevor, who had founded the Labour Church in 1891. Both Roper and Gore-Booth gave lectures and talks in the Labour Church in the late 1890s.[55] At some point Gore-Booth became interested in theosophy, as reflected in the poems in *The One and the Many,* published in 1904. In this collection, poems like "The Quest" expressed her immanentist vision: "I seek the One in every form, / Scorning no vision that a dewdrop holds." "The Ancient Wisdom," "The Great God Has Been Released from Darkness (Vedic Hymn)," and "Re-incarnation" also gestured toward theosophical themes.[56]

Gore-Booth's friend Margaret Wroe later recalled that "she always left the world of incident for the world of thought whenever she had the least excuse. 'Don't let us talk about politics,' was a frequent introduction to a conversation, and then she would plunge into whatever was filling her mind at the moment: a poem she was writing, or the Ancient Wisdom, or Buddha, or Astrology, or Theosophy, and in her later years, almost exclusively the New Testament and Christ."[57] Gore-Booth formally joined the TS in 1919, and she was a member of the Hampstead Theosophical Society until her death; many of her writings on Christian mysticism were first delivered to theosophical audiences.[58]

Like Despard, Gore-Booth blurred the boundaries between public and private and between secular and sacred. She preached a gospel of universal love, which, she claimed, made sense of both her feminism and her uncompromising pacifism. Pacifist themes were central to all her plays; whether she drew on Celtic myth or Egyptian mysticism, the central struggle pitted universal love against the false gods that supported war, divisiveness, and selfishness. These themes are developed most clearly in *The Buried Life of Deirdre,* written between 1908 and 1912.[59] The play introduces the theme of reincarnation, which she claimed was not "exclusively an Eastern doctrine" but one to be found in Celtic and Druidic teaching as well. The theme of the play, according to Gore-Booth, was the conflict between "the possessive and exclusive passion of love" and "the freedom and universality of loving." That conflict is worked out through the "law of evolution," which leads the soul to union with the "Spirit of the One."[60]

These themes were more fully worked out in her *Psychological and Poetic Approach to the Study of Christ*, published in 1923. Although she presented her insights as merely "personal intuitions and ideas," with no claim to scholarship, she had spent considerable time learning both Greek and Latin in order to make her own translations from manuscripts in the British Museum.[61] She began by defining "God" as "Love and Truth and Life," and proceeded on the basis that anything that was not in harmony with "Universal Infinite Love" must be false. Cautiously, and with much recourse to the early manuscripts and the original Greek, she stripped away the attribution of masculinity to the divine, and developed her own interpretation of God, the universe, and the individual self. This was, with some qualifications, an immanentist vision, in which the Divine Self inhabited and animated every living thing. In this view, the whole "Kosmos" was alive. There was no clear distinction between matter and spirit, and all life was bound together in an indissoluble unity.[62]

God and the universe were not, however, coextensive: war, violence, exclusiveness, and discord were not of God. As an absolutely uncompromising pacifist Gore-Booth could not countenance the notion of a just war, nor could she accept that war and violence could be the means for working out a divine plan. She resolved that conflict by drawing a distinction between "psyche" and "spirit": the "psyche" was the desire-nature, a response to the vibrations of the Life of God, and it was in this psychic sense that the Kosmos was "One Life." The life force that animated the Kosmos contained both good and evil. Because, for Gore-Booth, God was all love and contained no evil, she returned to the idea of God's transcendence: God had to be transcendent to be separate from the evil in creation.[63]

Spiritual evolution, a concept Gore-Booth shared with many of her contemporaries, involved attuning oneself to the higher vibrations: first of Life, which vivified and unified the Kosmos; then of Truth, which separated and divided, purifying the "psyche" of evil; and finally of Love, which produced a reunion, not only with God, but with a redeemed universe.[64] The self, for Gore-Booth, was the psyche purified and transmuted; it was all that was good and divine in the human being. Recondite as these claims may appear, they provided a crucial context for Gore-Booth's justification of her pacifist convictions. "I am," she claimed at one pacifist meeting, "one of those quite hopeless people who do not believe in fighting in any circumstances."[65] Violence, even in the best of causes, was of the psyche and not the self, it was out of tune with the vibrations of divine love. Therefore, she argued, "there's only one real alternative to violence, and that's Christ. Because there is *no passive* alternative to violence, nothing but Love."[66]

Political activity, Gore-Booth argued, had to be undertaken in light of the knowledge that the material world was ephemeral, less real than the eternal, spiritual world. In her autobiographical writings and letters, as in her explicitly theological work, Gore-Booth continually located the real in the spiritual rather than the material world: "How tremendous the idea of God is and marvellous, and how easy to lessen it. It seems the only real Idea in the world worth understanding, *the* Reality."[67] But since identification with God/Christ was simultaneously identification with God/Christ-in-the-Kosmos, "we shall find our desires and thoughts rushing out in sympathy and love towards every living thing."[68] This was clearly not a privatized spirituality, and though it was profoundly antimaterialist, it did not therefore neglect material conditions and the need to intervene politically in the material world.

Gore-Booth's emphasis on the self, or spirit, as the "real" self, as opposed to the body and the psyche, also enabled a radical rethinking of gender relations and sexuality that drew more directly on theosophical debates about reincarnation and the Divine Uranian. She laid out her views in a new journal called *Urania,* which grew out of the Aëthnic Union, a group founded by Thomas Baty in 1912 and dedicated to liberating men and women from the "soul-murder" of sexual difference. Both Roper and Gore-Booth joined the group shortly after it was founded. In 1916 some members of the Aëthnic Union founded *Urania* as a privately printed and privately circulated journal, which took for its motto the biblical phrase "All' eisin hôs angeloi" ("But they are like angels"). While none of the articles in *Urania* can be definitely attributed to Gore-Booth, she and Roper were among the journal's founders, and they edited some of the early issues.[69]

The group that coalesced around the journal stressed the erasure of sexual difference and the emergence of a new type of human being:

> Urania denotes the company of those who are firmly determined to ignore the dual organization of humanity in all its manifestations.
>
> They are convinced that this duality has resulted in the formation of two warped and imperfect types. They are further convinced that in order to get rid of this state of things no measures of "emancipation" or "equality" will suffice, which do not begin by a complete refusal to recognize or tolerate the duality itself.

If the world is to see sweetness and independence combined in the same individual, *all* recognition of that duality must be given up. For it inevitably brings in its train the suggestion of the conventional distortions of character which are based on it.

There are no "men" or "women" in Urania.

"All' eisin hôs angeloi."[70]

There are similarities here to the theosophical notion of the Divine Uranian, but the clear rejection of the notion of the dual humanity would have alienated many theosophists.

While Gore-Booth's vision was far from orthodox Christianity, it was still based in the Christian tradition and represented Christianity as normative. In some of her writings she did attempt to formulate a vision that included all the world's religions. For example, in a series of articles she planned to write for *The Herald of the Star*, the journal of the OSE, she wanted to emphasize that the real divisions were not between Christianity, Buddhism, Islam, and Hinduism but between "those who follow 'the path of love and prayer' in each, and those who put their faith in organization and goodness and churches."[71] But her vision concluded with the reinscription of Christianity as the true religion; only in Christianity, she believed, could one find the idea of "Eternal Life in Christ"; her belief in the ultimate reunion of the self with Divine Love in "active rapture" was fundamental to her gospel of love.[72]

Both Despard and Gore-Booth turned to esoteric spirituality to authorize different kinds of political solidarity. Each of them privileged different elements within the esoteric tradition: Despard looked to ancient India and Gore-Booth to early Christianity. But for both women, an emphasis on the unity of all life was central. The anarchist-feminist Dora Marsden, however, articulated a very different spiritual and political vision. Marsden's esoteric writings explicitly rejected theosophy's collectivist vision of the One Life in favor of a radically individualist version of esoteric Christianity. A teacher with a B.A. from Victoria University in Manchester, Marsden joined the WSPU in 1908; a year later she resigned her teaching post to become a full-time paid organizer for the union. Marsden's radical individualism soon brought her into conflict with the WSPU leadership, and she resigned in 1911 amid mutual recriminations.[73]

In November 1911 Marsden launched a new weekly paper, *The Freewoman*. Feminist reactions to the paper were mixed, to say the least. Marsden's outspoken attacks on the WSPU and its leadership, and the paper's uncompromisingly open discussion of sex and sexual morality, generated fierce criticism from all sides.[74] Judging from the paper's correspondence columns, *The Freewoman* was also one of the few feminist papers willing to tolerate an open discussion of atheism and criticisms of religious orthodoxy.[75] *The Freewoman* folded after less than a year. It reappeared briefly as *The New Freewoman*, primarily a literary rather than a feminist journal, and became associated under yet another name, as *The Egoist*, with Ezra Pound and the Imagists. The paper never had a large circulation, and it appealed primarily to the literary and political avant-garde; contributors included H. G. Wells and Rebecca West, Edward Carpenter, the suffragists Teresa Billington-Grieg and Ada Nield Chew, and anarchists Guy Aldred and Rose Witcop.[76] Alongside discussions of Uranianism, prostitution, and free love, the paper published many articles on spirituality, and women's spirituality in particular.

Marsden's contacts with occult and esoteric circles were extensive and formed an important context for the development of her own spiritual vision. She attended the Blavatsky Institute's summer school two years in a row. Further, Winifred W. Leisenring, the secretary of the Blavatsky Institute, was also the secretary of the British Thousand Club, which was set up to raise money to relaunch *The Freewoman* after it suspended publication; the Blavatsky Institute provided Marsden's paper with office space in its own London headquarters in Bloomsbury.[77] According to Ezra Pound, both Marsden and Shaw Weaver also attended lectures sponsored by Mead and the Quest Society.[78]

When *The Freewoman* was founded, Marsden's nominal co-editor was Mary Gawthorpe, also of the WSPU. Although she never joined the TS, Gawthorpe had a lifelong interest in theosophical ideas. She encountered Besant's work on karma in the Leeds Arts Club around 1904 and recorded in her autobiography that the book had had a profound effect on her, putting her into contact with powerful spiritual forces. Gawthorpe's later correspondence revealed a continuing, but intensely personal interest in both theosophy and Christian Science. Her published memoirs suggested only that theosophical teachings "rested in quiet spaces at a certain, unknown level, where talking was not allowed."[79]

The theosophist Ellen S. Gaskell was also a regular reader of *The Freewoman* and contributed articles to the paper in which she put forward a theosophical analysis of the suffrage movement. In a response to Sir Almroth Wright's notorious letter to the *Times* in 1912, which argued that suffrage militancy was the result of women's mental and emotional unbalance, Gaskell argued that if women were "less balanced than men," it was because they represented the "finer forces" in spiritual evolution, while men represented the grosser, more physical forces. Using the same logic, she claimed that "the rule of Force, whether physical or mechanical," was being superseded by the "reign of Peaceful Arbitration." Similarly, in the first issue of *The New Freewoman* the theosophist Francis Grierson attempted to assimilate Marsden's teachings to Blavatsky's, linking both to the emergence of a new, more spiritual era.[80]

Marsden herself explicitly rejected both theosophy and the TS. In 1913 she participated in a Blavatsky Institute summer school in Peebles where, according to her friend Harriet Shaw Weaver, she trounced the theosophists in debate and sold many copies of *The New Freewoman*. "The 'Freewoman' doctrine," Marsden claimed, "is just the rooting out of 'Theosophia.'"[81] Marsden's hostility to theosophy, however, was not extended to spiritual issues in general or esotericism in particular; her own political claims were also articulated in the language of esoteric spirituality. In the first issues of *The Freewoman* Marsden laid out the distinctions between the "Freewoman" and the "Bondwoman," arguing that women had to recognize their responsibility for their own emancipation. As we shall see, the same elements that distinguished the Freewoman from the woman enslaved also distinguished the immortal soul from the soulless masses.

In April 1912 Marsden began to develop a highly individualistic understanding of spirituality: "to be religious is to have a religious sense, as distinct as the sense of sight or sound . . . it has nothing to do with an intellectual outlook or concept. It is an extra, an added, channel of consciousness." Typically, Marsden's emphasis was on the individual's own experience and authority: no priest, no church, no text could override the authority of the individual's religious sense. Marsden's characterization of this religious sense was a profoundly physical, experiential, and personal vision. "The man with the religious sense" was one who "had God consciously beating in his brain, swelling out his heart, throbbing at every nerve-ending. . . . [he] cannot be rid of God, because God is part of his personal substance and goes wherever he goes." Marsden reinterpreted Christianity to make individual experience its central feature. She argued, for example, that the Christian account of the resurrection was true not because it had happened historically, but because in an act of individual self-creation all believers made it true, enacted it for themselves within their own souls: "Because we divine that the Resurrection is true, we ourselves shape the method of it. . . . He who thinks he will rise again in the body, doubtless will, and he who knows he will continue to live in spirit, *will* live in spirit." Christ, Marsden argued, was divine simply because he had declared himself to be divine. "Any man" who could say, "I am the Resurrection and the Life," and believe it sincerely, "*is* the Resurrection and the Life." This was (at least for Marsden, though possibly she had lost the majority of her readers by this point) the truth that was "self-evident" to the "Superman," whose religiosity was a kind of Nietzschean will-to-immortality.[82]

Throughout these writings, Marsden grappled with the inadequacies of language to express her concerns. Popular speech, she argued, was a form of "intellectual immorality," and readers of *The Freewoman* might do well to compile a "Select Glossary" that would help them make sense of "the multiplicity of meanings of the words 'spiritual' and 'material.'"[83] Many of Marsden's arguments on the subject became virtually incomprehensible, as she created an increasingly specialized vocabulary to convey her intensely individual philosophy. In Marsden's attempt to define *passion* and its relationship to both sex and the spirit, for example, she quickly reached the limits of popular speech. Passion, for Marsden, was clearly related to the sexual, but the sexual could be understood to exclude its physical aspects. The closest she came to a definition of *passion* was "intensified expansion of being," which was approached but could not be realized in "the attraction in sex-anticipation."[84] Sexual attraction was the most democratic form of passion, the form in which passion was most accessible to the average man or woman. These claims were an important part of Marsden's advocacy of free love, but her concern in these passages was not at all with sexual passion as it is generally understood.[85]

For Marsden, passion was the quality that transformed the undifferentiated cosmic life force into an individual soul. The purpose of evolution was to produce individuated forms, which Marsden called souls; the mark of the soul was personality, which Marsden defined as the "characterised, form-impregnated life with articulated differentiation." At "dissolution," or, more prosaically, death, the "worn out sheath" of the body would fall away and the "articulated soul" would remain, its "spatiality" greater or smaller in proportion to the greatness or meanness of the personality. Passion therefore ensured immortality, for the man or woman without passion was a soulless nonentity:

> If we now turn to that conception of ideal sexual passion, which shuns all relations in the physical, we find its real solution in this conception of continued existence of personality. A great spiritual experience such as a passion is must have a spiritual consequence, and its consequence is found in the individual spiritual entity, which is personality. Passion creates personality, and personality is the differentiated form of life which will not sink back into the undifferentiated.

The "ideal sexual passion," therefore, precluded "relations in the physical." Physical sexual relations ensured one form of immortality, through the production of children. This, Marsden argued, was a trivial form of immortality compared to the immortality that "creative mind-force" could bring, once it was separated "from its baser exploitations." The "modern interpretation of sex" was "putrid": "It heads straight for putrefaction and decay—in the physical." But the "passionate conception of sex . . . leads to increased life-force here and now, to the creation of personality, which is, we believe, the master of death."[86]

Creativity and willpower were tied to the individual soul's active process of self-creation. Passion was the individual's portion of the great cosmic life force. The achievement of an articulated individual personality therefore became, for Marsden, the most creative and permanent act in the universe. In her view, the Freewoman was well placed to become an articulated individual because women were most closely associated to the life force. The masculine ideal was "logical, mechanistic" and allowed "no room for the real life forces of the mind—the feminine, intuitive forces—to live." The Freewoman movement, she argued, stood for both the masculine and the feminine forces, but "if one must be absent, it had better be the logical, the masculinist; the feminist, the intuitive, is more vital, more fundamental, and can best save itself." The feminist movement, like all movements for freedom, was therefore "the putting out of an advance feeler to prepare the way for the new, intuitive, life-expanding impulse."[87]

Marsden's emphasis on the sacred character of individuality was linked to the elitism of her feminism. Only the Freewoman and Freeman could achieve immortality; the masses of men and women were destined simply to disappear back into the undifferentiated life force. This elitism also led her to elevate Christianity over the "religions of the East." She argued that Christianity was evolutionarily superior because it valued individual salvation; it emphasized the separateness of the individual soul, while "Eastern faiths" emphasized unity, the erosion of the soul's boundaries. The goal was not to become one with God, but to become "the More-than-Man, the God" oneself.[88] This was another key element in her disagreement with the Theosophical Society. The theosophical teaching on unity, which drew Despard, for example, toward the ancient wisdom of the East, was precisely the emphasis that Marsden rejected.

These claims also alienated many of the paper's subscribers, who could not agree whether Marsden was attacking religion or defending it. After Marsden's introduction of the notion of passion, Hatty Baker, later one of the founders of the women's Church of the New Ideal, pleaded with Marsden not to be "pagan." Baker argued that it was only "the Divine in a movement" that allowed it to endure. Women were "at core religious in the highest sense. . . . true religion is deeply rooted in woman, and no cause will be furthered by ignoring such." On the same page, Frances Prewett suggested that Marsden was perhaps not pagan enough, arguing that true Freewomen rejected all man-made creeds "and find a living and sufficient faith in Nature incorporate in their own souls." Rather than "frittering away her energies in cherishing the delusions of faith . . . woman should bring the whole force of her spiritual power into motherhood and other feminine work for humanity."[89]

Marsden's radically individualistic theology was reinforced by her study of anarchistic individualism in the work of the philosopher Max Stirner, whose ideal was the Egoist, the individual in permanent conflict with all other individuals.[90] When *The New Freewoman* was launched in June 1913, Stirner's influence was increasingly clear. *The New Freewoman* was intended, Marsden editorialized, "not for the advancement of Woman, but for the empowering of individuals—men and women; it is not to set women free but to demonstrate the fact that 'freeing' is the individual's affair and must be done first hand, and that individual power is the first step thereto."[91] Leaving the day-to-day work of putting out a paper to Harriet Shaw Weaver, Marsden dedicated herself to developing her own linguistic philosophy. She had come to believe that words like *Man* and *Woman,* along with *Equality, Justice,* and *Humanity,* were empty concepts, used to enslave actual men and women: "If we take away female reproductive organs from the concept 'Woman,' what have we left? Absolutely nothing, save a mountain of sentimental mush."[92]

For the next two decades, Marsden withdrew into isolation and dedicated herself to a multivolume study of space and time, which attempted to provide an objective proof of the existence of God through a comparative study of all religion, philosophy, and science. Her efforts culminated in the publication of *The Definition of the Godhead* (1928) and *Mysteries of Christianity* (1930), both issued by the Egoist Press. *The Definition of the Godhead* was dedicated to "The Great Name Hushed Among Us for So Long of Her Heaven the Mighty Mother of All," and the two books elaborated a vision of a feminine God and a feminine Trinity that had been deliberately obscured by what she called a "masculinist monotheism." The novelist Storm Jameson, a close friend of Marsden's and a member of the TS, thought *The Definition of the Godhead* a "great work of sensational merit and revolutionary in effect," but Marsden's difficult and obscure work had no real audience. Marsden continued to struggle with the remaining volumes, but sales were virtually non-existent. In 1935, she was diagnosed with "deep melancholia" and spent the rest of her life, until she died in 1960, in Crichton Royal Hospital, Dumfries.[93]

Marsden's *Freewoman* is generally characterized as the most "modern" of feminist periodicals during this period. This is partly because of the key role Marsden played in the emergence of literary modernism.[94] It is also due to the relative openness of *The Freewoman* to discussions of female desire and to the work of the sexologists and sex reformers.[95] The amount of attention Marsden gave to developing a feminist spirituality in *The Freewoman* suggests that mysticism and esotericism, as much as science and sexology, helped to shape the paper's "modernity." Most studies of Marsden deemphasize these religious debates. Her most recent biographer, Bruce Clarke, rereads Marsden's "dated participation in outmoded phenomenologies" (such as "the soul") as "equivocal early modernist anticipations of, as well as resistances to, the poststructuralist critique of the self or unified subject."[96] His reading erases the fact that these claims were formulated in explicitly spiritual terms. Marsden's esotericism was as fully implicated in her modernism as it was in her feminism and her "egoistic anarchism." Other accounts take Marsden's religious writings more seriously: Gillian Hanscombe and Virginia Smyers, for example, acknowledge the spiritual context of Marsden's writings, but they assume that a "spiritual" and a political analysis are mutually exclusive, and characterize the spiritual as "an analysis where all individuals somehow end up equal in the quest for enlightenment."[97] Both claims clearly misrepresent Marsden's position.

For Charlotte Despard and Eva Gore-Booth, the "things of the spirit" were more "real" than political or material conditions; in their view, political and material conditions were symptoms of a more profound spiritual malaise. Marsden's elitist anarchist-feminism was similarly validated by her own rendering of the relationship between individual autonomy and immortality. Each of these women represented the suffrage movement as a spiritual movement. They did not simply invoke a religious rhetoric to give the suffrage movement the status of a religious crusade or to borrow the authority of spirituality for suffrage; rather, they believed that the women's movement was a religious crusade, that it was a symptom of a larger set of spiritual changes. Gertrude Colmore, the author of the suffrage novel *Suffragette Sally* and of *The Life of Emily Davison,* written to commemorate the WSPU's first "martyr," reveals an even more explicit conflation of the spiritual and political in her own feminist political theology.

Colmore, a Quaker by birth, was married to Harold Baillie-Weaver, who was general secretary of the TS in England from 1916 to 1921. Colmore and Baillie-Weaver, who married in 1901, joined the TS together in 1906. Over the next decade, the couple poured their energies into a wide range of causes. Colmore was already a published novelist and poet, and she continued to explore political issues, from antivivisection to prostitution and venereal disease, in her novels; her last novel, *A Brother of the Shadow* (1926), dealt most explicitly with occult themes. Harold Baillie-Weaver was not only general secretary of the TS, but also a member of the Esoteric Section, the Order of the Star in the East, and the Universal Order of Co-Freemasonry. Colmore played a prominent role in the Theosophical Order of Service, especially through the TOS League to Help the Woman's Movement (of which Baillie-Weaver was chairman) and the TOS Anti-Vivisection League.[98]

Colmore herself was active in the WSPU from 1907 until late in 1918, and she was an early member of the Women's Freedom League. Her short stories appeared in the WFL paper, *The Vote*. Her husband was active in the Men's League for Women's Suffrage. With the Pethick-Lawrences and Evelyn Sharp, they were founding members of the United Suffragists in 1914. Harold Baillie-Weaver's support for the women's suffrage movement was clearly more than nominal: he spoke on behalf of "the Cause" on several occasions, and once shared the platform at the London Pavilion with Emmeline Pankhurst and Annie Kenney of the WSPU. He also wrote a series of articles for the WSPU's *Suffragette*, dealing with the legal issues raised by the prosecution of WSPU members. The couple were also active in animal-welfare organizations, and during the war they devoted much of their time to the pacifist movement, Colmore as a member of the Women's International League for Peace and Freedom, and Baillie-Weaver as chairman of the Peace Council, which campaigned for a negotiated peace.[99]

Colmore's *Suffragette Sally* was a kind of collective biography of the suffrage movement, tracing the ways in which women of different classes and political convictions came together in the suffrage struggle.[100] As Shirley Peterson argues, the concern with "spiritual progress" is central to both *Suffragette Sally* and *The Life of Emily Davison*. While Peterson quite rightly notes that the invocation of "religious metaphors" served "to emphasize the suffrage campaign as an evangelical quest or holy crusade," for Colmore herself these were not metaphors but truths.[101]

In *Suffragette Sally* Colmore located both the causes and the effects of the women's movement not in the political but in the spiritual realm:

Evolution has its own methods, and those who work them out are evolution's instruments. Individually the women who are working

in all their different ways to bring about the next phase in the development of humanity are working, each one according to the be-
hests of her conscience, her character, her circumstances. Cos-
mically they are tools, with just the qualities . . . which fit them to
do the work which at this particular time in the world's history
has to be done. You may praise or blame them, but the things
they do have been planned by a mightier than they.

This "evolutionary" force, Colmore argued, was identical with God,
who "moves in a mysterious way / His wonders to perform." The suffrage movement is thus represented as a symptom of cosmic forces, a
material and political reflection of spiritual realities. Colmore articulated these claims through the character of Rachel Cullen, who, at the
end of the novel, dies of injuries sustained on "Black Friday" when suffrage demonstrators clashed with police in a brutal battle. In the conversation quoted here, Cullen makes explicit the spiritual implications
of political martyrdom: women might have to die for their beliefs, and
on that day "the soul of the movement will be set free from the vile
body in which it has been constrained to dwell."[102] For Colmore, the
spiritual victories achieved by the WSPU outweighed and outlasted any
political defeats. The spirit, she argued, saw more clearly than the physical eye, and in every conflict between women's spirituality and men's
materialism—whether between women and their unsympathetic male
partners, between women protesters and police, or between hunger-
striking prisoners and male doctors—the material victory might go to
the men, but the spiritual victory belonged to the women.[103]

The triumph of the spirit over the flesh is represented as a specifically
feminine triumph over male materialism. The same themes framed Colmore's presentation of the life of Emily Davison. Immediately after
Davison's death from injuries sustained when she threw herself into the
path of the king's horse at the Derby, Colmore published a tribute to
Davison in *The Vote*, in which she made a direct link between Davison's
sacrifice and the New Age. According to Colmore, she heard of Davison's death as she was leaving a lecture at The Queen's Hall, a lecture
(doubtless sponsored by the TS or OSE) on the Coming Christ; in Colmore's article, Davison's martyrdom became an anticipation of the
Coming and the New Age.[104] (The link between Davison's sacrifice and
the work of preparation for a New Age was bizarrely confirmed a few
days later when Harold Hewitt, a member of the OSE, attempted to
replicate Davison's sacrifice during the Gold Cup at Ascot.)[105] In *The
Life of Emily Davison*, published in 1913, Colmore again located the
significance of suffrage militancy in its spiritual dimensions. Colmore's

Davison is "innately religious" and a "practical mystic," a woman who was "fully convinced that she was called by God, not only to work but also to fight for the cause she had espoused." All of Davison's militancy, Colmore claimed, was carried out under a mystical "Influence"; Davison's motto was "Rebellion against tyrants is obedience to God," and her political rebellions were therefore, according to Colmore, inseparable from religion.[106]

Colmore did not privilege the spiritual over the material and political; instead, she conflated the spiritual and political realms. The result was a sacralization of the political that eroded the boundaries between secular and sacred. In her characterization of what it meant to be a suffragette, the eponymous heroine of *Suffragette Sally* put the case another way: "It's religion an' politics; an' woman's place-is-the-'ome all in one. For religion's 'elpin' them as is put upon; an' that's wot we do. An' politics is fightin' agin the Government an' that's wot we do. . . . An' woman's-place-is-the-'ome, is lookin' after children and widders an' such like; an' that's wot we want to do if they'd only let us 'ave a look in."[107] Although Colmore's transcription of working-class speech betrays her own class privilege, Sally's words are as much an articulation of Colmore's own views as Rachel Cullen's evocation of "cosmic forces." Both emphasized the blurring of the boundaries between the political and the spiritual, and stood in opposition to those who would privatize spirituality and secularize politics. The real meaning of the women's movement, then, for Colmore, was its inner and spiritual meaning, its sacramental character.

The spiritual vision of the women's movement articulated here privileged spiritual understandings of material and political conditions. This valorization of the spiritual dimensions of feminism clearly relied in crucial ways on middle-class English women's insulation from the exigencies of a day-to-day struggle for material existence; this vision of women's spiritual superiority was drawn from and articulated within a middle-class ideology that rested on the economic, cultural, and political privileges of a middle-class elite. Those few working-class feminists who joined the TS could be alienated by its self-consciously elite culture; the theosophist Eva Slawson, for example, a legal secretary from Walthamstow, recorded in her diary her fears that a TS summer school would prove "too stylish."[108]

At the same time, it is crucial to recognize that assumptions about the inherent oppositions between the spiritual and the material and political did not operate in the same way for all early twentieth-century feminists. For Colmore, the spiritual included, rather than opposed, the material and political. Insofar as the suffrage movement was understood as a spiritual rather than "merely" political struggle, what some historians characterize as a "retreat" into spirituality in the 1920s could also be interpreted as an effort to continue by other means the larger struggle of which the suffrage movement was a symptom. The goal was women's emancipation, but the means could be spiritual as well as political. Spirituality was not, in this context, understood as a privatized and individual alternative to political action but as a higher form of political action.

The effort to reclaim the public, political realm as a sacred space was a crucial part of much feminist activity. After women's limited enfranchisement in 1918, it became increasingly clear that their participation in parliamentary politics was not going to sacralize the public sphere. Christabel Pankhurst's apparent defection to Seventh Day Adventism, for example, can also be understood as an effort to pursue feminist politics by spiritual means.[109] Even at the height of the suffrage struggle, Pankhurst had made women's spiritual claims central to her definitions of feminism: it was "the militant women crusaders" of the WSPU, she claimed in 1914, "in whom the spirit of Christ is living to-day." Women who were in prison for suffrage activities were reenacting Christ's crucifixion; like the martyrs of the early Church they endured physical tortures that could not compel their "spiritual submission." The WSPU's 1914 campaign to disrupt church services until the churches took a principled stand on the treatment of suffrage prisoners was similarly linked to this construction of women as martyrs for their faith.[110]

According to the prominent suffrage leader Emmeline Pethick-Lawrence, women were fighting "not [for] the Vote only, but what the Vote means—the moral, the mental, economic and spiritual enfranchisement of Womanhood; the release of women, the repairing, the rebuilding of that great temple of womanhood, which has been so ruined and defaced."[111] To fully appreciate the dynamics of this passage, it is necessary to take seriously Pethick-Lawrence's claims for "spiritual enfranchisement" and her characterization of women as "that great temple of womanhood." For Pethick-Lawrence, who joined the TS in 1922, women's "spiritual enfranchisement" was intimately bound up with more secular forms of enfranchisement.

Similarly, Cicely Hamilton located the struggle for women's suffrage within the context of the struggle of the spirit against materialism: "I believe the women's movement is one of those movements which occur every now and then in the history of the world, as if people suddenly revolted from the materialism with which perhaps they had been contented for generations, and as if they had been stirred by a wave of what I call the Spirit, and they have tried to get a little nearer to what they felt things ought to be."[112] If the cause of women's political activity was that women had been "stirred by the Spirit," then the most profound effects of that activity were also spiritual rather than material. As Charlotte Despard put it, "The women's movement is linked by the thread of love . . . [it] has opened women up to one another. . . . The vote may go, Parliament may go, but love will remain—spiritual love *is* the women's movement."[113] This is not to suggest that women's spirituality provided the motive force for secular activities; it is rather to suggest that historians need to rethink assumptions about distinctions between secular and sacred in women's politics during this period. For at least a significant minority of women, feminism was a kind of theology as much as a political ideology. The current tendency to conflate political with secular makes it difficult to perceive the extent to which, in much early twentieth-century feminist writing, the political realm was reconstituted as a sacred space.

Chapter Eight

Ancient Wisdom, Modern Motherhood

In April 1928 Annie Besant announced the formation of a new movement, organized to herald the Coming of "a great Spiritual Being who represents the feminine side of Divinity, the Ideal Womanhood, the 'World Mother.'" The public recognition of the World Mother, the incarnation of that Divine Feminine principle that had ever been active on a spiritual level, was intended to reflect the increased importance of women in public affairs. The World Mother, represented in the past by Isis and by Mary, the mother of Jesus, was now to be represented by Shrimati Rukmini Devi, the young Brahman wife of the theosophist George Arundale.[1] The World Mother was to be the "representative of Womanhood, Womanhood in its highest function, the function of the Mother." This World Mother, Besant explained as she announced the New Annunciation, summed up in herself all that was best and highest in womanhood. The World Mother movement was to complement, not to challenge or displace, the work of the Order of the Star in the East. As a dutiful wife, the World Mother recognized the headship and lordship of the World Teacher, the masculine aspect of God, represented in the TS by Krishnamurti: "The World-Mother speaks of the World-Teacher as Our Lord; recognises His high place."[2]

Strictly speaking, the World Mother movement can only be accounted a failure. It never gained a real following even among the most dedicated theosophists, and it suffered from a lack of commitment at the highest level. In a 1979 interview with Gregory Tillett, Rukmini Devi denied what might be described as the occult interpretation of the events of 1928 and refused to identify herself with any kind of Coming. She claimed "that she had never regarded the concept of representing the World Mother in the way in which it has come to be interpreted but thought it meant simply doing work in the arts and for humanity. . . . She denied ever being a 'representative' of the World Mother."[3] In England the World Mother movement had almost no following; its most prominent English exponent, Emily Lutyens, rejected many of Besant's claims and remained ambivalent about the implications of Besant's vision of womanhood and motherhood for feminism.

The World Mother movement, however, was only one of a much broader set of initiatives that did have a significant impact, not only in England but also in India. It was also the culmination of a process that had begun within the TS in the 1870s and 1880s—the effort to create a usable version of both eastern and feminine authority. Both images contained many conflicting possibilities. Theosophists had invoked many different visions of the East: as glamorous and exotic, as manly and rational, and as an ideal political state. Now the East, especially India, was primarily represented as the repository of the sacred, and the "Indian mother" became the best exemplar of India's spiritual traditions. The ancient wisdom of India was to provide a blueprint for the New Age, and one of the crucial features of the New Age was that it would achieve modernity without secularization. This was not simply an antimodernist call for a return to tradition, but an effort to create a new synthesis of East and West that would be both spiritual and modern.

The authority vested in India as the locus of the ancient wisdom, and in women as the mothers both of the race and of individual children, took a different shape in different historical and cultural locations. The implications of the theosophists' synthesis of East and West therefore varied widely. In England, the combination of ancient wisdom and modern motherhood tended to collapse into one of two extremes: a eugenic concern with the future of the race or an intensely privatized understanding of the role of motherhood in individual spiritual development. In India, in contrast, Rukmini Devi used the rhetoric of the World Mother movement to claim a political role for women, especially elite women, in the Indian nationalist movement and later in an independent India. This image of Indian motherhood was then re-exported to England, where it became a crucial resource in the interventions by English theosophists in feminist and anticolonial debates.

The TS in India had long been one of the society's largest national sections; in the mid-1930s there were more lodges and more members in India than in England.[4] In this period the Indian Section played an increasingly important role in setting the agenda for the society worldwide, a process that continued throughout the twentieth century. By the late 1920s Rukmini Devi Arundale was easily the most prominent Indian woman in the TS, and when her husband became president of the society after Besant's death in 1933, she became one of the most influential women in the TS as a whole. In the 1920s and 1930s the most significant feminist initiatives within the TS also took place in India, and the European women who were members of the TS often played a more important role in feminist activity in India than they did in their home countries.

The two most famous British feminists who were active in the TS in India, Margaret Cousins and Dorothy Jinarajadasa, were from Ireland and Scotland respectively. But many less well-known feminists within the English TS also moved to India to take up educational and philanthropic work. Ethelwyn Mary Amery, for example, left England for educational work in India; Dr. Louise Appel gave up her position as head of the Theosophical Order of Service in England to work with the Seva Sedan in Bombay and became the superintendent of the Theosophical High School, Madanapalle, in 1912. Francesca Arundale, George's aunt, was principal of the Central Hindu College Girls' School in Benares and of the National Girls' School at Mylapore, near Madras, for many years, and in 1922 she became the honorary head of the Women's Branch of the Education Department of the Holkar State. Mary W. Barrie served as principal of the Government Training College for Women Teachers in Madras in the mid-1920s, and Kate Browning was principal of the Girls' College in Benares in 1916. These were only a few of the many European women in the TS who followed a similar trajectory.

In the 1920s and 1930s Indian women theosophists also took an increasingly prominent part in the society's activities. Many pursued active political and educational work both within the TS and on behalf of Indian feminism: Shrimati Parvati Ammal Chandarashekara Iyer, for example, was the president of the Mysore Child Welfare Society and the vice president of the Mysore Constituent Conference of the All India Women's Conference on Educational Reform. D. Lakshmi Gurumurti was elected to the Chittoor District Board in 1935, and Shrimati Padmabai Sanjiva Rao took over as principal of the Girls' Theosophical College in Benares from 1916.[5]

Once in India, British women worked in many Indian feminist organizations. The Women's Indian Association (WIA), for example, was formed in Madras in 1917 by the theosophists Margaret Cousins and Dorothy Jinarajadasa (who married C. Jinarajadasa in 1916). With Besant as its honorary president, the WIA exploited the network of theosophical lodges throughout India to build an important women's reform organization that took the lead in the campaign for women's suffrage in India. Cousins, Jinarajadasa, and the theosophist A. Louise Huidekoper were also instrumental in the formation of the All India Women's Conference, which first met in Poona in January 1927.[6]

Even though much of the feminist activity among theosophists now took place in India, women in the English Section did continue to pursue feminist objectives. In the 1920s and 1930s, however, English feminism in general operated within an increasingly conservative political climate. Since at least the turn of the century fears of racial decline had prompted campaigns to increase the quality and quantity of the nation's births, and therefore the numbers of the nation's workers and soldiers. The Great War of 1914–18, which demonstrated the dependency of modern warfare on the supply of "cannon fodder," made the case seem even more urgent. Late nineteenth-century fears of racial degeneration were given a scientific gloss with the emergence of an active and vocal eugenics movement, which provided the underpinning for a variety of legislative initiatives.[7] The war experience also produced a new concern to promote harmony between the sexes, as opposed to the so-called sex war of the suffrage movement, thus eroding feminism's oppositional stance.[8] A self-consciously new feminism emerged, which demonstrated a renewed interest in improving the position of women as wives and mothers. Led by Eleanor Rathbone and the National Union of Societies for Equal Citizenship (formerly the NUWSS), new feminists argued that motherhood had been undervalued both by old feminists and by the state. Many of the campaigns adopted by the new feminists—for maternal health, improved working-class housing, family allowances, and protective legislation for women workers—were efforts to respond to the demands of working-class women and women in the labor movement. But the risk of new feminist campaigns was that they could perpetuate women's subordination even while attempting to formulate a radical critique of the sexual status quo.[9]

Like English feminism more broadly, feminist activity within the TS took new directions within this more conservative climate. Both before and after the war, members of the TS in England participated in campaigns that linked motherhood to a concern with the health of the race. Like their contemporaries in more mainstream organizations, theosophists attempted to assert their authority, on both scientific and spiritual grounds, to intervene in the rearing of an "imperial race." Leslie Haden Guest, for example, a socialist, suffragist, and prominent theosophist, explicitly linked women's enfranchisement to public health, arguing that since women were the acknowledged experts on child rearing and home conditions, they should therefore be included in state, national, and imperial policy making.[10] In 1916 Gertrude Holt Gerlach advertised in the pages of *The Vāhan* for assistance in founding a small home in the country for babies "in dire need of intelligent care," arguing that conditions in the slums did not "contribute towards an improved race."[11] In 1917 the TS inaugurated its most ambitious and long-lasting effort in this field—Brackenhill Theosophical Home School, directed by Kate Harvey, a former organizer with the Women's Freedom League. Brackenhill was founded to provide a new home for children with disabilities, orphans, deserted children, and those whose "homes are undesirable"; the school cared for children from the ages of two to sixteen and supplied them with vocational training.[12]

Over the course of the war, maternity and child welfare became increasingly central to the Theosophical Society's sense of its mission. As theosophists talked more of the coming New Age and of the reconstruction of society after the war, motherhood was a recurrent theme. In 1917 Charlotte Despard argued that the coming of the New Age was dependent on a transformation of the conditions of motherhood: "The recognition of the Mother," she argued (using the word in "its very largest meaning"), "and her return as a living force into the social, political and religious life of the nations—is the big thing that lies at the back of the whole of the modern democratic movement."[13] Despard's emphasis on the social and political aspects of motherhood, however, was increasingly displaced by a concern to intervene in the lives of individual mothers, and this concern was now formulated in terms of the individual mother's contribution to the health of the race.

In 1914 Besant argued that society had an obligation to pay attention to the health of mothers before the birth of their children, to make schools for mothers part of the educational system, and to surround mothers with conditions not only of health but also of beauty.[14] In a piece called "Mother and Child," written a few years later, Josephine Ransom, who became general secretary of the TS in England in 1933, echoed Besant's sentiments. She stressed that "it is the mother's sane and obvious duty to provide the finest physical materials which she can obtain for the nourishment of the child," and added that pregnant women should avoid trams and trains, which were rife with both physical and astral contagions.[15] Miss Bothwell-Gosse, head of the TS Sociological Department, was even more forthright, arguing that people should not "be allowed to spoil their own lives and to ruin the race" by indulging in racial poisons such as alcohol, and that "regulations dealing with the safety and health of the mother and the child should be enforced by law . . . and legislation should see that these infants have a chance in life and are not handicapped by race-poisons."[16] For those women members of the TS who took these strictures seriously, Stone Field Maternity Home, managed by resident physicians who were Fellows of the TS, was willing to provide care based on "Theosophical and New Era methods" of care for mother and child.[17]

The concern with the conditions under which individual mothers gave birth moved in two different directions in theosophical writing. The public and political concern with the health of the race coexisted uneasily with an emphasis on the private and personal ways in which the act of giving birth functioned as an important part of individual women's spiritual journey. Both elements can be traced in the writings of Emily Lutyens, the most prominent exponent of the new feminism within the English TS. Lutyens, who joined the TS in 1910, was the wife of the architect Edwin Landseer Lutyens. She came to the TS with a history of involvement in political and social reform that was in many ways typical of a progressive woman of her class: she had interested herself in the question of the state regulation of prostitution and served as a visitor to a local Lock (venereal) Hospital, where she read and sang to the patients. She joined the Moral Education League, formed to promote moral instruction in schools, one wing of which was instrumental in the formation of the Eugenics Education Society in 1907. Lutyens became an "ardent supporter" of the women's suffrage movement, although, unlike her sister Constance Lytton, she never became a militant. At the first meeting of the TS that she attended, Lutyens met Leslie Haden Guest, a "fellow-spirit" committed to social and political reform, and the two of them soon founded the Central London Lodge of the TS, a lodge "specially devoted to the practical application of Theosophy to social problems."[18]

In her own writings, Lutyens made a consistent effort to articulate the spiritual meanings of political, and especially feminist, activity. Lutyens's first major work on the subject, *The Sacramental Life*, published in 1917, was in many ways a new feminist document, a plea that feminists give serious attention to the hardships under which mothers, and particularly working-class mothers, labored every day. Egalitarian concerns remained important; she argued, for example, that women had a spiritual as well as a political obligation to "express themselves as human beings *first*," rather than as wives and mothers, and that some women required a "bigger scope" than marriage and motherhood in which to express their humanity. But new feminist concerns informed both her analysis of the problem and her proffered solution: Lutyens went on to argue that "if we really believe that motherhood is the finest profession that any woman can adopt, we must prove it by the endowment of motherhood, and so make it possible for the mother to remain at home and care for her children."[19]

In *The Call of the Mother*, published in 1926, Lutyens offered an extended treatment of motherhood that attempted to combine a new feminist analysis of motherhood with a profound sense of spiritual mission.[20] The book moved from "Motherhood As It Is" to "Motherhood

As It Might Be" and the "Motherhood of God." Lutyens's work fused actual and spiritual motherhood. She saw the physical and material degradation of motherhood as a reflection of the degradation of the Divine Feminine principle itself. Eugenic concerns were central to her work; quoting extensively from a range of standard eugenic texts, she argued that "you cannot produce a race of gods and heroes from diseased, overworked, idle, selfish, or materialistic parents."[21] Motherhood became the defining characteristic of femininity. All women were first and foremost, at least potentially, mothers. "A woman will remain a woman, and thereby a potential Mother, even if she be a doctor, lawyer, or a member of Parliament. Men are men and women are women, and there is no neuter gender. . . . In degrading women you degrade the potential Mother, and thus life is poisoned at its source." Lutyens argued that the feminists' emphasis on equality was misdirected. Sexual difference, with its implications for reproduction, had to be acknowledged: "I know there are many feminists who would ignore this fact of sex, who would have women regarded and treated as if sex played no part in their economy; but Nature is stronger than theory, and the dual aspect of the male and female, the positive and the negative, will persist while manifestation [i.e., the physical universe] lasts." Every woman was a potential mother, "and for that reason, her sex should set her apart as something sacred."[22]

Motherhood was not an adjunct to other vocations or professions, but "a vocation by itself, and one of the highest in the world. It is a vocation which requires the most careful and specialised training, it is the one which at present receives the least." Lutyens demanded that motherhood be recognized as "a profession valuable to the State, and remunerated as such, and when this is the case specialised training will form part of the school curriculum, and the Mother who accepts her high calling will be enabled by the State to fulfil it adequately, at least as far as the financial side of the question is concerned."[23] On that basis, Lutyens, like Rathbone, called for the endowment of motherhood, the state support of women's "high calling" to be mothers.

A key text in Lutyens's argument was a note written by the Master Koot Hoomi in 1883. Lutyens quoted it in the closing pages of her text. According to KH, "woman's mission is to become the mother of future occultists—of those who will be born without sin." KH's original note went on to present the "elevation of woman" as crucial to "racial" and spiritual salvation:

> On the elevation of woman the world's redemption and salvation hinge. And not till woman bursts the bonds of her sexual slavery,

to which she has ever been subjected, will the world obtain an in-kling of what she really is and of her proper place in the economy of nature. Old India, the India of the Rishis, made the first sound-ing with her plummet line in this ocean of Truth, but the post Ma-habaratean India, with all her profundity of learning, has ne-glected and forgotten it.

The light that will come to it and to the world at large, when the latter shall discover and really appreciate the truths that under-lie this vast problem of sex, will be like "the light that never shone on sea or land," and has come to men through the Theosophical Society. That light will lead on and up to the *true spiritual intu-ition*. Then the world will have a race of Buddhas and Christs, for the world will have discovered that individuals *have it in their own power* to procreate Buddha-like children or—demons. When that knowledge comes, all dogmatic religions and with these the demons, will die out.[24]

The "elevation of woman," then, was the key to the world's redemption and salvation; only a true valuation of motherhood (one drawn from "Old India") could usher in the millennium, which was conceived as a eugenic utopia, populated by Buddhas and Christs.

When Lutyens reproduced this passage, she elided the specific refer-ences to India.[25] But her overall argument held up "Old India" as a model for the elevation of women and motherhood. Lutyens criticized Christianity, and Protestantism in particular, for its erasure of the femi-nine aspects of the divine. Even Roman Catholicism, with its devotion to the Blessed Virgin, did not ascribe to this figure the attributes of God. Only Hinduism had preserved some form of the true understanding of the feminine aspect of God. But even Hinduism was the corruption of a more ancient wisdom. Lutyens's ultimate source of inspiration was "that oldest of all religions, the great mystery religion of Creation," by implication a pre-Vedic nature religion that was prepatriarchal and neither phallic nor monotheistic.[26]

In her discussion of the spiritual aspects of motherhood, Lutyens's concern with the health of the race was replaced by an emphasis on the expansion of spiritual consciousness that came through childbearing. Moving seamlessly from an evocation of the "great Earth-Mother" to the rhetoric of Anglican sacramentalism, Lutyens claimed that woman's function was to "transmute the lower into the higher, to consecrate the outward and visible signs that they may better show forth the inward spiritual grace." Motherhood was literally divine, because creative— not merely a physical symbol of divine creativity, but itself a manifestation of that divinity. The material facts of conception, pregnancy, and childbirth were thus consecrated and made sacred. As a priestess, the mother presided over the sacrament of birth. According to Lutyens, the mother was not only a priest, but also a Christ-figure: bearing children in blood and pain, like Christ crucified, "she has descended into hell in order to bring back heaven, she has passed through the valley of the shadow of death in order to give birth to life." Motherhood was therefore a great initiation into spiritual mysteries, a transfiguration, an illumination, and an expansion of consciousness.[27]

Lutyens embedded both her arguments, regarding the health of the race and the individual spiritual journey, in the context of a feminist analysis, albeit a relatively conservative one. Other members of the TS in England pursued these ideas in even more conservative directions. In the argument that women's primary function was to be the mothers of a reinvigorated race, motherhood was redefined as a public and political function, and came to be characterized as a racial duty and a service to the state. That characterization of motherhood echoed fascist and corporatist positions: women's claims to a social and political identity were intimately bound up with their potential for maternity, and motherhood was the way they earned their rights as citizens. This was Besant's argument in *Civilisation's Deadlocks and the Keys* (1924): "the motherhood of the citizen is surely one of the highest claims to citizenship that any human being can possess." In childbirth and childcare women paid their social and political dues, risking suffering and death to give "a new citizen to the State."[28]

But motherhood was not only a racial duty, it was also part of a very individual personal and spiritual quest, and it therefore required protection from an invasive state. This claim could also have conservative implications. George Arundale, for example, used it to deny feminist demands. Defending the exclusion of women from the Liberal Catholic priesthood (Arundale was at this point a bishop in the LCC), he argued that "each woman is a temple of Motherhood." "How can any woman envy us who are within this [LCC] Sanctuary when she is an Altar, when she is a Priest, when she is a Sacrament, when she is an Offering all in one? Unfortunately in the world today women do not realize this splendid priesthood. Some of them seek after other priesthoods. . . . War . . . unemployment . . . these crimes exist in our midst in no small degree because woman has forgotten, or perchance does not yet know, her mission, her power, her purpose."[29] Drawing on the gendered division of spiritual labor that had been developed within the LCC, Arundale made feminists, who sought "other priesthoods" than biological motherhood, responsible for all society's problems.

We can trace the collapse of spiritual motherhood from a political ideology into an individual spiritual experience in the writings of the theosophist Leonard Bosman. Bosman was a Co-Mason and the founder of the Jewish Society for Psychical Research as well as a Liberal Catholic. He wrote widely on Jewish and Christian mysticism, on Masonry, Gnosticism, and the Kabbalah, as well as on "Brahminic lore." A generation earlier, he had written a piece for the WFL paper, *The Vote,* on "woman's place in ancient India," in which he had argued that women in "ancient Vedic times" were far in advance of women among "modern 'superior' people," such as the English. The deterioration of the race, which he linked to the influence of Islam and Judaism, had reduced women to slaves and chattels. But, Bosman went on, "the modern woman must not be cast down, for the day of freedom is nearer than she thinks. A heavy Karma, as Theosophists would say, is in store for man. This century is to be the woman's century."[30]

In 1928 Bosman reworked his reading of the philosophical traditions of classical Hinduism, of the *Upanishads* and Vedanta. He deemphasized the physical aspects of labor and childbirth, arguing that "the act of child-birth is just a natural and in some ways even mechanical process." The real meaning of motherhood, Bosman went on, was in the spiritual expansion of consciousness that came with it. Like Arundale, Bosman invoked well-developed ideas about occult biology. In the context of the World Mother movement, however, the emphasis on physical motherhood was increasingly marked. Bosman argued that "it is probable that no woman can become a real occultist unless she has gained such an expansion of consciousness." Spiritual development consisted in remaking oneself as a channel for divine power, and "while the male body is capable of being used as a channel for the positive-masculine-causative aspect of the Deity," the female body was best suited to express its "receptive-feminine-formative aspect."[31] Bosman's implication was that women's bodies were also literally receptive (to impregnation by semen) and formative (as the fetus developed in the womb); these physical facts dictated the possibilities for women's spiritual development. The conviction that the spirit of motherhood could elevate the race was thus displaced by the claim that motherhood could bring individual women an expansion of consciousness.

In India the rhetoric of spiritual motherhood was deployed in the very different context of the Indian nationalist movement. In the late 1920s and early 1930s debates over the morality and legitimacy of the British Empire were conducted, in part, around the question of the status of women and motherhood in British India. An important moment in these debates was the publication in 1927 of Katherine Mayo's

Mother India, which represented a degraded and pathologized Indian womanhood as a justification for the "civilizing" presence of the British. In *Mother India* Mayo presented a tendentious account of Indian society, and especially of the position of women within it, to make the case that India was incapable of self-rule. She concluded that the cause of all India's problems, materially as well as spiritually, was "[the Indian's] manner of getting into the world and his sex-life thenceforward." Despite Mayo's claim that her interest was only in questions of public health, it quickly became clear that her book was an indictment of India in general and Hinduism in particular. Hinduism, she argued, viewed male sexual license and the degradation of women as sacred duties; the result was the degeneration of the race, a degeneration evidenced by an incapacity in the individual for self-control and in the nation for self-rule: "Inertia, helplessness, lack of initiative and originality, lack of staying power and of sustained loyalties, sterility of enthusiasm, weakness of life-vigour itself—all are traits that truly characterize the Indian not only of to-day, but of long-past history."[32]

In India, the debate over *Mother India* drew Indian women reformers closer to the male nationalist elite and helped consolidate the class and caste politics of Indian feminism. Largely upper-caste and middle-class women's organizations constituted themselves as the "authentic" voice of Indian womanhood, using the controversy as a way to authorize their own interventions.[33] Mayo's construction of the case allowed her, as Sandhya Shetty argues, to oppose that variant of Indian, and especially Bengali, nationalism that was attempting to mobilize the image of the "mother-goddess" in support of nationalist claims. Where nationalists used the image of Indian motherhood to bolster India's claims to spiritual superiority, Mayo "reconstruct[ed] the 'real' indigenous mother as deviant and Indian maternity as pathological."[34]

In England, some feminists under the leadership of Eleanor Rathbone took up the cause of Indian women in ways that marginalized the contributions to social reform made by women (and men) in India. In 1928 she put the case to members of the National Union of Societies for Equal Citizenship in uncompromising terms: "So long as imperialism is an unescapable fact, its responsibilities are also an unescapable fact, and these, for the women of this country, include the welfare of all those women in India and the East whose wrongs, as compared to the worst wrongs of our past, are as scorpions to whips."[35] During the debate over Mayo's *Mother India,* Rathbone's new feminism was increasingly marked by a racist and imperialist rhetoric.[36] Theosophy's identification of India as the source of the ancient wisdom and of Indian womanhood as an ideal type of womanhood allowed feminist theosophists who were otherwise in sympathy with Rathbone and the new feminists to break ranks over this debate. The position that British members of the TS articulated in the *Mother India* debates—in print, at protest meetings, in the WIA and the AIWC, as well as through the World Mother movement—was authorized by their identification with an oppositional image of the Indian mother. In England women like Lutyens appropriated this image in order to call into question the racism and imperialism of Mayo and her supporters.

Since theosophists were prominent among those who had extolled the virtues of Hinduism to English and American audiences, members of the TS were inevitably implicated in Mayo's attack on Hinduism. As the *Nashville Tennessean* put it, after reading *Mother India* the American reader would want to "throw his theosophy book out of the window and wash his hands."[37] Writing for *The Theosophist,* Besant described *Mother India* as "a remarkably wicked book slandering the whole Indian people." If Mayo's version were an accurate picture of Hindu civilization, Besant argued, it would have "been smothered in its own putrefaction" centuries ago.[38] In 1929 the theosophist Ernest Wood, founder of the Theosophical College at Madanapalle and former principal of the Sind National College in Hyderabad, published *An Englishman Defends Mother India,* a 458-page rebuttal of Mayo's claims.[39] Theosophists were also well positioned to support a range of efforts that gave Indian women a forum in which to respond to Mayo's criticisms. In London Emily Lutyens was one of several British men and women, along with some Indian men and at least one Indian woman, on the platform at the London Protest Meeting that had been organized by the British Commonwealth Association.[40] Lutyens also wrote privately to Mayo, challenging her to admit that the real purpose of *Mother India* was to foment opposition to the extension of political rights to South Asians not only in India but also in America.[41]

The elevation of Rukmini Devi Arundale to the status of World Mother helped rehabilitate Indian womanhood and the ancient wisdom in the face of Mayo's criticisms. The effort to reformulate the relationship between the ancient wisdom and modern motherhood was both modern and antimodern; it was simultaneously a site of resistance to and accommodation of new political and cultural forms. The defense of the "traditional" Indian woman was an important part of the political rhetoric of feminists within the TS in India, but tradition was linked to the reforming and modernizing projects of women's emancipation and Indian self-rule.

Both Margaret Cousins and Dorothy Jinarajadasa explicitly linked the struggle for women's rights in India to what they argued was *the*

Indian model of feminism and reform. Theosophists justified the "Indian woman's" political claims in explicitly spiritual terms, redeploying nationalist constructions of traditional Indian womanhood in support of feminist initiatives. Since the late nineteenth century a powerful strand in Indian nationalist thought had argued that this neo-traditional Indian woman embodied the inner, spiritual, essence of the nation. In Indian politics the conflation of women and the spiritual functioned to create a space for women, at least for relatively privileged and elite women, within nationalist politics.[42]

Feminists within the TS exploited this space. Dorothy Jinarajadasa, for example, argued to a congress of theosophists in Vienna in 1923 that in "the marvellous civilisation of India of thousands of years ago. . . . women were not the suppressed, held-down kind of people that you would imagine from the way they are often spoken of in Europe." The introduction of "Mahomedan" customs had brought changes to the "life of the old Arian [sic] races," and she appealed to "modern and progressive Hindu young people" to undo the damage. The resources for reform lay in India's ancient wisdom and in Hindu tradition. The veneration of wifehood and motherhood in India was an extension of the Hindu recognition of the "great divine Shākti, the power of God in the woman side of Him." Indian women were "intensely religious" and "intensely patriotic," and unlike many Indian men they had "not been affected by the Western civilisation which has come to India." The Indian woman "remains what she was; she wears Indian clothes, keeps to all the old Indian customs and goes on wearing the beautiful saree."[43] Of course, this version of Indian feminism did not represent all Indian women. It was formulated without Muslim women, for example, and in explicit opposition to groups like the Self Respect movement that appealed to non-Brahman Tamil women who had been marginalized by the WIA.[44]

The World Mother movement was similarly based on a narrow definition of which Indian women would represent *the* Indian woman. The particular shape of the World Mother movement was also the product of Besant's shifting relationship to feminism in both England and India. Although she made frequent trips to England, Besant had more or less made her home in India since 1893, and she had endeavored to assimilate as fully as possible into Indian life. Besant's defense of Hindu social customs and her refusal to criticize women's status in India brought her into conflict, not only with Christian missionaries, but also with some Hindu social reformers and with Indian secularists who condemned what they saw as her romanticization of Hindu practices. In the early 1900s Besant began, though cautiously, to call for a purification of Hinduism and a return to the Hinduism of the Vedas, a time when she believed women had had greater freedom and authority. In 1911 she became an active supporter of the English suffrage movement. Two years later she abandoned her efforts to forge an alliance with orthodox Hindus and committed herself to a reform campaign that included both political autonomy for India and emancipation for Indian women. Although Besant refused to make women's suffrage a plank in the platform of her Home Rule for India League, founded in 1916, she did support the founding of the Women's Indian Association in 1917 and agreed to serve as the association's president.[45]

The World Mother movement had first been discussed in 1925, but it was overshadowed by the attention generated by Krishnamurti's role as the vehicle of the World Teacher. Besant's decision to revive the World Mother movement in 1928 was partly a reaction to Krishnamurti's increasing independence, which culminated in his abdication of the role of Messiah.[46] In the wake of the controversy over Mayo's *Mother India*, however, the claims made for the New Annunciation and Rukmini Devi's role as the vehicle of the World Mother took on new resonances. The Indian mother, theosophists seemed to suggest, was not degraded or pathological, but divine. Besant proclaimed that the World Mother had spoken to her directly and had asked her to announce the coming. The New Annunciation, according to Besant in the first issue of *The World-Mother* magazine, was to be "one in which the position of motherhood will be fully recognised." It was to begin in India and to be led by an Indian woman because "in India the sanctity of motherhood has ever been recognised, and the mother side of the Self has here its natural place, not of rivalry, as too often in the West, but as the other half of humanity." Where women in Europe had had to struggle for their rights, the women of India were now "taking what they have felt to be their natural place in the Nation." Where Mayo had made the term *Indian feminist* seem an oxymoron, Besant naturalized the relationship between the Indian feminist and nationalist movements. Since the Indian woman was, as Besant put it, the embodiment of "the Shakti, the Power of God," it was much easier for Indian men to recognize and reverence both the woman and the mother than it was for their European counterparts.[47]

Besant claimed that the World Mother herself knew "no differences of caste, color, rank." "All, to Her, are Her children."[48] But this universalizing claim was simultaneously and perhaps inevitably undercut by the announcement that the World Mother was to become incarnate through a particular "vehicle." However universal the abstract ideal of the World Mother was intended to be, the "vehicle" she was to use was ineluctably particular: Rukmini Devi herself was not "Indian woman-hood" (however often that status might be claimed on her behalf), but a woman with a particular location in the caste and class politics of South India, and with a particular investment in the theosophical effort to synthesize East and West.

Rukmini Devi was born in 1904 in Madurai, the daughter, as theo-sophical sources continually emphasized, of "high caste parents."[49] In 1920, when she was sixteen, Rukmini Devi married George Arundale, who was then forty-two. The marriage caused something of a scandal both within the TS and outside it; some social reformers saw it as an endorsement of the practice of child marriage, while some members of the TS argued that it was inappropriate for those who aspired to high occult progress (as both Arundale and Rukmini Devi were believed to do) to form "ties of the flesh."[50]

From the beginning it was unclear how actively Rukmini Devi identi-fied with her position as the vehicle for the World Mother. When the first (and only) issue of *The World-Mother* magazine appeared, Ruk-mini Devi was listed as the editor. But it was Besant, not Rukmini Devi, who dominated the magazine and established its tone. Besant's "New Annunication" was the first article, which also served as the magazine's editorial. Rukmini Devi's only direct contribution to the entire issue was a devotional poem dedicated "To the World-Mother." The poem displayed the blending of Hindu with Christian symbolism that was typical of theosophical writing: "Thou who art Parvati, Lakshmi, Thou who art Sarasvati, / Thou who art Our Holy Lady Mary. . . . Come Thou to us, Blessed Mother Divine."[51] In this hymn to the World Mother, Rukmini Devi spoke not with the authority of the World Mother, but as a humble devotee. When the World Mother herself spoke through the pages of the magazine, in "The Call of the World-Mother," Rukmini Devi was curiously absent. A note by Besant ex-plained that this "call" had been transmitted by the World Mother through the "inevitably imperfect channel of a pupil living in the outer world." Without naming Rukmini Devi, Besant drew attention to her role in shaping the images and impressions transmitted, making her responsible for any defects of style, but not quite making her respon-sible for the message itself.

From that ambivalent position Rukmini Devi spoke through the voice of the Divine Mother, not only on behalf of "Indian Mother-hood," but on behalf of motherhood worldwide. The message that she conveyed emphasized the divinity of motherhood even while recogniz-ing, though not specifying, the ways in which "false tradition and blas-phemous custom" had dishonored actual mothers, to the detriment of

George Arundale and Rukmini Devi in 1930.
(Adyar Library and Research Centre)

both the home and the race. At the same time, the ideal of the World Mother was implicitly connected both to a reformed Hinduism and to a reinvigorated India in which women's political rights were recognized: "In the outer world no less must woman have her honored place, for the Nation needs her as a perfect example of the power and sacrifice of citizenship, purifying and ennobling its life, and by the purity of her

Shakti burning away the dross of selfishness and unbrotherliness. Every woman must be a Star in the home and in the life of the Mother-land. . . . Where women are honored and fulfil their womanhood, there shall reign peace and prosperity."[52] The designation of an Indian woman as the representative of the World Mother, a model not only for the women of her own country but for all women, stood in stark contrast to Mayo's characterization of Indian womanhood as degenerate and degraded.

It was no coincidence that a woman of high caste had been chosen as the latest vehicle for the World Mother. The eugenic language that had underpinned Lutyens's *Call of the Mother* reappeared as evidence of Rukmini Devi's fitness for her task. As Besant put it in *The Theoso-phist* in June 1928, "only in India can be found the pure unmixed de-scent of Aryan blood for thousands of years, marked by the wonderful delicacy of the physical body, the utter purity and impersonality of the emotional nature and the subjection of the mind to the intuition."[53] The authentically Indian woman, in Besant's rendering, was therefore also the pure "Aryan" Brahman woman. Besant and the TS exploited the discourse that held that the distinction between Brahman and non-Brahman in South India was racial as well as social, cultural, and lin-guistic: high-caste Brahmans were associated with northern "Aryans," and non-Brahmans with the original Dravidian inhabitants of the re-gion. While these claims could be mobilized to support the political claims of the non-Brahman movement, they could also be used, as they were in this case, to reinforce Brahman supremacy.[54]

The rhetoric of purity, refinement, and delicacy—given a eugenic inflection in Besant's writings about World Motherhood—was de-ployed in a rather different way in Rukmini Devi's own works, espe-cially those written after Besant's death in 1933. In these writings, the rhetoric of purity and refinement was used to authorize an explicitly cultural program, which was linked to but distanced from the physio-logical and biological elements of actual motherhood. When Rukmini Devi spoke as a "Mother" she spoke of "the woman as she was in an-cient India, not as she is to-day; the woman who was the Warrior, the true Mother, the Priestess, the ideal for the world."[55] Speaking to the world congress of theosophists in Geneva in 1936, she made clear her own understanding of the link between motherhood and cultural cre-ativity, offering yet another rereading of the ancient wisdom for the modern mother:

In the Sanskrit philosophy Motherhood in its physical aspect is a representative of the divine power, so that when a woman has children . . . she is physically bringing a fragment of the Deity into incarnation. . . . To bring up children and to educate them. . . . is divine, and this was realized in ancient India. . . . The fact that she is a Woman brings out the spirit of Motherhood, and she should represent in all phases of life that great spirit of Motherhood whether she is a mother on the physical plane or not.

Rejecting a definition of equality that would attempt to make women more like men, she celebrated the uniqueness of "Woman," which she located above all in women's capacity to create "Beauty and Happiness."[56]

In her pamphlet *Woman as Artist,* written sometime after independence in 1947, Rukmini Devi again linked women's special contributions to their capacity for beauty, which was inherent in women's "purity" and "refinement." Her vision of the fine art of motherhood included a social and political mission:

> Is there a greater woman than she who mothers her nation, either as mother in the home, or the mother who is a statesman, the mother who is a true educationist, the mother who works for the poor, or the mother who expresses her tenderness to the young including the animal kingdom? I see women in modern life who take up different professions, carrying the personal motherhood which they express in their home to the greater motherhood which they express to their country, to all the nations of the world. Such compassion that stirs a woman's soul to forget the smallness of life, to become truly great in her understanding, whether she is a physical mother or not, such compassion creates the greatest artist, who is the mother, and such motherhood is the very soul and essence of womanhood.

Modern conceptions of sex, marriage, and motherhood degraded women and betrayed the "mysterious and sacred power which, in the Indian scriptures, as in others, finds beautiful and wonderful expression." The spirit of woman should "nourish and humanize the entire social order," and women's political engagement in postindependence India, she implied, had done precisely that. And that was in part because among Indian women "there is a culture and a refinement in these directions [sex and motherhood] which . . . are unequalled anywhere else in spite of the unhappy social conditions that exist in our land."[57]

Through her marriage to Arundale, who succeeded Besant as president of the TS, and through the World Mother campaign, Rukmini Devi achieved a position of prominence within the Theosophical Society beyond what any other Indian woman had reached. That the Arundales remained childless reaffirmed Rukmini Devi's claim, as an initiate, to sexual purity and may also have made it easier for her to disconnect motherhood from its specifically reproductive meanings in her speeches and writings. After George Arundale's death in 1945, Rukmini Devi devoted herself to humanitarian and cultural work, and especially to the revival of *bharatanatyam* dance through the Kalakshetra school at Adyar. In 1953 and 1980 she ran unsuccessfully for president of the TS and—a testament to her humanitarian and cultural contributions—sat in the Indian Senate.[58] For Rukmini Devi, her position as World Mother provided a platform from which she could articulate her own vision of women's political and cultural destiny. That vision was grounded in her own understanding of the sacred character of both motherhood and womanhood.

Characteristically, one of her earliest political initiatives, as a delegate to the All India Women's Conference at Poona in January 1927, was to endorse a resolution supporting compulsory religious training in schools and colleges; the combination of feminism, educational reform, and the emphasis on an essentialized connection between womanhood and spirituality was typical of Rukmini Devi's feminist writing.[59] This mobilization of spiritual motherhood for feminist ends was made possible by the ways in which both women and the spiritual had been positioned within Indian nationalist rhetoric.

In India, the intersections between theosophy and feminism took on new forms in response to the specificities of Indian nationalist and feminist politics. The Theosophical Society brought British women into contact with Indian feminists, but it was clear that British women could not simply apply the lessons learned in Britain in the political context of colonial India. The result was to reshape theosophical feminism. Margaret Cousins's experiences are a case in point. Cousins and her husband were Irish Protestants who were instrumental in refounding the TS in Dublin in the early twentieth century. While in England, Cousins became a member of the WSPU and went on to play an important role in the Irish suffrage movement. She and her husband moved to India during the war to work for the TS. When she arrived in India, she believed that "Votes for women" would have to wait at least a hundred years. Through her work with Indian women, first in the Abala Abhivardini Samaj (the Weaker Sex Improvement Society) and then in the Women's Indian Association, she was forced to rethink her assumptions both about Indian women and about the contributions that she, as an Irish woman, could make to the Indian feminist movement.[60] Cousins's identification with Indian women was clearly a partial one in many ways; for one thing, her theosophical commitments predisposed her to look to a relatively elite, Brahman constituency. This also helped shape the WIA's membership and limit its appeal. The sympathies of the WIA's official paper, *Stri-Dharma* (loosely translated, "justice for women") were primarily with Hinduism, even though there was some effort to show sympathy for women in other religious traditions, including Muslim women.[61]

The theosophists' efforts to spiritualize modern political and civic life, in both India and England, were closely connected to a vision of a reformed and purified womanhood and motherhood. Emily Lutyens, for example, incorporated both the ancient wisdom and the spirit of the mother into a universalist utopia that was simultaneously spiritual and scientific, modern and traditional, eastern and western. Rukmini Devi, in contrast, mobilized the spiritual claims of the traditional Indian mother to achieve political and cultural authority for herself as an elite Brahman woman, not only in India but throughout the Theosophical Society worldwide. That image, in turn, was pressed into service as part of debates within the English feminist movement, over what role, if any, English women should play in "rescuing" their Indian sisters. All these claims located women's political power and their individual fulfillment in their maternal mission. And all used what they believed were ancient and eastern spiritual traditions to authorize their own understandings of modern motherhood. But they were produced from particular and competing historical and cultural locations, and the relationship between the ancient wisdom and modern motherhood was, therefore, never entirely stable.

Conclusion

In 1929 the Theosophical Society entered its longest lasting crisis: Jiddu Krishnamurti dissolved the Order of the Star and abdicated his position as the World Teacher. In *The Dissolution of the Order of the Star,* he rejected all attempts to organize spirituality, arguing that "Truth is a pathless land . . . . Truth, being limitless, . . . cannot be organised; nor should any organisation be formed to lead or to coerce people along any particular path." His goal, he claimed, was not to found a new religion, but to set men free—from all religions, all philosophies, and all fears.[1] As William Kingsland put it, "the youth who was boomed and advertised for years as the great *Avatar,* and to whom credulous believers gave homage on their knees in London drawing-rooms and elsewhere, has now entirely repudiated the whole business."[2]

Krishnamurti's decision threw the TS into chaos. A member of the Hastings and St. Leonard's Lodge recalled returning from holiday to discover that the lodge officials had resigned, the lodge rooms become deserted, and the Liberal Catholic Oratory been dismantled, all virtually overnight.[3] Many members followed Emily Lutyens's lead, arguing that theosophists had to recognize that it was necessary to choose between the old ways, and the new spiritual directions represented by Krishnamurti.[4] Others attempted to reconcile Krishnamurti's teaching with the existence of the TS and its subsidiary organizations. "Truth is a pathless land": that claim called into question the whole of the complex edifice that the Adyar TS had become in the first decades of the twentieth century.

Some members continued to support the TS out of devotion to Annie Besant and Charles Leadbeater. But in 1933 Besant died, and Leadbeater died a few months later in 1934. George Arundale succeeded Besant as president of the TS and reoriented it toward what he described as "straight Theosophy." According to Arundale, theosophy itself was in danger of being forgotten, as all sorts of other interests and activities absorbed the energies of the society's members. Theosophy was not "some popular panacea for the ills of the world." Arundale therefore rejected the political engagements that Besant had encouraged during her term as president of the TS.[5] Members of the Theosophical Order of Service were soon complaining that Arundale's straight theosophy had caused a split between the TS and the TOS, and that the TOS no longer received the support, the recognition, or the resources that it once had.[6]

Women in particular no longer joined the TS in such numbers. In 1925 women had constituted almost three-quarters of new members (73 percent); by 1930 that percentage had fallen to just under two-thirds (65 percent), and by 1935 it had fallen slightly lower (62 percent). New members of either sex were also joining at much lower rates: in 1920, the TS in England had enrolled 750 new members; in 1925, 705. In 1930 only 310 new members joined, and in 1935, 276. Total membership of the TS in England fell from a high of 5,170 in 1928 to 3,520 in 1935. Part of the decline can be attributed to factors over which the TS had little control: Margaret Jackson, then general secretary in England, blamed the reduction in membership on the impact of the economic depression, which had eroded the incomes of many of the society's supporters.[7] The redistribution of income after World War I had permanently altered the face of Britain's class society, and the professional class from which the TS had drawn the bulk of its membership no longer enjoyed the relative benefits that had been taken for granted in the years before 1914.[8] Today, although the society still exists, it has declined substantially in numbers and influence.

Next to straight theosophy, Arundale stressed "personal development." Under Blavatsky, Besant, and Leadbeater, he argued, "authority and scientific revelation have loomed large" within the TS. Arundale's goal was "to swing the pendulum back to individual experience, to individual intuition, to the challenge of the individual 'I.'"[9] Krishnamurti's teachings also gave a crucial place to self-transformation: "I think most of us realize the urgency of an inward revolution, which alone can bring about a radical transformation of the outer, of society." The utopian link between the transformation of subjectivity and the transformation of the material world was still there, but the mechanisms that were to link the transformation of the inner and outer worlds were not at all clear. Religious ideologies, like political ideologies, whether of the right or of the left, were, according to Krishnamurti, opinions not truths. Social and political change were ultimately meaningless: "It is a fact that society is always crystallizing and absorbing the individual and that constant, creative revolution can only be in the individual, not in society, not in the outer."[10]

These shifts to a radically privatized spirituality are consonant with the broader shifts within what has come to be known as the New Age movement. The anthropologist Paul Heelas argues that a central characteristic of the modern New Age is an emphasis on what he characterizes as "self-spirituality," the assumption that the self is sacred. "The basic idea," Heelas states, "is that what lies within—experienced by way of 'intuition,' 'alignment' or an 'inner voice'—serves to inform the judgements, decisions and choices required for everyday life."[11] Heelas traces this concern with the "celebration of the self" throughout contemporary New Age movements. It can be found in the most recent theosophical writings as well as in Wiccan ritual, in the Pagan Federation, in the autobiographical writings of Shirley MacLaine, and in James Redfield's best-seller *The Celestine Prophecy* (1994).

The emphasis on the celebration of the self is itself part of a broader set of shifts. A similar concern can be traced in contemporary therapeutic culture. Nikolas Rose's *Governing the Soul,* for example, surveys the articulation of new understandings of subjectivity and the self in Britain in the second half of the twentieth century and concludes that "the desiring, relating, actualizing self" is a relatively recent invention, produced and sustained by a range of new techniques and practices from military and industrial psychology to family therapy, game theory, and Gestalt therapy.[12] The location of the "authentic self" in intimate, personal, and subjective spaces is clearly part of a longer historical process, which could also be linked to the Victorian celebration of the "cult of domesticity," to the emergence of the novel in the eighteenth century, or even to seventeenth-century Puritanism or Renaissance humanism. The emphasis on self-actualization, however, does appear to have emerged in its contemporary form only in the middle of the twentieth century.

The spiritual variant of self-actualization that Heelas describes as the "celebration of the self" is an important element in this broader process. Many of the resources critical to this kind of self-spirituality were developed and debated within the Theosophical Society in the late nineteenth and early twentieth centuries. By the early 1900s the emphasis on textual and intellectual encounters with spirituality had been displaced by a growing concern with the subjective elements of religious "experience," a shift that was consolidated and exaggerated during and after World War I. At the same time, the fascination with occultism and ritual magic provided a forum for the cultivation of another kind of self-actualization. The focus on the will, and on the acquisition of an extraordinary range of occult powers, was an extreme version of the desire for self-realization.

New Age spirituality is new in part because it has emerged in tandem with modern understandings of the self: these are modern strategies to cope with modern problems. The experience of modernity has produced at least as many new variants of spirituality as it has displaced. The contemporary New Age movement is now a multimillion-dollar industry. My local New Age bookstore stocks 27,000 separate titles, along with compact disks, cassettes, tarot decks and oracle sets, and other assorted spiritual paraphernalia. Theosophical writings are no longer prominent best-sellers, but the theosophical "classics" continue to sell. Most New Age bookshops dedicate at least a shelf to the writings of Blavatsky, Leadbeater, and Krishnamurti; in the mid-1980s the Theosophical Publishing House in America was still generating revenues of over $800,000 a year, and it seems likely that that figure has continued to increase.[13] Many of the concerns that animated theosophists in the late nineteenth and early twentieth centuries continue to be reworked in contemporary New Age writing.

The image of the mystic East, for example, is still very much present. A recent collection of interviews entitled *Turning East* tells the stories of twenty westerners who made spiritual journeys to the East. The East, and India in particular, is represented in terms that would have been familiar to many theosophists: "India seems the repository of potent energies and special wisdom, accumulated and intensified for centuries"; "India seems extremely foreign to us, and yet somehow familiar, as if our roots are there, as if we recognize still existing in India a way of being which was once the common experience of humanity."[14] The contemporary fascination with the mystic East, brilliantly dissected by writers like Gita Mehta in *Karma Cola,* occupies a space similar to that of Blavatsky's Tibetan Mahatmas. In this vision of the East as both ineffably Other and the source of ancient wisdom, the traces of colonial and orientalist paradigms remain clearly visible.

The results of the West's encounter with the mystic East have not always been predictable. The western fascination with eastern mysticism has also provided resources for challenges to colonial and neocolonial power. Theosophy's alliance with South Indian elites, for example, played a critical role in both the nationalist and feminist movements in colonial India. Today the Indian Section of the TS is the largest and most influential of all its national sections. According to Paul Heelas, the TS in India today can no longer be accurately described as New Age. It has been "comprehensively 'Indianized'" and now attracts "the upper echelon of Madras society." The TS is now one of many spiritual centers in the city (now known as Chennai), remarkable only for its wealth and its special appeal to local elites.[15]

The effort to bridge the apparent gulf between science and religion is, it seems, as much a preoccupation today as it was in the 1890s. L. Ron Hubbard's *Dianetics* continues the attempt to answer the "ultimate questions" of human existence in the scientistic language of "Engrams," "Auditors," and the "Life Force," and millions of copies have been sold since the 1950s. Dianetics is advertised as a "spiritual healing technology" and claims to provide scientific insights into life, death, and the self. The terrain on which science and religion meet has changed dramatically over the last century, and neither category has been stable over the interim. Which concerns become the "ultimate questions" within particular traditions, however, is still a historical and cultural process, and still reflects and refracts the organization of power in our own society. Homosexuality, for example, is characterized in *Dianetics* as the result of "hundreds and hundreds of vicious engrams"; the notion that women should compete with men is rejected in favor of "the separation of the fields of women and men."[16]

An overwhelming proportion of New Age writing centers on the body, sexuality, and healing, all themes that were important to theosophical writing. The therapeutic touch movement provides the most direct link to theosophy. Dora Kunz, the founder of therapeutic touch, was born into a theosophical family and served for many years as general secretary of the American Section of the TS. Her husband Fritz Kunz was one of Leadbeater's pupils.[17] Books on spiritual healing, yoga-for-health, and the healing power of the mind continue to draw on the tropes that were popularized in Leadbeater's writings on the auras and the chakras, and still blend references to the Christian sacraments, the Dalai Lama, the Kabbalah, and even "Tibetan masters."[18] Sexual magic, which was viewed with horror by most early twentieth-century theosophists, is now (especially in discussions that link Tantric philosophy to marital counseling) almost mainstream.

What Aldous Huxley, following the philosopher Leibniz, called the "perennial philosophy" is at the heart of many of these claims. What may appear to the outsider as cut-and-paste spirituality or as eclectic or syncretic is often validated, as it was within the TS, by an appeal to a hidden wisdom that underlies all religions, philosophies, and scientific systems. The perennial philosophy, Huxley argued, "may be found among the traditionary lore of primitive peoples in every region of the world, and in its fully developed forms it has a place in every one of the higher religions."[19] The history of theosophy's ancient wisdom alerts us to the dynamics of this perennializing project: how and why are particular versions of the ancient wisdom favored over and selected out of others? Whose traditions are being preserved (or invented)?

These questions are of value, not only with regard to New Age claims, but also in relationship to initiatives pursued within larger and more established faith communities. The commitment to multifaith dialogue has been an important component of a liberalizing trend within mainline Christianity, at least in North America. Michael Ingham, the Anglican bishop of New Westminster in British Columbia, has recently published *Mansions of the Spirit: The Gospel in a Multi-Faith World.* Ingham's effort to develop a pluralist Christianity, a Christianity that recognizes itself as only one among many world religions, has been praised by His Holiness the Dalai Lama as a move toward "mutual respect." The Anglican Church, Ingham argues, can no longer afford to warn its parishioners, as the Lambeth Conference of Bishops did in 1897, of the dangers of an exaggerated respect for other faiths. The 1897 conference resolved "that the tendency of many English-speaking Christians to entertain an exaggerated opinion of the excellencies of Hinduism and Buddhism, and to ignore the fact that Jesus Christ alone has been constituted Saviour and King of mankind, should be vigorously corrected."[20] At the same time, liberal efforts toward multifaith dialogue have involved important and often exclusionary choices about what counts as faith, which traditions count as world-religions, and which elements within each of those varied traditions will be invited into dialogue.

Perhaps the most significant questions that arise out of this study of the Theosophical Society are those that inform the second part of this book: what relationship does spirituality have to modern political life? Insofar as feminism or socialism has been construed as a "modern" political formation, it has been implicitly characterized as a secular formation. Any vestiges of an anachronistic religiosity will, many scholars still seem to assume, be discarded as the movement becomes more fully modern, and therefore secular.[21] Post-Enlightenment discourses of modernity have tended to map the opposition between the sacred and the secular as an opposition between the traditional and the modern; the result has been to make it difficult to perceive those moments when a "progressive" politics, such as feminism, has been founded on and grounded in claims that are as much spiritual as political or economic. That is not to suggest that religious concerns were the "real" motivating force behind this element of English feminism in the late nineteenth and early twentieth centuries. It is, rather, to take seriously the ways in which debates about the relationships between the spiritual and the political reshaped both alternative spirituality and feminist politics.

Paul Heelas argues that if the modern New Age has a politics, it has been for the most part the vaguely liberal "everyone needs to find their own Truth" sort of politics.[22] One of the central themes of this study of theosophy is that this has not always been the case. Intensely personal and subjective visions of the spiritual self could coexist with expansive social and political projects. The relationship between spirituality, the self, and the social needs to be located in very specific historical contexts. At the same time, it is worth noting that the shift toward self-spirituality, in the Theosophical Society and in the modern New Age, has provided some bulwark, however fragile, against the claims of more conservative and authoritarian forms of religiosity. Religious rhetoric is still a powerful resource that has been mobilized to great effect on the right. The appeal to "ultimate" and "transcendent" truths, Christian or otherwise, has become a common theme in the assault on the "secular humanism" of feminism, socialism, or the gay and lesbian movement.

There are also significant exceptions to the quietist trends that Heelas describes within alternative spirituality. The late 1960s and 1970s witnessed a revival of interest in women's spirituality that has continued to grow.[23] Feminist theology is now a significant, though still marginalized, presence within the Christian tradition. Women within the Hindu, Muslim, and Jewish communities have also articulated new critiques and new understandings of the place of women within each of these traditions. Outside the mainstream—for example, within the Wiccan and Pagan movements—women continue to experiment with new forms of spiritual praxis. These initiatives are extremely diverse. Some of these writings rehearse the essentialist connections between women and spirituality that characterized early theosophical writings on the subject, or are written to appeal largely to a white, middle-class audience. Others attempt to develop postmodern understandings of both feminist and "queer" spirituality, the political valence of which is not yet entirely clear. The concern with spirituality is an important part of our own political context, and it is still worth paying attention to the inclusions and exclusions it authorizes.

Notes

Abbreviated citations used for archival collections are given in full in Works Cited.

Introduction

1. K. M. Betts, "The Laying of the Foundation Stone," *The Vāhan,* October 1911, 39–43.

2. See Tickner, *Spectacle of Women,* 124–30.

3. Two excellent studies are Vicinus, "Male Space and Women's Bodies," in *Independent Women,* 247–80; and deVries, "Transforming the Pulpit."

4. On the Suffrage Atelier see Tickner, *Spectacle of Women,* 20–26. Tickner provides a short biography of Colman Smith on 247–48. On Colman Smith's work on the tarot, see Greer, *Women of the Golden Dawn,* 405–9. Greer also points out Colman Smith's connection with the Suffrage Atelier.

5. *The Suffragette,* 13 June 1913, 570.

6. Clarke, *Oriental Enlightenment,* 90, 105.

7. "Propaganda Activity," *The Vāhan,* July 1911, 189.

8. Tickner, *Spectacle of Women,* 130.

9. Ibid., 128; Betts, "Laying of the Foundation Stone," 40; *The Vote,* 17 June 1911, 95–97.

10. Levine, *Feminist Lives in Victorian England,* 31, 36.

11. This high percentage is also linked to the fact that theosophy appealed above all to the middle class, which, as Banks notes, is overrepresented here. For Banks's female sample, see Banks, *Becoming a Feminist,* 168–70.

12. Burfield, "Theosophy and Feminism"; Bednarowski, "Women in Occult America."

13. McLeod, *Religion and the People of Western Europe;* Obelkevich, "Religion," 311.

14. Elizabeth Severs, "The Co-Masons and the Women's Suffrage Procession," *The Co-Mason,* July 1911, 129.

15. See Davidoff and Hall, *Family Fortunes.*

16. Valenze, "Cottage Religion and the Politics of Survival"; Taylor, *Eve and the New Jerusalem;* Owen, *Darkened Room.* See also Malmgreen, ed., *Religion in the Lives of English Women;* and Coon, Haldane, and Sommer, eds., *That Gentle Strength.*

17. "Emergency Executive Committee Meeting, 6 August, 1911," Minute Book, Executive Committee of the TS in England, 3:12, TSE.

18. J. I. Wedgwood, "The Theosophical Society in England and Wales: From the Editor," *The Vāhan,* October 1911, 51.

19. K. M. Betts, "The Annual Report for 1913–14," *The Vāhan,* July 1914, 259; George Lansbury, "Towards Brotherhood," *The Vāhan,* May 1916, 229; "The Theosophists and L.B.I.F.," *Daily Herald,* 27 May 1914, 4.

20. Rowbotham, "Edward Carpenter," in Rowbotham and Weeks, *Socialism and the New Life;* Weinbren, "Against *All* Cruelty"; Kean, "Smooth Cool Men of Science." The quotation from Hyndman is found in Stephen Winsten, *Salt and His Circle* (London: Hutchinson, 1951), 64; cited in Rowbotham, "Edward Carpenter," 45.

21. Stoler, *Race and the Education of Desire;* Sinha, *Colonial Masculinity.*

22. For a review of the literature on travel between England and India, see Grewal, *Home and Harem.* For an account of Indian travelers to England, see Burton, *At the Heart of the Empire.*

23. Annie Besant, "The President's Address," *The Vāhan,* August 1911, 2.

24. On Lutyens's commissions, see *Dictionary of National Biography* (1941–50), 538–39.

25. See Albanese, "Exchanging Selves, Exchanging Souls."

26. Said, *Orientalism;* on this tradition in early theosophical writing, see Bevir, "West Turns Eastward."

27. King, *Orientalism and Religion,* 4.

28. Chakrabarty, "Postcoloniality and the Artifice of History," 21.

29. Stephen Prothero criticizes the notion of syncretism precisely because of its failure to take seriously this question of power, and characterizes these exchanges as a process of "creolization." The precision of Prothero's metaphor makes it difficult to transfer to other contexts, but he is correct to emphasize theosophy's orientalist reading of eastern mysticism. See Prothero, *White Buddhist,* 7–9, 186n.21. For a fuller discussion of the colonial syncretic, see Dixon, "Ancient Wisdom, Modern Motherhood."

30. Lewis, *Gendering Orientalism,* 237.

31. On the contact zone, see Pratt, *Imperial Eyes.*

32. Ann Braude has claimed that the notion of secularization itself makes sense only when men's religious affiliations are the focus of study. See Braude, "Women's History," 90–95, 104–5.

33. This kind of study is only possible in the context of recent work that has forced historians to be aware of the extent to which the category "women" is itself always contingent. See Riley, *Am I That Name?* and Scott, *Only Paradoxes to Offer.*

34. Holton, "Feminism, History and Movements of the Soul," 283.

35. Dipesh Chakrabarty, "Minority Histories, Subaltern Pasts," *Perspectives* 35, no. 8 (November 1997): 40; quoted in Hol-

ton, "Feminism, History and Movements of the Soul," 283.

36. Owen, *Darkened Room,* xvii–xviii. See also Braude, *Radical Spirits,* 9.

37. Michel Foucault, "What Is Enlightenment?" in *The Foucault Reader,* ed. Paul Rabinow (New York: Pantheon Books, 1984), 43; cited in Bernstein, "Foucault," 281.

38. Bright, *Ancient One,* 130.

Chapter One
The Undomesticated Occult

1. "Statement and Conclusions of the Committee," *Proceedings of the Society for Psychical Research* 3 (1885): 207.

2. "Modern Miracle Working," *Pall Mall Gazette,* 12 May 1891, 2. Blavatsky has now been rehabilitated even among the psychical researchers. In 1986 the *Journal of the Society for Psychical Research* published a reexamination of the case that returned a verdict of "not proven." An expanded version of the article was published as Harrison, *H. P. Blavatsky and the SPR.*

3. Barker, introduction to the first edition of the *Mahatma Letters,* quoted in preface to the third edition: *Mahatma Letters,* edited by Humphreys and Benjamin, ix (hereafter cited as *Mahatma Letters*).

4. The Tibetan government had refused to allow the India Survey to be extended into Tibet; the British finally invaded Tibet in 1903–4. See Bishop, *Myth of Shangri-La.*

5. Blavatsky to Sinnett, 26 August 1882, in Barker, ed., *Letters of Blavatsky to Sinnett,* 31 (emphasis in original).

6. "More about the Theosophists," *Pall Mall Gazette,* 26 April 1884, 3.

7. In the 1860s biblical anthropology (characterized by an emphasis on degeneration) began to be displaced by the evolutionary paradigm. Stocking, *Victorian Anthropology.*

8. See Adas, *Machines as the Measure of Men.* While Adas traces the use of science and technology as a measure of "civilization" to a much earlier period, the introduction of an explicitly evolutionary model of development and the transformation of science and religion into oppo-

sites gave the link between science and civilization a new charge.

9. See McClintock, *Imperial Leather,* 232–57.

10. Oppenheim, *Other World,* 1–2. Oppenheim's reference is to Owen Chadwick, *The Secularization of the European Mind in the Nineteenth Century* (Cambridge: Cambridge University Press, 1975).

11. On Myers, see Oppenheim, *Other World,* 124–25, 245.

12. Myers, introduction to Gurney, Myers, and Podmore, *Phantasms of the Living,* xlvi–xlvii, liv–lv (emphasis in original).

13. Doubt was often symbolically represented in literature and memoir as estrangement from one's wife. See Jay, *Faith and Doubt in Victorian Britain,* 123–26. Although there were many women in the SPR, its leaders and most prominent members (with the exception of Sidgwick) were all men. See Walker, "Between Fiction and Madness," 236.

14. J. H. Stack to Mr. Sidgwick, 17 October 1884, Papers, I/7, SPR Archives.

15. Podmore, "Madame Blavatsky and the Theosophical Society," 82.

16. A similar formulation is suggested in Hubel, *Whose India?* 117, 214n.7.

17. Blavatsky's early activities are much disputed. For a sympathetic account, see Cranston, *HPB;* for a more skeptical account, see Meade, *Madame Blavatsky.*

18. Blavatsky to Sinnett, 20 June [1882], in Barker, ed., *Letters of Blavatsky to Sinnett,* 18. Mrs. Grundy was a character in Thomas Morton's play *Speed the Plough* (1798); she never appeared on stage, but other characters continually asked, "What would Mrs. Grundy say?"

19. Blavatsky to Sinnett, 15 August [1883], in Barker, ed., *Letters of Blavatsky to Sinnett,* 45.

20. Olcott, *Old Diary Leaves,* 4–5.

21. Blavatsky to Sinnett, n.d., in Barker, ed., *Letters of Blavatsky to Sinnett,* 175.

22. Carlson, "*No Religion Higher than Truth,*" 152–54.

23. Blavatsky to Sinnett, n.d., in Barker, ed., *Letters of Blavatsky to Sinnett,* 145.

24. Olcott's theory was that the "real" Blavatsky had died years before at the Battle of Mentana and that (male) Masters occupied her body in turn. W. T. Stead, "Our Gallery of Borderlanders: Colonel Olcott's Madame Blavatsky," *Borderland,* October 1894, 513.

25. *The Theosophist,* June 1946; cited in Cranston, *HPB,* 255n (emphasis in Cranston).

26. See, for example, Charles Johnston, "A Memory of Madame Blavatsky," in *H. P. B. In Memory of Helena Petrovna Blavatsky,* 25.

27. W. T. Stead, "Our Gallery of Borderlanders: Annie Besant," *Borderland,* July 1895, 207–9.

28. Edmund Russell, "Isis Unveiled: Personal Recollections of Madame Blavatsky," *Occult Review,* November 1918, 260–61 (emphasis in original).

29. Many of these early theosophists were, like Massey, also active in the British National Association of Spiritualists. On the links between spiritualism and theosophy in Britain, see Oppenheim, *Other World,* 162–74, 178–82.

30. For the branch's by-laws (of which this was no. 5), see "The British (Branch) Theosophical Society," n.d., Papers, III/13, SPR Archives. On the meeting itself, see Ransom, *Short History,* 107; and Adelaide Gardner et al., "History of the T. S. in England," 8, undated typescript, XXIX/2, TSE. James Santucci makes a similar case for the early days of theosophy in New York. See Santucci, "Women in the Theosophical Movement."

31. Ransom, *Short History,* 100–101, 113.

32. Lillie, *Koot Hoomi Unveiled,* 24.

33. H. P. Blavatsky, "Mahatmas and Chelas," *The Theosophist,* July 1884; cited in Cranston, *HPB,* 207. Cranston notes that the use of this terminology was introduced by Damodar K. Mavalankar, son of a wealthy Brahman family who renounced caste and fortune on joining the Theosophical Society (206–7). The Mahatmas were sometimes also referred to as "Adepts," or experts in occultism, and their pupils as "chelas."

34. Although the brotherhood had an important base in Tibet, it claimed to be an international fraternity. M and KH

were from the Punjab and Kashmir, respectively. Cranston, *HPB,* 82.

35. Ibid., 216–20; Sinnett, *Occult World,* 53–64. On Hume, see Moulton, "Early Congress and the British Radical Connection."

36. KH to Sinnett, "Received through Mad. B. about February 20th, 1881," in *Mahatma Letters,* 33.

37. Sinnett later reconsidered his attitude, concluding that although the letters were inspired by the Masters, they were not produced entirely by occult means. Sinnett, *Early Days,* 27–28.

38. In H. S. Olcott, *Old Diary Leaves,* 3rd rev. ed., 2:131–33; cited in Cranston, *HPB,* 209.

39. KH to Sinnett, Letter No. 24B, in *Mahatma Letters,* 182, 187 (emphasis in original). Hume's letter is quoted in a letter from KH to Sinnett.

40. M to Sinnett, Letter No. 29, in ibid., 224 (emphasis in original).

41. *Pall Mall Gazette,* 14 December 1885, 4.

42. Paul Johnson argues that this was a deliberate strategy on Blavatsky's part, to confuse those who would identify the real figures behind the myth of the Masters. Johnson, *Masters Revealed,* 6.

43. HPB to Sinnett, 20 June [1882], in Barker, ed., *Letters of Blavatsky to Sinnett,* 18 (emphasis in original).

44. KH to Sinnett, received in Allahabad, 1880 or 1881, in *Mahatma Letters,* 433.

45. See Sinha, *Colonial Masculinity,* 76–79.

46. HPB to Sinnett, 26 August 1882, in Barker, ed., *Letters of Blavatsky to Sinnett,* 32–33.

47. KH to Hume, [1881?], and KH to Sinnett, n.d., in *Mahatma Letters,* 206, 427. Hume later claimed that his activities on behalf of Indian nationalism were inspired by another—and presumably more congenial—set of Adepts. Johnson, *Masters Revealed,* 235.

48. KH to Sinnett, 29 October [1880], and KH to Sinnett, n.d., in *Mahatma Letters,* 15, 18.

49. KH to Sinnett, received "6-1-1883" [6 January 1883], in ibid., 330 (emphasis in original).

50. HPB to Sinnett, 20 June [1882], in Barker, ed., *Letters of Blavatsky to Sinnett,* 20.

51. Skultans, "Mediums, Controls and Eminent Men."

52. "Review of *The Perfect Way,*" *The Theosophist,* May 1882, 210.

53. HPB to Sinnett, July [1883], and HPB to Sinnett, 17 November 1883, in Barker, ed., *Letters of Blavatsky to Sinnett,* 44, 65.

54. Kingsford resigned when Koot Hoomi's writings were found to bear an awkward similarity to the work of an American spiritualist named Kiddle. Blavatsky offered a complex occult explanation, but Kingsford viewed it as plagiarism. On Kingsford, see Oppenheim, *Other World,* 185–90.

55. HPB to Sinnett, 27 September [1883], in Barker, ed., *Letters of Blavatsky to Sinnett,* 59.

56. Sinnett, *Autobiography,* 26; Sinnett, *Early Days,* 45.

57. On these restrictions, see Grewal, *Home and Harem,* 139–41.

58. *Pall Mall Gazette,* 11 May 1891, 2.

59. Cranston, *HPB,* 254.

60. The image of the male Indian body as exotic spectacle had a long history in nineteenth-century England that can be traced, for example, in the response to Rammohun Roy's visit to London in the 1830s. See Burton, *At the Heart of the Empire,* 36–44.

61. Chatterji, *On the Higher Aspect of Theosophic Studies,* 13.

62. Supplement to *The Theosophist,* January 1886, liv.

63. Sinha, *Colonial Masculinity,* passim; Grewal, *Home and Harem,* 142.

64. HPB to Mrs. Patience Sinnett, n.d., in Barker, ed., *Letters of Blavatsky to Sinnett,* 220.

65. Cranston, *HPB,* 232; *International Theosophical Yearbook, 1937,* 194.

66. C. W. Leadbeater, secretary, "Report of the London Lodge," in *The TS in Europe: First Annual Convention, Held in London, 1891* (n.p., n.d.), 36, Reference Library, TSE.

67. See Sinnett, *Autobiography,* 27; and Sinnett, *Early Days,* 29–31, 44.

68. *Proceedings of the Society for Psychical Research* 1 (1882–83): 3. On the SPR see Oppenheim, *Other World;* and Turner, *Between Science and Religion,* 38–133.

69. "Third Report of the Literary Committee," *Proceedings of the Society for Psychical Research* 2 (1884): 112–13 (emphasis in original).

70. See Oppenheim, *Other World,* 135–41.

71. This was certainly true of handwriting analysis in France during this period. See Panchasi, "Graphology and the Science of Individual Identity."

72. See, for example, Cranston, *HPB,* 258, 261.

73. "Meetings of Council," *Journal of the Society for Psychical Research,* 1, no. 5 (June 1884): 69.

74. For an overview of the case and its interpretations from a theosophical point of view, see Michael Gomes, "The Coulomb Case, 1884–1984," *The Theosophist,* December 1984, 95–102; January 1985, 138–47; February 1985, 178–86.

75. "Statement of the Committee: Report on Phenomena Connected with Theosophy," *Proceedings of the Society for Psychical Research,* 3 (1885): 204–5.

76. Eleanor M. Sidgwick, "On Physical Tests, and the Line between the Possible and the Impossible," *Journal of the Society for Psychical Research* 1, no. 17 (June 1885): 430–31.

77. Sinnett, *Occult World,* 5.

78. Podmore, "Madame Blavatsky and the Theosophical Society," 82–83.

79. "Appendix IV: Statements of Witnesses Concerning the Shrine and Environment," *Proceedings of the Society for Psychical Research,* 3 (1885): 338.

80. "Page Proofs/First Draft" of *First Report of the Committee of the Society for Psychical Research on Phenomena in Connection with the Theosophical Society,* 5–6, Papers, III/6, SPR Archives.

81. J. H. Stack, "Rough Notes on Report," in Stack to Sidgwick, 17 October 1884, Papers, I/7, SPR Archives.

82. *Journal of the Society for Psychical Research,* 1, no. 16 (May 1885): 369;

[Hume], *Hints on Esoteric Theosophy. No. 1,* 45–46.

83. *First Report of the Committee of the Society for Psychical Research Appointed to Investigate the Evidence for Marvellous Phenomena Offered by Certain Members of the Theosophical Society,* 10, Papers, III/7, SPR Archives (hereafter cited as *First Report*). On mesmeric experiments in India, see Winter, *Mesmerized,* 187–212.

84. Blavatsky's explanation—that "Hindus are spiritually intellectual and we physically spiritual"—was sufficiently incoherent to the "exoteric" mind as to be unanswerable. HPB to Sinnett, 20 June [1882], and HPB to Sinnett, n.d., in Barker, ed., *Letters of Blavatsky to Sinnett,* 20, 237–38 (emphasis in original). In *The Secret Doctrine* Blavatsky was to claim that the late nineteenth century was an important turning point in spiritual evolution: evolution to date was the descent of spirit into matter; future evolution would see the evolution of matter into spirit.

85. HPB to Sinnett, n.d., in Barker, ed., *Letters of Blavatsky to Sinnett,* 203 (emphasis in original).

86. "Report on the Census of Hallucinations," *Proceedings of the Society for Psychical Research* 10 (1894): 152–54.

87. *Proceedings of the Society for Psychical Research,* 3 (1885): 313.

88. *First Report,* 9.

89. Sinnett, *Autobiography,* 11–15.

90. See Stack, "Rough Notes on Report." On the liberties psychical researchers occasionally took under the guise of "test conditions," see Owen, *Darkened Room,* 69–71.

91. Morgan, *Report of an Examination into the Blavatsky Correspondence,* 5.

92. Owen, *Darkened Room,* 75–106, especially 104–6.

93. Hamlin, "Scientific Method and Expert Witnessing," 504.

94. Richard Hodgson, "Madame Blavatsky and the Theosophical Society," 7, proofs of unpublished article for *Contemporary Review,* Papers III/8, SPR Archives.

95. Hume to KH, 20 November 1880, in *Mahatma Letters,* 431.

96. Sinnett, *Early Days,* 59, 63.

97. HPB to Sinnett, 27 September [1883], and HPB to Mrs. Patience Sinnett, 23 July [1885?], in Barker, ed., *Letters of Blavatsky to Sinnett*, 59, 102 (emphasis in original).

98. A. P. Sinnett, "The Society for Psychical Research and Madame Blavatsky," reprint of letter to the editor of *Light*, 12 October 1885, 1–2, Papers, III/16, SPR Archives.

99. HPB to Mrs. Sinnett, 9 October [1885], in Barker, ed., *Letters of Blavatsky to Sinnett*, 122.

100. Hartmann, *Report of Observations*, 16 (emphasis in original).

101. General Council of the Theosophical Society, *Report of the Result of an Investigation*, 40.

102. C. C. Massey, "The British Theosophical Society" (October 1882), 4, Papers, III/12, SPR Archives.

103. Brown, *My Life*, 25.

104. KH to Sinnett, received c. 15 October 1880, in *Mahatma Letters*, 1.

105. On the transformation of science, see Hiebert, "Transformation of Physics," 237–38, 245–46.

106. Carlo Ginzburg argues that a "divinatory" or "conjectural" paradigm emerged in a wide range of fields during this period. Ginzburg, *Clues, Myths and the Historical Method*.

107. Walkowitz, *City of Dreadful Delight*, 11, 41–80.

108. Sinha, *Colonial Masculinity*, 1–25.

Chapter Two
The Mahatmas in Clubland

1. The precise details of the founding of the TS in 1875 are much disputed. Those who followed Judge considered him a cofounder of the TS, with Olcott and Blavatsky. The Adyar TS minimizes his role. On the implications of these events for the various theosophical movements, see Campbell, *Ancient Wisdom Revived*. Because the focus of this study is on the Theosophical Society in England, where the TS (Adyar) continued to dominate, the fortunes of Judge's society and its successors enter this narrative only incidentally. On Tingley's Point Loma society, see Ashcraft, "Dawn of the New Cycle"; and

Waterstone, "Domesticating Universal Brotherhood."

2. See, for example, "The Editor's Remarks," *The Northern Theosophist*, September 1894, 74.

3. Codd, *So Rich a Life*, 84.

4. Cox, *English Churches*, 25–27, 35.

5. Braude, "Women's History," 103.

6. For the concept of amateur orientalism, see Billie Melman's discussion of English women in the Middle East. Melman, *Women's Orients*, 19, 38–39.

7. Bennett, *In Search of the Sacred*, 43–49.

8. Lillie, *Koot Hoomi Unveiled*, 24. On this aspect of Max Müller's thought, see Dowling, *Language and Decadence*, 61–77, especially 72–73.

9. Farquhar, *Modern Religious Movements*, 286–87. Farquhar makes an exception for G. R. S. Mead. The goal of the lecture series is taken from the page preceding the preface.

10. C. H. H. Franklin, "Vibratory Capacity, the Key of Personality," in *Transactions of the Second Annual Congress of the European Federation of the TS, Held in London, 1905* (London: Council of the Federation, 1907), 339.

11. Bertram Keightley, "The Adyar Convention Lectures: Theosophy in the West," *The Theosophist*, July 1891, 585. On Keightley, see entry in *International Theosophical Yearbook, 1937*, 215.

12. The early history of the TS was complicated by the coexistence of two types of power within the society: Blavatsky's charismatic authority and Olcott's authority of office. Since claims to direct contact with the Masters could always be used to challenge elected officials, the transformation of charismatic into organizational authority—what Max Weber described as the "routinization of charisma"—was always incomplete. Campbell, *Ancient Wisdom Revived*, 96–99, 187–90.

13. See Gilbert, *Golden Dawn*, 7.

14. W. R. Old, "Annual Report of the British Section Theosophical Society, 10 October 1890," in *Report of the General Meeting of the Council of the British Section*, 14, TSE. On Old, see entry in *International Theosophical Year Book, 1937*, 228.

15. Cleather, *H. P. Blavatsky: A Great*

Betrayal, 83. See also Cleather, *H. P. Blavatsky as I Knew Her.*

16. Anderson, "Bridging Cross-Cultural Feminisms," 563–65. For biographical studies of Besant, see Nethercot's two-volume study, *First Five Lives of Annie Besant* and *Last Four Lives of Annie Besant;* and Taylor, *Annie Besant.* See also Besant's own account of her life in Besant, *Autobiography.* When Besant left her husband, she changed the pronunciation of her name to rhyme with *pleasant.*

17. For her account of her first contact with theosophy and her meeting with Blavatsky, see Besant, *Autobiography*, 310.

18. "Chronique of the Quarter," *Borderland* 2, no. 10 (October 1895): 291.

19. Nethercot, *First Five Lives of Annie Besant*, 291.

20. Yet Blavatsky herself criticized academic orientalism for being overly textual. She argued that Buddhism, for example, could not be understood without insight into its "esoteric" meanings, and that a focus on texts alone had led exoteric orientalists into error. See Wickremeratne, *Genesis of an Orientalist*, 221.

21. Blavatsky, *The Secret Doctrine*, 1:vii, xxii, 21. For an account of the writing of *The Secret Doctrine*, which rejects its supernatural origins, see Meade, *Madame Blavatsky*, 370–413.

22. Gardner, "Freemasonry," 3; Blavatsky, *The Secret Doctrine*, 1:xxxviii, 78–79; Carpenter, *My Days and Dreams*, 244.

23. Blavatsky, *Key to Theosophy*, 63.

24. Blavatsky, *The Secret Doctrine*, 1:17; 2:46, 434–35, 779.

25. Ibid., 2:9.

26. Turner, *Between Science and Religion*, 8–37.

27. Blavatsky, *Voice of the Silence*, xi. The title page notes that these fragments have been "translated and annotated by 'H.P.B.'"

28. James, *Varieties of Religious Experience*, 330–31 (emphasis in original). James's selection is compiled from the first twenty pages of Blavatsky's text.

29. Ransom, *Short History*, 257.

30. Nethercot, *First Five Lives of Annie Besant*, 330–31.

31. "Appendix: Extracts from Lodge Reports," in *The TS in Europe: First Annual Convention, Held in London, 1891* (n.p., n.d.), 53, Reference Library, TSE.

32. The original notice is preserved in the general secretary's office at the headquarters of the TS in England.

33. Scrutator, "Madame Blavatsky: A Personal Reminiscence," *Occult Review*, March 1914, 139; Arthur A. Wells, "Correspondence," *The Vāhan*, April 1907, 71.

34. "The Departure of H. P. B.," *The Vāhan*, May 1891, 1–3.

35. "Activities," *The Vāhan*, June 1892, 7.

36. *Pall Mall Gazette*, 9, 11, and 12 May 1891; Lillie, *Koot Hoomi Unveiled*, 24.

37. "Preliminary Circular: To the Theosophists of Europe (25 August 1890)," Minute Book of the European Section of the TS, vol. 1 (1890–91), TSE. The European Section, headquartered in London, replaced the British Section in 1890. When other national sections were organized, the TS in England resumed the title of British (and, some years later, English) Section. Since the main focus of this study is on England, and since theosophical activity in Europe and Britain during these years was also almost exclusively centered in England, I have referred to the English society throughout, except when referring to formal conventions held under the title of European or British Section. The original reorganization of the British Section was part of the struggle between Blavatsky and Olcott.

38. "Appendix: Abstracts of Reports from Branches, London Lodge," in *TS, European Section, Fourth Annual Convention, Held in London, 1894* (n.p., n.d.), 38–39, Reference Library, TSE.

39. "Report of Proceedings," in *TS, European Section, Third Annual Convention, Held in London, 1893* (n.p., n.d.), 21–22, Reference Library, TSE.

40. P. Q. R., "The Enquirer," *The Vāhan*, July 1894, 5.

41. P., "The Enquirer," *The Vāhan*, July 1894, 5.

42. De Steiger, *Memorabilia*, 156.

43. See the reports by W. R. Old in *TS in Europe: First Annual Convention, Held in London, 1891* (n.p., n.d.), Reference

242 Notes to Pages 51–59

Library, TSE; by G. R. S. Mead and Constance Wachtmeister in *TS, European Section, Second Annual Convention, Held in London, 1892* (n.p., n.d.), Reference Library, TSE; by G. R. S. Mead in *TS, European Section, Third Annual Convention, Held in London, 1893* (n.p., n.d.), Reference Library, TSE; and "Editor's Note," *The Vāhan*, September 1891, 1.

44. Pember, *Theosophy, Buddhism, and the Signs of the End*, 11.

45. Yeats, *Memoirs*, 282.

46. Cranston, *HPB*, 342; "Mead, George Robert Stowe," in *International Theosophical Year Book, 1937*, 224; *Who Was Who, 1929–40*.

47. Ransom, *Short History*, 105.

48. Roe, *Beyond Belief*, 21–22.

49. Nethercot, *Last Four Lives of Annie Besant*, 28–32.

50. Quoted in Nethercot, *First Five Lives of Annie Besant*, 365.

51. Garrett, *Isis Very Much Unveiled* (4th ed.), 130.

52. Besant, *Autobiography*, 326.

53. Garrett, *Isis Very Much Unveiled* (3rd ed.), 11, 14, 21. For similar metaphors, see Lillie, *Madame Blavatsky and Her "Theosophy,"* 118, 210.

54. "A New Lodge," *The Vāhan*, February 1895, 14.

55. W. Q. Judge, "By Master's Direction," 3 November 1894, XXVI/1–10, TSE (hereafter cited as Judge, "By Master's Direction"). The ES was known as the Eastern School of Theosophy during this period, to dissociate it from the TS proper and to emphasize the eastern sources of theosophical teaching. To avoid confusion, I have referred to it as the Esoteric Section or ES throughout. Judge's pamphlet was reprinted in the *Westminster Gazette*.

56. Annie Besant, "E.S.T. Eastern Division, Extract from a Letter to the Council," February 1895, 2, XXVI/4, TSE.

57. T. Ousman, Hon. Sec., "Stoke-on-Trent Centre," *The Vāhan*, April 1895, 6.

58. Robert B. Holt, "Fellow Theosophists," 20 March 1895 (privately printed), XXVI/1–28, TSE.

59. G. R. S. Mead, quoted in "Report of the North of England Federation of the

T. S. Sixth Quarterly Conference," *The Northern Theosophist*, December 1894, 3.

60. George Wyld, letter to *Light*, quoted in Lillie, *Koot Hoomi Unveiled*, 16.

61. On Chakravarti, see Tillett, *Elder Brother*, 65; Jones, *Socio-religious Reform Movements*, 170, 174.

62. The reference to Bengali Tantrik is from Tillett, *Elder Brother*, 65. Judge, "By Master's Direction," 5–6, 11.

63. Judge, "By Master's Direction," 9–11 (emphasis in original).

64. Lillie, *Madame Blavatsky and Her "Theosophy,"* 228.

65. Bertram Keightley, "A Common-Sense View of Mr. Judge's Circular of November 3rd, 1894," privately printed (London: Women's Printing Society Limited, n.d.), 6–7, XXVI/1–11, TSE.

66. "Question 14," *The Vāhan*, October 1891, 5.

67. W. A. Bulmer, "The Editor's Remarks," *English Theosophist*, December 1895, 26–27.

68. W. A. Bulmer, "Holy Mother Church," *English Theosophist*, November 1895, 21.

69. "Question 234," *The Vāhan*, December 1894, 2–3.

70. Bederman, *Manliness and Civilization*.

71. See, for example, George W. Russell, F.T.S., "To the Fellows of the Theosophical Society," privately printed (Dublin: Irish Theosophist Press, [1894]), XXVI/1–2, TSE.

72. "3, Upper Ely Place, Dublin," dated 26 November 1894, *The Vāhan*, January 1895, 9.

73. "Secession of Mr. Judge's Supporters," *The Vāhan*, August 1895, 1.

74. On theosophy in Dublin, see Meyer, *D. N. Dunlop*, 33–38.

75. "Dublin Lodge," *The Vāhan*, May 1895, 8.

76. Innes, *Woman and Nation*, 43–57. On the influence of this Irish occultism on W. B. Yeats, see Regan, "W. B. Yeats."

77. Besant, *Autobiography*, 3–4.

78. Anderson, "Bridging Cross-Cultural Feminisms," 567.

79. Rich, *Race and Empire*, 13, 27.

80. Young, *Colonial Desire*, 70. For Arnold, these were less separate racial types than separate tendencies within the English character.

81. See, for example, KH to Sinnett, n.d., in *Mahatma Letters*, 145–54; Blavatsky, *The Secret Doctrine*, 2:423–36. The full elaboration of these theories would await C. W. Leadbeater's clairvoyant investigations.

82. "A Learned Milliner," *Pall Mall Gazette*, 10 December 1885, 1–2; A. L. C. [Alice Leighton Cleather], "Correspondence: Theosophy in Western Lands," *The Theosophist*, June 1890, 533.

83. "North of England Federation TS," *The Northern Theosophist*, September 1894, 75.

84. Leopold, "British Applications of the Aryan Theory of Race"; Trautmann, *Aryans and British India*. Viswanathan, *Outside the Fold*, 206–7, also points out the Aryanization of Celtic peoples in theosophical racial theory, but places much less emphasis on the simultaneous Aryanization of Englishness.

85. Che-Yew-Tsäng, "A Forgotten Pledge," 3 February 1895, XXVI/1–25, TSE.

86. *The Vāhan*, May 1895, 4.

87. G. R. S. Mead, "Report of Proceedings: General Secretary's Report," and "Appendix to General Secretary's Report," in *TS, European Section, Seventh Annual Convention, Held in London, 1897* (n.p., n.d.), 3, 13, Reference Library, TSE.

88. G. R. S. Mead, "Report of Proceedings," in *TS, European Section, Eighth Annual Convention, Held in London, 1898* (n.p., n.d.), 5 (emphasis in original), Reference Library, TSE.

89. "Theosophy and Its Divisions," *Borderland* 3, no. 3 (1896): 305.

90. Constance Wachtmeister and Alexander Fullerton, "The Theosophical Society and the Secession Therefrom," 3, XXVI/1–39, TSE.

91. For an account of the activities of these groups, see *The English Theosophist* (formerly *The Northern Theosophist*), edited by W. A. Bulmer and published in London, which ran from 1893 to 1900.

92. Tingley lectured to steerage passengers during her trip across the Atlantic, while Besant had spoken only to cabin passengers. Nethercot, *Last Four Lives of Annie Besant*, 57.

93. General Secretary's Office, "Notice, 20 August 1899," in Record Book of the European Section (now British Section) of TS, vol. 2 (1891–1911), 121, TSE.

94. *Who Was Who, 1929–40*.

95. "Report of Proceedings," in *TS, European Section, Ninth Annual Convention, Held in London, 1899* (n.p., n.d.), 7, Reference Library, TSE.

96. "Northern Federation Propaganda Scheme," *The Vāhan*, June 1905, 88.

97. In contrast, in 1920, 501 of the 763 new members were women.

98. Roe, *Beyond Belief*, 185.

99. "International Office Bearers" and "General Secretaries Past and Present," in *International Theosophical Year Book, 1937*, 42–46. On Edger, see ibid., 203.

100. Minutes of Brighton Lodge, vol. 1, "Founding Lodge Meeting, 1 June 1890," 3, TSE; the quotation is found in ibid., vol. 2, "9 June 1895," TSE.

101. Minutes of Sheffield Lodge, vol. 1, "7 November 1895," 6; "16 January 1896," 26; "23 January 1896," 30; "8 October 1896," 111, TSE.

102. Harrison, *Separate Spheres*, 97–98, 104.

103. Levine, *Feminist Lives in Victorian England*, 67.

104. Walkowitz, *City of Dreadful Delight*, 135–69.

105. C. W. L. [Charles W. Leadbeater], "The Enquirer," *The Vāhan*, February 1899, 5.

106. "The Enquirer," *The Vāhan*, September 1897, 3 (emphasis in original).

107. "Practice Discussion Class," *The Vāhan*, January 1904, 42.

108. E. M. M., "Social Committee," *The Vāhan*, March 1906, 58; on topics for debate, see notices in *The Vāhan*, October 1907, 26, and March 1908, 70.

109. "To Our Questioners," *The Vāhan*, September 1898, 1.

110. "Blavatsky Lodge," *The Vāhan*, March 1897, 5.

111. Elizabeth Moulson, "Delegate's Report: NEF Meeting, 27 November

1897," Minutes of Sheffield Lodge, 1:172–73 (emphasis in original), TSE.

112. See Godwin, *Theosophical Enlightenment.*

113. James, *Varieties of Religious Experience,* 389.

114. C. Corbett, "The Annual Convention," *The Northern Theosophist,* August 1894, 68.

Chapter Three
"A Deficiency of the Male Element"

1. Harding, *Woman's Mysteries,* 17. Harding, like Jung himself, relied extensively on esoteric writings to make her case. See also Jung, *Psychology and the Occult.*

2. Cox, *English Churches in a Secular Society,* 34.

3. James, *Varieties of Religious Experience,* 42 (emphasis in original).

4. See Arnstein et al., "Recent Studies in Victorian Religion," 149.

5. These figures are based on my own calculations from five-yearly samples of the membership registers of the Theosophical Society in England. Women made up 62 percent of new members in 1900, 57 percent in 1905, 59 percent in 1910, 74 percent in 1915, 66 percent in 1920, and 73 percent in 1925.

6. The term was popularized by F. T. Brooks. See Brooks, *Neo-Theosophy Exposed.*

7. See Bednarowski, "Outside the Mainstream."

8. For an overview, see Wessinger, "Introduction," in Wessinger, ed., *Women's Leadership.*

9. Ida Ellis, "Correspondence," *The Vāhan,* March 1904, 61.

10. Minnie B. Theobald, "Correspondence," *The Vāhan,* April 1904, 68. Theobald and her family left the TS over the Leadbeater crisis and joined G. R. S. Mead's Quest Society. Theobald, *Three Levels of Consciousness.*

11. D. N. Dunlop, "Correspondence," *The Vāhan,* November 1906, 29. Dunlop eventually joined the Anthroposophical Society. His Blavatsky Institute and *The Path* magazine, which he edited with Charles Lazenby, were an alternative but not a direct challenge to the Adyar society. On Dunlop, see Meyer, *D. N. Dunlop.*

12. G. K., "Correspondence," *The Vāhan,* March 1907, 63–64.

13. Henry S. Olcott, "To the Theosophical Society, Its Officers and Members," 7 January 1907, 2, in Record Book of the British Section of the TS, vol. 2 (1891–1911), TSE.

14. Annie Besant, "The Testing of the Theosophical Society" (Benares: Tara Printing Works, n.d.), 8, XXI/25, TSE.

15. Ransom, *Short History,* 372.

16. Codd, *So Rich a Life,* 87.

17. Owen, *Darkened Room,* 202–3, 209.

18. G. A. Gaskell, *Exeunt Mahatmas!* 4–5; Ellen S. Gaskell, "Correspondence," *The Vāhan,* February 1904, 53–54.

19. G. R. S. Mead, "The Coming Election to the Presidency" (n.p., 1907), XXI/24, TSE.

20. Mead, *"The Quest,"* 293–95.

21. Annie Besant, "To the Members of the British Section" (London: Women's Printing Society, [1907]), 8, XXI/26, TSE.

22. Codd, *So Rich a Life,* 87.

23. Annie Besant, in *The Theosophist* (October 1907), 33, quoted in Ernest Wood, "If I Were President: The Election Manifesto of Ernest Wood," 4, XVIII/2, TSE.

24. Besant, "To the Members of the British Section," 3, XXI/26, TSE.

25. Annie Besant, "President's Address: Twenty-first Annual Convention, 1911," in Convention Minute Book, 1911–27, TSE (uncatalogued).

26. G. C., "Notes for Wardens in Charge of Groups," *The Link,* May 1909, 17–25.

27. Annie Besant, O. H., "Behavior in an E. S. Lodge," *The Link,* May 1909, 25–27.

28. "Questions and Answers," *The Link,* August 1909, 62.

29. J. I. Wedgwood, "The Theosophical Society in England and Wales," *The Vāhan,* September 1911, 28; "Ceremony of Initiation into the Theosophical Society," *The Vāhan,* May 1912, 205.

30. "Ceremony of Initiation into the Theosophical Society," *The Vāhan,* December 1911, 83–84.

31. "Report of the West London Branch," in *TS, European Section, Ninth Annual Convention, Held in London, 1899* (n.p., n.d.), 24, Reference Library, TSE.

32. *The Vāhan,* January 1909, 57.

33. *The Vāhan,* December 1914, 95.

34. "Bureau of Theosophical Activities," *The Vāhan,* October 1909, 35.

35. Leadbeater, *Hidden Side of Lodge Meetings,* 11.

36. Marie Russak, "The President's Queen's Hall Lectures," *The Vāhan,* April 1912, 180.

37. Ernest Outhwaite, "The Purpose of a National Headquarters," *The Vāhan,* March 1909, 74.

38. "Emergency Executive Committee Meeting, 6 August 1911," in Minute Book of the Executive Committee of the TS in England, vol. 3 (July 1911–November 1918), 11–12, TSE; Annie Besant, "An Appeal," *The Vāhan,* September 1911, 17; and J. I. Wedgwood, "The Theosophical Society in England and Wales: From the Editor," *The Vāhan,* December 1911, 94.

39. Annie Besant, O. H., "A Choice," *The Link,* August 1911, 43.

40. Tillett, *Elder Brother,* 24, 30–31, 41–42; the material quoted is in "Leadbeater, Charles Webster," in *International Theosophical Year Book, 1937,* 219. Although theosophical accounts suggest a Norman French derivation, Leadbeater's name is probably derived from "lead beater," a worker in lead, and is pronounced accordingly. See Tillett, *Elder Brother,* 288–89n.2.

41. Blavatsky herself had declared that "no Master of Wisdom from the East will himself appear or send anyone to Europe or America . . . until the year 1975." See H. P. Blavatsky, *Preliminary Memorandum of the Esoteric Section* (Adyar, 1966), 71; cited in Tillett, *Elder Brother,* 107. On the discovery of Krishnamurti, see Tillett, *Elder Brother,* 103–4. For biographical studies of Krishnamurti, see Mary Lutyens, *Life and Death of Krishnamurti;* and Sloss, *Lives in the Shadow.*

42. Tillett, *Elder Brother,* 114. Since Krishnamurti, like other members of the TS, appeared in past lives sometimes as a man and sometimes as a woman, in new sets of familial relationships, and as an individual of different races, the convention of assigning astronomical and mythological names was adopted to avoid confusion.

43. Nethercot, *Last Four Lives of Annie Besant,* 153.

44. On the Madras meeting, see Nethercot, *Last Four Lives of Annie Besant,* 170–72; on the manifestation, see Annie Besant, O. H., "A Unique Ceremony," *The Link,* February 1912, 123–25.

45. "Declaration of Principles," in [E. A. Wodehouse], "Order of the Star in the East" (n.p., n.d.), 7, Adyar Library.

46. J. I. Wedgwood, "From the Editor," *The Vāhan,* August 1912, 2; Wedgwood, "Report of the T. S. in England and Wales," in *General Report of the Thirty-seventh Anniversary and Convention of the TS, Held at Adyar, 1912* (Adyar, Madras: Theosophical Publishing House, 1913), 71.

47. Emily Lutyens, *Sacramental Life,* 14, 24.

48. Elizabeth Severs, "The Lives of Alcyone," *The Vāhan,* March 1911, 120.

49. See, for example, Thompson, *Theosophy of Mrs. Besant,* 15.

50. *The Vāhan,* November 1912, 75.

51. *The Vāhan,* November 1913, 72–73.

52. Jean Delaire, "Virility in the T.S.," *The Vāhan,* December 1913, 90.

53. For letters by Susan E. Gay, C. G. M. Adams, and E. A. Palmer, see "Virility in the T.S.," *The Vāhan,* December 1913, 91–92.

54. Wedgwood, *Universal Co-Masonry,* 30. Co-Masonry was organized hierarchically; members proceeded through a complicated series of degrees, each marked by special ceremonies and privileges. *The Co-Mason,* January 1925, 58–59.

55. "From the Master's Chair," *The Co-Mason,* January 1909, 5.

56. Edith Ward, "Foreshadowings," *The Co-Mason,* January 1909, 9.

57. *The Co-Mason,* January 1912, 48–49.

58. On Wedgwood, see Tillett, *Elder Brother,* 166–70.

59. H. H. L., "The Temple of the Rosy Cross," *The Vāhan,* April 1912, 182–83.

60. For a later account of the work of this

Master, see Leadbeater, *Masters and the Path*, 286–87.

61. Emily Lutyens, *Candles in the Sun*, 39–40.

62. J. I. Wedgwood, "The Temple of the Rosy Cross," *The Vāhan*, August 1913, 17.

63. Thorstein Veblen, *The Theory of the Leisure Class* (1899; London: Unwin, 1970), 239, quoted in Bentley, *Ritualism and Politics*, 25.

64. Dangerfield, *Strange Death of Liberal England*.

65. Gertrude Baillie-Weaver, "Freemasonry," *The Co-Mason*, April 1913, 78.

66. Pigott, *Liberal Catholic Church*, 3–7, 10, 15. On the LCC, see Tillett, *Elder Brother*, 169–76. Liberal Catholics claimed apostolic succession through the Jansenists and the Old Catholic Church (OCC), which broke with Rome in 1870 over the question of papal infallibility. Conflicts between theosophists and the Old Catholic hierarchy soon led to the disbanding of the OCC, and the LCC was reconstituted as a subsidiary activity of the TS.

67. Tillett, *Elder Brother*, 161; *Theosophy in Australia*, March 1917; cited in ibid., 176.

68. Leadbeater, *Science of the Sacraments*, 201, 299. Leadbeater noted cautiously that when the Lord himself came into the world, these arrangements might be altered. See ibid., 349–50.

69. J. I. Wedgwood, "Women and the Priesthood," *The Vāhan*, August 1918, 5. On Masonry, see Wedgwood, *Universal Co-Masonry*, 21.

70. J. I. Wedgwood, "A Tract for the Times: An Open Letter Addressed to the Clergy of the Liberal Catholic Church on the Continent of Europe" (Huizen, Netherlands: privately printed, 1928), 14, Periodicals, Catalogues, Etc. XXXII/15 TSE.

71. Besant had announced that, due to the pressure of her political work, she had renounced "*physical brain* intercourse" with the Masters, but she claimed that the "superphysical" links had never been broken and that she could obtain approval or disapproval from her Master whenever necessary. Ransom, *Short History*, 448 (emphasis in original).

72. Annie Besant, "The Conditions of

Occult Research," in *Transactions of the Second Annual Congress of the European Federation, Held in London, 1905* (London: Council of the Federation, 1907), 442; "Questions and Answers," *The Vāhan*, February 1908, 67.

73. Annie Besant, "Presidential Address," in *General Report of the Forty-seventh Anniversary and Convention of the TS, Held at Adyar, 1922* (Adyar, Madras: Theosophical Publishing House, 1923), 14; Besant, "Occultism and Occult Training," in *Transactions of the First Annual Congress of the Federation of European Sections of the TS, Held in Amsterdam, 1904* (Amsterdam: Council of the Federation, 1906), 393, TSE.

74. Quoted in H. J. Strutton, "Mysticism or Occultism? A Review of Evelyn Underhill's *Mysticism*," *Occult Review*, June 1911, 330–33.

75. Lily Nightingale, "Occultist and Mystic: A Study in Differentiation," *Occult Review*, April 1914, 199.

76. According to Besant, this was because members of the Mystic School had not been required to take a pledge of obedience. Annie Besant, "A Choice," *The Link*, August 1911, and November 1911, 43–44, 78.

77. M. H. Charles, "'The Paths,'" and "New Lodge," *The Vāhan*, March 1912, 160, 169.

78. M. H. Charles, "T. S. as a Herald," *The Vāhan*, February 1912, 144.

79. M. H. Charles, "'The Paths,'" *The Vāhan*, March 1912, 160 (emphasis in original). Besant also discussed a third Path, the Path of Action.

80. Letter from M. H. Charles, *The Vāhan*, April 1913, 203–4.

81. Alice DuPont Oritz, secretary, Wilmington Theosophical Society (Autonomous), "Open Letter" (n.p., July 1914), XXIV/4, TSE.

82. See, for example, Steiner, *Christianity as Mystical Fact*.

83. "Theosophical Society in England and Wales: Report of War Work, 1914–18 and Roll of Honour," XVIII/4, TSE. Books were also sent to conscientious objectors.

84. "General Report of the Year's Work of the Theosophical Society in England and Wales, 1919–1920," 2, XV/1A, TSE.

85. Cannadine, "War and Death," 218–19.

86. "Report of War Work, 1914–18 and Roll of Honour," 3, XVIII/4, TSE.

87. Fussell, *Great War,* 114–54; Philip Gibbs, *Now It Can Be Told* (New York, 1920), 398–99; cited in ibid., 125.

88. Graham Pole, *War Letters,* 29, 104. See also Two Subalterns, *Theosophy on Active Service,* 9.

89. Showalter, *Female Malady,* 172–75.

90. Graham Pole, *War Letters,* 71.

91. Cannadine, "War and Death," 206–9; "Report of the Order of the Star in the East, 1917–1918," in *General Report of the Forty-third Anniversary and Convention of the TS, Held at Delhi, 1918* (Adyar, Madras: Theosophical Publishing House, 1919), 152–57.

92. Adas, *Machines as the Measure of Men,* 380–401.

93. These statistics are compiled from general secretaries' reports in the general reports of the TS, issued by the society's international annual conventions.

94. "Executive Committee, 20 March 1909," in Record Book of the British Section of the TS, vol. 2 (1891–1911), 267–68, TSE.

95. "Executive Committee, 20 March 1909," in Record Book of the British Section of the TS, vol. 2 (1891–1911), 270, TSE.

96. "The Independent Theosophical League" (London: Women's Printing Society, n.d.), 1, VIII/58, TSE.

97. Mead, *"The Quest,"* 297.

98. Harold Wolfe Murray to A. P. Sinnett, [1911], XI/23, TSE. Sinnett returned to the TS in 1911, on the advice of the Masters.

99. Ransom, *Short History,* 441–52.

100. B. P. Wadia, "To All Fellow Theosophists and Members of the Theosophical Society" (Los Angeles: n.p., 1922), 1, 8, 11, III/34, TSE.

101. On Besant and Leadbeater's opposition to Barker's project and on Barker's career, see the *O. E. Library Critic,* March 1938.

102. Bailey, *Unfinished Autobiography,* 77, 164, 192–93, 196.

103. C. L. Peacocke, "Special Convention: The Theosophical Society in England, 25 February 1924," 11, XXVII/1/10, TSE.

104. William Loftus Hare, "The Theosophical Society in England: 'To Your Tents, O Israel!'" 1, in Miscellaneous Papers of the London Federation of the TS; and Hare, "The London Federation Committee, 23 July 1923," 2, typescript, XXVII/3, TSE.

105. Special Convention Committee, "Special Convention: The Theosophical Society in England: Agenda," 1–2, XXVII/1/10, TSE.

106. "Reply of Mr. N. P. Subramania Iyer" (Adyar, Madras: Vasanta Press, [1922]), 5, III/35, TSE.

107. Annie Besant, "Presidential Address," in *General Report of the Fiftieth Annual Anniversary and Convention of the TS, Held at Adyar, 1925* (Adyar, Madras: Theosophical Publishing House, 1926), 9.

108. [Surya Lodge], *Prospectus and Syllabus* (privately printed, [1922]), 1–2, 6–7.

109. Despard, *Theosophy and the Woman's Movement,* 22.

Chapter Four
"Buggery and Humbuggery"

1. Copy of H. Dennis to A. Besant, 25 January 1906, Document "A," 1, III/46A, TSE. Most of the relevant documents in the case were published in [Nair], *Evolution of Mrs. Besant.* See ibid., 113–16, for copies of the charges. Mrs. Dennis later deposited the original documents at the Harper Library, University of Chicago, and copies at the Special Collections Department, Columbia University.

2. See Tillett, *Elder Brother,* 77–102. Since Leadbeater was a member of what was now known as the British Section, the decision on his readmission was made by that body.

3. An account of the wardship trial was printed, with other documents, in Veritas, *Mrs. Besant and the Alcyone Case.*

4. T. H. Martyn, "Letter from Mr. T. H. Martyn to Mrs. Annie Besant (May 1921)," 2, III/16, TSE. Martyn's letter was published by the *O. E. Library Critic.*

5. Cleather, *H. P. Blavatsky: A Great Betrayal,* 1.

6. Krafft-Ebing, *Psychopathia Sexualis,* 6.

7. Ellis, *Auto-Erotism,* in *Studies in the Psychology of Sex,* vol. 1, part 1:324–25.

8. Copy of H. Dennis to A. Besant, 25 January 1906, Document "A," 1, III/46A, TSE.

9. For the full text of the cipher letter, see Tillett, *Elder Brother,* 82–83.

10. Weeks, *Sex, Politics and Society,* 107, 113.

11. Hall, "Forbidden by God, Despised by Men."

12. Copy of C. W. Leadbeater to A. Fullerton, 27 February 1906, Document "A," 4, III/46A, TSE.

13. "Minutes of Meeting Called by Colonel Olcott to Discuss Charges, May 16th, 1906," 9, III/46R, TSE (hereafter cited as "Minutes of Meeting Called by Colonel Olcott").

14. W. G. Keagey, "Memorandum," 1, typescript, n.d., III/46J, TSE.

15. Mort, *Dangerous Sexualities,* 163.

16. On these shifts, see Mort, *Dangerous Sexualities,* 86–92, 173–79; Walkowitz, *Prostitution,* 254–55; and Walkowitz, *City of Dreadful Delight,* 209–10.

17. Walkowitz, *Prostitution.*

18. "Further Corroborative Evidence," Document "A," 10, III/46A, TSE. Dyer and the boys were identified in H. Whyte's "Analysis of and Comments upon Evidence," which he asked be placed before the Advisory Board (III/46Q2, TSE). Lesley Hall argues that the reformers' claim that this was a routine medical practice is largely apocryphal, and Dyer's prescription may be atypical. Hall, "Forbidden by God, Despised by Men," 370.

19. Annie Besant, "Judges and Opinions" (reprinted from *Indian Patriot,* 2 May 1913), in "For Private Circulation" (privately printed, n.d.), 1–2, XIX/24, TSE.

20. Dr. Rocke, "'Unconscious Hypocrisy'" (reprinted from *Madras Times,* 21 April 1913), in ibid., 7, XIX/24, TSE; "Note by Dr. Louise Appel re the Petition for the Re-instatement of Mr. C. W. Leadbeater," III/12, TSE.

21. [Burrows and Mead], *Leadbeater Case: Suppressed Speeches,* 14, 23.

22. "The Holbrook Budget," *Theosophic Voice* (Chicago), May 1908, 5.

23. Annie Besant, "Letter from the President," *The Vāhan,* July 1913, 276.

24. "Minutes of Meeting Called by Colonel Olcott," 14.

25. Leadbeater to Fullerton, 27 February 1906, Document "A," 7, III/46A, TSE; reprinted in [Nair], *Evolution of Mrs. Besant,* 116–20.

26. Letter from George Arundale, quoted by Annie Besant in "Presidential Address," in *General Report of the Forty-seventh Anniversary and Convention of the TS, Held at Adyar, 1922* (Adyar, Madras: Theosophical Publishing House 1923), 13.

27. W. G. Keagey, "General Memorandum on the Recent Attack against Mr. Leadbeater," 21 November 1906, 2, 6–7, III/46M, TSE.

28. Annie Besant, page proofs of "A Letter to the Members of the Theosophical Society," November 1908, 5–6, III/46F, TSE. The letter was reprinted in [Nair], *Evolution of Mrs. Besant* (incorrectly dated 7 September 1908), 255–70.

29. *International Theosophical Year Book, 1937,* 218.

30. [Burrows and Mead], *Leadbeater Case: Suppressed Speeches,* 24; Mead et al., *Leadbeater Case: A Reply,* 8, 14.

31. "An Independent Theosophical League" (London: Women's Printing Society, n.d.), 1, VIII/58(2), TSE.

32. Leadbeater to G. H. Whyte, 24 July 1908, 2, III/46L, TSE; copy of Leadbeater to A. P. Sinnett, 12 July 1908, 1, III/46T, TSE.

33. Sinnett, *Autobiography,* 46; "Minutes of Meeting Called by Colonel Olcott," 26–27.

34. "Minutes of Meeting Called by Colonel Olcott," 10–11 (emphasis in original).

35. [Burrows and Mead], *Leadbeater Case: Suppressed Speeches,* 9.

36. G. H. Whyte summarizing Leadbeater, "Analysis and Comments upon Evidence," 5, III/46Q2, TSE.

37. Olcott's comments are ambiguous and may reflect inaccuracies in the transcript, which was produced from shorthand notes taken at the meeting. The broader context of the conversation suggests this is the most likely reading.

38. "Minutes of Meeting Called by Colonel Olcott," 18, 22.

39. Tillett, *Elder Brother*, 89–90.

40. Ibid., 51–52, 91; *International Theosophical Year Book, 1937*, 213.

41. C. Jinarajadasa's circular of 26 April 1906, reprinted in Veritas, *Mrs. Besant and the Alcyone Case*, xxvi–xxviii.

42. Krafft-Ebing, *Psychopathia Sexualis*, 230–61, especially 253. According to Krafft-Ebing, however, effemination was never associated with "*boy-love*" (254 [emphasis in original]).

43. Ellis and Symonds, *Sexual Inversion*, xi, 1. Ellis distinguished "congenital sexual inversion," which he believed was relatively rare, from the more general category of "sexual attraction between persons of the same sex, due merely to the accidental absence of the natural objects of sexual attraction." In practice this distinction was relatively difficult to maintain. See Garber, *Vice Versa*, 237–48.

44. Ellis, *Sexual Inversion*, in *Studies in the Psychology of Sex*, vol. 1, part 4:287. For a review of the sexological literature and a discussion of both Krafft-Ebing and Ellis, see Weeks, *Sex, Politics and Society*, 141–52.

45. C. Jinarajadasa, "'To Form a Nucleus of the Universal Brotherhood of Humanity'" (privately printed, n.d.), 1, III/46P, TSE.

46. "Copy of a Letter from a Boy . . . 18 June, 1906," in "Evidence Rebutting Accusations by Messrs. Burrows and Mead," 1–2, III/46C, TSE. The author was probably Basil Hodgson-Smith.

47. A. Besant to C. W. Leadbeater, 17 May 1906, reprinted in [Nair], *Evolution of Mrs. Besant*, 131.

48. C. W. Leadbeater, "The Enquirer," *The Vāhan*, September 1899, 5.

49. E., "Some Experiences," *The Link*, August 1911, 72–73; Annie Besant, "The Enquirer," *The Vāhan*, March 1898, 6.

50. H. Percy Leonard, "Divine Alchemy," *The Northern Theosophist*, October 1894, 84.

51. Letter from H. X., in [Hume], *Hints on Esoteric Theosophy. No. 1*, 22–23.

52. Bh. D. [Bhagavan Das], "Answers to Questions," *The Link*, February 1910, 128.

53. [Burrows and Mead], *Leadbeater Case: Suppressed Speeches*, 25.

54. The final figure of 600 was given by Mrs. d'Ace in 1924, "Proceedings of the Special Convention (from shorthand notes by B. P. Howell)," 55, XXVII/1/17, TSE.

55. [Horatio Bottomley], "A Teacher of Filth," *John Bull*, 6 February 1909, 141; and [Bottomley], "Plain Words to Mrs. Besant," *John Bull*, 13 February 1909, 165.

56. E. J. Lauder, "On the Education of Children: Physical, Moral, Intellectual, and Religious," in *Transactions of the Second Annual Congress of the European Federation of the TS, Held in London, 1905* (London: Council of the Federation, 1907), 415.

57. Besant, page proofs of "A Letter to the Members of the Theosophical Society," November 1908, 12, III/46F, TSE.

58. Emily Lutyens, "Action Lodge," in *Transactions of the Eighth Annual Congress of the Federation of European National Societies of the TS, Held in Vienna, 1923* (Amsterdam: Council of the Federation, 1923), 91.

59. T. C. Humphreys, "Correspondence: Youth and Sex," *The Theosophist*, March 1923, 665–66; "Correspondence: Youth and Sex," editorial note, *The Theosophist*, June 1923, 351. Humphreys later became prominent in the British Buddhist movement.

60. Tillett, *Elder Brother*, 151.

61. Veritas, *Mrs. Besant and the Alcyone Case*, 50–51.

62. [Nair], *Evolution of Mrs. Besant*, app. 2, xl, xliv, xlv.

63. [Nair], *Evolution of Mrs. Besant*, app. 3, lxxiv. Besant appealed the case to the Privy Council in London, and the earlier decisions were thrown out on jurisdictional grounds.

64. Quoted in [Nair], *Evolution of Mrs. Besant*, 322.

65. *The Equinox*, September 1913; cited in Tillett, *Elder Brother*, 155.

66. Ernest Michel, *Anti-Homo* (Amsterdam: Christophore, 1929), 7, 31; cited in de Tollenaere, *Politics of Divine Wisdom*, 88.

67. "Minutes of Meeting Called by Colonel Olcott," 23.

68. [Burrows and Mead], *Leadbeater Case: Suppressed Speeches,* 12.

69. For a fuller account of the scandal, see Tillett, *Elder Brother,* 181–204; on the Martyn letter, ibid., 188–90.

70. Roe, *Beyond Belief,* 69, 84; Nethercot, *Last Four Lives of Annie Besant,* 312.

71. "The Leadbeater Police Enquiry, 1922" (privately printed, n.d.), III/29, TSE.

72. T. H. Martyn, "Letter from Mr. T. H. Martyn to Mrs. Annie Besant (May 1921)," 2, III/16, TSE.

73. Tillett, *Elder Brother,* 148; "Farrer's Confession, 28 February 1922," III/16A, TSE. Farrer withdrew his confession, which was also reprinted by the O. E. Library Critic, in 1926. Annie Besant, "1906 and 1908" (privately printed, [1922]), 2, III/40, TSE.

74. Tillett, *Elder Brother,* 188, 190–91.

75. Ernest G. Griffiths, "The 'Martyn' Letter," 5–6, XXVII/1/20, TSE.

76. C. W. Leadbeater, "The Enquirer," *The Vāhan,* December 1898, 4.

77. Nethercot, *Last Four Lives of Annie Besant,* 48; Besant and Leadbeater, *Lives of Alcyone,* 1:22, 2:498. For a skeptical account of the writing of the *Lives,* by Leadbeater's secretary, see Wood, *"Is This Theosophy . . . ?"* 197.

78. Joseph H. Fussell, "Is Theosophy Revolutionary? A Reply to *The Morning Post,*" 8, XXIV/17, TSE.

79. Cosgrove, "Pulch."

80. Charles Lazenby, "Sex," *The Path,* November 1910, 95–96. See also Elizabeth Severs, "Theosophy and Reincarnation," *Occult Review,* July 1915, 50. According to Severs, "This change of sex does, I think, throw some light on the reason for the effeminate man and the masculine woman. Each may be incarnating in a change of sex and still exhibiting the dominant traits of the last lives."

81. Dowling, *Hellenism and Homosexuality,* 115. See also her chapter "The Higher Sodomy," 104–54.

82. Weeks, *Sex, Politics and Society,* 104.

83. Charles J. Whitby, "Tertium Quid," *The Freewoman,* 18 January 1912, 169.

84. M. H. Charles, " 'The Paths,' " *The Vāhan,* March 1912, 160.

85. B. A. Ross, "The Founding of the T. S. and the New Cycle: An Astrological Interpretation," *The Theosophist,* August 1920, 429–30; for a similar reading of Blavatsky's horoscope, see Orchard and Fletcher, *Life and Horoscope of Madame Blavatsky,* 14.

86. Ellis, *Sexual Inversion,* in *Studies in the Psychology of Sex,* vol. 1, part 4:29. A more extensive discussion of Ellis, Carpenter, and the theosophical theories of reincarnation can be found in Dixon, "Sexology and the Occult."

87. Carpenter, *Intermediate Types,* 62.

88. G. E. Sutcliffe, "Scientific Notes: The Mystery of Sex," *The Theosophist,* June 1909, 379.

89. Kunz, *Sex Concepts for the New Age,* 30–31, also 16–17.

90. D. N. Dunlop, "The Secret Way," *The Path,* July 1913, 15.

91. C. Lazenby, "Sex III," *The Path,* May 1911, 235. Others rejected this claim. See, for example, the series of articles by de Steiger, originally published in *The Path* and reissued in book form. De Steiger, *Superhumanity,* 57.

92. D. N. Dunlop, 24 May 1922, privately printed (London: Women's Printing Society, 1922), TSE (uncatalogued).

93. Charles Lazenby, "An Open Letter to My Fellow-Members in the Theosophical Society" (privately printed, n.d.), 1, XXIV/6, TSE.

94. Alfred Wilkinson, "Open Letter to Lady Emily Lutyens," 25 October 1922, and letter from Wilkinson, 5 September 1922, XXVII/2, TSE.

95. William Loftus Hare to Major Graham Pole, 2 April 1922, 1, III/44, TSE.

96. Owen, "Sorcerer and His Apprentice," 99, 103–4, 132.

97. Tillett, *Elder Brother,* 283.

98. Richardson, *Magical Life of Dion Fortune,* discusses Fortune's campaign against Leadbeater in detail. Following Fortune, Richardson is highly critical of Leadbeater (123–31).

99. Fortune, *Psychic Self-Defense,* 147.

100. Fortune, *Esoteric Philosophy of Love and Marriage,* 40–41.

101. Tillett, *Elder Brother,* 279–84.

102. Mead et al., *Leadbeater Case: A Reply,* 10.

103. Hilliard, "Unenglish and Unmanly," 184.

104. Leadbeater, *Science of the Sacraments,* 337–38.

105. Tillett, *Elder Brother,* 233–34.

106. Gray, "Constance Wilde," 2.

107. Washington, *Madame Blavatsky's Baboon,* 146.

Chapter Five
Occult Body Politics

1. J. I. Wedgwood, "Theosophical Viewpoints," *The Vāhan,* May 1912, 208–9.

2. See, for example, Rowbotham and Weeks, *Socialism and the New Life.*

3. Eagleton, "Flight to the Real," 12.

4. Gould, *Early Green Politics,* 28.

5. Pierson, *British Socialists,* 2–3. On the collapse of ethical socialism, see ibid., 125–249.

6. Bevir, "Labour Church Movement," 218–19. See also Bevir, "Welfarism, Socialism and Religion," 651.

7. W. Jupp, *The Religion of Nature and of Human Experience* (London: P. Green, 1906), 3; cited in Bevir, "Welfarism, Socialism and Religion," 646.

8. Doughan and Sanchez, *Feminist Periodicals,* 16–17.

9. See, for example, Leneman, "Awakened Instinct." Leneman points to the importance of theosophy in both the feminist and vegetarian movements.

10. Blavatsky, *Key to Theosophy,* 63.

11. See, for example, Bakhtin, *Rabelais and His World;* and Duden, *Woman beneath the Skin.* On liberalism as "possessive individualism," see Macpherson, *Political Theory of Possessive Individualism.*

12. Mehta, "Liberal Strategies of Exclusion," 63, 79.

13. Poovey, *Making a Social Body,* 11, 24.

14. Pateman, *Sexual Contract,* 176–77.

15. The best known statement of this argument is in Chatterjee, *Nation and Its Fragments,* discussed in greater detail below.

16. On Huidekoper and the AIWC, see Basu and Ray, *Women's Struggle,* 181.

17. Annie Lambert [A. L. Huidekoper], "The Future I May Face," typescript, Adyar Library.

18. Codd, *So Rich a Life,* 165.

19. Leadbeater, *Chakras* (1994). This edition has been revised to remove references to Krishnamurti and the OSE; in many reprints of Leadbeater's writings, modifications have also been made where the vocabulary, especially on race and racial hierarchy, has become unpalatable. See Leadbeater, *Chakras: A Monograph* (1927). References in the notes are to the 1994 edition, as it is more readily available.

20. Leadbeater, *Chakras,* 2 (emphasis in original).

21. This is a schematic account of a subject to which theosophists devoted countless volumes. While the exact details varied over time and among writers, the "sevenfold constitution of man" was accepted by most theosophists. For one example, see Leadbeater, *Textbook of Theosophy.*

22. Leadbeater, *Chakras,* 1–5.

23. Besant, *Ancient Wisdom,* 71.

24. Besant and Leadbeater, *Thought-Forms,* 23, 27, 52–53.

25. See Walkowitz, *Prostitution.*

26. Codd, *So Rich a Life,* 317–18.

27. C. W. L., "The Enquirer," *The Vāhan,* April 1899, 8.

28. C. W. L., "The Enquirer," *The Vāhan,* February 1900, 8.

29. A Buddhist, "Eating and Sleeping Alone," *The Theosophist,* April 1900, 405–6.

30. Tillett, *Elder Brother,* 41–42.

31. Leadbeater, *Chakras,* 65, 83.

32. Chatterjee, *Nation and Its Fragments,* 198.

33. This is one of Chatterjee's central claims. Ibid., 147.

34. Prothero, *White Buddhist,* 76, 136–39.

35. Annie Besant, "England and India," 10.

Lecture no. 4 in Annie Besant, Lectures A. B. 1900, Reference Library, TSE. For Besant's use of the rhetoric of India's spiritual superiority in the context of Indian nationalist politics, see Bevir, "In Opposition to the Raj."

36. A. A. W., "The Enquirer," *The Vāhan,* June 1899, 5.

37. G. R. S. M., "The Enquirer," *The Vāhan,* April 1899, 7.

38. J. W. B-I., "The Enquirer," *The Vāhan,* April 1892, 5.

39. B. K., "The Enquirer," *The Vāhan,* April 1897, 7–8 (emphasis in original).

40. M. R. St. John, "Correspondence," *The Vāhan,* June 1912, 250–51.

41. Report of Besant's speech, in Frederick F. Laycock, "The Northern Federation," *The Vāhan,* August 1909, 9.

42. E. M. G. and A. W., "The Enquirer," *The Vāhan,* June 1901, 84–85 (emphasis in original).

43. "Enquiries," *The Vāhan,* 15 February 1891, 6.

44. L. Ll. and G. R. S. M., "The Enquirer," *The Vāhan,* December 1896, 6–7.

45. "The Club for Working Women and Girls, Founded by the Theosophical Society," *The Vāhan,* 14 December 1890, 5–6; *Second Annual Report of the Working Women's Club* (London: published at the Club, n.d.), Reference Library, TSE.

46. On these initiatives, see reports in *The Vāhan* for 1892–93.

47. G. R. S. Mead, "Correspondence: Reply to J. Stuart Lord," *The Vāhan,* August 1895, 5 (emphasis in original).

48. "North of England Federation T.S.," *The Northern Theosophist,* March 1895, 33.

49. Ward, *Vital Question,* 10–12, 23.

50. See the 1881 census for Ilkley, Yorkshire, and the 1891 census for Bradford, Yorkshire; E. Ward & Co., *Dress Reform Problem.*

51. See, for example, Pope, *Novel Dishes for Vegetarian Households.*

52. Edith Ward, "Shafts of Thought," *Shafts,* 3 November 1892, 2.

53. See Edith Ward, "Shafts of Thought, VII," *Shafts,* June 1893, 63.

54. Ward, *Theosophy and Modern Science;* Pope, *Mysticism.*

55. See, for example, Edith Ward, P. M., "Foreshadowings," *The Co-Mason,* January 1909, 7–9; "Executive Council for Great Britain, 1914–15," *The Co-Mason,* October 1914, 178.

56. McMillan's membership was marked as lapsed in 1895. She often lectured to TS audiences in later years, but it is not clear whether she ever rejoined the society.

57. Margaret McMillan to John Bruce Glasier, 2 August 1892, Glasier Papers, I.1, 1892/37, 2–8, and Barbara Fraser to John Bruce Glasier, 12 January 1893, I.1, 1893/21, 12–1, Sidney Jones Library, University of Liverpool; cited in Steedman, *Childhood, Culture and Class in Britain,* 124.

58. Montefiore, *From a Victorian to a Modern,* 220–22.

59. Dora B. Montefiore, "Thoughts on the Heights," *Shafts,* February–March 1898, 19.

60. Dora B. Montefiore, "My Garden," *Shafts,* July–August 1898, 117.

61. See Elton Bligh, "The Responsibility of Women," *Shafts,* June 1893, 64. Bligh's article was critical of women and blamed them not only for their own oppression but for most other social problems as well.

62. E. M. Whyte, "Correspondence," *The Vāhan,* March 1912, 165–66.

63. Prochaska, *Women and Philanthropy;* Riley, *Am I That Name?*

64. Annie Besant, "The Pilgrimage of the Soul," *The Northern Theosophist,* July 1895, 71. On the persistence of this ideal through the many phases of Besant's life, see Wessinger, *Annie Besant and Progressive Messianism.*

65. Annie Besant, "Brotherhood," 1–4, in Lectures A. B. 1900, Reference Library, TSE.

66. This version is found in Annie Besant, "An Address to New Members: On Their Admission to the Theosophical Society," in *Yearbook of the Theosophical Society in England: 1930,* 10 (emphasis in original). In Yearbooks, 1930–33, Reference Library, TSE.

67. Annie Besant, "Theosophy and Cur-

rent Events," 1, in Lectures A. B. 1900, Reference Library, TSE.

68. Annie Besant, "Spiritual Life for Men in the World," 2 (emphasis in original), in Lectures A. B. 1900, Reference Library, TSE.

69. Besant and Leadbeater, *Man: Whence, How and Whither,* 329–30 (emphasis in original).

70. George S. Arundale, "To the Members of the Order of the Star in the East," *The Dayspring,* August 1913, 119.

71. S. Maud Sharpe, "T.S. in Britain: Annual Report," *The Vāhan,* July 1909, 123. Numbers had fallen by 1909, presumably as members resigned over the Leadbeater crisis.

72. Elizabeth Severs, "The Theosophical Order of Service," *The Vāhan,* December 1910, 72 (emphasis in original).

73. L. Haden Guest, "Channels of Propaganda," *The Vāhan,* January 1911, 84–85.

74. Joseph Bibby, "Correspondence: National Life," *The Vāhan,* December 1908, 43–44.

75. "The T. S. Order of Service," *The Vāhan,* November 1908, 27; Caroline Spurgeon, "The International Moral Education Congress," *The Vāhan,* November 1908, 31.

76. E. M. Mallet, "The T. S. Order of Service," *The Vāhan,* July 1909, 126.

77. "The President of the Theosophical Society and the Universal Races Congress," *The Vāhan,* July 1911, 190. On the congress, see Rich, *Race and Empire,* 44–49.

78. Helen Lübke, "Report of the T. S. Order of Service," in *General Report of the Thirty-fourth Anniversary and Convention of the TS, Held at Benares, 1909* (n.p., n.d.), 77; Ethel M. Whyte, "Report of the T.S. Order of Service—England," in *General Report of the Thirty-seventh Anniversary and Convention of the TS, Held at Adyar, 1912* (Adyar, Madras: Theosophical Publishing House, 1913), 181–82.

79. The motto was drawn from Psalm 82. Arthur St. John, "TS Order of Service—League of Redemption," *The Vāhan,* September 1912, 37.

80. "TS Order of Service—'The Redemp-

tion League,'" *The Vāhan,* May 1914, 219; "TOS Leagues in Bath—Redemption League," *The Vāhan,* November 1914, 71.

81. See, for example, E. M. Green, "Grail-Glimpses II: God's Scavenger," *The Theosophist,* February 1915, 458–64; and "The Light That Did Not Fail," *The Theosophist,* March 1919, 587–600. On Green's wartime activities, see *The Theosophist,* May 1915, 96.

82. Eva M. Martin, "Theosophical War Service," *The Vāhan,* October 1914, 48.

83. "On the Watch-Tower," *The Theosophist,* November 1914, 103.

84. "Bow Road Club on Active Service," *The Vāhan,* February 1917, 151.

85. G. S. Arundale and H. Baillie-Weaver, "Proposed League to Help a Right Settlement of the Present War," *The Vāhan,* August 1915, 1.

86. [E. A. Wodehouse], "Order of the Star in the East," 4–5, Adyar Library.

87. Beatrice de Normann, "The Theosophical Educational Trust in Great Britain and Ireland, Ltd.," in educational supplement to *The Vāhan,* April 1917, 1–2, Unbound Pamphlets, 1917–18, TSE.

88. Emily Lutyens, *Sacramental Life,* 8–11 (emphasis in original).

89. M. R. St. John, "Correspondence: Individual and Collective Responsibility," *The Vāhan,* December 1911, 92.

90. Jessie Davis, "Correspondence: Individual and Collective Responsibility," *The Vāhan,* January 1912, 114.

91. Orwell, *Road to Wigan Pier,* 152, 162, 195–96.

92. Webb, *Occult Establishment,* passim. De Tollenaere, in *Politics of Divine Wisdom,* 138–244, makes a similar claim.

93. Margherita Ruspoli, "A Few of the Lessons to Be Learned at Adyar," *The Vāhan,* April 1911, 137–38.

94. Besant, *Some Problems of Life,* 40, 58.

95. Marion Holmes, "Mrs. Annie Besant and Militant Tactics," *The Vote,* 29 January 1910, 160–61.

96. *The Patteran* (n.p., n.d.), 7–8, TS/16/61, Adyar Archives.

97. Haden Guest, *Theosophy and Social Reconstruction,* 24.

98. Annie Besant, "The Problem of Gov-

ernment: Autocracy, Aristocracy, Democracy," 12–13, notes of a lecture delivered in London, 18 October 1925, Besant V/XXIII/31, TSE.

99. Perkin, *Rise of Professional Society*, 117.

100. Besant, "Theosophy and Social Reform," 7.

101. Interview with Annie Besant in *Sheffield Daily Telegraph*, 23 June 1909, in Minutes of Sheffield Lodge, vol. 2 (1906–12), TSE.

102. Dora St. John, "Correspondence: Methods of Propaganda," *The Vāhan*, April 1912, 199.

103. M. R. St. John, "Theosophy and Socialism," *The Vāhan*, March 1912, 161.

104. Haden Guest, *Theosophy and Social Reconstruction*, 49.

105. Bibby, *Study in Social and Economic Welfare*, 30, 38–39.

106. Annie Besant, "The Problem of Nationality—To Whom Does a Nation's Land Belong?" 7–8, lecture delivered in London, 27 September 1925, Besant V/XXIII/28, TSE.

107. Annie Besant, "From the Front," in *Round Table* (1914), 6–7, 9.

108. Wolfe, *From Radicalism to Socialism*, 263–65. While Wolfe is concerned with Besant's earlier socialist thought, his claims apply equally well to her later theosophical views.

109. Andreski, "Introductory Essay," in *Herbert Spencer*, 13.

110. Dyhouse, "Mothers and Daughters in the Middle-Class Home," 27–28.

111. Annie Besant, "The Problem of Nationality," 32, Besant V/XXIII/28, TSE.

112. Bibby, *Study in Social and Economic Welfare*, 13, 24.

113. Besant, *Bearing of Religious Ideals on Social Reconstruction*, 6.

114. Besant, *Ancient Indian Ideal of Duty*, 9; Annie Besant, "From the Front," in *Round Table* (1914), 9.

115. Geraint [Annie Besant], "The Ideal Knight," in *Round Table* (1914), 12–13.

116. Brockhouse, "Socialism and Theosophy," 317–20.

117. Pierson, *British Socialists*, 30–34, 74–75, 126–27, 144–46.

118. *New Age*, 4 April 1907, quoted in Finlay, *Social Credit*, 241.

119. A. J. Penty's *Restoration of the Gild System* (London: Swan Sonnenschein, 1906) was a rejection of both capitalism and collectivism; Penty offered instead a vision of society organized into associations of producers along the lines of medieval guilds. Finlay, *Social Credit*, 47. Penty was a member of the TS from 1901 to 1903. Mairet, *A. R. Orage*, 22, 37. See also Pierson, *British Socialists*, 192–200.

120. Farr, *Modern Woman*, 7, 65–67, 92.

121. The Centre Group, *The Centre Policy* (London, 1932), 13, V/4, TSE. For a discussion of members of the TS elected to Parliament, see Tingay, "English Section and the House of Commons."

122. A. G. Pape, "The National Centre Policy of Action" (n.p., n.d.), 1, V/4, TSE; Pape, *National Centre Policy of Action*, 7.

123. Centre Group, *The Centre Policy* (London, 1932), 6, V/4, TSE.

124. Durham's work suggests that considerable caution needs to be exercised in generalizing about fascism in Britain on the basis of fascist policy (and practice) in Germany or Italy. See Durham, "Women and the British Union of Fascists"; and Durham, "Gender and the British Union of Fascists."

125. Michel Foucault, *Power/Knowledge: Selected Interviews and Other Writings, 1972–1977*, edited by Colin Gordon (New York: Pantheon, 1980), 78–92, cited in Chatterjee, *Nation and Its Fragments*, 236–37. See also Chatterjee's commentary, 261n.22.

Chapter Six
The Divine Hermaphrodite and the Female Messiah

1. Bland, "Married Woman," 141. Bland's recent work has provided a much fuller account of this period. See Bland, *Banishing the Beast*.

2. See, for example, the discussion of Quakerism in Holton, *Suffrage Days;* and the articles in Holton, Mackinnon, and Allen, eds., *Between Rationality and Revelation*.

3. Kent, *Sex and Suffrage*, 102.

4. This is the assumption that guides, for example, Jeffreys, *Spinster and Her Enemies*. See especially 27–53.

5. Rendall, "A Moral Engine?"

6. See Hammerton, *Cruelty and Companionship*, 155–63.

7. H. P. B., "The Mote and the Beam," *Lucifer*, August 1890, 472.

8. Blavatsky, *The Secret Doctrine*, 1:136.

9. One account of this process can be found in Blavatsky, *E.S.T. Instructions*, 545. Not all theosophists accepted this interpretation as authoritative; these teachings marked the Adyar theosophists as distinctive.

10. Blavatsky, *The Secret Doctrine*, 1:xliv, 185–86.

11. C. Lazenby, "Sex II," *The Path*, February 1911, 170–71.

12. Burton, *Burdens of History*, 28, 73.

13. Blavatsky, *Isis Unveiled*, 2:iv.

14. Alexander Fullerton, "The Phallicism in the Fifth Commandment," *Lucifer*, April 1893, 110.

15. The interpretation of the Siva-*lingam* as the worship of the male genitalia had a long history in European writing about Hinduism: in 1927 Katherine Mayo repeated the claim in *Mother India* (31), citing as her authority a work written in the early nineteenth century.

16. European Buddhist, "The Women of Ceylon as Compared with Christian Women," *Lucifer*, October 1889, 103.

17. "Progress and Culture," *Lucifer*, August 1890, 442–44.

18. D. Harij, "Theosophy and the Social Evil," *Lucifer*, May 1891, 189 (emphasis in original).

19. See Beals, "Fabian Feminism," 22–92.

20. Owen, *Darkened Room*, 159–60.

21. S. E. Gay, *Womanhood in Its Eternal Aspect*, 2.

22. S. E. G., "The Future of Women," *Lucifer*, October 1890, 116–22.

23. The British Library catalogue identifies Gay as the author of pamphlets originally published by Libra. Internal evidence in these articles tends to confirm the identification.

24. A., "Sex in Reincarnation," *Lucifer*, May 1894, 253–54.

25. Sinha, *Colonial Masculinity*.

26. J. W. B.-I., "The Enquirer," *The Vāhan*, August 1892, 4. Brodie-Innes noted that "some by a strain of language use the words male and female instead of positive and negative, but this practice causes much confusion."

27. Annie Besant, "The Pilgrimage of the Soul (Report of an Address given at Harrogate, 12 May 1895, contributed by K. C.)," *The Northern Theosophist*, July 1895, 70.

28. See, for example, A. W., "The Enquirer," *The Vāhan*, June 1901, 85.

29. See, for example, S. E. G., "Sex Symbology," *Lucifer*, September 1895, 79.

30. Gyanendra N. Chakravarti, "Hindu Marriage," *The Theosophist*, October 1888, 54.

31. Editorial note, *The Theosophist*, March 1889, 369.

32. Anderson, "Reincarnation as Applied to the Sex Problem," 63.

33. Kali Prasana Mukherji, "Scraps from a Hindu Notebook: Sex in Reincarnation," *Lucifer*, March 1894, 161.

34. Three Mlechchhas, "Fragments from an English Notebook," *Lucifer*, May 1894, 249–50. By calling themselves "Mlechchhas" ("foreigners" or "outcastes" in Sanskrit), they reemphasized their status as English rather than Indian.

35. Mukherji, "Scraps from a Hindu Notebook," *Lucifer*, March 1894, 161.

36. Three Mlechchhas, "Fragments from an English Notebook," *Lucifer*, May 1894, 249–50.

37. Chakravarti, "Whatever Happened to the Vedic *Dasi*?" 29–30. This picture was based on particular regions like Bengal and generalized to the whole of India. Ibid., 27–28, 42.

38. Chatterjee, *Nation and Its Fragments*, 130.

39. Most such women, she argued, would have lived as men in their last incarnation. E. M. G., "The Enquirer," *The Vāhan*, June 1901, 85.

40. G. R. S. Mead, "The Enquirer," *The Vāhan*, May 1901, 80.

41. Forbes, "Caged Tigers," 527.

42. Minute Book of Blavatsky Lodge, vol. 1 (15 October 1891), 115, Blavatsky Lodge; Membership Registers, TSE.

43. "Womanhood and Religious Mis-education," *Shafts,* 3 November 1892, 7. The Christmas supplement in 1892 reprinted Eliphas Levi's kabbalistic interpretation of Genesis.

44. Libra, "Womanhood from the Theosophical Point of View," *Shafts,* 31 December 1892, 131–32, and 7 January 1893, 152–53.

45. Antoinette Burton, in contrast, interprets this article as evidence of a secular, scientific evolutionism that set the modern West against a primitive East. See Burton, *Burdens of History,* 82.

46. See Susan E. Gay, "The Garment of Womanhood," *The Theosophist,* February 1914, 737–57.

47. Libra, "The Legal Value of the Unrepresented," *Shafts,* 11 February 1893, 233, and 25 February 1893, 259–60; S. E. G., review of Annie Besant's *Autobiography, Shafts,* January 1894, 192–95; Susan E. Gay, "The Higher Companionship of Man and Woman," *Shafts,* December 1895, 132–33 (reprinted from *Bibby's Magazine*).

48. Mrs. A. Phillips, "Why Women Are Women," *Shafts,* 18 February 1893, 249, and 25 February 1893, 267.

49. See, for example, J.A.O'N., "Heredity versus Theosophy," *Shafts,* 25 February 1893, 267.

50. H., "Attributes of the Sexes," *Shafts,* 11 February 1893, 238; and "Attributes of Sex," *Shafts,* April 1893, 38. H.'s attack on Vivekananda similarly made "Oriental impurity" and "*contempt for woman-hood*" the basis for rejecting Hinduism. H., "The Parliament of Religions at Chicago," *Shafts,* November 1893, 168 (emphasis in original).

51. Editorial note, *Shafts,* June 1893, 84.

52. Tweed, *American Encounter with Buddhism,* 63.

53. Jones, *Socio-religious Reform Movements,* 30–39.

54. Walker, "Vivekananda and American Occultism."

55. Jones, *Socio-religious Reform Move-ments,* 95–103, 169–70. The quotation is on p. 96.

56. On the persistence of a version of Christian manliness that included apparently feminine values, see Peter Gay, "The Manliness of Christ"; on the Salvation Army, see Walker, "I Live But Yet Not I."

57. Veldman, "Dutiful Daughter versus All-Boy," 3–4. On muscular Christianity see Vance, *Sinews of the Spirit.*

58. Bland, *Banishing the Beast,* 67–68.

59. Alice M. Callow, "Edward Maitland: In Memoriam," *Shafts,* December 1897, 338–41.

60. Kingsford and Maitland, *Perfect Way,* Lecture VII, para. 38, p. 169. The first edition of the book was based on Kingsford's 1881 lectures; some revisions were made in subsequent editions to incorporate her later "illuminations."

61. A Pioneer, "Women in the Mission Field: Should They Assimilate What Is Good in the Great Religions of the East with Christianity?" *Shafts,* June 1896, 72–73, and July 1896, 88–90.

62. Thanks to David Doughan for biographical information on Swiney. The fullest account of Swiney's life and writings is in Robb, "Eugenics, Spirituality, and Sex Differentiation."

63. "Books Worth Reading," *Shafts,* July–September 1899, 84.

64. B. K., "Review of *The Awakening of Women," Theosophical Review,* June 1899, 381.

65. Jeffreys, *Spinster and Her Enemies,* 35; Burton, *Burdens of History,* 85–86.

66. Swiney, *Het ontwaken der vrouw.* Thanks to Francisca de Haan for the identification of Kramers.

67. Swiney, *Awakening of Women,* 20, 53, 56, 86, 221, 275. Paradoxically, she also held up "Eastern adepts" as the forerunners of a new humanity, in which the "spiritual nature" was to be developed "at the expense of the animal" (36).

68. Swiney, *Cosmic Procession,* 126.

69. Ibid., 54; Swiney, *Mystery of the Circle and the Cross,* 66.

70. Swiney, *Ancient Road,* 77; Swiney, *Cosmic Procession,* 213.

71. Swiney, *Cosmic Procession,* 73. On

Geddes and Thompson, and on the uses to which this and other variants of evolutionary biology were put, see Russett, *Sexual Science.*

72. Swiney, *Cosmic Procession,* 12–14.

73. Swiney, *Ancient Road,* 306–7, 349.

74. Young, *Colonial Desire,* 126–33.

75. See, for example, Swiney, *Cosmic Procession,* 96–97; Swiney, *Esoteric Teaching of the Gnostics,* passim.

76. Swiney, *Ancient Road,* 376; Swiney, *Cosmic Procession,* 75.

77. Bland, *Banishing the Beast,* 219. On the Malthusian League, see 202–17.

78. Swiney, *Cosmic Procession,* 20, 33, 42–43, 213.

79. Swiney, *Bar of Isis,* 19.

80. Ibid., 29–30; Swiney, *Cosmic Procession,* 181.

81. Swiney, *Mystery of the Circle and the Cross,* 66; Swiney, *Ancient Road,* 86.

82. Swiney, *Cosmic Procession,* 94.

83. Ibid., 175–76.

84. Swiney, *Ancient Road,* 62, 122.

85. Swiney, *Cosmic Procession,* xii.

86. These claims were discussed in some detail by the members of Karl Pearson's Men and Women's Club, for example. See Bland, *Banishing the Beast,* 14–22.

87. Ignota [Elizabeth Wolstenholme Elmy], "The Awakening of Women," *Westminster Review,* July 1899; cited in Bland, *Banishing the Beast,* 353n.95; Jeffreys, *Spinster and Her Enemies,* 35. For a full discussion of Wolstenholme Elmy's career, see Holton, *Suffrage Days.* On the Women's Emancipation Union and marital rape, see ibid., p. 83.

88. G. R. S. M., "The Enquirer," *The Vāhan,* December 1896, 7; G. R. S. Mead, "Astral Plague and Looking-Glass," *Lucifer,* September 1889, 63.

89. G. V. K., "Married State a Stepping-Stone to Brahmacharya: The True Relation of the Sexes," *The Theosophist,* November 1896, 95–98.

90. See, for example, An American Buddhist, "Chastity," *The Theosophist,* April 1884, 161–62.

91. On Mills, see Bland, *Banishing the Beast,* 166–68. See also Membership Registers, TSE.

92. Collette, "Socialism and Scandal."

93. The entry in the TSE Membership Register is dated 1891, but this appears to be a clerical error. On Lanchester, see Banks, *Biographical Dictionary of British Feminists,* 2: 122.

94. Despard joined the TS the following year; Burrows had joined some years earlier. For ridicule of theosophy's advocacy of celibacy, see Court Jester, "At Low Street Fleece Court," *The Adult,* November 1898, 305–7. On the Free Press Defense Committee, see *The Adult,* August 1898, 191.

95. On Müller, see Bland, *Banishing the Beast,* 164–68. Since Müller was also instrumental in founding the Women's Printing Society, she may have appreciated the fact that the vast majority of theosophical publications were printed there.

96. Müller, "Theosophy and Woman," 169.

97. Minute Book of Blavatsky Lodge, vol. 1 (15 October 1891), 115, Blavatsky Lodge.

98. Burton, *Burdens of History,* 120.

99. A. L. C., "Correspondence: Theosophy in Western Lands," *The Theosophist,* October 1891, 57.

100. *The Theosophist,* February 1895, 344.

101. Transcript of Karl Pearson to Maria Sharpe Pearson, 7/1/96, Hacker Papers, box 13, 1986 Biographical Series, University College London.

102. Burke, *Swami Vivekananda,* 70.

103. *Times* (London), 17 January 1906, 6.

Chapter Seven
A New Age for Women

1. Codd, *So Rich a Life,* 5, 11, 41–76, 83.

2. Ibid., 89.

3. Codd, "Theosophy and the Relationship of the Sexes," 91–93.

4. Codd, *Looking Forward,* 33.

5. Codd, *So Rich a Life,* 48. Kenney's speeches also stressed the spiritual dimensions of the suffrage movement. See Annie Kenney, "To Help Humanity," *The Suffragette,* 24 April 1914, 37.

6. On Kenney, see "From the Editor," *The Vāhan*, August 1912, 3.

7. Vicinus, *Independent Women*, 251–52.

8. Banks, *Faces of Feminism*, 95–102; Tickner, *Spectacle of Women*, 213–25.

9. Mrs. K. E. Roy-Rothwell, "International Woman's Suffrage League," *The Theosophist*, November 1912, 319–20.

10. M. E. Allwork, "TS Order of Service: League to Help the Woman's Movement," *The Vāhan*, February 1914, 149.

11. Josephine and Sidney Ransom, "Letter to the General Secretary," *The Vāhan*, August 1914, 17.

12. On the Call to Prayer and the bishop of Kensington's speech, see *The Vāhan*, November 1913, 68. On the CLWS, see Heeney, *Women's Movement in the Church of England*, 105–15.

13. Fulford, *Votes for Women*, 240–41. See also the League's manifesto, *The Vote*, 2 May 1913, 15.

14. Mystic, "Correspondence: The Mystic Reunion," *Occult Review*, August 1912, 109–10 (emphasis in original).

15. Florence Wyman Richardson, "Evolution and Related Matters from a Theosophical Point of View," *Theosophical Review*, May 1905, 222–23.

16. Codd, "Theosophy and the Relationship of the Sexes," 91.

17. See, for example, Mrs. F. Hallett, "Some Reflections, Correspondences and Questionings," *The Theosophist*, April 1913, 31.

18. H. S. Green, "Men and Women as Types," *Theosophical Review*, November 1907, 229.

19. Annie Besant, page proofs of "A Letter to the Members of the Theosophical Society (November 1908)," 4, III/46F, TSE.

20. James Cousins, in Cousins and Cousins, *We Two Together*, 81.

21. I. M. P., "The Enquirer," *The Vāhan*, January 1908, 58.

22. Edith Ward, "Foreshadowings," *The Co-Mason*, January 1909, 9.

23. Holton, *Suffrage Days*, 25, 29, 31, 62, 77.

24. Bright, *Ancient One*, 9–10.

25. Bright, *Old Memories*, 32, 107.

26. On Despard, see Linklater, *Unhusbanded Life;* for a feminist account, see Mulvihill, *Charlotte Despard*.

27. On Despard's work in Nine Elms, see Linklater, *Unhusbanded Life*, 65–72; and Mulvihill, *Charlotte Despard*, 39–45.

28. See, for example, Despard's account of her adoption of the suffrage cause, written from Holloway in 1907, quoted in Mulvihill, *Charlotte Despard*, 54.

29. "Our New Editor," *The Vote*, 11 March 1911, 241. On Despard's reading of Shelley, see Linklater, *Unhusbanded Life*, 30–35.

30. Linklater, *Unhusbanded Life*, 52–53; Mulvihill, *Charlotte Despard*, 34; Membership Registers, TSE.

31. L. J. Bendit, general secretary of the TS in England, to Teresa Billington-Grieg, 1/7/1960, Charlotte Despard Collection, box 374, Fawcett Library, London.

32. Charlotte Despard, *The Rajah's Heir* (London: Smith, Elder & Co., 1890); cited in Mulvihill, *Charlotte Despard*, 34.

33. H. L., "The Summer School," *The Vāhan*, October 1911, 46–47; Helen F. R. Veale and M. R. St. John, "Secretary's Report for 1914–15," in Blavatsky Lodge: Annual Reports, Blavatsky Lodge Archives; K. Douglas Fox, "Country Gossip: From Bath," *The Vāhan*, January 1916, 124.

34. Despard and Collins, *Outlawed;* "A Suffrage Play," *The Vāhan*, November 1911, 67.

35. Despard, "Woman in the New Era," in Villiers, ed., *Case for Women's Suffrage*, 190–91.

36. Despard, *Woman's Franchise*, 7.

37. Charlotte Despard lecturing in Glasgow, cited in Linklater, *Unhusbanded Life*, 164.

38. Despard, *Theosophy and the Woman's Movement*, 5–7, 16.

39. Ibid., 15; see also Despard, *Woman in the New Era*, 33–34.

40. Despard, *Woman in the New Era*, 46.

41. Ibid., 34–40.

42. Despard, *Theosophy and the Woman's Movement*, 10–12, 23.

43. Despard, cited in Linklater, *Unhusbanded Life*, 177.

44. Ibid., 141, 193. For Despard's claim that the woman's movement was "in the direct line of spiritual evolution," see Despard, *Theosophy and the Woman's Movement,* 1.

45. Despard, *Theosophy and the Woman's Movement,* 15–16.

46. "Lecture List," *The Vāhan,* January 1901, 42–43. Philip Snowden's lectures were published as *The Christ That Is to Be* (London, 1904). See Pierson, *British Socialists,* 48–49.

47. "The Movement in Great Britain," *The Dayspring,* 11 January 1913, 18. A lecture in Glasgow on 18 November 1912 drew six or seven hundred people.

48. Charlotte Despard, "The Return of the 'Mother,'" in reconstruction supplement to *The Vāhan,* July 1917, 16–18.

49. Mulvihill, *Charlotte Despard,* 120–21; Linklater, *Unhusbanded Life,* 189–202.

50. Cited in Mulvihill, *Charlotte Despard,* 156 (emphasis in original).

51. Despard transferred from the English to the Irish Section of the TS in 1922, and left the society in 1934. Letter from the TS in Ireland, 24 July 1961, Charlotte Despard Collection, box 375/12, Fawcett Library, London.

52. On Roper and Gore-Booth's contribution to the suffrage movement and to the women's union movement, see Liddington and Norris, *One Hand Tied behind Us,* especially 77–83, 163.

53. Biographical information on Gore-Booth and Roper is drawn from Lewis, *Eva Gore-Booth.*

54. See Gore-Booth, "Inner Life of a Child," and Esther Roper, "Introduction," in Gore-Booth, *Poems.*

55. Lewis, *Eva Gore-Booth,* 66–67.

56. Gore-Booth, *Poems,* 215, 220–21, 255–56.

57. Quoted in Roper, "Introduction," in Gore-Booth, *Poems,* 37. It is difficult to date precisely the phases of Gore-Booth's religious thought. Gore-Booth provides a brief account in *Psychological and Poetic Approach,* 140.

58. Lewis, *Eva Gore-Booth,* 150–62; see also Membership Registers, TSE.

59. Frederick Lapisardi, "Introduction," in Gore-Booth, *Plays,* viii.

60. Gore-Booth, introduction to *The Buried Life of Deirdre,* in Gore-Booth, *Plays,* 152.

61. Gore-Booth, *Psychological and Poetic Approach,* xii; Roper, "Introduction," in Gore-Booth, *Poems,* 27; Lewis, *Eva Gore-Booth,* 156.

62. Gore-Booth, *Psychological and Poetic Approach,* ix–xi; 3–4, 16, 17, 113, 148.

63. Ibid., 12, 17, 61.

64. Ibid., 19, 70, 78.

65. R. M. Fox, *Rebel Irish Women* (Dublin: Progress House, 1935), 24; cited by Lapisardi in Gore-Booth, *Plays,* 128.

66. Eva Gore-Booth to T. P. Conwil-Evans, 1924, in Gore-Booth, *Poems,* 96 (emphasis in original). Gore-Booth explored the implications of this claim most directly in *The Sword of Justice,* written in 1918.

67. Eva Gore-Booth to Clare Annesley, 14 May 1925, in Gore-Booth, *Poems,* 75 (emphasis in original).

68. Gore-Booth, *Psychological and Poetic Approach,* 92, 98.

69. The motto was taken from Matthew 22:30, "For in the resurrection they neither marry, nor are given in marriage, but are as the angels of God in heaven." On Roper and Gore-Booth's association with the Aëthnic Union and the founding of *Urania,* see "Eva Gore-Booth," *Urania,* May–August 1926, 1. On Baty, *Urania,* and the Aëthnic Union, see Patai and Ingram, "Fantasy and Identity." According to Patai and Ingram, although Gore-Booth clearly played a significant role in the journal, there is no evidence to link her directly to any of the articles (295n.25).

70. This statement of purpose appeared regularly in *Urania* in the late 1920s.

71. Gore-Booth to Margaret Wroe, 1920, in Gore-Booth, *Poems,* 80.

72. Gore-Booth, *Psychological and Poetic Approach,* 185, 252; see also Gore-Booth to Margaret Wroe, October 1925, in Gore-Booth, *Poems,* 89.

73. Garner, *Brave and Beautiful Spirit,* 14, 22.

74. Bland, *Banishing the Beast,* 265.

75. See, for example, the letter from

Rachel Graham, *The Freewoman,* 23 May 1912, 18–19.

76. See Bland, *Banishing the Beast,* 268; Garner, *Brave and Beautiful Spirit,* 84.

77. Garner, *Brave and Beautiful Spirit,* 97. The Blavatsky Institute's *Path* magazine contained the most explicit discussions of sex, sexuality, and homosexuality of all the theosophical papers during this period, and the institute's leaders, Charles Lazenby and D. N. Dunlop, were relatively sympathetic to many of the causes championed in *The Freewoman.*

78. Ezra Pound to Patricia Hutchins, no. 19 (30 October [1953]), Patricia Hutchins Collection, Add. 57725, British Library, London; cited in Surette, *Birth of Modernism,* 132.

79. On Gawthorpe's later life, see Holton, *Suffrage Days,* 247; the quotation is found in Gawthorpe, *Up Hill to Holloway,* 193.

80. Ellen S. Gaskell, "The Value of the Quick Unbalance of Women," *The Freewoman,* 18 April 1912, 438; on Grierson, see Clarke, *Dora Marsden,* 122.

81. Harriet Shaw Weaver to Dora Marsden, 1 August 1913; cited in Garner, *Brave and Beautiful Spirit,* 97; Dora Marsden to Harriet Shaw Weaver, 2 September 1913, Harriet Shaw Weaver Papers, MS 57354, British Library, London; cited in Clarke, *Dora Marsden,* 123. Shaw Weaver was a self-declared atheist and had little sympathy either with theosophy or with Marsden's esotericism.

82. "Topics of the Week: Some Thoughts on Religion," *The Freewoman,* 18 April 1912, 423–24 (emphasis in original).

83. "Topics of the Week: Freewomen and Evolution," *The Freewoman,* 16 May 1912, 503.

84. Dora Marsden, editorial note, *The Freewoman,* 6 June 1912, 59.

85. See Bland's exploration of the notion of passion in Marsden's writings and in *The Freewoman,* in *Banishing the Beast,* 273–77.

86. Dora Marsden, "Interpretations of Sex: IV," *The Freewoman,* 23 May 1912, 1–2. In this issue the paper's subtitle changed from "A Weekly Feminist Review" to "A Weekly Humanist Review."

87. "Topics of the Week: Freewomen and Evolution," *The Freewoman,* 16 May 1912, 503–4.

88. Dora Marsden, "Concerning the Idea of God," *The Freewoman,* 27 June 1912, 102.

89. Hatty Baker, "Religious or Pagan," and Frances Prewett, "Atheists," *The Freewoman,* 6 June 1912, 58–59.

90. On the influence of Stirner, especially his *Ego and His Own,* on Marsden's thinking, see Garner, *Brave and Beautiful Spirit,* 101–4; and Clarke, *Dora Marsden,* 20.

91. Dora Marsden, in *The New Freewoman,* 1 July 1913; cited in Garner, *Brave and Beautiful Spirit,* 103.

92. Ibid., 145; Dora Marsden, in *The New Freewoman,* 1 July 1913 and 1 August 1913; cited in ibid., 103, 107.

93. Ibid., 159–72, 184–85. For Jameson's comments on Marsden's work, see Margaret Storm Jameson to Dora Marsden, 1 September 1928; cited in ibid., 166.

94. Bruce Clarke makes this case in *Dora Marsden;* on feminism and modernism in *The Freewoman,* see Barash, "Dora Marsden's Feminism."

95. See, for example, Banks, *Becoming a Feminist,* 100; Rendall, "Introduction," in *Equal or Different,* 21; Jeffreys, *Spinster and Her Enemies,* 93–97. Jeffreys sees the alliance with sexology as a retrograde step.

96. See Clarke, *Dora Marsden,* 154, 215.

97. Hanscombe and Smyers, *Writing for Their Lives,* 150–75, especially 172.

98. On Colmore and Baillie-Weaver, see Morley with Stanley, *Life and Death of Emily Wilding Davison.* Gertrude Colmore's *Life of Emily Davison* is reprinted in Morley and Stanley. Colmore's suffrage novel, *Suffragette Sally* (1911), has been reprinted as *Suffragettes,* edited by Dale Spender. To avoid confusion, I have referred to Gertrude Baillie-Weaver by her professional name of Colmore and to Harold Baillie-Weaver as Baillie-Weaver.

99. Morley and Stanley, *Life and Death of Emily Wilding Davison,* 100–107, 180. On animal welfare, see Colmore, *Trades That Transgress.*

100. The title character, Sally, is a maid of all work who becomes a full-time orga-

nizer for the WSPU. The two other major characters, Lady Geraldine Hill and Edith Carstairs, represent upper- and middle-class women.

101. Peterson, "Politics of a Moral Crusade," 107.

102. Colmore, *Suffragettes,* 164–66. Colmore explicitly endorses this position in her author's note at the end of the novel (320).

103. See, for example, ibid., 86, 278–79. See also Peterson's discussion of Colmore's use of the Calvary metaphor. Peterson, "Politics of a Moral Crusade," 106.

104. Gertrude Colmore, "Unbalanced," *The Vote,* 13 June 1913, 113.

105. See Fulford, *Votes for Women,* 286; and "Mr. H. Hewitt," *The Dayspring,* 11 July 1913, 101.

106. Colmore, *Life of Emily Davison,* 19–20, 23.

107. Colmore, *Suffragettes,* 300.

108. Thompson, ed., *Dear Girl,* 241.

109. See deVries, "Transforming the Pulpit."

110. Christabel Pankhurst, "'Thou That Killest the Prophets,'" *The Suffragette,* 10 April 1914, 590; on the 1914 campaign, see reports "Suffragettes and the Church" throughout *The Suffragette* for 1914.

111. Emmeline Pethick-Lawrence, *The Faith That Is in Us* (London: Woman's Press, [1908?]), 4; cited in Vicinus, *Independent Women,* 249.

112. Cicely Hamilton, in *The Vote,* 14 January 1911, 141.

113. Charlotte Despard, cited in Linklater, *Unhusbanded Life,* 244.

Chapter Eight
Ancient Wisdom, Modern Motherhood

1. Ransom, *Short History,* 485–86. Some of the material in this chapter has also appeared in Dixon, "Ancient Wisdom, Modern Motherhood."

2. Annie Besant, "The New Annunciation," *World-Mother,* May 1928, 2.

3. Tillett, *Elder Brother,* 311n.8. According to Nethercot, when he interviewed Krishnamurti on the subject of the World Mother, he blurted out, "Oh, that

was all cooked u——," before catching himself. Nethercot, *Last Four Lives of Annie Besant,* 404.

4. See *International Theosophical Yearbook, 1937,* 47.

5. On the women in this and the preceding paragraph, see entries in "Who's Who in the Theosophical Society," in *International Theosophical Year Book, 1937.* On Appel, see also "The President's Return to India," *The Vāhan,* November 1911, 64.

6. On the WIA, see Forbes, "Caged Tigers," 528; Candy, "Relating Feminisms, Nationalisms, and Imperialisms," 587. For more general accounts that include discussions of British theosophists, see Ramusack, "Cultural Missionaries"; and Jayawardena, *White Woman's Other Burden,* especially 107–55.

7. See Davin, "Imperialism and Motherhood," 90–101, 123–24; Soloway, *Demography and Degeneration,* 3–17, 138–62.

8. Kent, *Making Peace,* 114–39.

9. Lewis, "Feminism and Welfare," 92–94. For an overview, see Banks, *Politics of British Feminism,* 28–44. Eleanor Rathbone's "Old and the New Feminism" appeared in the *Woman's Leader,* March 1925, 52.

10. Haden Guest published several books and pamphlets on maternal and child welfare. On suffrage and public health, see Haden Guest, *Votes for Women and the Public Health,* 2, 6.

11. Gertrude Holt Gerlach, "Babies," *The Vāhan,* April 1916, 206; see also Gerlach, "War Babies," *The Vāhan,* May 1915, 160; Jean R. Bindley, "Correspondence: Unwanted Children," *The Vāhan,* February 1919, 190.

12. "Brackenhill Theosophical Home School—Collecting Card," insert in *The Vāhan,* July 1920.

13. Charlotte Despard, "The Return of the 'Mother,'" in reconstruction supplement to *The Vāhan,* July 1917, 17.

14. "The Educational Conference: Summary of Mrs. Besant's Opening Address," *The Vāhan,* July 1914, 247.

15. Josephine Ransom, "Mother and Child," in educational supplement to *The Vāhan,* April 1917, 31, in Unbound Pamphlets, 1917–18. TSE.

16. A. Bothwell-Gosse, "The Problem of

the Declining Birthrate and of Infant Mortality," in reconstruction supplement to *The Vāhan,* July 1917, 20–21.

17. Advertisement for Stone Field Maternity Home in Theosophical Diaries, vol. 2, 1923–29, April–July 1927, 88, Reference Library, TSE.

18. Emily Lutyens, *Candles in the Sun,* 14, 17.

19. Emily Lutyens, *Sacramental Life,* 110–12.

20. Emily Lutyens, *Call of the Mother.* The book went into a second edition in 1927.

21. Ibid., vii–viii. Lutyens also referred to the "accidentally conceived" progeny of the leisured classes.

22. Ibid., 32–33.

23. Ibid., 70–73.

24. [Hume], "Note by an 'Eminent Occultist,'" *Theosophical Miscellanies. No. 2,* 115 (emphasis in original).

25. For Lutyens's version, see *Call of the Mother,* 95–96; for a fuller discussion of the differences between the two versions, see Dixon, "Ancient Wisdom, Modern Motherhood," 199.

26. See, for example, Emily Lutyens, *Call of the Mother,* 76–77, 90–93.

27. Ibid., 76–79.

28. Besant, *Civilisation's Deadlocks and the Keys,* 63.

29. George Arundale, "Motherhood," *The Theosophist,* July 1930, 569–71; cited, with ellipses, in de Tollenaere, *Politics of Divine Wisdom,* 378.

30. On Bosman, see *International Theosophical Year Book, 1937,* 191; on the range of his writings, see the advertisements on the back pages of Bosman, *World Mother;* L. A. Bosman, "Woman's Place in Ancient India," *The Vote,* 14 May 1910, 33.

31. Bosman, *World Mother,* 5, 19–20.

32. Mayo, *Mother India,* 24, 29.

33. Sinha, "Reading *Mother India,*" 23, 30–31, 33.

34. Shetty, "(Dis)figuring the Nation," 61.

35. Eleanor Rathbone, in *Women's Leader,* 13 July 1928, quoted in Mary D. Stocks, *Eleanor Rathbone: A Biography* (London:

Victor Gollancz, 1949), 127, and in Ramusack, "Catalysts or Helpers?" 113.

36. Ramusack, "Cultural Missionaries," 315–16; Sinha, "Reading *Mother India,*" 29–32.

37. *Nashville Tennessean,* 10 July 1927; cited in Jha, *Katherine Mayo,* 76.

38. Annie Besant, in *The Theosophist,* reprinted as appendix 11 of Natarajan, *Miss Mayo's Mother India,* 113.

39. On Wood, who was also for many years private secretary to C. W. Leadbeater, see *International Theosophical Yearbook, 1937,* 243.

40. See Sinha, "Reading *Mother India,*" 30. Extracts from speeches given at the meeting were printed as appendices in Natarajan, *Miss Mayo's Mother India.*

41. Emily Lutyens to Mayo, 19 May 1928, Mayo Collection, box 11, Sterling Memorial Library, Yale University; cited in Jha, *Katherine Mayo,* 51–52.

42. Chatterjee, *Nation and Its Fragments,* 130–31.

43. D. Jinarajadasa, "The Emancipation of Indian Women," in *Transactions of the Eighth Annual Congress of the Federation of European National Societies of the TS, Held in Vienna 1923* (Amsterdam: Council of the Federation, 1923), 82–85, 87.

44. Candy, "Occult Feminism," 125.

45. Anderson, "Bridging Cross-Cultural Feminisms," 567, 569, 571–75.

46. See Nethercot, *Last Four Lives of Annie Besant,* 402–3.

47. Annie Besant, "The New Annunciation," *World-Mother,* May 1928, 1–2. Besant's article was the text of a speech delivered at the Liberal Catholic Church of St. Michael and All Angels at Adyar on the feast of the Annunciation.

48. Ibid., 3.

49. See, for example, "Arundale, Rukmini," in *International Theosophical Year Book, 1937,* 186.

50. The phrase is Emily Lutyens's. See Lutyens, *Candles in the Sun,* 81. Lutyens noted that Jinarajadasa's marriage to Dorothy Graham had caused a greater scandal among theosophists in 1916. Whether this was because English theosophists were more willing to accept an interracial

marriage when the man was English is unclear.

51. Rukmini, "To the World-Mother," *World-Mother*, May 1928, 13.

52. [Rukmini Devi Arundale], "The Call of the World-Mother," *World-Mother*, May 1928, 8–9.

53. Annie Besant, in *The Theosophist*, June 1928; cited in Bosman, *World Mother*, 29.

54. Irschick, *Politics and Social Conflict in South India*, xiv–xvii. For an analysis of the impact of these kinds of claims on women, see Chakravarti, "Whatever Happened to the Vedic *Dasi?*"

55. Rukmini Devi, cited in Nethercot, *Last Four Lives of Annie Besant*, 367.

56. Rukmini Devi, "The Spirit of Motherhood," *The Theosophist*, October 1936, 16–19.

57. Devi, *Woman as Artist*, 1–2, 7–10, 16.

58. Tillett, *Elder Brother*, 257. Rukmini Devi was defeated in 1953 by her brother, N. Sri Ram, and in 1980 by her niece, Radha Burnier. See Mills, *One Hundred Years of Theosophy*, 141, 194. On her political career, see Nethercot, *Last Four Lives of Annie Besant*, 406.

59. Basu and Ray, *Women's Struggle*, 8.

60. Margaret Cousins, in Cousins and Cousins, *We Two Together*, 298–99.

61. On *Stri-Dharma*, which was published from Bombay between 1919 and 1936, see Doughan and Sanchez, *Feminist Periodicals*, 41–42.

Conclusion

1. Krishnamurti, *Dissolution of the Order of the Star*, 3–4, 6.

2. Kingsland, *Work of a Theosophical Organisation*, 11.

3. "A Brief History of the Formation and Work of the Hastings and St. Leonard's Theosophical Lodge," typescript with holograph additions, TSE (uncatalogued).

4. "Notes of Meeting Held at the Cowdray Club, January 1930," 1, in Miscellaneous Papers of the London Federation of the Theosophical Society, TSE.

5. George Arundale, "World-Wide Campaigns," *News and Notes of the Theosophical Society in the British Isles*, August–September 1934, 5.

6. "Meeting of the Theosophical Order of Service," 4 October 1934, in Addresses by the President: 1934, 7–8, V/21, TSE.

7. Margaret Jackson, "T.S. in England," in *Fifty-fourth Annual General Report of the Theosophical Society for 1929* (Adyar, Madras: The Recording Secretary, Theosophical Society, 1930), 45.

8. See, for example, Perkin, *Rise of Professional Society*, 218–85.

9. Josephine Ransom, "From the General Secretary," *News and Notes*, December 1934, 1; George S. Arundale, "What Is My Policy?" in *International Theosophical Yearbook, 1937*, 23.

10. Krishnamurti, *Penguin Krishnamurti Reader*, 14–15, 18.

11. Heelas, *New Age Movement*, 23.

12. Rose, *Governing the Soul*, xii.

13. Mills, *One Hundred Years of Theosophy*, 196.

14. Giles, "Editor's Introduction," in Tillis and Giles, eds., *Turning East*, xv–xvi.

15. Heelas, *New Age Movement*, 122.

16. Hubbard, *Dianetics*, 140–41, 215.

17. Mills, *One Hundred Years of Theosophy*, 186, 197.

18. See, for example, Myss, *Anatomy of the Spirit*.

19. Huxley, *Perennial Philosophy*, iv.

20. Lambeth Conference, 1897, resolution 15; cited in Ingham, *Mansions of the Spirit*, 31.

21. I am indebted here to Peter van der Veer's discussion of modernity and secularization in *Religious Nationalism*, 12–18.

22. Heelas, *New Age Movement*, passim.

23. See, for example, the essays in Spretnak, ed., *Politics of Women's Spirituality*; and Garcia and Maitland, eds., *Walking on the Water*.

Works Cited

The literature on theosophy is vast, and only a fraction of it has been cited here. For a comprehensive listing of relevant literature for the nineteenth century, see Michael Gomes, *Theosophy in the Nineteenth Century: An Annotated Bibliography* (New York: Garland, 1994). No comparable study exists for the twentieth century.

Archival Collections

Abbreviated citations used in the notes are given in parentheses.

Adyar Library and Resarch Centre, and Archives of the International Headquarters of the Theosophical Society, Adyar, Chennai, India. (Adyar Library; Adyar Archives)

Archives of the Blavatsky Lodge of the Theosophical Society in England, London. (Blavatsky Lodge)

Archives of the Theosophical Society in England, London. (TSE)

Charlotte Despard Collection, Fawcett Library, London.

Hacker Papers, University College London Library.

Mahatma Papers, British Library, Manuscripts Room, London.

Papers Relating to the Investigation of Madame Blavatsky, Archives of the Society for Psychical Research, Cambridge, England. (SPR Archives)

Primary Sources

Anderson, Jerome A. "Reincarnation as Applied to the Sex Problem." In *The Theosophical Congress Held by the Theosophical Society at the Parliament of Religions: Report of Proceedings and Documents*, 59–64. New York: American Section Hea.lquarters TS, 1893.

Bailey, Alice A. *The Unfinished Autobiography.* New York: Lucis Publishing, 1951.

Barker, A. T., ed. *The Letters of H. P. Blavatsky to A. P. Sinnett and Other Miscellaneous Letters.* New York: Frederick A. Stokes, [1923].

Besant, Annie. *The Ancient Indian Ideal of Duty.* Adyar, Madras: Theosophical Publishing House, 1917.

———. *The Ancient Wisdom.* 1897; reprint, Adyar, Madras: Theosophical Publishing House, 1939.

———. *An Autobiography*. 1st ed., 1893; 3rd ed., 1939; reprint, Adyar, Madras: Theosophical Publishing House, 1983.

———. *The Bearing of Religious Ideals on Social Reconstruction*. Adyar, Madras: Theosophical Publishing House, 1916.

———. *Civilisation's Deadlocks and the Keys*. Adyar, Madras: Theosophical Publishing House, 1924.

———. *Some Problems of Life*. London: Theosophical Publishing Society, 1900.

———. "Theosophy and Social Reform." In Annie Besant et al., *Theosophical Ideals and the Immediate Future*. London: Theosophical Publishing Society, 1914.

Besant, Annie, and Charles W. Leadbeater. *The Lives of Alcyone*. 2 vols. Adyar, Madras: Theosophical Publishing House, 1924.

———. *Man: Whence, How and Whither: A Record of Clairvoyant Investigation*. 1913; reprint, Wheaton, Ill.: Theosophical Press, 1947.

———. *Thought-Forms*. 1901; reprint, London: Theosophical Publishing House, 1925.

Bibby, Joseph. *A Study in Social and Economic Welfare: Part Two*. Liverpool: P. P. Press, n.d.

Blavatsky, H. P. *E.S.T. Instructions*. In *H. P. Blavatsky: Collected Writings, 1889–1890*. Vol. 12. Wheaton, Ill.: Theosophical Publishing House, 1980.

———. *Isis Unveiled: A Master-Key to the Mysteries of Ancient and Modern Science and Theology*. 2 vols. 1877; reprint, Pasadena, Calif.: Theosophical University Press, 1988.

———. *The Key to Theosophy*. 1889; reprint, London: Theosophical Publishing House London, [1968].

———. *The Secret Doctrine: The Synthesis of Science, Religion, and Philosophy*. 2 vols. London: Theosophical Publishing, 1888; facsimile ed., Pasadena, Calif.: Theosophical University Press, 1988.

———. *The Voice of the Silence, Being Chosen Fragments from the "Book of the Golden Precepts."* 1889; reprint, Pasadena, Calif.: Theosophical University Press, 1976.

Bosman, Leonard. *The World Mother*. London: Dharma Press, [1928].

Bright, Esther. *The Ancient One: To the Young Folks at Home*. London: Theosophical Publishing House, 1927.

———. *Old Memories and Letters of Annie Besant*. London: Theosophical Publishing House, 1936.

Brockhouse, H. "Socialism and Theosophy." *Socialist Review,* June 1913: 314–20.

Brooks, F. T. *Neo-Theosophy Exposed . . . Part II of "The Theosophical Society and Its Esoteric Bogeydom."* Mylapore, Madras: Vyasashrama Bookshop, 1914.

Brown, W. T. *My Life*. Freiburg: D. Lauber, n.d.

[Burrows, Herbert, and G. R. S. Mead.] *The Leadbeater Case: The Suppressed Speeches of Herbert Burrows and G. R. S. Mead at the Annual Convention of the British Section of the Theosophical Society*. London: privately printed, [1908].

Carpenter, Edward. *Intermediate Types among Primitive Folk: A Study in Social Evolution*. London: George Allen & Co., 1914.

———. *My Days and Dreams: Being Autobiographical Notes*. London: George Allen & Unwin, [1916].

Chatterji, Mohini M. *On the Higher Aspect of Theosophic Studies*. Transactions of the London Lodge of the Theosophical Society 3. N.p., January 1885.

Cleather, A. L. *H. P. Blavatsky: A Great Betrayal*. Calcutta: Thacker, Spink & Co., 1922.

———. *H. P. Blavatsky as I Knew Her*. Calcutta: Thacker, Spink & Co., 1923.

Codd, Clara M. *Looking Forward: The Coming Faith and the Coming Social Order*. Edinburgh: Orpheus Publishing House, 1918.

———. *So Rich a Life*. Pretoria: Institute for Theosophical Publicity, 1951.

———. "Theosophy and the Relationship of the Sexes." In *Lectures of the Forty-fourth Annual Convention and Third Wheaton Summer School*. Held at Wheaton, Ill., 5–15 July, 1930. N.p., n.d.

Colmore, Gertrude. *The Life of Emily Davison: An Outline*. London: Woman's Press, 1913. Reprinted in Ann Morley with Liz Stanley, *The Life and Death of Emily Wilding Davison: A Biographical Detective Story*. London: Women's Press, 1988.

———. *Suffragettes: A Story of Three Women*. Edited by Dale Spender. London: Pandora Press, 1984.

———. *Trades That Transgress*. London: Theosophical Order of Service, [1923].

Cousins, James H., and Margaret E. Cousins. *We Two Together*. Madras: Ganesh & Co., 1950.

De Steiger, Isabelle. *Memorabilia: Reminiscences of a Woman Artist and Writer*. London: Rider & Co., n.d.

———. *Superhumanity*. London: Elliot Stock, 1916.

Despard, Charlotte. *Theosophy and the Woman's Movement*. London: Theosophical Publishing Society, 1913.

———. *Woman in the New Era*. [London]: Suffrage Shop, 1910.

———. "Woman in the New Era." In *The Case for Women's Suffrage*. Edited by Brougham Villiers. London: T. Fisher Unwin, [1907].

———. *Woman's Franchise and Industry*. London: Women's Freedom League, n.d.

Despard, Charlotte, and Mabel Collins. *Outlawed: A Novel on the Woman Suffrage Question*. London: Henry J. Drane, [1908].

Devi, Rukmini. *Woman as Artist*. Adyar, Madras: Vasanta Press, n.d.

Ellis, H. Havelock. *Studies in the Psychology of Sex.* 2 vols. New York: Random House, 1942.

Ellis, H. Havelock, and John Addington Symonds. *Sexual Inversion.* London: Wilson & Macmillan, 1897; reprint, New York: Arno Press, 1975.

Farquhar, J. N. *Modern Religious Movements in India.* [1914]; reprint, Delhi: Munshiram Manoharlal, Oriental Publishers and Booksellers, 1967.

Farr, Florence. *Modern Woman: Her Intentions.* London: Frank Palmer, 1910.

Fortune, Dion. *The Esoteric Philosophy of Love and Marriage and the Problem of Purity.* Wellingborough, Northamptonshire: Aquarian Press, 1988.

———. *Psychic Self-Defense: A Study in Occult Pathology and Criminality.* London: Rider & Co., [1930]; reprint, Wellingborough, Northamptonshire: Aquarian Press, 1988.

Frazer, James G. *The Golden Bough: A Study in Magic and Religion.* Abridged ed. with introduction by Robert Fraser. London: Oxford University Press, 1994.

Garcia, Jo, and Sara Maitland, eds. *Walking on the Water: Women Talk about Spirituality.* London: Virago Press, 1983.

Gardner, E. L. *Freemasonry Being a Progressive Science.* Transaction 1, Universal Co-Masonry, British Federation. London: Office of the Grand Secretary, [1930].

Garrett, Edmund. *Isis Very Much Unveiled, Being the Story of the Great Mahatma Hoax.* 3rd ed. London: Westminster Gazette Office, [1894]. 4th ed. London: Westminster Gazette Office, n.d.

Gaskell, G. A. *Exeunt Mahatmas!* London: Watts & Co., 1907.

Gawthorpe, Mary. *Up Hill to Holloway.* Penobscot, Maine: Traversity Press, 1962.

Gay, S. E. *Womanhood in Its Eternal Aspect.* Reprinted from *Modern Thought,* 15 December 1879. N.p., n.d.

General Council of the Theosophical Society. *Report of the Result of an Investigation into the Charges against Madame Blavatsky.* Madras: Theosophical Society at Adyar, printed by Graves, Cookson & Co., n.d.

Gore-Booth, Eva. *The Plays of Eva Gore-Booth.* Edited with an introduction by Frederick S. Lapisardi. San Francisco: EMText, 1991.

———. *Poems of Eva Gore-Booth: Complete Edition with The Inner Life of a Child and Letters and a Biographical Introduction by Esther Roper.* London: Longmans, Green & Co., 1929.

———. *A Psychological and Poetic Approach to the Study of Christ in the Fourth Gospel.* London: Longmans, Green & Co., 1923.

Graham Pole, David. *War Letters and Autobiography.* London: J. Burrow & Co., n.d.

Haden Guest, Leslie. *Theosophy and Social Reconstruction.* London: Theosophical Publishing Society, 1912.

——. *Votes for Women and the Public Health*. London: Women's Freedom League, n.d.

Harding, M. Esther. *Woman's Mysteries Ancient and Modern: A Psychological Interpretation of the Feminine Principle as Portrayed in Myth, Story, and Dreams*. 2nd ed. 1971; reprint, New York: Harper Colophon Books, 1976.

Hartmann, F. *Report of Observations Made during a Nine Months' Stay at the Head-quarters of the Theosophical Society at Adyar (Madras) India*. Madras: Graves, Cookson & Co., 1884.

H. P. B. *In Memory of Helena Petrovna Blavatsky, by Some of Her Pupils*. London: Theosophical Publishing Society, 1891.

Hubbard, L. Ron. *Dianetics: The Modern Science of Mental Health*. New ed. Los Angeles: Bridge Publications, 1985.

[Hume, A. O.]. *Hints on Esoteric Theosophy. No. 1. Is Theosophy a Delusion? Do the Brothers Exist?* 2nd ed. Calcutta: Calcutta Central Press, 1882.

——. *Theosophical Miscellanies. No. 2. Unpublished Writings of Eliphas Levi. The Paradoxes of the Highest Science*. Calcutta: Calcutta Central Press, 1883.

Humphreys, Christmas, and Elsie Benjamin, eds. *The Mahatma Letters to A. P. Sinnett from the Mahatmas M. and K. H.* 3rd rev. ed. Adyar, Madras: Theosophical Publishing House, 1962, 1979.

Huxley, Aldous. *The Perennial Philosophy*. 1944; reprint, Cleveland: World Publishing, 1962.

Ingham, Michael. *Mansions of the Spirit: The Gospel in a Multi-Faith World*. Toronto: Anglican Book Centre, 1997.

The International Theosophical Yearbook, 1937. Adyar, Madras: Theosophical Publishing House, 1937.

James, William. *The Varieties of Religious Experience: A Study in Human Nature*. 1902; reprint, New York: Macmillan, 1961.

Jung, C. G. *Psychology and the Occult*. Translated by R. F. C. Hull. Bollingen Series 20. Princeton, N.J.: Princeton University Press, 1977.

Kingsford, Anna Bonus, and Edward Maitland. *The Perfect Way; or, the Finding of Christ*. 1st ed., 1882; 4th ed., London: John M. Watkins, 1909.

Kingsland, William. *The Work of a Theosophical Organisation*. London: privately printed, 1930.

Krafft-Ebing, Richard von. *Psychopathia Sexualis*. Translated by Franklin S. Klaf. New York: Bell Publishing, 1965.

Krishnamurti, J. *The Dissolution of the Order of the Star*. Ommen, Netherlands: Star Publishing Trust, 1929.

——. *The Penguin Krishnamurti Reader*. Compiled by Mary Lutyens. London: Penguin Books, 1970.

Kunz, Fritz. *Sex Concepts for the New Age*. Chicago: Theosophical Press, 1926.

Leadbeater, C. W. *The Chakras*. Adyar, Madras: Theosophical Publishing House, 1927; Wheaton, Ill.: Quest Books, Theosophical Publishing House, 1994.

———. *The Hidden Side of Lodge Meetings*. N.p., n.d.

———. *The Masters and the Path*. Adyar, Madras: Theosophical Publishing House, 1925.

———. *The Science of the Sacraments*. Los Angeles: St. Alban Press, 1920.

———. *A Textbook of Theosophy*. 1912; reprint, Adyar, Madras: Theosophical Publishing House, 1975.

Lillie, Arthur. *Koot Hoomi Unveiled; or, Tibetan "Buddhists" versus the Buddhists of Tibet*. London: Psychological Press Association and E. W. Allen, n.d.

———. *Madame Blavatsky and Her "Theosophy": A Study*. London: Swan Sonnenschein & Co., 1895.

Lutyens, Emily. *The Call of the Mother*. London: Methuen & Co., 1926.

———. *Candles in the Sun*. London: Rupert Hart-Davis, 1957.

———. *The Sacramental Life*. Glasgow: Star Publishing Trust, 1917.

Mairet, Philip. *A. R. Orage: A Memoir*. New Hyde Park, N.Y.: University Books, 1966.

Mayo, Katherine. *Mother India*. London: Jonathan Cape, 1927.

Mead, G. R. S. *"The Quest"—Old and New: A Retrospect and a Prospect*. Quest Reprint Series 1. London: John M. Watkins, n.d. Originally published in *The Quest: A Quarterly Review* 17, no. 3 (April 1926).

Mead, G. R. S., Herbert Burrows, W. Kingsland, and Edith Ward. *The Leadbeater Case: A Reply to the President's Letter of November 1908*. London: privately printed, 1908.

Montefiore, Dora B. *From a Victorian to a Modern*. London: E. Archer, 1927.

Morgan, H. R. *Report of an Examination into the Blavatsky Correspondence by J. D. B. Gribble*. Ootacamund: Observer Press, 1884.

Müller, F. Henrietta. "Theosophy and Woman." In *The Theosophical Congress Held by the Theosophical Society at the Parliament of Religions: Report of Proceedings and Documents*, 168–70. New York: American Section Headquarters TS, 1893.

Myers, F. W. H. Introduction to Edmund Gurney, F. W. H. Myers, and Frank Podmore, *Phantasms of the Living*. 2 vols. London: Trübner & Co., 1886.

Myss, Caroline. *Anatomy of the Spirit: The Seven Stages of Power and Healing*. New York: Crown Publishers, 1996.

[Nair, T. M.]. *The Evolution of Mrs. Besant*. Madras: Justice Printing Works, 1918.

Natarajan, K. *Miss Mayo's Mother India: A Rejoinder*. 2nd ed. Madras: G. A. Nateson & Co., 1928.

Olcott, H. S. *Old Diary Leaves: America 1874–1878*. 1st ser. 1895; reprint, Adyar, Madras: Theosophical Publishing House, 1941.

Orchard, A. F., and A. Fletcher. *The Life and Horoscope of Madame Blavatsky.* Epsom: Birch & Whittington, [1924].

Orwell, George. *The Road to Wigan Pier.* 1937; reprint, Harmondsworth, England: Penguin Books, 1962.

Pape, A. G. *The National Centre Policy of Action.* London: Office of the National Centre Group, n.d.

Pember, G. H. *Theosophy, Buddhism, and the Signs of the End.* London: Hodder & Stoughton, 1891.

Pigott, F. W. *The Liberal Catholic Church: Its Origin, History, Purpose and Teachings.* London: St. Alban Press, 1925.

Podmore, Frank. "Madame Blavatsky and the Theosophical Society." *Good Words,* February 1892: 82–86.

Pope, Mary. *Mysticism.* London: Theosophical Publishing Society, 1908.

———. *Novel Dishes for Vegetarian Households: A Complete and Trustworthy Guide to Vegetarian Cookery.* 2nd ed. London: Percy Lund & Co., 1893.

Ransom, Josephine. *A Short History of the Theosophical Society, 1875–1937.* Adyar, Madras: Theosophical Publishing House, 1938.

Round Table Year Book, Easter 1914. N.p., [1914].

Sinnett, A. P. *Autobiography of Alfred Percy Sinnett.* London: Theosophical History Centre, 1986.

———. *The Early Days of Theosophy in Europe.* London: Theosophical Publishing House, 1922.

———. *Karma: A Novel.* 2 vols. London: Chapman & Hall, 1885.

———. *The Occult World.* 3rd ed. London: Trübner & Co., 1883.

———. *The Social Upheaval in Progress.* London: Theosophical Publishing House, 1920.

Spretnak, Charlene, ed. *The Politics of Women's Spirituality: Essays on the Rise of Spiritual Power within the Feminist Movement.* Garden City, N.Y.: Anchor Books, 1982.

Steiner, Rudolf. *Christianity as Mystical Fact and the Mysteries of Antiquity.* 2nd ed. 1947; reprint, New York: Anthroposophic Press, 1972.

[Surya Lodge]. *Prospectus and Syllabus.* London: n.p., 1922.

Swiney, Frances. *The Ancient Road or the Development of the Soul.* London: G. Bell & Sons, 1918.

———. *The Awakening of Women or Woman's Part in Evolution.* London: George Redway, 1899.

———. *The Bar of Isis: The Law of the Mother.* London: C. W. Daniel, 1912.

———. *The Cosmic Procession or The Feminine Principle in Evolution.* London: Ernest Bell, 1906.

———. *The Esoteric Teaching of the Gnostics.* London: Yellon, Williams & Co., 1909.

———. *The Mystery of the Circle and the Cross or The Interpretation of Sex.* London: Open Road Publishing, 1908.

———. *Het ontwaken der vrouw, of, De rol der vrouw in de evolutie der menschheid.* Translated by M. Kramers. Almelo: W. Hilarius, 1902.

Theobald, Minnie B. *Three Levels of Consciousness: An Autobiography.* London: John M. Watkins, 1960.

Thompson, E. W. *The Theosophy of Mrs. Besant.* Mysore City: Wesleyan Mission Press, 1913.

Tillis, Malcolm, and Cynthia Giles, eds. *Turning East: New Lives in India: Twenty Westerners and Their Spiritual Quests.* New York: Paragon House, 1989.

Two Subalterns. *Theosophy on Active Service.* 3rd ed. Folkestone: Bewley, Printer, n.d.

Veritas. *Mrs. Besant and the Alcyone Case.* Madras: Goodwin & Co., 1913.

Ward, E., & Co. *The Dress Reform Problem: A Chapter for Women.* London: Hamilton, Adams & Co., 1886.

Ward, Edith. *Theosophy and Modern Science.* London: Theosophical Publishing Society, 1906.

———. *The Vital Question: An Address on Social Purity to All English-Speaking Women.* [2nd ed.] London: Percy Lund & Co., 1892.

Wedgwood, J. I. *Universal Co-Masonry, What Is It?* 2nd Australasian ed. Sydney: Universal Printing, 1917.

Wells, H. G. *Ann Veronica: A Modern Love Story.* New York: Harper & Brothers, 1909.

Wood, Ernest Egerton. *An Englishman Defends Mother India: A Complete Constructive Reply to "Mother India."* Madras: Ganesh & Co., 1929.

———. *"Is This Theosophy . . . ?"* London: Rider & Co., 1936.

Yeats, W. B. *Memoirs: Autobiography—First Draft, Journal.* Transcribed and edited by Denis Donoghue. London: Macmillan, 1972.

Secondary Sources

Adas, Michael. *Machines as the Measure of Men: Science, Technology, and Ideologies of Western Dominance.* Ithaca, N.Y.: Cornell University Press, 1989.

Albanese, Catherine L. "Exchanging Selves, Exchanging Souls: Contact, Combination, and American Religious History." In *Retelling U.S. Religious History.* Edited by Thomas A. Tweed. Berkeley: University of California Press, 1997.

Anderson, Nancy Fix. "Bridging Cross-Cultural Feminisms: Annie Besant and Women's Rights in England and India, 1874–1933." *Women's History Review* 3, no. 4 (1994): 563–80.

Andreski, Stanislav. "Introductory Essay." In *Herbert Spencer: Structure, Function and Evolution.* London: Michael Joseph, 1971.

Arnstein, Walter, et al. "Recent Studies in Victorian Religion." *Victorian Studies* 33, no. 1 (1989): 149–75.

Ashcraft, William Michael. "'The Dawn of the New Cycle': Point Loma Theosophists and American Culture, 1896–1929." Ph.D. diss., University of Virginia, 1995.

Bakhtin, Mikhail. *Rabelais and His World.* Translated by Helene Iswolsky. Cambridge, Mass.: MIT Press, 1968; reprint, Bloomington: Indiana University Press, 1984.

Banks, Olive. *Becoming a Feminist: The Social Origins of "First Wave" Feminism.* Brighton, England: Wheatsheaf Books, 1986.

———. *The Biographical Dictionary of British Feminists.* Vol. 2, *A Supplement, 1900–1945.* Brighton, England: Harvester Wheatsheaf, 1990.

———. *Faces of Feminism: A Study of Feminism as a Social Movement.* 1981; reprint, Oxford: Basil Blackwell, 1986.

———. *The Politics of British Feminism, 1918–1970.* Aldershot, England: Edward Elgar Publishing, 1993.

Barash, Carol. "Dora Marsden's Feminism, the *Freewoman,* and the Gender Politics of Early Modernism." *Princeton University Library Chronicle* 49, no. 1 (1987): 31–56.

Basu, Aparna, and Bharati Ray. *Women's Struggle: A History of the All India Women's Conference, 1927–1990.* New Delhi: Manohar Publications, 1990.

Beals, Polly A. "Fabian Feminism: Gender, Politics and Culture in London, 1880–1930." Ph.D. diss., Rutgers: The State University of New Jersey, 1989.

Bederman, Gail. *Manliness and Civilization: A Cultural History of Gender and Race in the United States, 1880–1917.* Chicago: University of Chicago Press, 1995.

Bednarowski, Mary Farrell. "Outside the Mainstream: Women's Religion and Women Religious Leaders in Nineteenth Century America." *Journal of the American Academy of Religion* 48 (1980): 207–31.

———. "Women in Occult America." In *The Occult in America: New Historical Perspectives.* Edited by Howard Kerr and Charles L. Crow. Urbana: University of Illinois Press, 1983.

Bennett, Clinton. *In Search of the Sacred: Anthropology and the Study of Religions.* London: Cassell, 1996.

Bentley, James. *Ritualism and Politics in Victorian Britain: The Attempt to Legislate for Belief.* Oxford: Oxford University Press, 1978.

Bernstein, Richard J. "Foucault: Critique as Philosophical Ethos." In *Philosophical Interventions in the Unfinished Project of Enlightenment.* Edited by Axel Honneth, Thomas McCarthy, Claus Offe, and Albrecht Wellmar. Cambridge, Mass.: MIT Press, 1992.

Bevir, Mark. "In Opposition to the Raj: Annie Besant and the Dialectic of Empire." *History of Political Thought* 19, no. 1 (1998): 61–77.

———. "The Labour Church Movement, 1891–1902." *Journal of British Studies* 38, no. 2 (1999): 217–45.

———. "Welfarism, Socialism and Religion: On T. H. Green and Others." *Review of Politics* 55, no. 4 (1993): 639–61.

———. "The West Turns Eastward: Madame Blavatsky and the Transformation of the Occult Tradition." *Journal of the American Academy of Religion* 62, no. 3 (1994): 747–67.

Bishop, Peter. *The Myth of Shangri-La: Tibet, Travel Writing and the Western Creation of Sacred Landscape.* Berkeley: University of California Press, 1989.

Bland, Lucy. *Banishing the Beast: English Feminism and Sexual Morality, 1885–1918.* London: Penguin Books, 1995.

———. "The Married Woman, the 'New Woman' and the Feminist: Sexual Politics of the 1890s." In *Equal or Different: Women's Politics, 1800–1914.* Edited by Jane Rendall. Oxford: Basil Blackwell, 1987.

Braude, Ann. *Radical Spirits: Spiritualism and Women's Rights in Nineteenth-Century America.* Boston: Beacon Press, 1989.

———. "Women's History *Is* American Religious History." In *Retelling U.S. Religious History.* Edited by Thomas A. Tweed. Berkeley: University of California Press, 1997.

Burfield, Diana. "Theosophy and Feminism: Some Explorations in Nineteenth-Century Biography." In *Women's Religious Experience: Cross-cultural Perspectives.* Edited by Pat Holden. London: Croom Helm, 1983.

Burke, Marie Louise. *Swami Vivekananda in the West: New Discoveries. Part One: A New Gospel.* 3rd ed. Calcutta: Advaita Ashrama, 1987.

Burton, Antoinette. *At the Heart of the Empire: Indians and the Colonial Encounter in Late-Victorian Britain.* Berkeley: University of California Press, 1998.

———. *Burdens of History: British Feminists, Indian Women, and Imperial Culture, 1865–1915.* Chapel Hill: University of North Carolina Press, 1994.

Campbell, Bruce F. *Ancient Wisdom Revived: A History of the Theosophical Movement.* Berkeley: University of California Press, 1980.

Candy, Catherine. "The Occult Feminism of Margaret Cousins in Modern Ireland and India, 1878–1954." Ph.D. diss., Loyola University Chicago, 1996.

———. "Relating Feminisms, Nationalisms, and Imperialisms: Ireland, India and Margaret Cousins's Sexual Politics." *Women's History Review* 3, no. 4 (1994): 581–94.

Cannadine, David. "War and Death, Grief and Mourning in Modern Britain." In *Mirrors of Mortality: Studies in the Social History of Death.* Edited by Joachim Whaley. London: Europa Publications, 1981.

Carlson, Maria. *"No Religion Higher Than Truth": A History of the Theo-*

sophical Movement in Russia, 1875–1922. Princeton, N.J.: Princeton University Press, 1993.

Chakrabarty, Dipesh. "Postcoloniality and the Artifice of History: Who Speaks for 'Indian' Pasts?" *Representations* 37 (1992): 1–26.

Chakravarti, Uma. "Whatever Happened to the Vedic *Dasi*? Orientalism, Nationalism and a Script for the Past." In *Recasting Women: Essays in Colonial History.* Edited by Kumkum Sangari and Sudesh Vaid. New Delhi: Kali for Women, 1989.

Chatterjee, Partha. *The Nation and Its Fragments: Colonial and Postcolonial Histories.* Princeton, N.J.: Princeton University Press, 1993.

Clarke, Bruce. *Dora Marsden and Early Modernism: Gender, Individualism, Science.* Ann Arbor: University of Michigan Press, 1996.

Clarke, J. J. *Oriental Enlightenment: The Encounter between Asian and Western Thought.* New York: Routledge, 1997.

Collette, Christine. "Socialism and Scandal: The Sexual Politics of the Early Labour Movement." *History Workshop* 23 (1987): 102–11.

Coon, Lynda L., Katherine J. Haldane, and Elisabeth W. Sommer, eds. *That Gentle Strength: Historical Perspectives on Women in Christianity.* Charlottesville: University Press of Virginia, 1990.

Cosgrove, P. D. "'Pulch': A Brief Sketch of the Life of Charles Lazenby by His Daughter." *Canadian Theosophist* 69, no. 5 (1988): 101–6.

Cox, Jeffrey. *The English Churches in a Secular Society, Lambeth, 1870–1930.* New York: Oxford University Press, 1982.

Cranston, Sylvia. *HPB: The Extraordinary Life and Influence of Helena Blavatsky, Founder of the Modern Theosophical Movement.* New York: G. P. Putnam's Sons, 1993.

Dangerfield, George. *The Strange Death of Liberal England.* London: McGibbon & Kay, 1935.

Davidoff, Leonore, and Catherine Hall. *Family Fortunes: Men and Women of the English Middle Class, 1780–1850.* Chicago: University of Chicago Press, 1987.

Davin, Anna. "Imperialism and Motherhood." In *Tensions of Empire: Colonial Cultures in a Bourgeois World.* Berkeley: University of California Press, 1997. Originally published in *History Workshop* 5 (1978): 9–65.

De Tollenaere, Herman A. O. *The Politics of Divine Wisdom: Theosophy and Labour, National, and Women's Movements in Indonesia and South Asia, 1875–1947.* Nijmegen: Uitgeverij Katholieke Universiteit Nijmegen, 1996.

DeVries, Jacqueline R. "Transforming the Pulpit: Preaching and Prophecy in the British Women's Suffrage Movement." In *Women Preachers and Prophets through Two Millennia of Christianity.* Edited by Beverly Mayne Kienzle and Pamela J. Walker. Berkeley: University of California Press, 1998.

Dixon, Joy. "Ancient Wisdom, Modern Motherhood: Theosophy and the

Colonial Syncretic." In *Gender, Sexuality and Colonial Modernities*. Edited by Antoinette Burton. London: Routledge, 1999.

———. "Sexology and the Occult: Sexuality and Subjectivity in Theosophy's New Age." *Journal of the History of Sexuality* 7, no. 3 (1997): 409–33.

Doughan, David, and Denise Sanchez. *Feminist Periodicals, 1855–1984: An Annotated Critical Bibliography of British, Irish, Commonwealth and International Titles*. Brighton, England: Harvester Press, 1987.

Dowling, Linda. *Hellenism and Homosexuality in Victorian Oxford*. Ithaca, N.Y.: Cornell University Press, 1994.

———. *Language and Decadence in the Victorian Fin de Siècle*. Princeton, N.J.: Princeton University Press, 1986.

Duden, Barbara. *The Woman beneath the Skin: A Doctor's Patients in Eighteenth-Century Germany*. Translated by Thomas Dunlap. Cambridge, Mass.: Harvard University Press, 1991.

Durham, Martin. "Gender and the British Union of Fascists." *Journal of Contemporary History* 27 (1992): 513–29.

———. "Women and the British Union of Fascists, 1932–1940." In *The Politics of Marginality: Race, the Radical Right and Minorities in Twentieth-Century Britain*. Edited by Tony Kushner and Kenneth Lunn. London: Frank Cass & Co., 1990.

Dyhouse, Carol. "Mothers and Daughters in the Middle-Class Home, c. 1870–1914." In *Labour and Love: Women's Experience of Home and Family, 1850–1940*. Edited by Jane Lewis. Oxford: Basil Blackwell, 1986.

Eagleton, Terry. "The Flight to the Real." In *Cultural Politics at the Fin de Siècle*. Edited by Sally Ledger and Scott McCracken. Cambridge, England: Cambridge University Press, 1995.

Finlay, John L. *Social Credit: The English Origins*. Montreal: McGill-Queen's University Press, 1972.

Forbes, Geraldine H. "Caged Tigers: 'First Wave' Feminists in India." *Women's Studies International Forum* 5, no. 6 (1982): 525–36.

Fulford, Roger. *Votes for Women: The Story of a Struggle*. London: Faber & Faber, 1957.

Fussell, Paul. *The Great War and Modern Memory*. New York: Oxford University Press, 1975.

Garber, Marjorie. *Vice Versa: Bisexuality and the Eroticism of Everyday Life*. New York: Simon & Schuster, 1995.

Garner, Les. *A Brave and Beautiful Spirit: Dora Marsden, 1882–1960*. Brookfield, Vt.: Gower Publishing, 1990.

Gay, Peter. "The Manliness of Christ." In *Religion and Irreligion in Victorian Society: Essays in Honor of R. K. Webb*. Edited by R. W. Davis and R. J. Helmstadter. New York: Routledge, 1992.

Gilbert, R. A. *The Golden Dawn and the Esoteric Section*. London: Theosophical History Centre, 1987.

Ginzburg, Carlo. *Clues, Myths and the Historical Method.* Translated by John Tedeschi and Anne C. Tedeschi. Baltimore: Johns Hopkins University Press, 1989.

Godwin, Joscelyn. *The Theosophical Enlightenment.* Albany: State University of New York Press, 1994.

Gould, Peter C. *Early Green Politics: Back to Nature, Back to the Land, and Socialism in Britain, 1880–1900.* New York: St. Martin's Press, 1988.

Gray, Natasha. "Constance Wilde: A Modest Mystic." *Cauda Pavonis: Studies in Hermeticism* 9, no. 1 (1990): 1–4.

Greer, Mary K. *Women of the Golden Dawn: Rebels and Priestesses.* Rochester, Vt.: Park Street Press, 1995.

Grewal, Inderpal. *Home and Harem: Nation, Gender, Empire, and the Cultures of Travel.* Durham, N.C.: Duke University Press, 1996.

Hall, Lesley A. "Forbidden by God, Despised by Men: Masturbation, Medical Warnings, Moral Panic, and Manhood in Great Britain, 1850–1950." *Journal of the History of Sexuality* 2, no. 3 (1992): 365–87.

Hamlin, Christopher. "Scientific Method and Expert Witnessing: Victorian Perspectives on a Modern Problem." *Social Studies of Science* 16, no. 3 (1986): 485–513.

Hammerton, A. James. *Cruelty and Companionship: Conflict in Nineteenth-Century Married Life.* New York: Routledge, 1992.

Hanscombe, Gillian, and Virginia L. Smyers. *Writing for Their Lives: The Modernist Women, 1910–1940.* London: Women's Press, 1987.

Harrison, Brian. *Separate Spheres: The Opposition to Women's Suffrage in Britain.* London: Croom Helm, 1978.

Harrison, Vernon. *H. P. Blavatsky and the SPR: An Examination of the Hodgson Report of 1885.* Pasadena, Calif.: Theosophical University Press, 1997.

Heelas, Paul. *The New Age Movement: The Celebration of the Self and the Sacralization of Modernity.* Oxford: Blackwell Publishers, 1996.

Heeney, Brian. *The Women's Movement in the Church of England: 1850–1930.* Oxford: Clarendon Press, 1988.

Hiebert, Erwin N. "The Transformation of Physics." In *Fin de Siècle and Its Legacy.* Edited by Mikuláš Teich and Roy Porter. New York: Cambridge University Press, 1990.

Hilliard, David. "Unenglish and Unmanly: Anglo-Catholicism and Homosexuality." *Victorian Studies* 25 (1982): 181–210.

Holton, Sandra Stanley. "Feminism, History and Movements of the Soul: Christian Science in the Life of Alice Clark (1874–1934)." *Australian Feminist Studies* 13, no. 28 (1998): 281–94.

———. *Suffrage Days: Stories from the Women's Suffrage Movement.* New York: Routledge, 1996.

Holton, Sandra Stanley, Alison Mackinnon, and Margaret Allen, eds. *Between Rationality and Revelation: Women, Faith and Public Roles in the Nineteenth and Twentieth Centuries. Women's History Review* 7, no. 2 (1998).

Hubel, Teresa. *Whose India? The Independence Struggle in British and Indian Fiction and History.* Durham, N.C.: Duke University Press, 1996.

Innes, C. L. *Woman and Nation in Irish Literature and Society, 1880–1935.* Athens: University of Georgia Press, 1993.

Irschick, Eugene F. *Politics and Social Conflict in South India: The Non-Brahman Movement and Tamil Separatism, 1916–1929.* Berkeley: University of California Press, 1969.

Jay, Elisabeth. *Faith and Doubt in Victorian Britain.* London: Macmillan Education, 1986.

Jayawardena, Kumari. *The White Woman's Other Burden: Western Women and South Asia during British Rule.* New York: Routledge, 1995.

Jeffreys, Sheila. *The Spinster and Her Enemies: Feminism and Sexuality, 1880–1930.* London: Pandora Press, 1985.

Jha, Manoranjan. *Katherine Mayo and India.* New Delhi: People's Publishing House, 1971.

Johnson, K. Paul. *The Masters Revealed: Madame Blavatsky and the Myth of the Great White Lodge.* Albany: State University of New York Press, 1994.

Jones, Kenneth W. *Socio-religious Reform Movements in British India. New Cambridge History of India* III.1. New York: Cambridge University Press, 1989.

Kean, Hilda. "The 'Smooth Cool Men of Science': The Feminist and Socialist Response to Vivisection." *History Workshop Journal* 40 (1995): 16–38.

Kent, Susan Kingsley. *Making Peace: The Reconstruction of Gender in Interwar Britain.* Princeton, N.J.: Princeton University Press, 1993.

———. *Sex and Suffrage in Britain, 1860–1914.* Princeton, N.J.: Princeton University Press, 1987.

King, Richard. *Orientalism and Religion: Postcolonial Theory, India and "The Mystic East."* London: Routledge, 1999.

Leneman, Leah. "The Awakened Instinct: Vegetarianism and the Women's Suffrage Movement in Britain." *Women's History Review* 6, no. 2 (1997): 271–87.

Leopold, Joan. "British Applications of the Aryan Theory of Race to India, 1850–1870." *English Historical Review* 89 (1974): 578–603.

Levine, Philippa. *Feminist Lives in Victorian England: Private Roles and Public Commitment.* Oxford: Basil Blackwell, 1990.

Lewis, Gifford. *Eva Gore-Booth and Esther Roper: A Biography.* London: Pandora Press, 1988.

Lewis, Jane. "Feminism and Welfare." In *What Is Feminism? A Reexamination.* Edited by Juliet Mitchell and Ann Oakley. New York: Pantheon Books, 1986.

Lewis, Reina. *Gendering Orientalism: Race, Femininity and Representation.* London: Routledge, 1996.

Liddington, Jill, and Jill Norris. *One Hand Tied behind Us: The Rise of the Women's Suffrage Movement.* London: Virago Press, 1978.

Linklater, Andro. *An Unhusbanded Life: Charlotte Despard, Suffragette, Socialist and Sinn Feiner.* London: Hutchinson & Co., 1980.

Lutyens, Mary. *The Life and Death of Krishnamurti.* London: John Murray, 1990.

Macpherson, C. B. *The Political Theory of Possessive Individualism: Hobbes to Locke.* Oxford: Clarendon Press, 1962.

Malmgreen, Gail, ed. *Religion in the Lives of English Women, 1760–1930.* London: Croom Helm, 1986.

McClintock, Anne. *Imperial Leather: Race, Gender and Sexuality in the Colonial Contest.* New York: Routledge, 1995.

McLeod, Hugh. *Religion and the People of Western Europe, 1789–1970.* Oxford: Oxford University Press, 1981.

Meade, Marion. *Madame Blavatsky: The Woman behind the Myth.* New York: G. P. Putnam's Sons, 1980.

Mehta, Gita. *Karma Cola: The Marketing of the Mystic East.* London: Jonathan Cape, 1980; reprint, London: Minerva, 1990.

Mehta, Uday S. "Liberal Strategies of Exclusion." In *Tensions of Empire: Colonial Cultures in a Bourgeois World.* Edited by Frederick Cooper and Ann Laura Stoler. Berkeley: University of California Press, 1997. Originally published in *Politics and Society* 18, no. 4 (1990): 427–54.

Melman, Billie. *Women's Orients: English Women and the Middle East, 1718–1918: Sexuality, Religion and Work.* London: Macmillan Academic & Professional, 1992.

Meyer, T. H. *D. N. Dunlop: A Man of Our Time.* London: Temple Lodge Publishing, 1992.

Mills, Joy. *One Hundred Years of Theosophy: A History of the Theosophical Society in America.* Wheaton, Ill.: Theosophical Publishing House, 1987.

Morley, Ann, with Liz Stanley. *The Life and Death of Emily Wilding Davison: A Biographical Detective Story.* London: Women's Press, 1988.

Mort, Frank. *Dangerous Sexualities: Medico-Moral Politics in England since 1830.* New York: Routledge & Kegan Paul, 1987.

Moulton, Edward C. "The Early Congress and the British Radical Connection." In *The Indian National Congress: Centenary Hindsights.* Edited by D. A. Low. Delhi: Oxford University Press, 1988.

Mulvihill, Margaret. *Charlotte Despard: A Biography.* London: Pandora Press, 1989.

Nethercot, Arthur H. *The First Five Lives of Annie Besant.* Chicago: University of Chicago Press, 1960.

———. *The Last Four Lives of Annie Besant*. London: Rupert Hart-Davis, 1963.

Obelkevich, James. "Religion." In *The Cambridge Social History of Britain, 1750–1950*. Vol. 3, *Social Agencies and Institutions*. Edited by F. M. L. Thompson. New York: Cambridge University Press, 1990.

Oppenheim, Janet. *The Other World: Spiritualism and Psychical Research in England, 1850–1914*. New York: Cambridge University Press, 1985.

Owen, Alex. *The Darkened Room: Women, Power, and Spiritualism in Late Victorian England*. London: Virago Press, 1989.

———. "The Sorcerer and His Apprentice: Aleister Crowley and the Magical Exploration of Edwardian Subjectivity." *Journal of British Studies* 36 (1997): 99–133.

Panchasi, Roxanne. "Graphology and the Science of Individual Identity in Modern France." *Configurations* 4, no. 1 (1996): 1–31.

Patai, Daphne, and Angela Ingram. "Fantasy and Identity: The Double Life of a Victorian Sexual Radical." In *Rediscovering Forgotten Radicals: British Women Writers, 1889–1939*. Edited by Angela Ingram and Daphne Patai. Chapel Hill: University of North Carolina Press, 1993.

Pateman, Carole. *The Sexual Contract*. Stanford, Calif.: Stanford University Press, 1988.

Perkin, Harold. *The Rise of Professional Society: England since 1880*. New York: Routledge, 1989.

Peterson, Shirley. "The Politics of a Moral Crusade: Gertrude Colmore's *Suffragette Sally*." In *Rediscovering Forgotten Radicals: British Women Writers, 1889–1939*. Edited by Angela Ingram and Daphne Patai. Chapel Hill: University of North Carolina Press, 1993.

Pierson, Stanley. *British Socialists: The Journey from Fantasy to Politics*. Cambridge, Mass.: Harvard University Press, 1979.

Poovey, Mary. *Making a Social Body: British Cultural Formation, 1830–1864*. Chicago: University of Chicago Press, 1995.

Pratt, Mary Louise. *Imperial Eyes: Travel Writing and Transculturation*. New York: Routledge, 1992.

Prochaska, F. K. *Women and Philanthropy in Nineteenth-Century England*. Oxford: Oxford University Press, 1980.

Prothero, Stephen. *The White Buddhist: The Asian Odyssey of Henry Steel Olcott*. Bloomington: Indiana University Press, 1996.

Ramusack, Barbara N. "Catalysts or Helpers? British Feminists, Indian Women's Rights, and Indian Independence." In *The Extended Family: Women and Political Participation in India and Pakistan*. Edited by Gail Minault. Columbia, Mo.: South Asia Books, 1981.

———. "Cultural Missionaries, Maternal Imperialists, Feminist Allies: British Women Activists in India, 1865–1945." *Women's Studies International Forum* 13, no. 4 (1990): 309–21.

Regan, Stephen. "W. B. Yeats and Irish Cultural Politics in the 1890s." In *Cul-*

tural Politics at the Fin de Siècle. Edited by Sally Ledger and Scott McCracken. New York: Cambridge University Press, 1995.

Rendall, Jane. "Introduction" and "'A Moral Engine'? Feminism, Liberalism and *The English Woman's Journal.*" In *Equal or Different: Women's Politics, 1800–1914.* Edited by Jane Rendall. Oxford: Basil Blackwell, 1987.

Rich, Paul B. *Race and Empire in British Politics.* 2nd ed. New York: Cambridge University Press, 1990.

Richardson, Alan. *The Magical Life of Dion Fortune: Priestess of the Twentieth Century.* London: Aquarian Press, 1991. Originally published as *Priestess.* London: Aquarian Press, 1987.

Riley, Denise. *"Am I That Name?" Feminism and the Category of "Women" in History.* Minneapolis: University of Minnesota Press, 1988.

Robb, George. "Eugenics, Spirituality, and Sex Differentiation in Edwardian England: The Case of Frances Swiney." *Journal of Women's History* 10, no. 3 (1998): 97–117.

Roe, Jill. *Beyond Belief: Theosophy in Australia, 1879–1939.* Kensington: New South Wales University Press, 1986.

Rose, Nikolas. *Governing the Soul: The Shaping of the Private Self.* New York: Routledge, 1990.

Rowbotham, Sheila, and Jeffrey Weeks. *Socialism and the New Life: The Personal and Sexual Politics of Edward Carpenter and Havelock Ellis.* London: Pluto Press, 1977.

Russett, Cynthia Eagle. *Sexual Science: The Victorian Construction of Womanhood.* Cambridge, Mass.: Harvard University Press, 1989.

Said, Edward W. *Orientalism.* New York: Vintage Books, 1979.

Santucci, James. "Women in the Theosophical Movement." Originally published in *Explorations: Journal for Adventurous Thought* 9, no. 1 (1990). Available electronically at *http://idt.net/~pdeveney/womenints.html*

Scott, Joan Wallach. *Only Paradoxes to Offer: French Feminists and the Rights of Man.* Cambridge, Mass.: Harvard University Press, 1996.

Shetty, Sandhya. "(Dis)figuring the Nation: Mother, Metaphor, Metonymy." *Differences: A Journal of Feminist Cultural Studies* 7, no. 3 (1995): 50–79.

Showalter, Elaine. *The Female Malady: Women, Madness, and English Culture, 1830–1980.* New York: Pantheon Books, 1985.

Sinha, Mrinalini. *Colonial Masculinity: The "Manly Englishman" and the "Effeminate Bengali" in the Late Nineteenth Century.* Manchester: Manchester University Press, 1995.

———. "Reading *Mother India:* Empire, Nation, and the Female Voice." *Journal of Women's History* 6, no. 2 (1994): 6–44.

Skultans, Vieda. "Mediums, Controls, and Eminent Men." In *Women's Religious Experience: Cross-cultural Perspectives.* Edited by Pat Holden. London: Croom Helm, 1983.

Sloss, Radha Rajagopal. *Lives in the Shadow with J Krishnamurti*. London: Bloomsbury Publishing, 1991.

Soloway, Richard A. *Demography and Degeneration: Eugenics and the Declining Birthrate in Twentieth-Century Britain*. Chapel Hill: University of North Carolina Press, 1990.

Steedman, Carolyn. *Childhood, Culture and Class in Britain: Margaret McMillan, 1860–1931*. London: Virago Press, 1990.

Stocking, George. *Victorian Anthropology*. New York: Free Press, 1987.

Stoler, Ann. *Race and the Education of Desire: Foucault's History of Sexuality and the Colonial Order of Things*. Durham, N.C.: Duke University Press, 1995.

Surette, Leon. *The Birth of Modernism: Ezra Pound, T. S. Eliot, W. B. Yeats, and the Occult*. Montreal: McGill-Queen's University Press, 1993.

Taylor, Anne. *Annie Besant: A Biography*. New York: Oxford University Press, 1992.

Taylor, Barbara. *Eve and the New Jerusalem: Socialism and Feminism in the Nineteenth Century*. London: Virago Press, 1983.

Thompson, Tierl, ed. *Dear Girl: The Diaries and Letters of Two Working Women, 1897–1917*. London: Women's Press, 1987.

Tickner, Lisa. *The Spectacle of Women: Imagery of the Suffrage Campaign 1907–14*. Chicago: University of Chicago Press, 1988.

Tillett, Gregory. *The Elder Brother: A Biography of Charles Webster Leadbeater*. London: Routledge & Kegan Paul, 1982.

Tingay, Kevin. "The English Section and the House of Commons." *Theosophical History* 2, no. 6 (1988): 221–25.

Trautmann, Thomas R. *Aryans and British India*. Berkeley: University of California Press, 1997.

Turner, Frank Miller. *Between Science and Religion: The Reaction to Scientific Naturalism in Victorian England*. New Haven: Yale University Press, 1974.

Tweed, Thomas A. *The American Encounter with Buddhism, 1844–1912: Victorian Culture and the Limits of Dissent*. Bloomington: Indiana University Press, 1992.

Valenze, Deborah. "Cottage Religion and the Politics of Survival." In *Equal or Different: Women's Politics 1800–1914*. Edited by Jane Rendall. Oxford: Basil Blackwell, 1987.

Vance, Norman. *The Sinews of the Spirit: The Ideal of Christian Manliness in Victorian Literature and Religious Thought*. Cambridge, England: Cambridge University Press, 1985.

van der Veer, Peter. *Religious Nationalism: Hindus and Muslims in India*. Berkeley: University of California Press, 1994.

Veldman, Meredith. "Dutiful Daughter versus All-Boy: Jesus, Gender, and the Secularization of Victorian Society." *Nineteenth Century Studies* 11 (1997): 1–24.

Vicinus, Martha. *Independent Women: Work and Community for Single Women, 1850–1920.* London: Virago Press, 1985.

Viswanathan, Gauri. *Outside the Fold: Conversion, Modernity, and Belief.* Princeton, N.J.: Princeton University Press, 1998.

Walker, Mary. "Between Fiction and Madness: The Relationship of Women to the Supernatural in Late Victorian Britain." In *That Gentle Strength: Historical Perspectives on Women in Christianity.* Edited by Lynda J. Coon, Katherine J. Haldane, and Elisabeth W. Sommer. Charlottesville: University Press of Virginia, 1990.

Walker, Pamela J. "'I Live But Yet Not I, for Christ Liveth in Me': Men and Masculinity in the Salvation Army, 1865–90." In *Manful Assertions: Masculinities in Britain since 1800.* New York: Routledge, 1991.

Walker, Steven F. "Vivekananda and American Occultism." In *The Occult in America: New Historical Perspectives.* Edited by Howard Kerr and Charles L. Crow. Urbana: University of Illinois Press, 1983.

Walkowitz, Judith R. *City of Dreadful Delight: Narratives of Sexual Danger in Late-Victorian London.* Chicago: University of Chicago Press, 1992.

———. *Prostitution and Victorian Society: Women, Class, and the State.* London: Cambridge University Press, 1980.

Washington, Peter. *Madame Blavatsky's Baboon: Theosophy and the Emergence of the Western Guru.* London: Secker & Warburg, 1993.

Waterstone, Penny Brown. "Domesticating Universal Brotherhood: Feminine Values and the Construction of Utopia, Point Loma Homestead, 1897–1920." Ph.D. diss., University of Arizona, 1995.

Webb, James. *The Occult Establishment.* La Salle, Ill.: Open Court Publishing Company, 1976.

Weeks, Jeffrey. *Sex, Politics and Society: The Regulation of Sexuality since 1800.* 2nd ed. New York: Longman, 1989.

Weinbren, Dan. "Against *All* Cruelty: The Humanitarian League, 1891–1919." *History Workshop Journal* 38 (1994): 86–105.

Wessinger, Catherine Lowman. *Annie Besant and Progressive Messianism, 1847–1933.* Lewiston, N.Y.: Edwin Mellen Press, 1988.

———. Introduction to *Women's Leadership in Marginal Religions: Explorations Outside the Mainstream.* Edited by Catherine Wessinger. Urbana: University of Illinois Press, 1993.

Wickremeratne, Ananda. *The Genesis of an Orientalist: Thomas William Rhys Davids and Buddhism in Sri Lanka.* Delhi: Motilal Banarsidass, 1984.

Winter, Alison. *Mesmerized: Powers of Mind in Victorian Britain.* Chicago: University of Chicago Press, 1998.

Wolfe, Willard. *From Radicalism to Socialism: Men and Ideas in the Formation of Fabian Socialist Doctrines, 1881–1889.* New Haven: Yale University Press, 1975.

Young, Robert J. C. *Colonial Desire: Hybridity in Theory, Culture and Race.* New York: Routledge, 1995.

Index

Doughan, David, 122
Dowling, Linda, 114
dress reform, 134
Drummond, Flora, 6, 179
Dublin Lodge (TS), 57
Dunlop, D. N., 69–70, 115–16, 244n.11,
 260n.77
Durham, Martin, 150, 254n.124
Dyer, Dr., 99

Eagleton, Terry, 121
eastern mysticism. *See* mystic East
Eastern School of Theosophy, 242n.55
Edger, Miss Lilian, 62
effemination, Krafft-Ebing's concept of,
 105–6
Egoist, The, 195
Egyptology, 169
Eleusinian Society, 90
Ellis, Havelock, 96, 98, 105, 114–15,
 249n.43; *Sexual Inversion,* 114
Englishness, theosophy and, 59
English Section (TS), 209. *See also* British
 Section (TS); British Theosophical Society; Theosophical Society (TS)
equality, of women, 158. *See also* feminism;
 suffrage movement
Esoteric Christian Union (ECU), 166
esotericism, Christian, 165–67, 190–94,
 196–200
Esoteric Section (TS), 45, 52, 54, 68, 72–74,
 76, 86, 91–93, 242n.55
eugenics movement, 169–71, 209, 212
European Section (TS), 50, 241n.37
evolution, 19–20, 43, 132–33, 146, 163, 192,
 236n.7, 236n.8, 239n.84. *See also* science,
 modern

Fabianism, 122
Fabian Society, 157
"faddists and cranks," theosophists as, 142–
 43, 150–51
family, rhetoric of, 145–46
Farquhar, J. N., *Modern Religious Movements in India,* 43–44
Farr, Florence, *Modern Woman: Her Intentions,* 148–49
Farrer, Reginald, "Confession," 111
fascism, 143–44, 149–50
feminism, 147–50, 152–53, 155, 167–72, 179,
 214; and Christianity, 153, 156–58, 162–
 64, 169, 213; and immanentism, 122–23,
 134–37; in India, 208, 218–19, 221–22;
 and racism, 167–72; and theosophy, 5–7,
 154–64, 209–10, 224–25. *See also* suffrage
 movement; women's spirituality
feminism, new, 209, 211, 216–17

feminization: and the body, 132–33; of
 Christianity, 165–67, 175–76; of theoso-
 phy, 68–75, 118
Finch, Mr., 30
Forbes, Geraldine, 162
Fortune, Dion (Violet Firth), 116–17
Foucault, Michel, 13, 151
Fraternity of the Inner Light, 116
Freemasonry. *See* Co-Masonry
Freewoman, Marsden's conception of, 196,
 198
Freewoman, The, 114, 194–96, 200
Fullerton, Alexander, 156
Fussell, Joseph, 112

Gandhi, M. K., 188
Gardner, E. L., 46–47
Garrett, Edmund, *Isis Very Much Unveiled,*
 52–54
Gaskell, Ellen, 72, 195–96
Gaskell, G. A., *Exeunt Mahatmas!,* 71–72
Gawthorpe, Mary, 6, 195
Gay, Susan E. (Libra), 79, 158, 255n.23;
 "Future of Women, The," 157; *Prophet of
 Nazareth, The,* 158; "Womanhood from
 the Theosophical Point of View," 162–63;
 Womanhood in Its Eternal Aspect, 157–59
Geddes, Patrick, 168
gender: and reincarnation, 157–58, 160; and
 religion, 42, 59–60, 67–69; and sexuality,
 111–18. *See also* feminization; manliness;
 Uranian, the
gender roles, 157–59
gentleman's club, TS as, 41–42, 49, 51–52,
 62–66
gentlemen, European, as witnesses, 36–37.
 See also manliness
Gerlach, Gertrude Holt, 209
German Section (TS), 88
Gibbs, Philip, *Now It Can Be Told,* 88–89
Ginzburg, Carol, 240n.106
Gnosticism, 169
Golden Dawn, 45, 65
Gore-Booth, Eva, 6, 179–80, 190–94; *Buried
 Life of Deirdre, The,* 191–92; *One and the
 Many, The,* 191; *Psychological and Poetic
 Approach to the Study of Christ,* 192
Graham Pole, David, 89
graphology, 239n.71
Green, Emily Maud, 132, 141, 161
Green, Henry Selby, 183
Grewal, Inderpal, 31
Grierson, Francis, 196
Griffiths, Ernest, 111
Guild Socialism, 8, 149
Gurney, Edmund, 21
Gurumurti, D. Lakshmi, 208